First World War

and Army of Occupation

War Diary

France, Belgium and Germany

42 DIVISION
125 Infantry Brigade
Headquarters
1 March 1917 - 11 April 1919

WO95/2654/1

The Naval & Military Press Ltd
www.nmarchive.com
Published in association with The National Archives

Published by

The Naval & Military Press Ltd

Unit 10 Ridgewood Industrial Park,

Uckfield, East Sussex,

TN22 5QE England

Tel: +44 (0) 1825 749494

www.naval-military-press.com

www.nmarchive.com

This diary has been reprinted in facsimile from the original. Any imperfections are inevitably reproduced and the quality may fall short of modern type and cartographic standards.

Contents

Document type	Place/Title	Date From	Date To
Heading	WO95/2654/1 125 Infantry Brigade Headquarters Mar 1917-Apr 1919		
Heading	42nd Division 125th Infy Bde Bde Headquarters Mar-1917-Apr 1919		
Heading	War Diary Of 125/42 Bde H.Q. From March 1st To March 31st 1917 Volume 32. May 17 Apr 19		
War Diary	France	01/03/1917	01/03/1917
War Diary	Pont-Remy	02/03/1917	17/03/1917
War Diary	Hamel	18/03/1917	26/03/1917
War Diary	Frise	27/03/1917	06/04/1917
War Diary	Peronne	06/04/1917	12/04/1917
War Diary	Villers-Faucon	12/04/1917	14/04/1917
War Diary	Peronne	15/04/1917	17/04/1917
War Diary	Frise	18/04/1917	20/04/1917
War Diary	Peronne	21/04/1917	29/04/1917
War Diary	Tincourt	30/04/1917	30/04/1917
Heading	War Diary Of 125th Infantry Brigade May 1st-May 31st 1917 Volume 34		
War Diary	Peronne Tincourt	01/05/1917	02/05/1917
War Diary	St Emilie Area.	03/05/1917	03/05/1917
War Diary	St. Emilie	04/05/1917	06/05/1917
War Diary	Longavesnes	07/05/1917	09/05/1917
War Diary	St Emilie	10/05/1917	13/05/1917
War Diary	Epehy	14/05/1917	18/05/1917
War Diary	Longavesnes	19/05/1917	20/05/1917
War Diary	Equancourt	21/05/1917	22/05/1917
War Diary	Dessart Wood	23/05/1917	27/05/1917
War Diary	Ytres	28/05/1917	31/05/1917
Heading	War Diary Of 125th Infy Bde Ivne 1st-30th 1917 Vol No 35		
Heading	War Diary Of 125th Infy Bde From June 1st. 30th 1917 Vol No 36		
War Diary	Ytres	01/06/1917	05/06/1917
War Diary	Ytres Havrincourt Wood	06/06/1917	06/06/1917
War Diary	Havrincourt Wood	07/06/1917	21/06/1917
War Diary	Ytres	22/06/1917	30/06/1917
Heading	War Diary Of 125th Trench Mortar Battery. June The 1st-30th 1917 Vol No. 2		
War Diary	Ytres	01/06/1917	07/06/1917
War Diary	Peronne	08/06/1917	08/06/1917
War Diary	Vaux-En-Amienois	09/06/1917	19/06/1917
War Diary	Peronne	20/06/1917	20/06/1917
War Diary	Ytres	21/06/1917	21/06/1917
War Diary	In The Line	22/06/1917	29/06/1917
War Diary	Ytres	30/06/1917	30/06/1917
Operation(al) Order(s)	125th. Brigade Warning Order No. 23	01/07/1917	01/07/1917
Operation(al) Order(s)	125th. Brigade Order No. 26		
Miscellaneous			
Operation(al) Order(s)	125th Brigade O.O. No. 20		
Operation(al) Order(s)	Addendum No. 1 To O.O. No 20	03/06/1917	03/06/1917

Operation(al) Order(s)	125th Brigade O.O. No. 21	07/06/1917	07/06/1917
Miscellaneous	5th L.F.	09/06/1917	09/06/1917
Miscellaneous	5th L.F.	10/06/1917	10/06/1917
Operation(al) Order(s)	125th Brigade O.O. Number 22	11/06/1917	11/06/1917
Miscellaneous	5th Lan Fus.	15/06/1917	15/06/1917
Operation(al) Order(s)	125th Infantry Brigade O.O. No. 23	19/06/1917	19/06/1917
Miscellaneous	Table "A" Of Working Parties Found By 125th Brigade.		
Miscellaneous	Table "B"		
Operation(al) Order(s)	Addendum No. 1 To 106th Brigade O.O. No. 23	20/02/1917	20/02/1917
Operation(al) Order(s)	125th Brigade Order No. 24		
Operation(al) Order(s)	125th Brigade Operation Order No. 25	25/06/1917	25/06/1917
Operation(al) Order(s)	Addendum To 125th Brigade Order No 24	26/06/1917	26/06/1917
Operation(al) Order(s)	Addendum No. 2 To 125th. Brigade Order No. 24		
Heading	War Diary Of 125th Infy Bde July 1st-31st 1917 Volume No 37		
War Diary	Ytres	01/07/1917	08/07/1917
War Diary	Gomiecourt	09/07/1917	31/07/1917
War Diary	France Sheet 57D	01/07/1917	01/07/1917
War Diary	Bde. H.Q. at Bus-Les-Artois	02/07/1917	10/07/1917
War Diary	Ref. Sheet 57D	11/07/1917	22/07/1917
War Diary	K28c 1525 J30 d 3000	23/07/1917	23/07/1917
War Diary	K31b 3090	24/07/1917	31/07/1917
Heading	War Diary Of 125th Infy. Bde August 1st-31st 1917 Volume No 38		
Miscellaneous			
War Diary	Gomiecourt	01/08/1917	19/08/1917
War Diary	Bouzincourt	20/08/1917	21/08/1917
War Diary	Albert	22/08/1917	22/08/1917
War Diary	Near Godewaersvelde L.13	23/08/1917	24/08/1917
War Diary	L.13	24/08/1917	31/08/1917
War Diary	Ypres Area	01/09/1917	08/09/1917
War Diary	Brandhoek	09/09/1917	14/09/1917
War Diary	Ypres Area	15/09/1917	17/09/1917
War Diary	Brandhoek	18/09/1917	19/09/1917
War Diary	St Janter Biezen	20/09/1917	22/09/1917
War Diary	Arneke Area.	23/09/1917	24/09/1917
War Diary	Ghyvelde	25/09/1917	30/09/1917
Miscellaneous	125th Inf Bde Intelligence Summary	31/08/1917	31/08/1917
Miscellaneous	Patrol Report. Attached 125 Bde Sat Summary No2	01/09/1917	01/09/1917
Miscellaneous	Patrol Report Attached To 125 Inf. Bde. 2 at Summ. No 3	02/09/1917	02/09/1917
Miscellaneous	125th Inf. Bde. Intelligence Summary. No 3	01/09/1917	01/09/1917
Miscellaneous	125 Bde. Intelligence Summary No 4	03/09/1917	03/09/1917
Miscellaneous	125th Inf. Bde. Intelligence Summary No 4	02/09/1917	02/09/1917
Miscellaneous	125th Inf. Bde. Intelligence Summary No. 5	03/09/1917	03/09/1917
Miscellaneous	Patrol Report From Jasper	03/09/1917	03/09/1917
Miscellaneous	Report Of NCO In/C. of Patrol	03/09/1917	03/09/1917
Miscellaneous	42nd Div.	04/09/1917	04/09/1917
Miscellaneous	125th Inf. Bde Intelligence Summary No 6	04/09/1917	04/09/1917
Miscellaneous	125th Inf. Bde Intelligence Summary No 7	05/09/1917	05/09/1917
Miscellaneous	125th Inf. Bde. Intelligence Summary No 8	06/09/1917	06/09/1917
Miscellaneous	5. Lan. Fus.	22/07/1918	22/07/1918
Miscellaneous	5 Lancs Fus.	22/07/1918	22/07/1918
Miscellaneous	5 Lan Fus	01/09/1917	01/09/1917
Operation(al) Order(s)	125th Brigade Operation Order Number 33	01/09/1917	01/09/1917

Heading	War Diary Of Inf 125 Bde-October 1st-31st 1917 Vol No 40		
War Diary	St Idesbald	01/10/1917	05/10/1917
War Diary	Nieuport	06/10/1917	20/10/1917
War Diary	Lapanne Area	21/10/1917	31/10/1917
Heading	War Diary Of 125th Infy Bde Nov 1st-30th 1917 Vol No. 40		
War Diary	La Panne	01/11/1917	06/11/1917
War Diary	Nieuport	07/11/1917	18/11/1917
War Diary	Leffrincouke	19/11/1917	19/11/1917
War Diary	Wormhoudt	20/11/1917	20/11/1917
War Diary	Zermezeele	21/11/1917	21/11/1917
War Diary	Staple	22/11/1917	22/11/1917
War Diary	Thiennes	23/11/1917	26/11/1917
War Diary	Bethune	27/11/1917	30/11/1917
Heading	War Diary Of 125th Infy Bde Vol No 41. Dec 1917. Vol 11		
War Diary	Canal Sector Bethune	01/12/1917	09/12/1917
War Diary	Bethune	10/12/1917	10/12/1917
War Diary	Vendin Lez Bethune	11/12/1917	21/12/1917
War Diary	Loisne	22/12/1917	31/12/1917
Heading	War Diary Of 125 Infy Bde Jan 1st-31st 1918 Vol No 43		
War Diary	Bethune Area	01/01/1918	06/01/1918
War Diary	Bethune	07/01/1918	08/01/1918
War Diary	Bethune Area	09/01/1918	16/01/1918
War Diary	Bethune (Givenchy Sector)	17/01/1918	24/01/1918
War Diary	Bethune	25/01/1918	25/01/1918
War Diary	(Canal Sector)	26/01/1918	31/01/1918
Operation(al) Order(s)	125th. Brigade Order No. 67	07/01/1918	07/01/1918
Operation(al) Order(s)	125th Brigade Order 68	12/01/1918	12/01/1918
Miscellaneous			
Miscellaneous	Defence Scheme. 125th. Infantry Brigade		
Operation(al) Order(s)	Corrigendum To 125th. Inf. Bde Order No. 68		
Heading	WD Vollumes		
Operation(al) Order(s)	Amendment To 125th. Infantry Brigade Order No. 68	15/01/1918	15/01/1918
Operation(al) Order(s)	125th Infantry Brigade Order No. 69	26/01/1918	26/01/1918
Operation(al) Order(s)	Relief Table Issued With 125th Infantry Brigade Order No. 69. Table "A"	26/01/1918	26/01/1918
Operation(al) Order(s)	Working Party Table To Accompany 125th Infantry Brigade Order No. 69. Table "B"		
Miscellaneous	125th Brigade Defence Scheme. Givenchy Sector.	08/01/1918	08/01/1918
Miscellaneous	6th. L.n Fus.	08/01/1918	08/01/1918
Miscellaneous	On Front Of Flanking Brigades.	07/01/1918	07/01/1918
Miscellaneous	Disposition of Machine Guns. Appendix. 1		
Miscellaneous	Gun Positions. 12th. L.T.M. Battery. Appendix 2		
Miscellaneous	Signal Communications. Appendix. IV.		
Diagram etc	Communications Givenchy Sector.		
Miscellaneous	Administrative Arrangements. Appendix 6		
Heading	War Diary Of 125th Infy Brigade Feb 1918 Vol No 44		
War Diary	Bethune Area	01/02/1918	28/02/1918
Heading	42nd Division B.H.Q. 125th Infantry Brigade March 1918		
War Diary	Bethune Area E21b80	01/03/1918	03/03/1918
War Diary	K3d22	04/03/1918	12/03/1918
War Diary	Bethune Area.	13/03/1918	13/03/1918

War Diary	Drouvin K3d22	14/03/1918	23/03/1918
War Diary	51c S.E. Adinferwood X27b13	23/03/1918	23/03/1918
War Diary	57c NW. Logeast Wood A25d 27	24/03/1918	24/03/1918
War Diary	57C N.W. Gomiecourt A23d12	24/03/1918	25/03/1918
War Diary	57C NW. Gomiecourt. A 22 b34	25/03/1918	25/03/1918
War Diary	57c NW Ablainzevelle F23d73	26/03/1918	26/03/1918
War Diary	57D NE Essarts E24d79	26/03/1918	29/03/1918
War Diary	57 D.N.E. Gonnecourt E28d66	30/03/1918	31/03/1918
Heading	Appendices A.1 to A.28 and A.30 to A.43		
Operation(al) Order(s)	125th, Infantry Brigade Order No. 73	01/03/1918	01/03/1918
Miscellaneous	7th L.I.	22/03/1918	22/03/1918
Operation(al) Order(s)	125th. Brigade Order No. 74	23/03/1918	23/03/1918
Miscellaneous	A Form. Messages And Signals.		
Miscellaneous	Messages And Signals.		
Miscellaneous	Special Order Of The Day. By Major-General A. Solly-Flood, C.M.G., D.S.O. Commanding 42nd (East Lancs.) Division.	24/03/1918	24/03/1918
Miscellaneous	A Form. Messages And Signals.		
Miscellaneous	126 Inf Bde		
Miscellaneous	Messages And Signals.		
Miscellaneous	A Form. Messages And Signals.		
Miscellaneous	42nd Division (Warning) Order.	25/03/1918	25/03/1918
Miscellaneous	Messages And Signals.		
War Diary	Messages And Signals.		
Miscellaneous	Messages And Signals.		
Miscellaneous	A Form. Messages And Signals.		
Miscellaneous	Messages And Signals.		
Miscellaneous	A Form Messages And Signals.		
Miscellaneous	Messages And Signals.		
Miscellaneous	A Form Messages And Signals.		
Miscellaneous	Messages And Signals.		
Miscellaneous	A Form. Messages And Signals.		
Heading	42nd Div IV. Corps. War Diary Headquarters. 125th Infantry Brigade. April 1918		
Heading	125 Inf Bde War Diary Vol. 46 1st-30 April 1918		
War Diary	57D NE Gommecourt E 28d66 Essarts E24d79	01/04/1918	03/04/1918
War Diary	57D NE Essarts E24d79	04/04/1918	07/04/1918
War Diary	57D NE Essarts E24d79 57D Vauchelles I 32b87	08/04/1918	10/04/1918
War Diary	57D Vauchelles I32b19	11/04/1918	12/04/1918
War Diary	St. Leger I.12C17	13/04/1918	13/04/1918
War Diary	57D. St. Leger. I2C17	14/04/1918	15/04/1918
War Diary	57D.N.E. Gommecourt. E28d89	16/04/1918	17/04/1918
War Diary	57D NE E27C96	18/04/1918	24/04/1918
War Diary	57D NE E27C96 Fonquevillers	25/04/1918	27/04/1918
War Diary	57D NE Couin JId65	28/04/1918	30/04/1918
Heading	Appendices 1 to 31		
Miscellaneous	Ref 57 D.N.E. 1.20.000	01/04/1918	01/04/1918
Miscellaneous	B.M. 198	03/04/1918	03/04/1918
Miscellaneous	Random.		
Miscellaneous	1/8 LE		
Miscellaneous	42 Div 112 Inf Bn		
Miscellaneous	125 Bde.		
Miscellaneous			
Miscellaneous	48th L.F. 1/5th L.F.		
Miscellaneous	42 Div. 127 Inf Bde.		
Miscellaneous			

Miscellaneous	125 Bde.		
Miscellaneous			
Miscellaneous	125 Bde.	05/04/1918	05/04/1918
Miscellaneous	42 Divn. 127 I.B. 112 I.B.		
Miscellaneous	125 Inf. Bde.	05/04/1918	05/04/1918
Miscellaneous	Razor		
Miscellaneous	42 Div		
Miscellaneous	Razor		
Miscellaneous	125 Inf. Bde.		
Miscellaneous	5th L.F. 7 L.F. 8 L.F.		
Miscellaneous	Razor Refail Rasp Raul		
Miscellaneous	Razor		
Miscellaneous	5 L.F. 7 L.F. 8 L.F.		
Miscellaneous	125 Bde.	06/04/1918	06/04/1918
Miscellaneous	125 Inf. Bde	06/04/1918	06/04/1918
Miscellaneous	Inter Battalion Relief Order	06/04/1918	06/04/1918
Miscellaneous	1/5th. L.F. 1/17th L.F 18th Manchester B.M. 279	06/04/1918	06/04/1918
Miscellaneous	Special Telegram.		
Operation(al) Order(s)	125th Infy Bde Order No. 75	07/04/1918	07/04/1918
Operation(al) Order(s)	125 Inf Bde Order No 75	07/04/1918	07/04/1918
Operation(al) Order(s)	125th. Infantry Brigade Order No. 76	12/04/1918	12/04/1918
Operation(al) Order(s)	125th. Infantry Brigade Order No. 77	15/04/1918	15/04/1918
Operation(al) Order(s)	125 Inf Bde Order No. 78	23/04/1918	23/04/1918
Operation(al) Order(s)	125 Inf Bde Order No 79	27/04/1918	27/04/1918
Heading	125 Inf Bde War Diary Vol 47 May 1st-31st 1918 Vol 16		
War Diary	57.DNE Couin. J1.d65	01/05/1918	01/05/1918
War Diary	57D NE Gommecourt E28d 16	02/05/1918	05/05/1918
War Diary	Couin J1d65	06/05/1918	11/05/1918
War Diary	Couin. 57DNE J1D65	12/05/1918	31/05/1918
Operation(al) Order(s)	125th. Infantry Brigade Order No. 80	01/05/1918	01/05/1918
Operation(al) Order(s)	125 Inf Bde Order No. 81	03/05/1918	03/05/1918
Operation(al) Order(s)	125 Inf Bde Order No 82	05/05/1918	05/05/1918
Heading	War Diary 125 Inf. Bde. June 1918. Vol.48		
War Diary	57D NE Couin J1Db5	01/06/1918	13/06/1918
War Diary	57D.N.E. J18.b.1.9	13/06/1918	30/06/1918
Operation(al) Order(s)	125th. Infantry Brigade Order No. 83	04/06/1918	04/06/1918
Operation(al) Order(s)	Addendum To 125th Infantry Brigade Order No. 83	05/06/1918	05/06/1918
Operation(al) Order(s)	Corrigendum To 125th Infantry Brigade Order No. 83	06/06/1918	06/06/1918
Operation(al) Order(s)	125th. Infantry Brigade Order No. 84	12/06/1918	12/06/1918
Operation(al) Order(s)	Table Issued With 125th Infantry Brigade Order No. 84		
Operation(al) Order(s)	Addendum To 125th. Infantry Brigade Order No. 84	12/06/1918	12/06/1918
Operation(al) Order(s)	125th Ind Bde Order No. 85	19/06/1918	19/06/1918
Operation(al) Order(s)	125 Inf. Bde. Order No. 85	19/06/1918	19/06/1918
Miscellaneous	Warning Order.	28/06/1918	28/06/1918
Operation(al) Order(s)	125th Bde Order No. 86	29/06/1918	29/06/1918
Miscellaneous			
Miscellaneous	A Form Messages And Signals.		
Heading	War Diary For July 1918 HQ 125 Infy Bde Vol 18		
Miscellaneous	5 Lancs Fus	23/07/1918	23/07/1918
Operation(al) Order(s)	125th. Infantry Brigade Order No. 88	24/07/1918	24/07/1918
Operation(al) Order(s)	Relief Table To Accompany Bde. Order 88		
Heading	125 Infantry Brigade From 1st August 1918 To 31st August 1918 Volume No 49		
War Diary	Ref. Sheet 57D 1/40000 J26a95	01/08/1918	03/08/1918
War Diary	J17C31	03/08/1918	14/08/1918

War Diary	Ref Sheet 57D 1/40000 Bde H.Q. J17C31	15/08/1918	19/08/1918
War Diary	Ref Sheets 57D 157C 1/40000 K31b48	20/08/1918	21/08/1918
War Diary	Ref 57D 57C 1/40000 K31b48 (Bde HQ)	22/08/1918	23/08/1918
War Diary	K25a85	24/08/1918	24/08/1918
War Diary	K36a76	24/08/1918	24/08/1918
War Diary	Ref Sheets 57D 57C R5d78	26/08/1918	26/08/1918
War Diary	M2d24	27/08/1918	30/08/1918
War Diary	M1Za59	31/08/1918	31/08/1918
Operation(al) Order(s)	125th Infantry Brigade Order No. 89	02/08/1918	02/08/1918
Operation(al) Order(s)	Table To Accompany 125th Infantry Brigade Order. No. 89		
Operation(al) Order(s)	125th. Infantry Brigade Order. No. 90	15/08/1918	15/08/1918
Operation(al) Order(s)	125th. Infantry Brigade Order. No. 91	15/08/1918	15/08/1918
Operation(al) Order(s)	125th. Infantry Brigade Order No. 92	15/08/1918	15/08/1918
Operation(al) Order(s)	125 Inf Bde Order No:97	25/08/1918	25/08/1918
Operation(al) Order(s)	125th Inf Bde Order No. 98	27/08/1918	27/08/1918
Operation(al) Order(s)	125th Inf Bde Order No. 99	30/08/1918	30/08/1918
Operation(al) Order(s)	125th Inf Bde Order No. 100	31/08/1918	31/08/1918
Operation(al) Order(s)	125th Inf Bde Order No. 101	30/08/1918	30/08/1918
Operation(al) Order(s)	125th. Infantry Brigade Order No. 93	17/08/1918	17/08/1918
Operation(al) Order(s)	125th. Infantry Brigade Order No. 94	17/08/1918	17/08/1918
Operation(al) Order(s)	Reference 125th. Infantry Brigade Order No. 95	20/08/1918	20/08/1918
Operation(al) Order(s)	125th. Infantry Brigade Order No. 95	20/08/1918	20/08/1918
Miscellaneous	Time Table 'E'.Dispositions Of Battalions Of 125th Infantry Brigade.		
Miscellaneous	Artillery Programme.	20/08/1918	20/08/1918
Operation(al) Order(s)	125th. Infantry Brigade Order No. 96	22/08/1918	22/08/1918
Heading	War Diary 125 Inf Bde HQ Sept 1918 Vol 50		
War Diary	Ref 57C 1/40000 M12a 59	01/09/1918	02/09/1918
War Diary	IN3C26	03/09/1918	03/09/1918
War Diary	Ref. 57C 1/40000 O7b95 O15b99	03/09/1918	05/09/1918
War Diary	57C M2d54	06/09/1918	21/09/1918
War Diary	I 30 a 98	22/09/1918	26/09/1918
War Diary	Q10 Central	27/09/1918	27/09/1918
War Diary	57C Q10 Central	27/09/1918	29/09/1918
War Diary	Q3b32	30/09/1918	30/09/1918
Miscellaneous	5 Lan Fus.	27/09/1918	27/09/1918
Operation(al) Order(s)	125 Inf Bde Order No. 102	02/09/1918	02/09/1918
Operation(al) Order(s)	125 Inf Bde Order No 103	02/09/1918	02/09/1918
Operation(al) Order(s)	125 Inf Bde Order No. 104	03/09/1918	03/09/1918
Operation(al) Order(s)	125 Inf Bde Order No. 105	04/09/1918	04/09/1918
Operation(al) Order(s)	125 Infantry Brigade Order No. 106	04/09/1918	04/09/1918
Operation(al) Order(s)	25 Inf Bde Order No. 104	05/09/1918	05/09/1918
Operation(al) Order(s)	125 Inf Bde Order No. 108	05/09/1918	05/09/1918
Operation(al) Order(s)	125th. Infantry Brigade Order No. 110	19/09/1918	19/09/1918
Operation(al) Order(s)	March Table To Accompany 125th. Infantry Brigade Order No. 110		
Operation(al) Order(s)	125th. Infantry Brigade Order No. 111	20/09/1918	20/09/1918
Operation(al) Order(s)	Table 'A'-To Accompany 125th. Infantry Brigade Order No. 111		
Operation(al) Order(s)	Table 'B'-To Accompany 125th. Infantry Brigade Order No. 111		
Heading	War Diary 125 Inf. Bde. H.Q. Oct. 1918 Vol 51		
War Diary	57C Q3b32	01/10/1918	07/10/1918
War Diary	R13d.9.5	08/10/1918	08/10/1918
War Diary	27B M11C2.7	09/10/1918	09/10/1918

War Diary	N4.b.4.0	10/10/1918	10/10/1918
War Diary	I 15.C.8.8	10/10/1918	10/10/1918
War Diary	57.B.J1a.5.5	10/10/1918	12/10/1918
War Diary	J 3.C.5.8	12/10/1918	12/10/1918
War Diary	J 3.C.5.8 Bde HQ	12/10/1918	17/10/1918
War Diary	I 10 a.5.9	18/10/1918	19/10/1918
War Diary	J.1 a 5.5	20/10/1918	20/10/1918
War Diary	J 1a.5.5 Bde HQ.	20/10/1918	21/10/1918
War Diary	E19.a.3.2	22/10/1918	22/10/1918
War Diary	E19.a.3.2 Bde H.Q.	23/10/1918	23/10/1918
War Diary	D28.a.5.1	23/10/1918	23/10/1918
War Diary	I 15.d 2.6	24/10/1918	31/10/1918
Miscellaneous	A Form. Messages And Signals.		
Operation(al) Order(s)	125th. Infantry Brigade Order No. 113	07/10/1918	07/10/1918
Operation(al) Order(s)	125th. Infantry Brigade Order No. 115	10/10/1918	10/10/1918
Operation(al) Order(s)	125th. Infantry Brigade Order No. 116	10/10/1918	10/10/1918
Operation(al) Order(s)	125th. Infantry Brigade Order No. 117	12/10/1918	12/10/1918
Operation(al) Order(s)	Relief Table To Accompany 125th Inf Bde Order No. 117	12/10/1918	12/10/1918
Miscellaneous	13 Inf Bde Bde On Left Group R.F.A. 126 Inf Bde.	14/10/1918	14/10/1918
Miscellaneous	42nd Division	14/10/1918	14/10/1918
Miscellaneous	8th. Lancs. Fus. Summary Of Operations-October 13th.1918	13/10/1918	13/10/1918
Operation(al) Order(s)	125th. Infantry Brigade Order No. 118	15/10/1918	15/10/1918
Operation(al) Order(s)	125th. Infantry Brigade Order No. 119	17/10/1918	17/10/1918
Operation(al) Order(s)	Relief Table Issued With 125th. Infantry Brigade Order No. 119	18/10/1918	18/10/1918
Operation(al) Order(s)	125th. Infantry Brigade Order No. 120	19/10/1918	19/10/1918
Operation(al) Order(s)	125th. Infantry Brigade Order No. 122	22/10/1918	22/10/1918
Operation(al) Order(s)	Time Table For 125th. Infantry Brigade Order No. 122		
Operation(al) Order(s)	125th. Infantry Brigade Order No. 124	23/10/1918	23/10/1918
Operation(al) Order(s)	Amendment No. 1. To 125th. Infantry Brigade Order No. 124	23/10/1918	23/10/1918
Miscellaneous	5th. Lan Fus.	22/10/1918	22/10/1918
Miscellaneous	Instructions No 1. Signalling Arrangements		
Heading	125 Inf Bde HQ War Diary November 1918 Vol 52		
War Diary	Map 57B I15d 26	01/11/1918	03/11/1918
War Diary	Solesmes	04/11/1918	04/11/1918
War Diary	51A R32 Beaudignies	05/11/1918	05/11/1918
War Diary	51 Herpignies	06/11/1918	07/11/1918
War Diary	O34a97	07/11/1918	07/11/1918
War Diary	51 1/40000 O34a97	07/11/1918	08/11/1918
War Diary	Boussieres P31d88	08/11/1918	08/11/1918
War Diary	Ref. 51.1/40000 Boussieres P31d88	08/11/1918	09/11/1918
War Diary	Hautmont P29C88	10/11/1918	10/11/1918
War Diary	Hautmont H/51. 1/40000 & 52. 1/40000	10/11/1918	11/11/1918
War Diary	51. P23C70	12/11/1918	30/11/1918
Operation(al) Order(s)	125th. Infantry Brigade Order No. 125	03/11/1918	03/11/1918
Operation(al) Order(s)	125th. Infantry Brigade Order No. 126	04/11/1918	04/11/1918
Miscellaneous	A Form Messages And Signals.		
Miscellaneous	Messages And Signals.		
Miscellaneous	A Form Messages And Signals.		
Operation(al) Order(s)	125th. Infantry Brigade Order No. 132	11/11/1918	11/11/1918
Miscellaneous	42nd (East Lancashire) Division. Summary Of Operations	05/11/1918	05/11/1918
Heading	War Diary December 1918 125 Infy Bde H.Qrs Vol 23		

War Diary	Ref 51.1/40000 Hautmont	01/12/1918	01/12/1918
War Diary	P 23 C70	02/12/1918	13/12/1918
War Diary	Mauberge	14/12/1918	14/12/1918
War Diary	Estinne Au Mont	15/12/1918	15/12/1918
War Diary	Anderlues	16/12/1918	17/12/1918
War Diary	Charleroi	18/12/1918	31/12/1918
Operation(al) Order(s)	125th. Infantry Brigade Order No. 135	10/12/1918	10/12/1918
Operation(al) Order(s)	Appendix To 125th. Infantry Brigade Order No. 135		
Operation(al) Order(s)	March Table To Accompany 125th. Bde Order No. 135		
Operation(al) Order(s)	Amendment No. 2. To 125th. Inf Brigade Order No. 135	13/12/1918	13/12/1918
Operation(al) Order(s)	Addendum And Amendment No. 1 To 125th. Infantry Brigade Order No. 135	11/12/1918	11/12/1918
Heading	War Diary For January 1919 125 Inf Bde H.Qrs Vol 24		
War Diary	Rue De Montigny Charleroi	01/01/1919	31/01/1919
Heading	125 Light Trench Mortar Battery. From 1st January 1919 To 31st January 1919 Volume No. 24		
War Diary		01/01/1919	31/01/1919
Heading	125 Inf Bde H Qrs. War Diary For February 1919 Vol 55		
War Diary	Rue de Montigny Charleroi	01/02/1919	28/02/1919
Heading	125 Inf Bde H.Qrs War Diary For March 1919 Vol 56		
War Diary	Rue de Montigny Charleroi	01/03/1919	11/04/1919
Map	Map "A" Showing S.O.S. Lines Close Defence In Front System 125. M.G.Coy		
Map	Map "B" Showing S.O.S. Lines Of 125. T.M.B.		

(1)

WO95/2654

125 Infantry Brigade Headquarters

Mar 1917 - Apr 1919

42ND DIVISION
125TH INFY BDE

BDE HEADQUARTERS

MAR-1917-APR 1919

Vol 2

CONFIDENTIAL.

WAR DIARY OF 125 BDE / 42 H.Q.

FROM MARCH 1ST TO MARCH 31ST.

1917.

VOLUME 32.

Sept. 17
Apr. 19

Army Form C. 2118

Instructions regarding War Diaries and Intelligence Summaries are contained in F. S. Regs., Part II. and the Staff Manual respectively. Title Pages will be prepared in manuscript.

WAR DIARY
or
~~INTELLIGENCE SUMMARY~~ of 125 BDE

Vol. 32. Page 1. (Erase heading not required.) MARCH 1ST – MARCH 1917.

Place	Date	Hour	Summary of Events and Information	Remarks and references to Appendices
	MARCH.			
FRANCE	1.		In the train journeying from MARSEILLES to PONT REMY. &c. Ref Map. 1/100 000 ABBEVILLE 14, &c.	
PONT-REMY	2.		Arrived PONT REMY. Cold + wet. Occupied Billets. Bde HQ & M. Gun Coy at VIEULAINE 5 LF at LIERCOURT. 6 LF at SOREL & WANEL. &c.	
	4.		Officers' chargers arrived PONT REMY from EGYPT. Snow. &c.	
	5		7 L.F. and 8 L.F. arrived – & occupied Billets. &c.	
	6.		Transport drawn at ABBEVILLE to complete establishment as per Pt VII W.E.	
	11.		Three Interpreters arrived at Battns – Mr STRUB arrived Bde HQ as Bde Interpreter. &c	
	12.		Orders received re Musketry Course. – 2/LT ZIMMERN, 8 L.F. joined Bde HQ as Intelligence Offr. Brig-Gen H.C. FRITH C.B. returned to Bde from Div. and resumed command – Lt Col R.L. Lees D.S.O. returning to 6 L.F. &c.	
	13.		Machine Gun Coy carried out firing on Boyd range off FONTAINE – SOREL RD. Orders recd for move of Bde Group to HAMEL. Ref map 1/100 000 AMIENS 17. ABBEVILLE 14. Orders issued by Bde &c	(A). Div letter GS 11/15 A 21/4/286. Bde Orders No1 + No 2.
	14.		Horses + transport moved by march route to HAMEL. Billeted at S. SAUVEURS night 14/15th &c.	
	15.		Horses + transport arrived HAMEL via FOUILLOY. Ref map 1/100 000 AMIENS 17 – ABBEVILLE 14.	
		10³⁰ a.m.	Bde Group entrained at LONGPRÉ and proceeded to CORBIE – detrained there and marched to HAMEL – and occupied Billets &c.	
	17.		Advance Party returned from trenches – Major R.P. LEWIS (Bde Major) resumed duty with Bde. &c	

1875 Wt. W593/826 1,000,000 4/15 J.B.C. & A. A.D.S.S./Forms/C. 2118.

Instructions regarding War Diaries and Intelligence Summaries are contained in F. S. Regs., Part II. and the Staff Manual respectively. Title Pages will be prepared in manuscript.

WAR DIARY

or

~~INTELLIGENCE SUMMARY~~ of 125 BDE

(Erase heading not required.)

Army Form C. 2118

VOL. 32. PAGE 2. MARCH 1ST – 31ST 1917.

Place	Date	Hour	Summary of Events and Information	Remarks and references to Appendices
	MARCH.			
HAMEL	18	10.0 am	Party of officers + O.R. proceeded to trenches, to be attached to Bde for 48hrs – This party included Brig. Gen FRITH. 7c	
	20		Brig. Gen FRITH and party returned from trenches. Weather cold and damp. 7c	
	22		427 Coy R.E. ordered to move to ESTREES Ref map 62D. 7c	42 DW wire G741.
	23		427 Coy R.E. proceeded to ESTREES for work on BRIE Bridge and ESTREES-BRIE Road. Frost and Snow. 7c	
HAMEL	24		Recd orders for Bde Group, less 427 Coy RE, to move by march route to FRISE. Bde orders issued Ref. Map 62c. 62D. Fine and dry. Summer-Time adopted at 11pm. 7c	III Corps order No 188. Bde order No 3
	25.	7 a.m.	Bde Group (less RE) marched to FRISE. 5LF. ~~6LF~~ billetted in BUSCOURT. 6LF at ECLUSIER. 7LF at ECLUSIER. 8LF at FEUILLERES. Bde HQ at FRISE – MGun Coy at FRISE. 1/1st Field Ambulance at No 56 CAMP. Hour of march 7.0 a.m. mid-day halt 12.30 – 1.30 p.m. Head of column arrived 1.30 p.m. Route via CERISY – MERICOURT – FROISSY – CAPPY. Weather Dry and fine. 7c	
	26.		Orders received re supplying working parties on roads in District. 125 Lt. TRENCH MORTAR BATTERY arrived FRISE. 7c	
FRISE	27		5LF moved from BUSCOURT to FLAUCOURT. Working parties on roads between HERBECOURT and FLAUCOURT also in BIACHES area. Dry + fine. 7c	
	28		Working parties cleaning roads. Hard frost.	
	29		Working parties cleaning road. Heavy rain.	
	30		Working parties cleaning roads.	
	31.	9 a.m.	7LF moved to PERONNE, attached to 48 Divn, for work on roads.	

R P Lewis Major
for Brigdr Genl.
Commanding 125 Bde

1875 Wt. W593/826 1,000,000 4/15 J.B.C. & A. A.D.S.S./Forms/C. 2118.

Instructions regarding War Diaries and Intelligence Summaries are contained in F. S. Regs., Part II. and the Staff Manual respectively. Title Pages will be prepared in manuscript.

WAR DIARY
or
~~INTELLIGENCE SUMMARY~~
(Erase heading not required.)

Army Form C. 2118

VOL 30 — 125 BDE. APRIL 1st – APRIL 30th 1917.

Place	Date APRIL	Hour	MAP REFERENCE	Summary of Events and Information	WEATHER	Remarks and references to Appendices
			62c. FRANCE 1/40,000.			
FRISE	1st			Bde employed in road-mending. Capt R.V. GERY (4th City of London M.G.C) assumed command of 125 MG Coy	Fine.	JC.
"	2ND.			Lt R.S. NEWTON returned to Bde HQ from leave in ENGLAND	Snowstorms.	JC.
"	3RD.			Lt B. SHELMERDINE (7L.F.) arrived at Bde HQ to assume duties of Staff Capt. during absence of Capt A.O. NEEDHAM on leave in ENGLAND	Heavy Snow	JC.
"	4TH.			Capt A.O. NEEDHAM proceeded to ENGLAND on leave.	Heavy snow	JC
"	5TH		" "	1/5TH LAN FUS marched from DESIRÉE VALLEY to CARTIGNY. 6LF moved from ÉCLUSIER to DESIRÉE VALLEY. Worked on road there, and proceeded to PERONNE. 8LF marched from FEULLIERES to PERONNE. 7LF moved from PERONNE to TINCOURT, moved thence to LONGAVESNES)	Fine & dry	JC.
"	6TH	2pm		BDE HQ moved, by march route, to PERONNE, arriving there at 5pm.	Cold & wet.	JC
PERONNE			62c. FRANCE 1/40,000.	5LF marched to TEMPLEUX LA FOSSE		
	7TH			125 M.GUN COY and 125 T.M BATTY arrived, by march route, from FRISE at 5pm. Orders received from 48 DIV. re move of Bde to VILLERS-FAUCON area. Bde warned.	Cold & wet	JC.
"	8TH	9a.m.	62c 1/40,000. 62c NE 1/20,000	Brig Gen FRITH and Bde Major and a/Staff Captn. proceeded to VILLERS-FAUCON to view line and billets. Bde HQ changed billets in PERONNE.	Fine.	JC
			62c SE. 1/20,000.	5 LAN FUS, relieved 5th Battn R. WARWICKS at SAULCOURT. 7LF relieved 7th Battn R. WARWICKS in Right Sector. EPEHY.		Bde Op. Ord.s No 4.
	9TH	12 Noon	" "	5 LAN FUS. relieved 8th Battn R. WARWICKS in left Sector - PEZIERES. 6 LAN FUS relieved 7 R. WARWICKS at LONGAVESNES. 23rd Inf Bde holding line on left of 5LF. and 144TH BDE holding line on right of 7LF. 125 M Gun Coy moved to LONGAVESNES.	wet.	JC " "
	10TH	11a.m.		6 LAN FUS relieved 8th R. WARWICKS at SAULCOURT. 125 M. GUN COY relieved 143 M. Gun Coy. at SAULCOURT. 125 TRENCH M. BATTY relieved 143 T.M.B. at LONGAVESNES. 125 BDE HQ. moved to VILLERS FAUCON. relief of 143 BDE completed. 6LF working on roads. 8LF moved to LONGAVESNES.	wet	JC.
	11TH.			Orders issued for relief of 7 LAN FUS by 6 LAN FUS and for 8LF to proceed to SAULCOURT. Orders received from 48 DIVN for seizing of No 12 COPSE, NAMELESS COPSE, & RED RUIN. Bde orders issued.	wet.	JC Bde O.O. No 5. JC 48 Div O.O. No 177 Bde O.O. No 6.
	12TH.			Preparations for attack on COPSES etc. Two companies 6LF ordered up in support of 7LF. Two companies 8LF relieved two companies 6LF at SAULCOURT.	Warmer but wet	JC

1875 Wt. W593/826 1,000,000 4/15 J.B.C. & A. A.D.S.S./Forms/C. 2118.

Instructions regarding War Diaries and Intelligence Summaries are contained in F. S. Regs., Part II. and the Staff Manual respectively. Title Pages will be prepared in manuscript.

Army Form C. 2118

WAR DIARY

~~or~~

~~INTELLIGENCE SUMMARY~~ OF 125 BDE

(Erase heading not required.)

Page 2. FROM APRIL 1st TO APRIL 30th. 1917.

Place	Date	Hour	MAP REFERENCE	Summary of Events and Information	WEATHER	Remarks and references to Appendices
VILLERS-FAUCON	NIGHT 12/13.	9pm.	62 C. FRANCE NE 1/20000. + 57 C. SE.	No 12 COPSE, NAMELESS COPSE, & RED RUIN SEIZED. Casualties 1 Off + 3 men wounded. A party consisting of Lt JENKINS, Lt WAUGH, and Lt HARRISON, + 25 O.R. all from 5 LF. proceeded to establish an advanced post and dug position in which they remained during night of 12/13 + until 11pm 13th when they withdrew + returned to EPEHY.	Snow.	Bde report F/9/c.
"	13th		"	Orders issued for relief of Bde by 143 Bde. MALASSISE FARM (62 C N.E. F 8 B 1.9.) shelled and direct hit caused collapse of cellar (several casualties). 6 LF relieved 7 LF, who moved to LONGAVESNES.		Bde O.O. No 7.
"	14th.	(1) 4 pm (2) 7 45 pm (3) 7 45 pm	"	(1) 8 LAN FUS marched to CARTIGNY. (2) 5 LAN FUS. moved to SAULCOURT from Left Sector, being relieved by 6th R. WARWICKS at 7 45 pm. (3) 6th LAN FUS. marched to VILLERS FAUCON from Right Sector, being relieved by 5th R. WARWICKS.	Fine.	" "
PERONNE	15th			5th LAN FUS marched to PERONNE, being relieved by 8th R. WARWICKS. 6th LAN FUS marched to PERONNE + were relieved by 7th R. WARWICKS. 125 M. GUN COY proceeded to LONGAVESNES, relieved by 143 M. GUN COY. 125 TRENCH M. BATTY marched to PERONNE, being relieved by 143 T.M.B. 125 Bde HQ proceeded to PERONNE, being relieved by 143 Bde HQ.	Cold & Dry	" "
PERONNE	16th	2 pm. 10 pm.		125 M GUN Coy marched to PERONNE. 5 LF working on roads, also 6 LF. CAPT A.O. NEEDHAM returned from leave. 125 Bde came under orders of 42nd DIVISION.	Wet	
PERONNE	17th	(1) 9 a.m. (2) 11 30 am	62 C 1/40.000.	(1) 7 LAN FUS marched to H 35. (FLAUCOURT) (2) Bde HQ. 5 LF, 6 LF, M GUN Coy + TM Batty proceeded to FRISE area. 5 LAN FUS billetted in ECLUSIER, also 6 LAN FUS. Bde HQ, MG Coy + TM Batty billetted at FRISE. 8th LAN FUS marched from CARTIGNY to FEUILLERES, leaving 2 platoons at CARTIGNY. Bde relieved by 126 Bde.	Rain.	
FRISE	18th.			Brig. Gen FRITH granted 10 day's leave. Lt B. SHELMERDINE returned to 7 LF, handing over to Capt A.O. NEEDHAM. 6 LF training.	Rain.	

1875 Wt. W593/826 1,000,000 4/15 J.B.C. & A. A.D.S.S./Forms/C. 2118.

Instructions regarding War Diaries and Intelligence Summaries are contained in F. S. Regs., Part II. and the Staff Manual respectively. Title Pages will be prepared in manuscript.

Army Form C. 2118

WAR DIARY

~~or~~

~~INTELLIGENCE SUMMARY~~ of 125th Inf Bde.
from APRIL 1st—APRIL 30th, 1917.

(Erase heading not required.)

Place	Date	Hour	Summary of Events and Information	WEATHER.	MAP REFERENCE	Remarks and references to Appendices
FRISE	19th		Lt Col P.V. HOLBERTON (1/5 LAN FUS) assumed command of Bde vice Brig Gen FRITH to ENGLAND on leave. 6LF training. Fc	Dry & warm		
"	20th.		Battns working on roads. 6LF training. Fc	do		
PERONNE.	21st.	9AM.	125th Bde HQ moved by march route to PERONNE. 7th LAN FUS marched to CARTIGNY and ×LE MESNIL BRUNTEL & billetted there. 8th LAN FUS moved to ESTREES-EN-CHAUSSEE (1 Coy) and MONS-EN-CHAUSSEE (Battn HQ & 2 Coys) and ×1 Coy there, and 100 men to BRIE. VILLERS-CARBONNEL (1 Coy), Fc	do.	1/40000 FRANCE 62C.	Bde O.O. No 9.
PERONNE	22nd		125 M Gun Coy & 125 TM Batty. moved by march route to PERONNE, also 6LF. Fc.			
"	23rd		Battns working on roads. One Section each of Bombers, Rifle Grenadiers, Lewis Gunners & Signallers training in each Battn. 5LF marched to NOBESCOURT FARM (K32B).			
"	24th		Battns working on roads. CAPT LAWRENCE (K.R.R.) succeeded MAJOR R.P. LEWIS 1st DEVON REGT (to 10th MANCHESTERS as Commdg Offr) as Bde Major.	Sunny & warm.		
"	25th.		Battns working on roads. Fc.	Dull but fine		
"	26th		Battns working on roads. 1 Coy 7LF to PERONNE. 2 platoons 8LF moved to FOUCAUCOURT. 2 coys 8LF to CERISY. 8LF HQ to PERONNE. Fc	Dry & warm		
"	27th.		do. do. Fc	do.		
"	28th.		Units informed that they must be prepared to move to support either of the Divisions of 3rd Corps [illegible] in line or either of flank Corps.	Fine.		

1875 Wt. W593/826 1,000,000 4/15 J.B.C. & A. A.D.S.S./Forms/C. 2118.

Instructions regarding War Diaries and Intelligence Summaries are contained in F. S. Regs., Part II. and the Staff Manual respectively. Title Pages will be prepared in manuscript.

Army Form C. 2118

WAR DIARY
or
~~INTELLIGENCE SUMMARY~~ OF 125TH INF BDE

(Erase heading not required.) FROM APRIL 1ST – APRIL 30TH 1917.

Place	Date	Hour	MAP REFERENCE	Summary of Events and Information	WEATHER	Remarks and references to Appendices
PERONNE	APRIL 28TH		FRANCE 62 C. 1/40,000.	G.O.C III CORPS conferred MILITARY MEDAL upon: No 7274 PTE STOCK. 1/6 LAN FUS and; No 281252 " J. DAVIES. 1/7 LAN FUS for assistance rendered in rescue of men buried by collapse of cellar at MALASSISE FARM on 13TH inst. Fe.	Dry & warm	After order to B.R.O. No 68.
" "	29TH	2 PM. 1.30 PM	" " / " "	6 LF moved by march route to BUIRE. Took over accommodation from 9th Man Rgt. 8 LF moved by march route to DOIGNT. (less 3½ Coys). Drew tents from D.A.D.O.S at DOIGNT & occupied same. Fe.	Sunny & warm.	Bde O.O. No 10.
TINCOURT.	30TH.	10 am	" "	5 LF marched to Camp K5 Central. 6 LF ordered to march to VILLERS FAUCON, units warned re relief of 48 Div by 42 Div. Detached Coys of 7 LF at BRIE and PERONNE rejoined. 125 M Gun Coy moved to TINCOURT. Bde HQ moved by march route to TINCOURT & occupied huts vacated by 145 Bde. Fe.	Fe. Dry & warm.	Bde O.O. No 11.

Hubert C. Frith
Brigadier General
Cmndg 125 Inf Bde.

1875 Wt. W593/826 1,000,000 4/15 J.B.C. & A. A.D.S.S./Forms/C. 2118.

Vol 4

CONFIDENTIAL

WAR DIARY

of

125TH INFANTRY BRIGADE

MAY 1ST — MAY 31ST

1917

VOLUME 34

May 31.17.

Army Form C. 2118

WAR DIARY
or
~~INTELLIGENCE SUMMARY~~
(Erase heading not required.)

Instructions regarding War Diaries and Intelligence Summaries are contained in F. S. Regs., Part II. and the Staff Manual respectively. Title Pages will be prepared in manuscript.

PAGE 1 MAY 1917. of 125TH INFY BDE VOL 34

Place	Date	Hour	MAP REFERENCE	Summary of Events and Information	WEATHER	Remarks and references to Appendices
PERONNE TINCOURT	MAY. 1ST	7am.	FRANCE 62C 1/40000.	Orders issued for relief of 144th Inf Bde by 125 Inf Bde. Time Table issued in Conjunction with Orders. 7LF marches to ROISEL (camp K5 central) Night 1/2 MAY:- 5LF moved to Right Subsector of Rt Bde Front. 6LF moved to E29a 88. 7LF moved from camp K5 central. 125 Bde HQ moved to TINCOURT. 125 T.M.B. moved to TINCOURT. 1/2 MGun Coy moved to Right Sub. Sector of Rt Bde Front. 7LF relieved 7th WORCESTERS (HQ at F27c 4.4)		Bde Op.O. No 11. Addendum No 1. JC
	2ND.		FRANCE 62 C NE.	Orders issued for relief of 5th LF and 6LF by 7th and 8th LF. 8LF moved to camp S.E. of VILLERS. FAUCON. 125 BDE HQ & TMB moved to F20b 25. HQ MGun Coy moved to HQ in line. Night 2/3 - 6LF moved to left Sub Sector of Rt Bde Front.		Bde Op.O. No 11. Addendum No 2. JC
ST EMILIE area.	3RD		do	Orders issued for relief of 125 Bde by 126 Bde. Relief of 144 Bde by 125 Bde completed NIGHT 2/3 MAY. (Bde HQ then being in RONSSOY WOOD) 8LF relieved 1/4 GLOS. REGT. supporting 1/6 LF. Bde HQ moved from RONSSOY WOOD to ST EMILIE. Bde Transport Lines established at K10 central. Brig Gen HC FRITH retd from leave.	Fine	Bde Op.O. No 12. JC
STEMILIE	4TH.		do	Lt Col PV HOLBERTON resumed command 1/5 LAN FUS. night 4/5. 6LF relieved by 10th Manchesters. 7LF relieved by 4th E. Lancs., & moved to K5 central camp as Divnl Reserve. 6LF moved to VILLERS FAUCON.		
ST. EMILIE	5TH	3pm.	do	Orders issued re Line of Resistance and work on BROWN LINE. night 5/6:- 5LF relieved by 9th Manchesters. 8LF relieved by 5th E Lancs. 125 TMB relieved by 126 TMB. Bde HQ relieved. 125 MGCoy (1/2) relieved by 126 MGCoy (1/2).		Bde Op.O. No 13. JC
ST. EMILIE	6TH	8pm.	do	Orders issued re relief of 127 Inf Bde by 125 Bde in Divnl Left Sector. 5LF at VILLERS FAUCON. night 6/7. HQ + 1/2 125 MG Coy relieved by HQ + 1/2 126 MG Coy. Bde HQ moved to LONGAVESNES.		Bde Op.O. No 14. JC
LONGAVESNES	7TH.		do.	5LF billeted in VILLERS FAUCON. Situation in line quiet.		JC
LONGAVESNES	8TH		FRANCE, 62c NE 57c SE } 1/20000	Night 8/9. 8LF relieved 6th Manchesters. HQ at '14 WILLOWS' X26c. - with 2 coys in BROWN LINE. 6LF relieved 7th Manchesters. HQ at EPEHY F1c27. Part 125 MGun Coy relieved part 127 MGCoy. HQ at PEIZIERES.		JC

1875 Wt. W593/826 1,000,000 4/15 J.B.C. & A. A.D.S.S./Forms/C. 2118.

Army Form C. 2118

Instructions regarding War Diaries and Intelligence Summaries are contained in F. S. Regs., Part II. and the Staff Manual respectively. Title Pages will be prepared in manuscript. PAGE 21

WAR DIARY
or
~~INTELLIGENCE SUMMARY~~
(Erase heading not required.)

MAY. 1917. of 125TH INF. BDE VOL No 34

Place	MAY Date	Hour	MAP REFERENCE	Summary of Events and Information	WEATHER	Remarks and references to Appendices
LONGAVESNES	9TH		FRANCE. 62C NE. and 57C SE 1/20 000.	5LF marched from VILLERS FAUCON to PEIZIERES. (in Bde Reserve)		
STEMILIE	10TH		do	On night 9/10 Bde HQ moved to S.EMILIE relieving 127 Bde HQ. 7LF moved to F1c58, relieving 5th Manchesters. 5LF relieved 8th Manchesters W30d42. HQ & remainder MGCoy relieved HQ & remainder 127 MGCoy in Left Sub Sector HQ (PEIZIERE) and Reserve. 125 TM Batty relieved 127 TMB at VILLERS-FAUCON (HQ) & in line. One of our aeroplanes brought down near CATELET COPSE as result of air fight between six of our machines and two enemy 'planes.	Very warm.	FC
STEMILIE	11TH		do	Orders recd. from GOC 42 Div. to move Bde HQ to EPEHY.	Very warm	FC
STEMILIE	12TH		do	5LF moved from PEIZIERES to 14 WILLOWS. (in LINE) relieving 8LF. Night 12/13. 8LF moved to PEIZIERES into 'support of left subsector'. Situation in line very quiet.	warm, and Thunder-showers.	FC
STEMILIE	13TH		do.	Night 13/14. Bde HQ moved to EPEHY. 7/LF relieved by 1/6LF, & moved to EPEHY.	warm and Showery	FC
EPEHY	14TH		do	Trenches & billets flooded by violent storm in night. LITTLE PRIEL FARM heavily shelled during afternoon.	Violent storm during night.	FC
EPEHY	15TH.		do.	1/7 LF. whole battn digging communication trench to outpost line at night.		FC
EPEHY	16TH	7am.	62 C 1/40.000. 62c NE 1/20,000	Bde op orders issued for relief of 125 BDE by 3rd CAVALRY BDE. Preparations made for relief. 5LF relieved by 8LF. former moving back to PEIZIERES. Situation in line quiet. Night 16/17 8LF ~~[illegible]~~ moved to 14 WILLOWS.		Bde Op. Ord. No16. FC

1875 Wt. W593/826 1,000,000 4/15 J.B.C. & A. A.D.S.S./Forms/C. 2118.

Army Form C. 2118

WAR DIARY

~~or~~

~~INTELLIGENCE SUMMARY~~ of

(Erase heading not required.) 125TH INFY BDE VOL 34

Instructions regarding War Diaries and Intelligence Summaries are contained in F. S. Regs., Part II. and the Staff Manual respectively. Title Pages will be prepared in manuscript.

PAGE 3 MAY 1917

Place	Date	Hour	MAP REFERENCE	Summary of Events and Information	WEATHER	Remarks and references to Appendices
EPEHY	17TH		62C 1/40.000 62 NE 1/20.000 57 C SE 1/20.000	Night 17/8. 7 LAN FUS relieved by 16th LANCERS – and moved to CAMP K5 CENTRAL ~~VILLERS FAUCON~~. 5 LAN FUS relieved by 5th LANCERS & moved to SAULCOURT. 125 M GUN COY relieved by No 3 MG Squadron & moved to VILLERS-FAUCON – 125 TMB moved to VILLERS FAUCON – ~~7LF~~	Fine.	JC
EPEHY	18TH		do.	5 LF camped in CHAUFFOURS WOOD – SAULCOURT. Night 18/19. 125 Bde HQ moved to LONGAVESNES. 8 LF relieved by 5th LANCERS and 1 squadron of 4th HUSSARS – and moved to VILLERS FAUCON. 6 LF relieved by 16th LANCERS and 1 squadron SCOTS GREYS. 6 LF moved to VILLERS FAUCON.		JC
LONGAVESNES	19TH		do.	Bde op orders issued for move of 125 Bde Group to EQUANCOURT. 5 LAN FUS at SAULCOURT; 6 LAN FUS, 7 LAN FUS, 8 LAN FUS AT VILLERS FAUCON. TM BATTY, M GUN COY AT VILLERS FAUCON 5 LF marched to EQUANCOURT.		Bde op order No 17. JC
LONGAVESNES	20TH	1pm.	62 C 1/40000	Bde Group marched to EQUANCOURT – Bde HQ offices opened there at 4pm. Bde HQ billetted at EQUANCOURT. 7 LAN FUS do – do – 8 LAN FUS do – do – 5 LAN FUS billetted in CAMP V 10 a; 6 LAN FUS do do do; M GUN COY do do V 11 a; T M Batty do do do. (429 Coy RE at FINS. 429 ASC at CAMP V 3 c)	Sunny and very warm	Bde op order No 17. JC
EQUANCOURT	21ST.		do.	Preparations made for relief of 60th Bde in line.	Close and Showery.	JC
EQUANCOURT	22ND	6pm	57C SE 1/20000	5 LF left EQUANCOURT and relieved 6TH OX & BUCKS REGT in line (Battn HQ VILLERS PLOUICH). Bde HQ moved to DESSART WOOD. (W 1 b 0 7) and relieved 60th Bde HQ. 7 LF in left sector of line – 5 LF in centre – 8 LF in right sector – 6th LF in GOUZEAUCOURT WOOD (reserve)	Wet.	JC
DESSART WOOD.	23RD	9.45pm.	do.	Situation quiet. Trenches improved – drained etc. Cloud-Gas alarm raised – but cancelled at about 10pm. Situation quiet.	Hot.	JC
DESSART WOOD	24TH		do.	Bde op orders issued for relief of 5 LF. 8 LF. & 1/2 Sections M. Gun Coy by 13th YORKS REGT & 21st MIDDLESEX REGT, & 121 M Gun Coy. also for relief of 7 LF by 6 LF.	Hot.	Bde op order No 19. JC

1875 Wt. W593/826 1,000,000 4/15 J.B.C. & A. A.D.S.S./Forms/C. 2118.

Army Form C. 2118

Instructions regarding War Diaries and Intelligence Summaries are contained in F. S. Regs., Part II. and the Staff Manual respectively. Title Pages will be prepared in manuscript. PAGE 4 VOL. 34.

WAR DIARY
~~or~~
~~INTELLIGENCE SUMMARY~~

(Erase heading not required.) of 125TH INFY BDE MAY 1917.

Place	Date	Hour	MAP REFERENCE	Summary of Events and Information	WEATHER	Remarks and references to Appendices
DESSART WOOD	25TH		57c SE 1/20.000	Night 25/26. 8LF relieved by 21st Middlesex Regt. 5LF relieved by 13TH Yorks Regt.	Hot.	Bde op. Order No 19. JC
DESSART WOOD.	26TH	1 am	ditto	The Germans raided post held by 21st MIDDLESEX Regt. a barrage of shell and rifle grenade (rie accompanying the raid. Raiding party entered our trench and then withdrew - taking one prisoner and one Lewis Gun. 8LF's last platoon was moving down communication trench when barrage commenced & casualties (8LF) were 1.OR killed & 1.OR wounded. 8LF moved to BERTINCOURT. 7LF relieved by 6 LF, & marched to BERTINCOURT.	Hot	JC
DESSART WOOD	27TH	5 pm.	57C SE 1/20000	Bde HQ marched to YTRES.	Hot	Addendum No1 Bde op. Order No 19.
			57c 1/40.000.	Night 27/28. 6th Lan Fus relieved by 2/5th Leicester Regt. 5th Lan Fus relieved by 5th Lincoln Regt. Situation Quiet. 125 Bde HQ relieved by 121 Bde HQ. 5LF moved to YTRES.		JC
YTRES	28TH		ditto	Battalions, MG Coy & TM Batty training. Working parties provided for R.E and Town Major YTRES. 6LF marched to YTRES (P20d).	Hot	JC
YTRES	29TH		ditto	Battalions & MG Coy training (& TM Batty). Working parties provided for R.E. and TOWN MAJOR YTRES.	Fine but dull.	JC
YTRES	30TH	330pm 430pm.	ditto	Battalions & MG Coy training (& TM Batty) Working parties provided for R.E. & Town Major YTRES 1/7 Lan Fus } 1/8 Lan Fus } inspected by GOC Bde.	Sunny	JC
YTRES	31ST.	945 am	ditto.	Inspection of personnel & transport of Bde HQ. by Brig Gen FRITH. Battalions training. 1/6 Lan Fus inspected by GOC Bde. Working parties provided for RE & Town Major YTRES.	Fine	JC
	31.5.17					

[signature] Frith
Brigadier. General
Commanding 125TH INF. BDE

CONFIDENTIAL

Vol 5

WAR DIARY

of

125TH INFY BDE

JUNE 1ST – 30TH.

1917

VOL No. 35.

CONFIDENTIAL

WAR DIARY

of

125TH INFY BDE

from

JUNE 1ST - 30TH
1917

VOL, NO 36.

Army Form C. 2118

Instructions regarding War Diaries and Intelligence Summaries are contained in F. S. Regs., Part II. and the Staff Manual respectively. Title Pages will be prepared in manuscript.

WAR DIARY

~~or~~ ~~INTELLIGENCE SUMMARY~~ of

(Erase heading not required.)

JUNE 1917. 125th INFY BDE. PAGE 1. VOL NO. 35

Place	Date	Hour	MAP REFERENCE	Summary of Events and Information	WEATHER.	Remarks and references to Appendices
YTRES	1st.		FRANCE MAP. 57c. 1/40.000 57c.S.E. 1/20.000.	Bde training under Battn arrangements. Working parties for R.E. 5 LF inspected by Brig. Gen. H.C. FRITH. 7 LF " " " " "	Fine	JC
YTRES	2nd.		do.	Bde training under Battn arrangements. Working parties for R.E.	do	JC
YTRES	3rd		do.	Orders issued for relief of 126th Bde in the line. 2 Sections M.G.Coy assisted 126 M.G.Coy in barrage from HAVRINCOURT WOOD.	do.	Bde Op.O. No 20. Addendum No 1. to Op.O. No 20. JC
YTRES	4th		do.	Advance parties from units 125 Bde visited Front and Reserve Lines, and remained there.	do	Addendum No 1. and Bde JC
YTRES	5th		do.	Afternoon. 5 LF relieved 4 E. LANCS in Right Reserve. 6 LF relieved 10th MANCHrs in Left Reserve. night 5/6. 7 LF relieved 9th MANCHESTERS in Right Subsector. 8 LF relieved 5th E. LANCS in left Subsector. 127 Bde on left of 8 LF. 178 Bde on right of 7 LF. (6th Notts & Derby Regt).	do	Operatn. Order No 20. JC
YTRES - HAVRINCOURT WOOD	6th	8 a.m.	do.	Bde HQ moved to HAVRINCOURT WOOD. Q14d.1.7. and relieved 126 Bde HQ. 5 LF HQ. P18d.7.3. 6 LF HQ. Q7d.3.4. 7 LF HQ. Q14b5.3. 8 LF HQ. Q8d.2.4. M.Gun Coy HQ. Q13d.8.8. night 6/7. 125 Machine Gun Coy relieved 126 M.Gun Coy.	do	JC
HAVRINCOURT WOOD	7th		do.	Orders issued re co-operation of 125 Bde with 127 Bde. in Consolidation of line K33c.7.0. K32b2.1. K32b1.7. K32a.9.9. Situation quiet.	do	Bde Op.O. No 21. JC
HAVRINCOURT WOOD	8th		do.	Situation quiet. night 8/9. 125 M.Gun Coy & 8 LF. assisted 127 Bde in consolidation of new line.	do	JC

1875 Wt. W593/826 1,000,000 4/15 J.B.C. & A. A.D.S.S./Forms/C. 2118.

Instructions regarding War Diaries and Intelligence Summaries are contained in F. S. Regs., Part II. and the Staff Manual respectively. Title Pages will be prepared in manuscript.

WAR DIARY

~~or~~

~~INTELLIGENCE SUMMARY~~

(Erase heading not required.)

Army Form C. 2118

JUNE 1917. of 125TH INFY BDE. PAGE 2. VOL. 35

Place	Date	Hour	MAP REFERENCE.	Summary of Events and Information	WEATHER.	Remarks and references to Appendices
HAVRINCOURT WOOD.	9TH		FRANCE. 57C 1/40000 57CSE. 1/20000.	Orders issued for 5th LF and 6LF to relieve 7th & 8LF respectively in line on night 11/12. Situation Quiet.	Fine. Thundery.	Bde order Y.14. JC
do.	10TH		do.	Orders issued postponing relief of 7th & 8LF until night 12/13. Situation very Quiet.	Fine. Thunder Showers. Wet night	Bde order Y.14/1. JC
do.	11TH.		do.	Orders issued for relief of 7LF by 5LF and for taking over portion of Line from 127 Bde – 5LF relieved 7LF in Right sub. sector – 7LF going into Bde Reserve –	Fine.	Bde Op. Order No 22. JC
do.	12TH		do.	night 12/13. 6LF took over portion of line from 6th MANCHESTERS (HQ. Q7 b 34) Bde Left Boundary extended to include that portion of line held by 6 M/c Regt	Sunny.	Bde Op order No 22 JC
do.	13TH		do.	7LF moved into 6LF HQs (vacated). 9th MANCHESTERS moved up from Second Line to act as Bde Reserve. taking over HQs vacated by 7LF. night 13/14. 125 M. GUN coy took over from 127 M GUN Coy up to New Bde Left Boundary.		" " JC
do	14TH.		do	Line quiet in day but hostile Minenwerfer & MGs active during night. General work on defences.		JC
do	15TH		do	7LF relieved 8LF in Centre Sub-Sector – 8LF going into Bde Reserve. 7LF advanced H.Q. moved into Dug out at Q3 c 9.3.		Bde Letter Y19. JC
do	16TH		do.	Situation Quiet – Line improved – patrols sent to EMY WOOD etc.		JC

1875 Wt. W593/826 1,000,000 4/15 J.B.C. & A. A.D.S.S./Forms/C. 2118.

Instructions regarding War Diaries and Intelligence Summaries are contained in F. S. Regs., Part II. and the Staff Manual respectively. Title Pages will be prepared in manuscript.

WAR DIARY

or

~~INTELLIGENCE SUMMARY~~ of 125TH. INFY BDE

(Erase heading not required.) JUNE 1917.

Army Form C. 2118

PAGE 3.

VOL. 35.

Place	Date	Hour	MAP REFERENCES	Summary of Events and Information	WEATHER	Remarks and references to Appendices
HAVRINCOURT WOOD	JUNE 17TH	12.30 am	FRANCE 57C SE 1/20.000.	Hostile raid on post dispersed by L.G. fire (6LF). Situation quiet otherwise.	Fine	
do	18TH		" "	Enemy positions in FEMY WOOD bombed by fighting patrol, and subjected to M. Gun barrage during night.	Fine	
do	19TH		" "	Orders issued for relief of 125 Bde by 126 Bde — Heavy rain.	Thundery	Bde Op Order No 23.
do	20TH		" "	Trenches flooded. heavy rain storms.	Heavy rain.	
do.	21ST		" "	night 21/22. 125 Bde relieved by 126 Bde — 5LF by 5E.LANCS Right S. Sector, 6LF by 4E. LANCS in left Sub Sector — 7LF by 10 MANCHESTERS in Centre Sub-sector. 8LAN FUS remaining in Bde left Reserve — and 9th MANCHESTERS relieving 4E.LANCS in Bde Right Reserve — 5LF & 6LF to YTRES. 7LF to BERTINCOURT		Bde Op Order No 23
YTRES	22ND		" "	125 Bde HQ relieved by 126 Bde HQ — & proceeded to YTRES. night 22/23. 125 T. MORTAR BATTY relieved 126 TMB in line — also M Gun Coy		"
YTRES	23RD		" "	Bde Training — General inspection by G.O.C. Gen. H.C. FRITH CB relinquished command of 125 Bde & proceeded to ENGLAND — "X". 125 Bde HQ at YTRES. 5LF at YTRES. 7LF at BERTINCOURT. 6LF at YTRES. 125 M Gun Coy at YTRES. (HQ & 1 section).	Sunny. Storms.	
do.	24TH		" "	Bde Training — General inspection by G.O.C. Orders issued for relief of 8LF by 5LF.	Sunny	Bde Op Order No 24

"X". Brig. Gen H. FARGUS. CMG. DSO. assumed Command of 125 Infy Bde vice Brig Gen HC FRITH.

1875 Wt. W593/826 1,000,000 4/15 J.B.C. & A. A.D.S.S./Forms/C. 2118.

Instructions regarding War Diaries and Intelligence Summaries are contained in F. S. Regs., Part II. and the Staff Manual respectively. Title Pages will be prepared in manuscript.

WAR DIARY

~~INTELLIGENCE SUMMARY~~ Of 125TH INFY BDE . JUNE 1917.

(Erase heading not required.)

Army Form C. 2118

PAGE 4

VOL: 35.

Place	Date	Hour	MAP REFERENCE	Summary of Events and Information	WEATHER	Remarks and references to Appendices
YTRES	JUNE 25TH		57C SE 1/20000. FRANCE	Orders issued for relief of 125 LIGHT TRENCH MORTAR BATTY by 126 TMB. 5LF & 7LF. route marching.	Fine.	Bde Op Order No 25
" "	26th		ditto	CAPT. A.E. LAWRENCE (Bde Major) proceeded to PARIS on six day's leave. Orders issued for ~~with~~ withdrawal of 2 coys of 6LF from HAURINCOURT WOOD. Bde training. 5LF inspected by Brig. Gen FARGUS C.M.G. D.S.O.	Fine	addendum to Bde Op. Order No 24
" "	27th		ditto	Bde training – Attack formations – bombing – musketry etc.	Showery	
" "	28th		ditto	Bde training – Further orders issued re relief of 8LF by 5LF.	Showery	addendum No 2 to Bde Op Order No. 24.
" "	29th		ditto	Bde training: 8LF relieved by 5LF. in left Reserve to 126 Bde. 2 coys 6LF withdrawn from HAURINCOURT WOOD to YTRES.	Showery	Bde Op Order No 24 & addendum to same.
" "	30th		ditto.	Bde training –	Showery	

Harold Fargus Brig. Genl Cmmdg 125th Infy Bde

1875 Wt. W593/826 1,000,000 4/15 J.B.C. & A. A.D.S.S./Forms/C. 2118.

CONFIDENTIAL

WAR DIARY

OF

125TH TRENCH MORTAR BATTERY.

JUNE THE 1ST — 30TH, 1917.

VOL. No 2.

Army Form C. 2118. 1.

Instructions regarding War Diaries and Intelligence Summaries are contained in F. S. Regs., Part II. and the Staff Manual respectively. Title pages will be prepared in manuscript.

VOL 35

WAR DIARY ~~or INTELLIGENCE SUMMARY~~ OF 125 TRENCH MORTAR BATTERY for month of June 1917.

(Erase heading not required.)

Place	Date	SEET ~~Hour~~ REFERENCE	Summary of Events and Information	Remarks and references to Appendices
YTRES.	1/6/17	57C.S.E.	Battery at YTRES in camp (P.20.b.2.1) at rest. Training being carried on. Strength of Battery 4 officers and 40 O.R.S	J.B.S.
YTRES	2/6/17 to 6/6/17	"	Battery continues its training in camp here (P.20.b.2.1.). Weather fine & hot.	J.B.S.
YTRES	7/6/17		The Battery, having received instructions to proceed to the IVth Army School of Mortars for course of instruction, march to FINS & proceed therefrom by train (DECAUVILLE) to PERONNE and spend night there in 42nd Divisional Reinforcement Camp	J.B.S.
PERONNE	8/6/17		Battery leaves PERONNE (LA CHAPALETTE station) and proceed by train to AMIENS leaving PERONNE at midday & arriving AMIENS at 4:15 p.m. The Battery is then marched to IVth Army School of Mortars at VAUX-EN-AMIENOIS, lorry transport being provided for guns & battery stores.	J.B.S.
VAUX-EN-AMIENOIS	9/6/17 to 19/6/17		Battery attends refresher course at IVth Army School of Mortars – Instruction is given in the use of the new rings (BALLISTITE). Strength of Battery is reduced by four (N.C.O's) who, under instruction from Brigade & Division, rejoin their own Divisions	J.B.S.
VAUX-EN-AMIENOIS	19/6/17		Battery leaves IVth Army School of Mortars at 3 o'c a.m. by route march to LONGUEAU where it entrains for PERONNE (LA CHAPALETTE station) & arrives there at 3 o'c. p.m. Night spent at 42nd Divl Reinforcement camp	J.B.S.

1577 Wt. W10791/1773 500,000 1/15 D. D. & L. A.D.S.S./Forms/C. 2118.

Army Form C. 2118.

2.

Instructions regarding War Diaries and Intelligence Summaries are contained in F. S. Regs., Part II. and the Staff Manual respectively. Title pages will be prepared in manuscript.

WAR DIARY ~~or INTELLIGENCE SUMMARY~~ OF 125 TRENCH MORTAR BATTERY

(Erase heading not required.)

Place	Date	SHEET ~~Hour~~ REF'NCE.	Summary of Events and Information	Remarks and references to Appendices
PERONNE	20/6/17	57C S.E.	Battery leaves PERONNE (QUINCONCE Station) at 1:30 p.m. & arrive at FINS Station at 4:30 p.m. & proceed by route march to camp at YTRES (P.20.b.2.1).	JBS
YTRES	21/6/17		Battery relieves 126 TRENCH MORTAR BATTERY in line at HAVRINCOURT WOOD - headquarters being at Q.14.c.5.3., Section headquarters Q.4.c.6.6. One mortar at Q4.b.50.55 one at Q.3.b.75.75, one at Q.3.a.70.90 and one with Section headquarters. During relief in TRESCAULT, Q.10.a.8.7 1 N.C.O + 6 men were hit by hostile shell (4.2") one of these was subsequently able to return to duty after treatment at dressing Station.	JBS
IN THE LINE	22/6/17		From mortar at Q.3.a.7.9. we fired at 10.30 p.m. 11:45 p.m & 12:45 am (23/6/17) 16 rounds in all - Retaliation by hostile T.M.'s & 4.2's was experienced	JBS
IN THE LINE	23/6/17		A quiet day in the line. The mortars were not fired (except at 12:45 a.m. as before mentioned).	JBS
IN THE LINE	24/6/17		At 11:50 a.m. one mortar at Q.3.a.7.9. received a direct hit from a medium MINENWERFER destroying gun and certain ammunition. No casualties to men, they having been withdrawn just prior to the gun's destruction, by the Officer in charge (2nd Lt. C.F. FRENCH) Later in the day this emplacement again received another direct ~~hit~~ from hostile Shell fire & was further demolished.	JBS

Instructions regarding War Diaries and Intelligence Summaries are contained in F. S. Regs., Part II. and the Staff Manual respectively. Title pages will be prepared in manuscript.

WAR DIARY OF 125 TRENCH MORTAR BATTERY.

~~INTELLIGENCE SUMMARY.~~

(Erase heading not required.)

Army Form C. 2118.

3.

Place	Date	~~Hour~~ SHEET REFNCE	Summary of Events and Information	Remarks and references to Appendices
IN THE LINE	24/6/17 (contd)	57C SE	At 10.10 p.m., 11.20 p.m. + 11.45 p.m. mortar at Q.3.b.75.75 fired 12 rounds, target being X.34.c.05.25. 2 Shells failed to explode. A new emplacement was made at Q.3.a.75.95 near "F" Sap in lieu of old one demolished by shell fire	J.B.E.
IN THE LINE	25/6/17		Line very quiet + no shooting of our mortars took place on this day. Under compliance with Brigade Orders both Sergeants of the Battery were returned to their own Divisions. Their names are 200235 SGT HOMAN. G.H 1/4 R.BERKS REGT, 48th DIV. and 43052 SGT EDGAR.T. 1st CAMERON REGT, 1st DIVISION	J.B.E.
IN THE LINE	26/6/17		A shoot ~~tat~~ took place at 11 o.c - 12 o.c midnight from mortar in the open near Section headquarters (Q.4.c.6.6) 16 rounds were fired, target being CHALK PIT in front of HARRISON TRENCH - No shells failed to explode.	J.B.E.
IN THE LINE	27/6/17		Line quiet, no shooting took place from our mortars.	J.B.E.
IN THE LINE	28/6/17		At 3 o'c a.m. 8 rounds were fired from new emplacement at Q.3.a.75.95 target being poplar trees on our immediate front - All shells exploded	J.B.E.
IN THE LINE	29/6/17		Battery was relieved in line by the 126th TRENCH MORTAR BATTERY.	J.B.E.

1577 Wt. W10791/1773 500,000 1/15 D. D. & L. A.D.S.S./Forms/C. 2118.

Instructions regarding War Diaries and Intelligence Summaries are contained in F. S. Regs., Part II. and the Staff Manual respectively. Title Pages will be prepared in manuscript.

WAR DIARY ~~or~~ ~~INTELLIGENCE SUMMARY~~ OF 125 TRENCH MORTAR BATTERY

(Erase heading not required.)

Army Form C. 2118

4.

Place	Date	SHEET ~~Hour~~ REFNCE	Summary of Events and Information	Remarks and references to Appendices
YTRES	30/6/17		Battery arrived at camp in YTRES (P.20.b.2.1) at 3 o'c. am. on this day. Battery strength 4 Offrs. + 38 O.R.S.	J.B.S.

J. B. [illegible] Capt

O/c 125 Trench Mortar Battery.

1875 Wt. W593/826 1,000,000 4/15 J.B.C. & A. A.D.S.S./Forms/C. 2118.

WO

SECRET. COPY NO. 10.

125th. BRIGADE WARNING ORDER NO. 23.

1-7-17

Ref: 57 c. 1.40,000.

1. The 58th. Division will shortly relieve the 59th., and 42nd. Divisions, and take over Command of their Divisional area.

2. The 42nd. Division on relief will move to an area about BAPAUME where it will be in Third Army Reserve.

3. The 125th. Infantry Brigade Group will probably march from its present billets to the BAPAUME area on 6th. July.

4. The 429 Coy. A.S.C. will move with 125th. Brigade Group.

5. ACKNOWLEDGE.

L.L. Robinson.

Capt.,

For Bde. Major,

125th. Brigade.

Issued at 9 am By Orderly.

Copy No. 1 to 5th. L.F.
2 6th. L.F.
3 7th. L.F.
4 8th. L.F.
5 125th. M.G. Coy.
6 125th T.M.B.
7. 429 Coy. A.S.C.
8. S.C.
9. 42nd. Div.
10 W.D.
11. W.D.
12 File.

SECRET. COPY NO....16...

125th.BRIGADE ORDER NO. 36.

Map Reference: 57 C. 1/40,000.

1. The 125th.Bde.Group will march from present area to GOMMIECOURT area on 6th.inst.,as per attached table.

2. All units will march closed up to regulation.distances with 1st. Line Transport. Baggage Wagons will march with the train. 400 yds.interval is to be kept between units.

3. Watches will be syncronized by an officer from each unit at Bde. H.Q. at 7.p.m.,5th.inst.

4. Completion of moves to be reported to Bde,H.Q.

5. Bde.H.Q. will close at YTRES at 5 a.m.,6th.inst.,and open at 1-p.m. same day at GOMMIECOURT.

6. Details of the relief of the Sections M.G.Coy.in HAVRINCOURT Wood will be issued later.

7. A C K N O W L E D G E.

A L Lawrence
Capt.,
Bde.Major,
125th.Bde.

Issued at..2.30 pm.......

Copy No.1 to 5th.L.F.
2 6th.L.F.
3 7th.L.F.
4 8th.L.F.
5 125th.M.G.C.
6 " T.M.B.
7 428 Fd.Coy.R.E.
8 1/2 E.L.Fd.Amb.
9. 429 Co.A.S.C.
10 Bde.T.O.
11 42nd.Div.
12 126th.Bde.
13 S.C.
14 B.G.O.
15 Signals.
16 W.D.
17 W.D.
18 and 19 FILE.

UNIT.	STARTING POINT.	TIME.	ROUTE.	REMARKS.
5th L.F.	Cross Roads, BUS. O 24 b 2.0.	6-0 a.m.	BUS-ROCQUIGNY-LE TRANSLOY BAPAUME-SAPIGNIES.	
7th L.F.	-do-	6-10 a.m.	-do-	
Brigade H.Q.	-do-	6-20 a.m.	-do-	
6th L.F.	-do-	6-25 a.m.	-do-	
8th L.F.	-do-	6-35 a.m.	-do-	
125th M.G.Coy.	-do-	6-45 a.m.	-do-	
125th T.M.Battery.	-do-	6-50 a.m.	-do-	
1/2nd E. Lancs. Field Ambulance.	-do-	7-10 a.m.	-do-	Not to enter YTRES before 6-25 a.m.
428 Field Coy. R.E.	-do-	7-20 a.m.	-do-	Headquarters and 2 sections to march direct to BIHUCOURT from BAPAUME.
429 Coy A.S.C.	Road junction ROCQUIGNY. O 27 c 2.6.	8-20 a.m.	-do-	

S E C R E T.

No.......

125th BRIGADE O.O. No. 20.

1. 125th Brigade will relieve 126th Brigade in the Line on Night 5/6 June, and 6/7 June.

2. 7th L.F. will relieve 9th Manchesters. Right Front.
8th L.F. " " 5th East Lancs. Left Front.
5th L.F. " " 4th " " Right Reserve.
6th L.F. " " 10th Manchesters. Left Reserve.

3. Commanding Officers will report to 126th Brigade Headquarters, Q 14 d 1.7. for guides at 12.30.p.m. 4th June. 1 Officer a Company, 1 N.C.O a Platoon of 2 Front Battalions, 2 guides per Company of Reserve Battalions and 1 man per each Vickers Gun in the Front ~~Line~~ and INTERMEDIATE Lines will report at same time. These representatives will remain in the line until their Units come in on relief.

4. All details of relief to be arranged between Commanding Officers concerned.

5. A C K N O W L E D G E.

[signature]

Captain,
Brigade Major,
125th BRIGADE.

Issued at.......

Copies to :-

1. 5th L.F.
2. 6th L.F.
3. 7th L.F.
4. 8th L.F.
5. 125 M.G.Coy.
7. 126th Brigade.
8. 42nd Division.
9. Signal Officer.
10. Staff Captain.
11.} War Diary.
12.}
13. F I L E.

S E C R E T.
****

Copy No. 10

ADDENDUM No. 1 TO O.O. No 20.

3/6/17.

1. Reference para 2 of O.O.20. Relief of Front line Battalions to take place on Night 5/6th June. Relief of Reserve Battalions to be completed by 5.p.m. 5th June.

2. Machine Gun Company will relieve on Night 6/7th June i,e. 24 hours later than the Infantry.

3. Prior to 10.a.m. 6th inst all Units to report relief complete to 126th Brigade using code word "WAZER".

4. All maps (except 57c $\frac{1}{40,000}$) photographs, S.A.A. Grenades, Rockets, Tools, Petrol Tins, Horns, Defence Schemes and Instructions re work policy to be taken over.

5. 126th Trench Mortar Battery ~~xxxxxxxxxxxxxxx~~ will be attached to 125th Brigade during absence of 125th T.M.B.

6. Dispositions will be :-

Brigade Headquarters.	Q 14 d 1.7.
Right Front Battalion.	Q 14 b 5.3.
Left " "	Q 8 d 2.4.
Right Reserve Battn.	P 18 d 7.3.
Left " "	Q 7 d 3.4.
Machine Gun Company.	Q 13 d 8.8.

7. Brigade Headquarters will close at YPRES at 8.a.m. 6th inst and open at Q 14 d 1.7 at 10.a.m. at which hour Command will pass.

8. A C K N O W L E D G E.

A. J. Lawrence
Captain,
Brigade Major,
126th BRIGADE.

Issued at 8.30.p.m.
Copies to:-

1. 5th L.F.
2. 6th L.F.
3. 7th L.F.
4. 8th L.F.
5. 125 M.G.Coy.
6. 123th Brigade.
7. 42nd Division.
8. Signal Officer.
9. Staff Captain.
10.) War Diary.
11.)
12. F I L E.
13. 429th Coy A.S.C.
14. Brigade Transport Officer.
15. 127 Bde
16. 178 Bde

W.D.

SECRET.

Copy No. 12

125th BRIGADE O.O.No.21. 7/6/17.

1. On the night of 8/9th June the 127th Brigade will establish a line on approximately Post F (K 33 c 7.0) to K 32 b 2.1 K 32 b 1.7 K 32 a 9.9.

2. During the consolidation of this line the 127th Brigade will avoid as far as possible encounters with the enemy but artillery, machine gun and trench mortar assistance has been arranged for.

3. 125th M.G.Coy will arrange for two guns to be in position to fire on the corner of the Wood at K 33 d 3.4 where an enemy M.G. is suspected.

4. On the same night 8th L.F. will dig a post at about K 33 d 30.15.

5. 8th L.F. will be prepared to assist the 127th BRIGADE with fire from their forward posts, should the enemy endeavour to prevent them digging in on the line mentioned in para 1.

6. ACKNOWLEDGE.

A.P. Lawrence
Captain,
Brigade Major,
125th BRIGADE.

Issued at :-

Copies to:-

1. 5th L.F.
2. 6th L.F.
3. 7th L.F.
4. 8th L.F.
5. 125 M.G.Coy.
6. 125 T.M.Batty.
7. 127th Brigade.
8. 178th "
9. 428th Fd Coy R.E.
10. 42nd Division.
11. 210th Brigade R.A.
12)
13) War Diary.
14 FILE.

SECRET.

Y.14.

5th L.F.
6th L.F.
7th L.F.
8th L.F.
125 M.G.Coy.
125 T.M.Batty.
428th Fd Coy R.E.
210th Bde R.A.
42nd Division.
127th Brigade.
178th "
Signal Officer.
Staff Captain.
F I L E.
War Diary.
" "

---

1. 5th and 6th L.F. will relieve 7th and 8th L.F. respectively in the line on the night of 11/12 June.

2. All details to be arranged by C.Os concerned.

3. Relief complete to be reported to Brigade Headquarters by code word "HOPS".

[signature]

Captain,
Brigade Major,
125th BRIGADE.

9/6/17.

S E C R E T.
==*=*=*=*

Y.14/1.

5th L.F.
6th L.F.
7th L.F.
8th L.F.
125th M.G.Coy.
125th T.M.Battery.
428th Fd Coy R.E.
210th Brigade R.A.
42nd Division.
127th Brigade.
178th "
Signal Officer.
Staff Captain.
F I L E.
War Diary.
" "

Reference No.Y.14/1 of 9/6/17, para 1.

The relief mentioned in para 1 will take place on the night 12/13 June.

A. Lawrence

Captain,
Brigade Major,
125th BRIGADE.

10/6/17.

Issued at 12.30.p.m.

S E C R E T.

Copy No..16..

125th BRIGADE O.O. NUMBER 22. June 11th 1917.

1. 5th L.F. are relieving 7th L.F. in Right Sub-Sector to-night. 7th L.F. will go into Brigade Reserve.

2. 125th Brigade are taking over a portion of 127th Brigade Line on night 12/13 June. The New Brigade Left Boundary will then run as follows:-
K 27 d 1.0 - K 33 a 7.0 - K 33 d 7.0 (in the Front Line) - X Roads Q 7 a 5.2 - P 6 c 2.1 - P 10 c 0.0 - P 9 central to the Corps Northern Boundary in P 2 b central.
The track running through K 32 d 8.0 to K 33 central is inclusive to 125th Brigade.

3. On night 12/13 June the 6th L.F. will take over this portion of the line from 6th Manchesters and also up to Sutton Post (K 33 d 4.0) exclusive from 8th L.F. 6th L.F. will take over 6th Manchesters Headquarters at Q 7 b 3.4. The stream running through Q 4 a and c will remain the Boundary between the Right and Centre Battalions.

4. On Night 13/14 June 125th Machine Gun Company will take over from 127th Brigade Machine Gun Company up to New Brigade Left Boundary.

5. On Night 12/13 June 7th L.F. will take over accommodation vacated by 6th L.F. Two Platoons will be the permanent Garrison of the Intermediate Line and hold Number 4 locality Q 8 a 6.2 - Q 8 a 3.4.

6. On Night 13/13th June One Battalion of 126th Brigade less one Company which will remain as permanent Garrison of Second Line (42nd Division O.O No 28 para 6 a) will move up into HAVRINCOURT WOOD and become Brigade Reserve.
The Headquarters and Three Companies will take over accommodation vacated by 7th L.F.
Battn less 1 Coy ~~The Battalion~~ will then be accommodated as follows:-
Headquarters, at P 18 d 7.3.
Three Companies in Intermediate Line and vicinity.
Two Platoons will be the permanent Garrison of the Intermediate Line and hold Number 2 Locality Q 8 d 7.3 - Q 8 d 50.45.

7. All details of relief to be arranged between C.Os concerned.

8. Relief complete to be reported ~~complete~~ to Brigade Headquarters by Code word "TEEK".

9. A C K N O W L E D G E.

A R Lawrence
Captain,
Brigade Major,
125th BRIGADE.

Issued at..11.P.M.
Copies To:-
1. 5th L.F.
2. 6th L.F.
3. 7th L.F.
4. 8th L.F.
5. 125th M.G.Coy.
6. 125th T.M.Batty.
7. Staff Captain.
8. Signal Officer.
9. Brigade T.O.
10.)
11.) 126th Brigade.
12. 127th Brigade.
13. 177th "
14. 42nd Division.
15. F I L E.
16.)
17.) War Diary.

S E C R E T.

Y.19.

5th Lan Fus.
6th " "
7th " "
~~7th " "~~
8th " "
9th Manchesters.
125th M.G.Coy.
126th T.M.Batty.
210th Brigade R.A.
42nd Division.
127th Brigade.
176th "
Staff Captain.
Brigade Transport Officer.

---

1. 7th Lan Fus will relieve the 8th Lan Fus in Centre Sub-Sector to-night.

8th Lan Fus going into Left Brigade Reserve.

2. Headquarters will change over.

3. 7th Lan Fus Advanced Headquarters will move into Dug-Out in Quarry Q 5 c 9.3 tomorrow.

4. A C K N O W L E D G E.

A Lawrence

Captain.
Brigade Major,
125th BRIGADE.

15/6/17.

SECRET. W.D Copy No. 21.

125th INFANTRY BRIGADE O.O. No.23.

19/6/17.

1. 126th Brigade will relieve 125th Brigade in the Line on night 21/22nd June.

2. (a). 5th East Lancs will relieve 5th Lan Fus in Right Sub-Sector.

(b). 10th Manchesters will relieve 7th Lan Fus in Centre Sub-Sector.

(c). 4th East Lancs will relieve 6th Lan Fus in Left Sub-Sector.

(d). 9th Manchesters will relieve 4th East Lancs in Brigade Right Reserve.

(e). 8th Lan Fus will remain in Brigade Left Reserve, sending one Company as permanent Garrison 2nd Line (P 18 d 3.3) to relieve one Company 4th East Lancs by 3.p.m. 21/6/17.

(f). No Battalions relieving in the Front Line will pass PLACE MORTMARE before 10.p.m. (except parties mentioned in Table "A" paras (g) and (h)).

3. After Relief:-

(a). 5th Lan Fus will be accommodated in YTRES, taking over from 9th Manchesters.

(b). 6th Lan Fus will be at YTRES taking over from ~~xxx~~ 10th Manchesters.

(c). 6th Lan Fus will detail two Companies with a total working strength of not less than 220 workers to take over from 5th East Lancs and 10th Manchesters to work on burying cable. They will be accommodated at P 18 b 5.3.
Captain LASKI will be in Command.
This party will not work before 6.a.m. 23rd inst.

(d). 7th Lan Fus will be in BERTINCOURT taking over from 5th East Lancs.

4. ~~126th M.G.Company will find the following permanent Garrisons~~

4. 126th M.G.Company will take over from 125th M.G.Company on night 22/23rd June.

125th M.G.Company will find the following permanent Garrisons :-

(a). One Section in INTERMEDIATE LINE (Right Sector)

(b). One Section in Second Line. (Right Sector)

(c). One Section in Second Line. (Left Sector)

5. 125th T.M.Battery will relieve 126th T.M.Battery in the Line 20/21st June.

6. All details of relief are to be arranged between C.O's concerned.

7. All sketches, photographs, and Orders connected with the Defence and working policy of the Line are to be handed over on relief.

P.T.O.

8. Working Parties found by Right Brigade will be relieved as per table "A".

9. Working parties to be found by REserve Brigade will be relieved as per Table "B".

10. Command of Sector will pass to G.O.C. 126th Brigade at 10.a.m. 22nd inst.

11. 125th Brigade will close at Q 14 d 1.7 at 10.a.m. 22nd inst, and open at 12.noon at YTRES.

12. Administrative Instructions will be issued by Staff Captain.

13. Relief Complete to be wired by Code Word "PRATT".

14. A C K N O W L E D G E.

[A. E. Lawrence]

Captain,
Brigade Major,
125th BRIGADE.

Issued at 8.p.m. by D.R.

Copies To:-

1. 5th Lan Fus.
2. 6th " "
3. 7th " "
4. 8th " "
5. 4th East Lancs.
6. 125th M.G.Company.
7. 126th T.M.Battery.
8. 125th T.M.Battery.
9. 428th Field Company R.E.
10. 428th Field Coy R.E.
11. 429th " " "
12. 256th Tunnelling Company. R.E.
13. 210thBrigade R.A.
14. 127th Brigade.
15. 176th Brigade.
16. 42nd Division.
17. Staff Captain.
18. Signal Officer.
19 17. Brigade Transport Officer.
20 18. 429th Company A.S.C.
21 19. } War Diary.
22 20. }
23 21. F I L E.

TABLE "A" OF WORKING PARTIES FOUND BY 125th BRIGADE.

	Location	Party	Relief / Arrangements
(a).	Right Brigade H.Q. Q 8 a 1.4.	24 men Daily. 3. 8 hour shifts of 8 men each.	8th Lan Fus will relieve 4th East Lancs at 4.p.m. 21/6/17.
(b).	TRESCAULT WELL. Q 10 a 4.6.	4 men.	10th Manchesters will relieve 5th Lanc Fus at an hour to be arranged between C.O's concerned.
(c).	Well. Q 9 a 1.4.	12 men Daily. 3. 8 hour shifts of 8 men each.	8th Lan Fus will relieve 4th East Lancs at 4.p.m. 21/6/17.
(d).	Brigade H.Q. COSY COPSE. Q 3 d 4.3.	60 men daily. 3. 8 hour shifts of 20 men each.	8th Lan Fus will relieve 4th East Lancs at 4.p.m. 21/6/17.
(e).	Divisional H.Q. MILL FARM P 13 d 3.3.	30 men Daily. 3. 8 hour shifts of 10 men each.	8th Lan Fus will relieve 4th East Lancs at 4.p.m. 21/6/17.
(f).	~~Brigade H.Q.~~ Battalion H.Q. OXFORD VALLEY. Q 3 a 4.3.	24 men Daily. 3. 8 hour shifts of 8 men each.	4th East Lancs to relieve 8th Lan Fus at 12 midnight. 21/6/17.
(g).	Battalion H.Q. Near WATER COPSE.	8 men nightly.	4th East Lancs to send party to WATER COPSE at 9.30.p.m. nightly commencing 21/6/17.
(h).	Battalion H.Q. Near "E" Sap.	8 men nightly.	5th East Lancs to send party to BUTLERS CROSS at 9.30.p.m. nightly, commencing 21/6/17.
	256th Tunnelling Company R.E. will arrange Guides to meet parties mentioned in (g) and (h).		
(i).	KANTARA R.E. Dump. Q 14 Central.	4 men nightly.	8th Lan Fus to send party nightly at 9.30.p.m. to report to Sapper BURSLEM commencing 21/6/17.
(j).	KANTARA R.E. Dump. Q 14 Central.	8 men daily.	8th Lan Fus to send party daily at 8.a.m. to report to Sapper BURSLEM commencing 22/6/17.

TABLE "B"

H.E.DUMP, RUYAULCOURT - 2 N.C.Os. and 36 men

8th L.F. will relieve 4th East Lancs at 12 noon

22nd instant.

ADDENDUM No.1 TO 125th BRIGADE O.O. No.35.

20/6/17.

1. Reference para 6 of above. The 125th T.M.Battery will now relieve the 126th T.M.Battery in the Line on the Night 21/22nd June.

[illegible signature]

Captain,
Brigade Major,
125th BRIGADE.

Issued at:- [illegible] p.m. by D.R.

Copies to:-
1. 125th T.M.Battery.
2. 126th T.M.Battery.
3. 429th Company R.E.
4. 255th Tunnelling Company R.E.
5. 210th Brigade R.A.
6. 127th Brigade.
7. 126th "
8. 42nd Division.
9. Staff Captain.
10. Brigade Transport Officer.
11. 429th Company A.S.C.
12 }
13 } War Diary.
14. F I L E.

ADDENDUM TO TABLE "B" ISSUED WITH 125th BRIGADE O.O. No.35.

The party detailed in Table "B" will be rationed by R.E. from 23rd inclusive. They will report to Sergeant Major [illegible], R.E.

Town Major. YPRES.	50 men daily 9.a.m.	6th Lan Fus and 5th Lan Fus alternate days, commencing 23rd with 6th Lan Fus.
Divisional H.Q. P 10 a 5.5. under 255th Tunnelling Coy R.E.	36 men Daily. 3 Shifts of 12 men each.	To be found by 5th Lan Fus commencing 12 midnight 22nd inst.

Copy No. 9

125th.BRIGADE ORDER NO.24.

1. The following reliefs will take place on 29th.inst.

(a). 5th.L.F. will relieve 8th.L.F. in Left Reserve to 126th.Brigade.

(b). 7th.L.F. will relieve the 2 coys.6th.L.F. in HAVRINCOURT WOOD and take over 6th.L.F. working parties.

2. Details of relief to be arranged between C.O's concerned. There must be no cessation of work.

L. Robinson Capt.,
for Bde.Major,
125th.Bde.

Copy No.1 5th.L.F.
2 6th.L.F.
3.7th.L.F.
4.8th.L.F.
5.428 Fd.Coy.R.E.
6.126th.Bde.
7.127th.Bde.

8.W.D.
9.W.D.
10.FILE.
11 42nd.Div.

S E C R E T.   COPY NO. ...8.....

125th BRIGADE OPERATION ORDER NO. 25.

25/6/17.

1. 125th Trench Mortar Battery will be relieved in the line by 126th Trench Mortar Battery on night 28th/29th.

A. Lawrence

Captain,
Brigade Major,
125th Brigade.

Copies to :-

1. 125th T.M.Battery.
2. 126th T.M.Battery.
3. 126th Brigade.
4. 42nd Division.
5. Staff Captain.
6. Signal Officer.
7. Brigade Transport Officer.
8. War Diary.
9. War Diary.
10. File.

SECRET

COPY NO 5

ADDENDUM TO 125TH BRIGADE ORDER NO 84

1. Reference Para (b) of above Order. The work being done by the 2 Companies of the 6th L.F. in HAVRINCOURT WOOD has been suspended. The 2 Companies 6th L.F. will remain at disposal of 126th Brigade until 29th inst when they will be withdrawn to YTRES. Time will be notified by 126th Brigade. No relief for this party will be sent by 7th L.F.

Copy No 1. 6th L.F.
2. 7th L.F.
3. 428 Fld Coy R.E.
4. 126 Brigade.
5. W.D.
6. W.D.
7. FILE.
8. 42nd Division.

[signature] for Captain,
For Brigade Major,
125th Brigade.

26/6/17.

SECRET   COPY NO. 8

ADDENDUM NO.2 TO 125th.BRIGADE ORDER NO.24.

1. Reference Para 1.(a) of above order, add :-

The 5th.L.F. will not leave YTRES until 10.0 p.m.

E Robinson Captain,

For Brigade Major,

125th.Infantry Brigade.

Copy No. 1 to 5th.L.F.
2 6th "
3 C.R.E.
4 126th.Bde.
5 127 Bde.
6 42nd.DIV
7 W.D.
8 W.D.
9 File.

Vol 6

CONFIDENTIAL

WAR DIARY

of

125TH INFY BDE

JULY 1ST — 31ST

1917

VOLUME No. 37.

Army Form C. 2118

Instructions regarding War Diaries and Intelligence Summaries are contained in F. S. Regs., Part II. and the Staff Manual respectively. Title Pages will be prepared in manuscript. Page 1. Vol 37

WAR DIARY
or
~~INTELLIGENCE SUMMARY~~ of 125th Infy Bde
(Erase heading not required.)
~~June~~ July 1917.

Place	Date July	Hour	Map Reference	Summary of Events and Information	Weather	Remarks and references to Appendices
YTRES	1st		FRANCE 57c. 57c S.E.	Warning order issued re relief of 42nd & 59th Divisions by 58th Divn. Bde Training - Musketry - bombing. attack formations etc.	Showery.	Bde warning order No 23.
"	2nd		" "	Bde Training " " " " " "	Fine	
"	3rd		" "	Bde Training " " " " "	Sunny	
	4th		" "	Bde Training " " " " "		
	5th		" "	Bde Training " " " " "		
	6th	6 a.m.	57c.	Bde Group marched to GOMIECOURT and moved into camps there. Bde HQ in chateau - Battns, MG Coy, TMB, & 427 Coy RE & 1/2nd F. Amb. & 429 Coy ASC under canvas.	Sunny.	Bde order No 26.
	7th		"	Gomiecourt AREA inspected with view to Bde Training - sites chosen for ranges, bombing pits etc.		
	8th		"	Bde Training commences.		

1875 Wt. W593/826 1,000,000 4/15 J.B.C. & A. A.D.S.S./Forms/C. 2118.

Army Form C. 2118

Instructions regarding War Diaries and Intelligence Summaries are contained in F. S. Regs., Part II. and the Staff Manual respectively. Title Pages will be prepared in manuscript.

WAR DIARY
~~or~~
~~INTELLIGENCE SUMMARY~~

(Erase heading not required.)

PAGE 2 VOL 37. of 125th INFY BDE JULY 1917.

Place	Date	Hour	MAP REF.	Summary of Events and Information	WEATHER	Remarks and references to Appendices
GOMIECOURT	9TH.		FRANCE. 57C.	Bde Training - musketry, bombing, Lewis + Vickers Gun work, signalling, bayonet work, attack formations etc. Range construction, improvement of camp areas.		
" "	10		"	Do.		
" "	11		"	Do.		
" "	12		"	Do.		
" "	13		"	Do		
" "	14		"	Do.		
" "	15		"	Do		
" "	16		"	Do.		

1875 Wt. W593/826 1,000,000 4/15 J.B.C. & A. A.D.S.S./Forms/C. 2118.

Army Form C. 2118

Instructions regarding War Diaries and Intelligence Summaries are contained in F. S. Regs., Part II. and the Staff Manual respectively. Title Pages will be prepared in manuscript.

WAR DIARY
or
~~INTELLIGENCE SUMMARY~~ of 125 INFY BDE

(Erase heading not required.)

PAGE 3 VOL 37. JULY 1917.

Place	Date	Hour	MAP REFERENCE	Summary of Events and Information	WEATHER	Remarks and references to Appendices
GOMIECOURT "	17th		FRANCE 57 C.	Bde Training.	Showery.	
"	18th		"	Do.	Showery	
"	19th		"	Do. Demonstration of attack by 1/5 LAN FUS. & T.M.BATTERY using live ammunition –	Windy. & Dull.	
"	20th		"	Do. Bde Training.	Fine but dull.	
"	21st.		"	Do Bde Training.	Fine but dull.	
"	22nd		"	Bde Parade Church Service & March past G.O.C. 42 Divn. at conclusion of service.	Sunny	
"	23rd		"	Bde Training.	Sunny	
"	24th.		"			

1875 Wt. W593/826 1,000,000 4/15 J.B.C. & A. A.D.S.S./Forms/C. 2118.

Army Form C. 2118

Instructions regarding War Diaries and Intelligence Summaries are contained in F. S. Regs., Part II. and the Staff Manual respectively. Title Pages will be prepared in manuscript.

WAR DIARY

~~or~~

~~INTELLIGENCE SUMMARY~~ OF 125 INFY. BDE

(Erase heading not required.)

PAGE 4. VOL 37.

JULY 1917.

Place	Date	Hour	MAP REFERENCE	Summary of Events and Information	WEATHER	Remarks and references to Appendices
GOMIECOURT	25th		FRANCE 57 C	Bde. Training.	FINE	
"	26th		"	Do.	Fine	
"	27th		"	Do	Showery	
"	28th		"	Do	Showery	
"	29th		"	Bde. Parade Church Service.	Sunny	
"	30th		"	BDE. Training	dull but fine	
"	31st		"	Do	dull	

Hamasfargus
Brigadier General
Commanding 125th Inf. Brigade.

1875 Wt. W593/826 1,000,000 4/15 J.B.C. & A. A.D.S.S./Forms/C. 2118.

Instructions regarding War Diaries and Intelligence Summaries are contained in F. S. Regs., Part II. and the Staff Manual respectively. Title pages will be prepared in manuscript.

WAR DIARY
or
~~INTELLIGENCE SUMMARY.~~
(Erase heading not required.)

Army Form C. 2118.

SHEET 1.
125. INFANTRY BRIGADE.

Place	Date	Hour	Summary of Events and Information	Remarks and references to Appendices
FRANCE SHEET 57D	July			
	1		Quiet day	M.L.
BDE. H.Q. at BUS-LES-ARTOIS	2		125 INFANTRY BRIGADE relieved by 126 INF. BRIGADE and 3rd NEW ZEALAND RIFLE BRIGADE. On completion of relief 125 BDE. H.Q. moved to BUS-LES-ARTOIS, 1/5 LANCASHIRE FUSILIERS moved to BUS-LES-ARTOIS woods with B.H.Q at J 20 a 8.0., 1/7 LANCASHIRE FUSILIERS moved into bivouacs S. of COURCELLES-au-BOIS with B.H.Q at J34 b 26, 1/8 LANCASHIRE FUSILIERS moved into bivouacs at J22c and in the PURPLE RESERVE LINE with B.H.Q at J22 c 1.5., 125 BDE. L.T.M. BATTERY moved to BUS woods at J20 c 98. The Brigade was in Divisional Reserve.	M.L.
	3 to 9		During this time brigade found working parties for trench digging, ~~burying~~ cable & wiring. Usual training was carried out by companies not working.	M.L.
	10		125 BDE. relieved 127 INF. BDE. in Right Section of Divisional Front with 1/7 LAN. FUS. in right subsection (1 company in front line - B.H.Q at K32 a 14), 1/8 LAN. FUS. in left subsection (2 companies in front line - B.H.Q. at K25 a 85) and 1/5 LAN. FUS. in Brigade Reserve - B.H.Q at Q1 b 05. On completion of relief 125 BDE. H.Q. moved to J24 d 68 and 125 L.T.M. BATTERY H.Q to K32 a 41	M.L.

1577 Wt. W10791/1773 500,000 1/15 D. D. & L. A.D.S.S./Forms/C. 2118.

Instructions regarding War Diaries and Intelligence Summaries are contained in F. S. Regs., Part II. and the Staff Manual respectively. Title pages will be prepared in manuscript.

WAR DIARY
or
~~INTELLIGENCE SUMMARY.~~
(Erase heading not required.)

Army Form C. 2118.

SHEET 2.

125 INFANTRY BDE.

Place	Date	Hour	Summary of Events and Information	Remarks and references to Appendices
REF. SHEET 57D	July 11 to 15		Quiet period - patrolling carried out by brigade every night - trenches improved and working parties found by battalion in brigade reserve	[illegible]
	16		125 INF. BDE. H.Q. moved to P5a 88	[illegible]
	17		1/7 LAN. FUS. in cooperation with artillery carried out a minor operation & captured 1 prisoner at Q4 b 14	[illegible]
	18		1/5 LAN. FUS relieved 1/8 LAN. FUS. in left subsection and 1/8 LAN. FUS. moved into Brigade Reserve.	[illegible]
	19		Enemy withdrew from ROSSIGNOL WOOD in K12b and 127 BRIGADE in left section of Divisional Front advanced 500 yards on 1000 yds. front	[illegible]
	20 to 21		Quiet period	[illegible]
	22		In order to conform with advance of 127 BRIGADE - 5TH LAN. FUS. established posts at K28c 20.75, K28c 30.55	[illegible]

1577 Wt. W10791/1773 500,000 1/15 D. D. & L. A.D.S.S./Forms/C. 2118.

Instructions regarding War Diaries and Intelligence Summaries are contained in F. S. Regs., Part II. and the Staff Manual respectively. Title pages will be prepared in manuscript.

WAR DIARY

or

~~INTELLIGENCE SUMMARY.~~

(Erase heading not required.)

Army Form C. 2118.

SHEET 3

125 INFANTRY BRIGADE

Place	Date	Hour	Summary of Events and Information	Remarks and references to Appendices
REF. SHEET 57D	July			
K28c 1525	23	5.0 AM	1/5 LAN. FUS. established post at K28c 15.25 in cooperation with artillery & Trench Mortar Batteries	MW
J30 d 3000		2.30 pm	1/8 LAN. FUS. moved into new B.H.Q. at J30 d 30.00	
K31b 3090	24	8.0 pm	1/5 LAN. FUS. moved into new B.H.Q. at K31b 30.90 - quiet day	MW
	25		Quiet day.	MW
	26		125 INFANTRY BDE. relieved by 126 INFANTRY BDE. On completion of relief brigade moved into Divisional Reserve with 125 BDE. H.Q. at BUS-les-ARTOIS, 1/5 LAN. FUS. ~~and~~ B.H.Q. ~~in~~ J22c24, 1/7 LAN. FUS. BHQ at J34b26, 1/8 LAN. FUS. B.H.Q and 125 L.T.M.B. in BUS WOODS.	MW
	26 to 31		Working parties supplied by battalions for trench digging, tunnelling and wiring. Training carried out by companies not working.	MW

[signature] for G.O.C. 125 Infty Bde

CONFIDENTIAL

Vol 7

WAR DIARY

OF

125TH INFY. BDE

AUGUST 1ST – 31ST 1917

VOLUME No 38.

Army Form C. 2118

Instructions regarding War Diaries and Intelligence Summaries are contained in F. S. Regs., Part II. and the Staff Manual respectively. Title Pages will be prepared in manuscript.

WAR DIARY
or
INTELLIGENCE SUMMARY
(Erase heading not required.)

Place	Date	Hour	Summary of Events and Information	Remarks and references to Appendices

1875 Wt. W593/826 1,000,000 4/15 J.B.C. & A. A.D.S.S./Forms/C. 2118.

Army Form C. 2118

WAR DIARY

~~or~~

~~INTELLIGENCE SUMMARY~~ of 125TH INFY BDE

(Erase heading not required.)

AUGUST 1ST — 31ST 1917.

Instructions regarding War Diaries and Intelligence Summaries are contained in F. S. Regs., Part II. and the Staff Manual respectively. Title Pages will be prepared in manuscript. PAGE 1. VOL 38.

Place	AUG Date 1917	Hour	MAP REFERENCE	Summary of Events and Information	WEATHER	Remarks and references to Appendices
GOMIECOURT	1ST		FRANCE 57c 1/20000	Bde Training - Bayonet Fighting - Bombing. Lewis Gunners. Signallers - Musketry. Assault practice. etc ..	Wet & Cold	JC
"	2ND		"	Do — do —	Rain	JC
"	3RD		"	Do. do.	Showery	JC
"	4TH		"	Do. do.	Showery & Cold	JC
"	5TH		"	Do. do	Fine & bright	JC
"	6TH		"	Do. do	Fine.	JC
"	7TH		"	Do. do	Dull.	JC
"	8TH		"	Do do.	Dull. Thunder.	JC

1875 Wt. W593/826 1,000,000 4/15 J.B.C. & A. A.D.S.S./Forms/C. 2118.

Army Form C. 2118

Instructions regarding War Diaries and Intelligence Summaries are contained in F. S. Regs., Part II. and the Staff Manual respectively. Title Pages will be prepared in manuscript. PAGE 2 . VOL No 38.

WAR DIARY ~~or~~ ~~INTELLIGENCE SUMMARY~~ of 125TH INFY BDE

(Erase heading not required.)

AUGUST 1ST – 31ST. 1917.

Place	AUG Date 1917	Hour	MAP REFERENCE	Summary of Events and Information	WEATHER	Remarks and references to Appendices
GOMIECOURT	9TH		FRANCE 57c 1/20000	Bde Training. Trench to Trench attack Practice. specialists training – Field Firing etc.	Heavy Rain.	JC
"	10TH		"	Do . do .	Heavy Rain	JC
"	11TH		"	Do . do .	Showery	JC
"	12TH		"	Do . do .	Showery	JC
"	13TH		"	Do do .	Showery	JC
"	14TH		"	Do do	Fine	JC
"	15TH		"	Do do	Fine	JC
"	16TH		"	Do do	Showery	JC.

1875 Wt. W593/826 1,000,000 4/15 J.B.C. & A. A.D.S.S./Forms/C. 2118.

Army Form C. 2118

Instructions regarding War Diaries and Intelligence Summaries are contained in F. S. Regs., Part II. and the Staff Manual respectively. Title Pages will be prepared in manuscript.

WAR DIARY
or
~~INTELLIGENCE SUMMARY~~ of 125 INFY BDE

(*Erase heading not required.*)

PAGE 3. VOL NO 38. AUGUST 1917.

Place	AUG Date 1917	Hour	MAP REFERENCE	Summary of Events and Information	WEATHER	Remarks and references to Appendices
GOMIECOURT	17th		FRANCE 57c 1/20000	Bde Training.	Showery	JC
"	18th		"	Do	Showery	JC
"	19th		"	Do. Bde Group preparing to move by march route to BOUZINCOURT. Bde Op Order No 29 issued.	Fine	Bde Op Or. No 29. JC
BOUZINCOURT	20th		"	Bde Group marched to BOUZINCOURT & billeted there.	Sunny	JC.
"	21st		"	Bde Group at BOUZINCOURT.	Sunny	JC
ALBERT	22nd		BELGIUM MAP. 27 SHEET 1/40000	Bde ~~Group~~ HQrs marched to ALBERT also M Gun Coy and proceeded by train to GODEWAERSVELDE and detrained there & marched to billets at L.13. Bde Group proceeded	Sunny	JC
near GODEWAERSVELDE L.13.	23rd		"	to GODEWAERSVELDE (Belgium) by train.		JC
L.13.	24th		"	Bde op order for move of 1/2nd E LANCS FIELD AMB. to RED FARM (Sheet 28. G5d 9 5) issued.	Showery	Bde op order No 30. JC.

Army Form C. 2118

WAR DIARY
or
~~INTELLIGENCE SUMMARY~~ of 125th INFY BDE

AUGUST 1917.

Instructions regarding War Diaries and Intelligence Summaries are contained in F. S. Regs., Part II. and the Staff Manual respectively. Title Pages will be prepared in manuscript.

PAGE 4. VOL NO 38 (Erase heading not required.)

Place	AUG Date 1917	Hour	MAP REFERENCE	Summary of Events and Information	WEATHER	Remarks and references to Appendices
L.13.	25th		BELGIUM SHEET 27 1/40000	Bde in billets - training.	Fine occasional showers	FC
"	26th		"	Capt AE LAWRENCE (Bde Major) visited line to be taken over by Bde near YPRES. Bde in billets - training.	Fine	FC
	27th		"	Bde in billets.	Showery	FC
	28th		SHEET 28 1/40000	Orders issued for move of Bde to YPRES SOUTH AREA - Bde marched to POPERINGHE - and entrained there - detraining at GOLDFISH CHATEAU.	Wet	Bde op Order No 31. FC
	29th		"	Bde proceeded to YPRES SOUTH	Wet	FC
	30th		"	Bde under canvas in YPRES SOUTH AREA. night 30/31. Bde took over Divl Front from 46th Infy Bde.	Showery	FC
	31st.		"	5 & 6 LF in Front line } Right & Left, 7 & 8 in Support } respectively. Left Bde Boundary POMMERN CASTLE right " " YPRES-ROULERS RLY. Adjacent Bde on left: 182nd. 142nd adjacent Bde on right.	Fine	FC

Harold Fargus
Brig. Genl
Commanding 125 Infy Bde

1875 Wt. W593/826 1,000,000 4/15 J.B.C. & A. A.D.S.S./Forms/C. 2118.

Instructions regarding War Diaries and Intelligence Summaries are contained in F. S. Regs., Part II. and the Staff Manual respectively. Title Pages will be prepared in manuscript.

PAGE 1.
VOL NO 39

WAR DIARY
or
~~INTELLIGENCE SUMMARY~~
(Erase heading not required.)

of 125 INFY BDE
SEPT. 1ST - 30TH 1917.

Army Form C. 2118

Place	Date	Hour	MAP REF.	Summary of Events and Information	WEATHER	Remarks and references to Appendices
YPRES area	SEPT 1ST		FREZENBURG 1/10000.	Bde in Line as 31/8/17 Bde HQs MILL COTT. on YPRES-ZONNEBEKE ROAD. 2 Battns in Line - 2 in Support - administrative portion of Bde in Camps in YPRES SOUTH - also Transport - night 1/2nd. 5 LF relieved by 7 LF.	Showery	Bde op Order No 33 FC
"	2ND		do.	8 LF relieved 6 LF. 2 coys 5 LF & 2 coys 6 LF proceeded to H.I.G.C and D. for special training	Fine	FC
"	3RD		do.	Orders issued for relief of 7 LF by 5 LF (less 2 coys) and 2 coys 6th M/c Regt & 8 LF by 6 LF (— 3 —) and 2 coys 6th M/c Regt.	Fine & hot	Bde op order No 34. FC
"	4TH		do	Orders issued for attack on BORRY FARM, BECK HSE, IBERIAN	"	Bde op order No 35 FC
"	5TH		do	Preparations for attack on BORRY FARM, BECK HSE, IBERIAN. Heavy barrage fire by enemy.	"	FC
	6TH		do	Attack on BORRY FARM, BECK HSE, IBERIAN by 2 coys 5 LF & 3 coys 6 LF. Attack failed. tho' BECK HSE was taken our forces were withdrawn. (Intelligence summary attd).	Fine	Intelligence Summary & map. FC
	7TH		do	Orders issued for relief of 125 Bde by 127 Bde.	Fine	Bde op order No 36 FC
	8TH		do.	Night 7/8. 125 Bde relieved in Left sector of 42 Div Front by 127 Bde - Bde marched to BRANDHOEK No 2 AREA. and encamped there, administrative portion & transport also moving there from YPRES SOUTH.	Fine warm	FC

1875 Wt. W593/826 1,000,000 4/15 J.B.C. & A. A.D.S.S./Forms/C. 2118.

Army Form C. 2118

Instructions regarding War Diaries and Intelligence Summaries are contained in F. S. Regs., Part II. and the Staff Manual respectively. Title Pages will be prepared in manuscript.

PAGE 2
VOL NO 39.

WAR DIARY
or
~~INTELLIGENCE SUMMARY~~
(Erase heading not required.)

of 125 INFY BDE
SEPT 1ST - 30TH 1917

Place	Date	Hour	MAP REF.	Summary of Events and Information	WEATHER	Remarks and references to Appendices
BRANDHOEK	SEPT. 9TH		~~Sheet~~ 28 G. 11.	Bde in camp. training, - baths - equipping etc.	Fine	
"	10TH		"	Do: " " "	Fine	
"	11TH		"	Do: " " "	Fine	
"	12TH		"	Do: " " "	Fine	
"	13TH			Orders issued for relief of 127 Bde in Left Sector by 125 Bde.	Fine	Bde op order No 37 JC
"	14TH		Sheet 28 NW 1/10,000	Night 14/15. Bde relieved 127 Bde in Left Sector of 42 Div Front. Bde HQs moved to MILL COTT.	Fine shot	JC
YPRES AREA	15TH		do.	Bde in line. (2 Battns in line - 2 in support).	Fine	
"	16TH		"	Bde Order issued for relief of Bde by South African Bde.	Fine	Bde op order No 38.

1875 Wt. W593/826 1,000,000 4/15 J.B.C. & A. A.D.S.S./Forms/C. 2118.

Army Form C. 2118

Instructions regarding War Diaries and Intelligence Summaries are contained in F. S. Regs., Part II. and the Staff Manual respectively. Title Pages will be prepared in manuscript.

PAGE 3

VOL No 39.

WAR DIARY

or

~~INTELLIGENCE SUMMARY~~

(Erase heading not required.)

of 125TH INFY BDE

SEPT. 1ST - 30TH 1917

Place	Date	Hour	MAP REF:	Summary of Events and Information	WEATHER	Remarks and references to Appendices
YPRES AREA.	SEP 17TH		FREZENBERG 1/10000 Sheet 28 NW 1/20000	Night 17/18th – Bde relieved by South African Bde. Bde Group marched to BRANDHOEK No 2 AREA &	Fine	FC
BRANDHOEK	18TH		do	encamped there – Administrative portion & transport moving there from YPRES SOUTH. Orders issued for move of Bde Group to ST JAN-TER-BIEZEN AREA	do	FC
" "	19TH		do. & 27 NE 1/20000	Bde Group marched to St JAN-TER-BIEZEN AREA & encamped there.	do	
ST JAN-TER BIEZEN	20TH		" "	In camp – Orders issued (warning) re move of Bde to ARNEKE AREA.	do.	Bde op Order No 40 FC
" "	21ST		" "	Addendum to warning order issued.	do	Addendum No. 1 to Bde op Order No 40.
" "	22ND		" "	Bde Group (less transport) proceeded to ARNEKE AREA – (Transport moved by road) and billetted there.	do	FC
ARNEKE AREA.	23RD		HAZEBROUCK 5A	In billets ~~camp~~ at ARNEKE –	do	FC
"	24TH		Sheet 19.D.	Bde proceeded by train to GHYVELDE – and billetted there. Warning order issued re move of Bde to ST. ISESBALD.	do	Bde op Order No 41 FC

1875 Wt. W593/826 1,000,000 4/15 J.B.C. & A. A.D.S.S./Forms/C. 2118.

Army Form C. 2118

WAR DIARY
~~or~~
~~INTELLIGENCE SUMMARY~~
(Erase heading not required.)

Instructions regarding War Diaries and Intelligence Summaries are contained in F. S. Regs., Part II. and the Staff Manual respectively. Title Pages will be prepared in manuscript.

PAGE 4
VOL NO 39.

of 125TH INFY BDE
SEP 1ST – 30TH 1917

Place	Date	Hour	MAP REF.	Summary of Events and Information	WEATHER	Remarks and references to Appendices
GHYVELDE	Sep. 25TH	6am 1pm.	BELGIUM SHEET 19.	Orders issued for move of Bde to ST ISESBALD AREA. Bde marched to ST IDESBALD AREA – huts and tents.	Fine	Bde op order No 42
" "	26TH		"	Camped at ST IDESBALD and COXSYDE BAINS – Route marches – training etc	Fine	
" "	27TH		"	Do Do	Fine & hot	
" "	28TH		"	Do Do	Fine	
" "	29TH		"	Do Do	Fine	
" "	30TH		"	Do Do.	Fine	

Hamabarghs[?] Brig. Genl
Cmmdg 125th Infy Bde.

1875 Wt. W593/826 1,000,000 4/15 J.B.C. & A. A.D.S.S./Forms/C. 2118.

125th Inf. Bde. Intelligence Summary
No 2

period noon 31/8/17 – noon 1/9/17.

1) OPERATIONS

a) ours. A new post to hold ½ platoon was dug at approx D25 ~~[illegible]~~ b 05 20

A small forward post for 1 NCO & 6 men was dug at D25 b 10 05

A new position for support Coy was dug & occupied between BILL COTT & GREY RUIN.

M.Gs at I6c 9980 fired 4000 rounds on line VAMPIR – ZEVENKOTE.

b) enemys. nil.

2) ARTILLERY ACTIVITY

a) ours.

active throughout the whole period

b) enemy's

active throughout the whole period

The following places were shelled

3.30–5 a.m. FREZENBERG RIDGE BILL COTT & WILDE WOOD.

The tank just W. of WILDE WOOD was set on

II b. Cont.

fire about 6.30 a.m.
during afternoon I 5. c+d & I 3+4 fairly heavily
during afternoon C 29 d Central & during night RUPPRECHT FARM
heavy fire on SQUARE FARM from 4 a.m – 5.30 a.m.

3) ENEMY DEFENCES

a) nil
b) nil
c) more active during night, one appeared to fire from BECK HOUSE on & over SQUARE FARM.
d) nil
e) during afternoon what seemed an explosion of an ammunition dump was observed in ZONNEBEKE.

4)
5) nil

6) 4 men with flag & stretcher seen on HILL 35 at 9.a.m. Occasional movement is seen here.

PATROL REPORT.

attached 125 Bde Int Summary No 2.

Right battalion sent out the following patrols.

1 NCO & 4 men left post at D25 d 94 at 11 pm. It went to the two tanks about 100 yds in front, staying there 20 minutes. a grenade & flare were fired from ruin at D26 c 18. Patrol moved into trench on left of tanks, & remained 5 minutes. Nothing was heard or seen

Patrol returned at 11.45 pm

Two patrols visited a line of old enemy dug outs at D25 b 0540, b 0550, & b 0560, found them unoccupied, & remained there till dawn. Nothing was seen or heard

Left battalion sent out the following Patrols

at 9.30 p.m 4 O.R left D25 a 67 to investigate trench running obliquely from line. They returned at 10 30 p.m & report trench unoccupied, 7-8 ft deep. 2ft 6 wide & knee deep in water. No wire behind. Remains of wire shell uncut in front a patrol of 1 officer + 4 O.R left D25 a 67 at 12.50 a.m to reconnoitre ground in front of trench running from D 25 a 67 – D19 c 82.

They proceeded 75 yds in front of advanced L.G post towards BECK HOUSE + report ground very broken. Sniper active from Point to right of BECK HOUSE. There appears to be little wire in front of BECK HOUSE.

1 officer + 3 O.R went to examine wire at D19 Central. Wire is judged to be about 250 yds in front of IBERIAN. Ground very cut up. Wire partially destroyed but still presents an obstacle. Very lights were fired by enemy from shell hole just his side of the wire hindering reconnaissance.

Patrol returned at 10.25 p.m.

[signature] Lt
for Brig Gen Comdg
125 Inf Bde.

1/9/17.

Patrol Report
attached to 125 Inf. Bde. Int. Summ. No 3.

Right Battalion 1/7 Lancs Fus.

1 NCO + 3 men went out from left sector at 2 a.m to reconnoitre the BORRY FARM position. They report a good deal of wire in front of the position also stakes, but the wire is broken up. The bright moon impeded progress. Patrol returned at 3 a.m.

[signature] Lt.
for Brig. Gen. Comdg
125th Inf Bde

2/9/17.

125th Inf Bde. Intelligence Summary. No 3

period noon 1/9/17 – noon 2/9/17.

I

OPERATIONS

a) ours 7th Batt Lancs Fus. relieved 5th Batt in right sector & 8th relieved 6th in left sector. our MGS engaged the following targets during the night

1) X roads D26 a 9590
2) redoubt D26 a 8095
3) X roads D20 c 98

about 4000 rounds were fired.

b) enemy's nil

II artillery activity

a) ours active throughout the period

b) enemys artillery was active, the following were particularly shelled.

10. pm – midnight. IBEX RES TRENCH & junction of CAMBRIDGE Rd & YPRES-ROULERS railway.

early morning on approx line from SQUARE FARM – FROST HOUSE.

12.20 a.m. hostile barrage on same line for 5 minutes, after a golden rain rocket had been sent up.

FREZENBERG RIDGE & POTIJZE intermittently shelled

III Enemy defences.

a) New Work

Repairs have been done to front part of BECK HOUSE.

b) ~~wd~~ wire nil

c) M.G.S. 3 MG's fired on our aeroplanes from GHELUVELT line Exact position unknown.

MG from direction of BECK HOUSE ~~FARM~~ was active at intervals during the night

d) T.M.'s a few rounds were fired at SQUARE FARM during the afternoon

e) dumps nil

IV ENEMY COMMUNICATIONS. nil

V ENEMY DISPOSITIONS

Snipers were active from direction of BECK HOUSE during night & from IBERIAN during the day.

MOVEMENT

VI occasional men seen on HILL 35

2 men seen walking about at 9.15 am at D 20 C 35 45.

VII E A ACTIVITY

7.30 p.m. 2 planes circled over our lines
10.15 a.m. 8 " " " " "
flying at about 10,000 ft.

8 MISCELLANEOUS.

Twice between 2.45 p.m & 3 p.m two green flares were sent up from enemy posts at IBERIAN.

9. WORK

75 boards put down, commencing the doubling of the G track to SQUARE FARM
SQUARE FARM repaired
Aid posts commenced & roads worked on.
Single duckboarding of F track completed to J1a 0095. 100 yds double duckboarding complete on F. Track
Preparing 250 yds for double boarding.

[illegible] Lt
for Brig Gen Comdg
125th Inf. Bde.

2/9/17

CORRECTION Ref. para 1a of Summary No 2, dated 1/9/17. for D25 b 05/20, substitute D25 a 9555 & for D25 b 1005 substitute D25 d 2095

Part II

125 Bde. Intelligence Summary No 4.

1 officer & 2 O.R. were captured by JABBER this morning.

Method of capture. Prisoners came towards our lines in error. They were fired upon & held up their hands. They were taken about 4 a.m at about D25 Central.

all belong to 1st. M.G. Coy. 1st Batt 120 I.R 27 Div. (normal)

The officer has only just returned from 14 days leave near STUTTGART, spent the night of Sept 1/2nd at HOOGLEDE, came up behind the line in a waggon during the day, & was given a map with some M.G positions marked on, & told to go up at night & relieve another officer. One of the O.R.s is his batman & the other ~~also~~ a guide who apparently lost his way. The guide had only been up one day, cannot read a map, is stupid & knows nothing.

The officer has not been here before knew nothing about his Coy. disposition or gun positions. He states the 1st Batt. is in front at present, with 1st M.G. Coy. He is uncertain of the position of the other two battalions. He confirms the order of battle on his flanks, i.e. left 60th I.R. (121 D.W.) right 124 I.R. 123 Gr. R (27 D) 204 D.

He states the coy had 8 guns, but that 2 had been lost.

Two men who started out with him last night were hit on the way up.

[illegible] Lt.
for Brig. Gen. Comdg
125 Inf. Bde.

8/9/17.

125th Inf. Bde Intelligence Summary
No 4
period noon 2/9/17 – noon 3/9/17

1) OPERATIONS.
a) ours. 1 officer + 2 O.R. taken prisoner (see Part II)
b) enemy nil.

2) ARTILLERY ACTIVITY
a) ours active throughout period, a bombardment of BORRY FARM by 6" Hows following by creeping barrage to farms beyond took place at 7 a.m.
b) enemy's rather less active till evening, but there has been much shelling during the night & this morning.
about 9 p.m. BAVARIA HOUSE & road,
2 a.m. – 2.30 region of BILL COTT & WILDE WOOD.
intermittently F track
After our barrage this morning the following shelling took place.
8 a.m. – 8.15. BATTERY Positions in rear
8.10 – 8.30. barrage on back area of FREZENBERG ridge between SQUARE FARM & BAVARIA HOUSE & on G track.
8.35 – 8.45 light barrage between SQUARE & LOW FARMS. The nearest shells to our positions were 50 yds in rear of support line immediately behind LOW FARM.
8 a.m. – 10 region of NEW COTT & MILL COTT.

3. ENEMY DEFENCES.

a) new work — nil
b) wire — nil.
c) MGS — fired from BECK during night
" " IBERIAN on FREZENBERG

Intermittent & indirect fire fell all down W slope of FREZENBURG RIDGE from railway to POTIJZE ROAD. The bullets were spent & came from direction of GALLIPOLI COPSE.

A party of enemy were seen at dusk entering emplacement at D19 b 18 with an MG

d) TMS }
e) Dumps } nil.

4) ENEMY COMMUNICATIONS. }
5) ENEMY DISPOSITIONS } nil

6) MOVEMENT. 1 man came out of dug out at D19 b 9.3. he was fired at & disappeared.

1.pm 3 enemy using field glasses seen in bush at D19 b 15.10. Disappeared when fired on.

There has been very little movement.

7) EA. activity
above normal.

4.30 p.m. 2 EA dropped 2 bombs near MILLCOTT
7 p.m. 20 EA reported over our lines,
2 ~~remaining~~ flew over BAVARIA HOUSE,
very low firing their M.G.s.

3/

7) Contd.

10 pm 3 bombs dropped near RUPPRECHT FARM & about 16 b 3.8

8) MISCELLANEOUS. O.B. were up at intervals.

Snipers appear to fire from about D19 b 25.15
A fire was seen at 9.50 pm which burnt all night at approx. D26 b 30.

9) Work done. right front battalion general improvement of trenches
Rifle pits dug on line D25 a 63 – D25 a 55 45

left front battalion. general improvement of trenches. Salvage collected

right support battalion. Making fire positions & draining old enemy dugouts in trench I5 b 73 – I6 c 23
IBEX RES. improved & latrines dug.
old front line at I5 d 37 improved & drained

left support battalion. Work on trenches & drainage

[signature] Lt
for Brig Gen. Cmdg
125 Inf. Bde.

3/9/17.

125th Inf. Bde. Intelligence Summary No 5.

period noon 3/9/17 – noon 4/9/17

) OPERATIONS.

a) ours. MG's fired about 5000 rounds on

1) X roads D26a 9580 2) BREMEN REDOUBT.

3) X roads D20c 98 4) POTSDAM. 6) VAMPIRE.

about 5.30 p.m. a few men from JASPER tried to get into BECK. They were seen 50 yds from their trench. A bugle sounded & rockets went up from various points. Men came out of dugouts at D19b 3013, D19d 3035 & 3531 & D25b 15, 6473 & 5490 & appeared to occupy posts. Men seemed to leave 3 dugouts at D19d Central & go back to their line. Barrage fell 4.5 minutes after first flare (above from our right batt – owing to barrage reports from left not yet to hand) –

b) enemy nil

) ARTILLERY.

a) ours active. Various prearranged shoots were carried out

b) enemy's more active than usual, especially from about 2 p.m. onwards. Gas shells were used against batteries & on area of our old front line, & tear gas near BAVARIA HOUSE. FREZENBERG RIDGE, SQUARE to FROST FARM & TRACK, W of WILDE WOOD. were all heavily shelled at times.

3) ENEMY DEFENCES.

a) new work. } nil.
b) wire }
c) M.G's. during barrage MGS from BORRY & BECK played on bridge on G track about D 25 a. 25 75. MG from IBERIAN active against FREZENBERG
d) TM } nil.
e) Dumps }

4) ENEMY COMMUNICATIONS } nil
5) " DISPOSITIONS. }

6.) MOVEMENT.
5.30. p.m. men seen moving round BORRY.
7.55 p.m 2 men went from VAMPIRE to POTSDAM. one was hit.
2 men with rifles left BECK during the Shelling.
12.30. p.m. 20 men crawled along trench in front of BORRY. they were fired on.

7) EA activity normal. EA flew very low over our front line, over IBER. RES. & over the evacuated position in front of LOW FARM.

8). MISCELLANEOUS.
Flares of various kinds went up all night. Green appears to call for Artillery

31

A corner of the roof of BECK HOUSE has been blown off.

A body, believed to be one of the party with the prisoners taken y'day was found. Underneath his identity disc

A German in front of POTSDAM was killed by our snipers this morning.

WORK DONE

General improvement & draining of trenches

Strong points for 50 rifles each at C 30 d 70 & C 30 d 33 taped out.

150 yds of F track duck boarded, & further boards brought up to CAMBRIDGE RD.

Wiring material for LOW FARM moved to RE dump A POTIJZE RD. 20% moved on to LOW FARM. Worked commenced on S.P at C 30 d 70. J track duck boarding improved. Shelter for cookers in CAMBRIDGE RD begun.

2 splinter proof dog kennels erected at Bde H.Q.

[illegible] Lt
for Brig. Gen. Comdg
125th Inf. Bde

4/9/17.

Patrol Report from JASPER.

A patrol was sent out this afternoon consisting of 1 NCO & 3 8 men (2 LGs with a gun, & one RG.) By report of patrol last night it was pretty certain nobody was in BECK FARM. The patrol this afternoon who could get forward under cover was sent out with a view to getting near the House & of course observing more if possible catching it. Attached is report of NCO i/c & the following is what was observed by me & others from LOW FARM.

The first lights to go up were rockets bursting into 5 to 6 white lights. A man was seen to run from IBERIAN to a concrete house marked NB on attached map. Another was seen to run from NB to a dug out marked DO. & 2 others from DO to a trench marked T. Lights continued to go up including many bursting into 2 reds. Sniping began & a bugle was heard. The call resembled the first half of the English officers call (without last 3 Gs) 2 red lights were then sent up one after the other from just behind BECK FARM.

Two EA came over & a barrage was opened. This started an hour after the first lights went up & was put down 150-200 YDS in rear of our front line. Rockets bursting into 2 pieces were sent up during the barrage. The barrage then seemed to go a bit further back, practically on top of the rise. It lasted ½ hour. Before it ceased ordinary Verey lights were sent up. If this is a signal to cease barrage it can of course only be a daylight signal. The main result of the patrol was the spotting absolutely of the enemy main line of defence. BECK FARM I should say is only manned in case of emergency & the garrison live in dugouts behind. The NCO's noticed no damage done to BECK FARM only one corner broken off.

3/9/17

Report of NCO i/c. of patrol

I made my way as ordered at 5 p m along the CT running towards BECK FARM. When about 70 yds from it I struck across half right to the road running to S of BECK FARM. I left the LG & the 2 men & went forward with my other man to a shell hole where I was 50 yds away from FARM (i.e. S of it). I saw lights going up 300 yds half right. I saw 3 Germans walking away from a dug out in rear of B.F. (30 yds E).
They had rifles but no equipment. On my right I saw the head of a sentry in an emplacement. There was no sign of movement at BECK FARM. Well lights continued to go up 300 yds away so I knew we had been noticed & decided to send word to the 2 LGs, to get back a bit & wait. The sentry in the emplacement did not see anything till they began to go back. He looked down & another man got up to look. His uniform was pale blue, he held a stick in his hand & his helmet resembled that of the English. Sniping began at my men. I a

bugle was blown from the dug out behind BECK & lights also went up. 2 EA came over flying very low & a heavy barrage was put down. I could not then get nearer BECK so I made my way back by the same route as I had come by getting back without anyone being hit at 7.30 p.m.

3/9/17

42nd Div.

Herewith copies of patrol reports, with maps attached, received from 1/8 Lancashire Fus., also their Int Summary & a report on the raid by the Commanding officer.

[illegible] Lt.
for Brig Genl Comdg
125 Inf Bde

4/9/17

125th Inf Bde Intelligence Summary
No 6.

period noon 4/9/17 - noon 5/9/17.

1) OPERATIONS.

a) ours. 2 Coys of JAPAN & 2 Coys. JEWEL relieved JABBER in right sector & 1 Coy JAUNT & 2 of JEWEL relieved 3 coys of JASPER in left sector

b) enemy's nil

2) ARTILLERY

a) ours active H.A. bombarded BORRY FARM a few shells fell short & over 13 blinds were counted.

b) enemys. less active than during preceding period, especially during the afternoon. FREZENBERG RIDGE, POTIJZE & batteries W of CAMBRIDGE RD were shelled at times.

3) ENEMY DEFENCES

a) New work } nil
b) wire } nil
c) MG.s 1 from BORRY fires on about D 25 Central.
d) TM's } nil
e) Dumps } nil

4) ENEMY COMMUNICATIONS
5) " DISPOSITIONS } nil
6) " MOVEMENT. Snipers fired from rear of BECK + D19b22.

7). E.A. active. many came over our lines & there was again low flying over LOW FARM

8) MISCELLANEOUS

When E.A were up during the night signals consisting of 3 lights one below the other in line were frequently sent up from enemy lines.

Enemy appear to be wearing black canvas helmet covers.

Their runners carry long pistols & wear no equipment.

9) WORK DONE.

General improvement of trenches. 30 yds trench dug 5' from C30d4 towards BILL.COTT.

Sandbagging 1st Elephant hut at I5a59 continued & ground prepared for 2nd. Material for 400 yds carrying taken to LOW FARM & 600 yds to front line at D19c78.

5/9/17.

[signature] Col
for Brig Gen Cmdg
125th Inf Bde

125th Inf. Bde Intelligence Summary
No 7
period noon 5/9/17 – noon 6/9/17.

I. OPERATIONS

a) ours. At 7.30 a.m this morning an attack was launched against IBERIAN, BECK HOUSE & BORRY FARM, after artillery preparation & under cover of a creeping barrage.

BECK HOUSE has been captured & is being consolidated. Of its garrison of 2 OFFS & 47 men, 1 OFF. & about 30 men have been taken prisoners & the rest killed or severely wounded.

At IBERIAN our troops are reported in trenches S of the farm at D19 b 25 00 & in the trenches N, in front of the tank at D19 b 03, but the position is not very clear.

At BORRY, we have been hampered by MG fire from VAMPIRE, and are at present held up in front of dug outs S of the farm. Contact aeroplane reports our flares at D25 b 55 & 48.

Enemy preparing for a counter attack near BREMEN REDOUBT have been dispersed by artillery & MG. fire.

b) enemy nil.

2). ARTILLERY

a) ours. Bombardments & barrages carried out as arranged

b) enemys his barrage on FREZENBER RIDGE & SQUARE FARM FROST came down from 8.45pm - 10.30.pm. It came down again on the usual places in answer to ours this morning. During this mornings operations, enemy activity has been confined almost exclusively to forward areas

WILDE WOOD was heavily shelled last night.

3.) DEFENCES.

c) M.G.s. one from IBERIAN active during the afternoon.

a) b) d) e) nil.

4.) ENEMY COMMUNICATIONS nil.

5.) 2nd Batt. 120th I.R. is now in the line

6.) ENEMY MOVEMENT

During y'days bombardment, 2 men left IBERIAN & ran back into at D19d77.

3)

7) E.A. were again very active, & though on several occasions they flew very low, as far over our lines as CAMBRIDGE Rd. very little fire was brought to bear on them.

4 O.B.s have been up all morning

8) MISCELLANEOUS

Hostile barrage came down last night after the sending up of a red, green & golden rain rockets

9). WORK DONE

Carrying parties preparing for the attack, assembly, & immediate support trenches of right battalion lengthened

Repairs to J track carried out & new route from F track to Right Batt. right Coy H.Q. & to left flank taped out

[illegible] Lt
for Brig Gen Comdg
12th Inf Bde

6/9/17

125th Inf. Bde Intelligence Summary.
No 8.

period noon 6/9/17 – noon 7/9/17.

1) OPERATIONS.

a) ours. Fighting took place all day yesterday for the possession of BORRY FARM, BECK HOUSE & IBERIAN.

The force attacking BORRY was held up by MG fire from the dugouts S of the farm & from VAMPIRE, but succeeded in digging itself ~~[illegible]~~ in in two lines running from D25b2820 – D25b1830 & from D25b0541 – D25b05.60 & in establishing a post at D25b0580, but owing to heavy MG fire was forced to withdraw to its original line in the evening. xx

BECK was taken early in the morning & consolidated, but after the withdrawal from IBERIAN, our left was in the air & a hostile counter attack succeeded in enveloping the place & retaking it.

The force attacking IBERIAN were at one time reported by RFC as being in possession of trenches S & N of the post, but this is probably incorrect, as most of it became casualties before the objective was reached.

M.G. fire from IBERIAN & more particularly from HILL 35 was very heavy & eventually caused a withdrawal to the original front line in the course of the afternoon.

During the counter attack on BECK our M.G. obtained an excellent target & caused the enemy severe casualties.

* Later reports state that the line D25 b 2520 – D25b 1530 has been consolidated the left being brought back & joined to our original line.

b) enemy's

Enemy assembled for counter attack from direction of VAMPIRE & the positions in BORRY FARM. Twice during the course of the day they were cut up by our artillery fire. At 7.45 p.m. S.O.S. went up from our left positions in direction of HILL 35.

Our barrage fire at 7.45 undoubtedly stopped a heavy counter attack on our left position.

2) ARTILLERY

a) ours
Very active carrying out programme & answering S.O.S. signals.

b) enemy's.

Barrage came down as usual

3

lines at 7.27 a.m 6/9/17.

3) ENEMY DEFENCES.

a) new work } nil
b) new wire }
c) M.G.S. reported to have fired from roof of IBERIAN during the attack, from the trenches in front of from HILL 35. Fire was intense from moment troops left the trenches, barrage apparently falling first on objectives. IBERIAN is a M.G. nest; exact locations uncertain as reports are conflicting.

M.G.S in strong points at BORRY fired through our barrage.

d) T.M.S. } nil
e) dumps }

4.) ENEMY COMMUNICATIONS ~~nil~~
5.) " dispositions

After morning attack, in the afternoon many enemy seen in trench W of BECK, where there seems to be concealed communication to BORRY.

6) MOVEMENT.

Considerable movement during afternoon at about D19 c 8 c.

where they seemed to be massing in trenches.
Enemy Burial + collecting parties, under red X flag have been hard at work since 3 pm This points to heavy casualties.
Enemy snipers very active.

7). E.A. below normal. One EA flew low just before the attack over our lines.
1. E.A. brought down ~~200 yds in~~ about D25 b 72.

8) Miscellaneous nil

9) WORK DONE.

General improvement of trenches in support areas.

[signature] Lt.
for Brig Gen Cmdg
125th Inf. Bde.

7/9/17.

Secret
Y169

5. L. Fus.
7 L. Fus.
8 L. Fus.
125 I. Bty.
X/42 T.M. Bty.
'C' Coy 42nd M.G. Bn.
Right Group.
127 Inf Bde.
128 Inf Bde.
Signals.
42nd Division
War Diary (2 copies)

Ref this office letter No. Y166 dated 21st inst.

1. 5 L. Fus will establish Post No. 3 K.28.c.15.25. tomorrow morning 23rd inst and form a defensive flank along SOUTHERN AVENUE.
2. During the night 22nd/23rd inst Post No. 2 K.28.c.30.55 will be doubled and two Lewis guns placed in position. This post must be defended at all costs.
3. The following artillery arrangements have been made
Zero -15 to ZERO. Field Artillery will put down a barrage on the following lines
K.27.d.95.15 – K.28.c.80.45 – K.28.a.47.10.

During this time two 4.5 Howitzers will fire on K.28.c.40.40 and two 4.5 Howitzers on BASIN WOOD at K.28.c.55.40.
Zero to Zero + 30 barrage on K.27.d.95.15 – K.28.c.80.45 will lift and thicken the barrage from K.28.c.45.40 – K.28.c.80.45. The barrage from K.28.c.80.45 – K.28.a.47.10 will be continued. During this time one 4.5 howitzer will fire on K.28.c.40.40, two on BASIN WOOD at K.28.c.55.45 and one on K.28.c.95.50.

If this second barrage is required after Zero + 30, O.C. 5 Lancs. Fus. will notify this office by code word GRACE.

From Zero – 15 to Zero + 30 harassing fire will be brought to bear on following points and surrounding trenches:–

(i) K.34.a 90.60.
(ii) K.34.a 30.30.

4. Co-operation of 6" Newton and 3" Stokes Mortars to be arranged by O.C. 5 Lancs. Fus.

5. When Post No 3 is established this office will be informed by code word THREE.

6. Zero hour will be 5 0 a.m (Five a.m 23rd inst.)

7. ACKNOWLEDGE.

[signature] Captain,
Brigade Major,
125 Inf Brigade

22-7-18

Issued thro' Signals 12 midnight 22/23rd inst.

SECRET   Y 167

5 Lancs Fus.
7 Lancs Fus.
8 Lancs Fus.
125 T M Battery.
127 Inf Bde.
Right Group.
"C" Coy. 42 M G Battn.
427 Fd. Coy R.E.
X/42 T M Battery.
42 Division
C R E 42 Division
252 Tunnelling Coy. R.E.

War Diary

---

5 Lan Fus will move into their New Head quarters ~~tomorrow~~ on 24th instant at K.31. b 30.90. Move to be complete by 8 p m.

8 Lan Fus will move into their New Head Quarters tomorrow 23rd inst. at J.30.d. 30.00. Move to be complete by 2.30 p.m. 252 Tunnelling Coy is sending a representative to take over this dugout. 8 Lan Fus will leave a NCO behind to hand it over.

[signature], Captain,
Brigade Major
125 Inf. Brigade.

22-7-18.

SECRET

5 Lan. Fus   Y.166

7 Lan. Fus

8 Lan. Fus

125 T.M. Battery

X/42 Bty Medium Trench Mortars

'C' Coy, 42 M.G. Battn.

Right Group

127 Inf Bde

188 Inf Bde

42 Division.

1 In order to conform with the advance of the 127 Infantry Brigade and to protect my front line with a line of Advanced Posts. Posts will be established tomorrow 22nd inst. at 11 a.m. at the following points.

i	K 28 c 20 75
ii	K 28 c 30 45
iii	K 28 c 15 25
iv	K 34 a 30 60
v	K 34 a 30 30
vi	K 34 c 20 95
vii	K 34 c 40 75
viii	K 34 c 60 60
ix	K 34 c 80 40

Posts Nos i-vi inclusive will be established by 8 Lan. Fus the remaining three by 7 Lan Fus

2 An officer will be in charge of at least every three posts

3. Small carrying parties will be detailed and held in readiness to move forward as soon as the posts are established, with wire, tools, etc. to assist in the consolidation.

4. There will be no artillery preparation, but field guns will be ready to open fire in the event of necessity on the following lines.

(1) K 28 c 30 90 – K 28 a 05 95 –
K 28 c 75 50 – K 28 c 60 40

(2) K 28 c 60 40 – K 28 a 10 45
K 34 b 30 55 – K 34 a 80 35

(3) K 34 b 00 50 – K 34 a 80 30 thence along
VALLADE TRENCH to K 34 a 25 30

If any one or more of these barrages are required units will wire to this office in code words as follows.

Barrage No 1 GRACE
" No 2 PHYLLIS
" No 3 MAUD

which will be forwarded to Right Group for ~~[illegible]~~ action.

These barrages will be maintained for twenty minutes. If Artillery fire is required for a longer period units will ask from this office.

5. When it is known that a post has been established the number shewn against the post in para 1 will be wired to this office.

6. ACKNOWLEDGE.

E.H. Sarton [illegible] Captain,
Brigade Major,
125 Inf. Brigade.

21-7-18.

3)

7) HOSTILE AEROPLANE ACTIVITY

2 Bombs dropped near POTIZJE at about 4.30 pm

12 E A over our lines between 6–7 pm, driven off by AA.

7.45 am. Aeroplane (nationality unknown) fell in enemy lines on our front

8) Miscellaneous

0 Balloons up from 4.15 pm – 5 pm.

on bearing 20° 30′
45° 30′ } grid from I 6 C 99 80
80°

1/9/17

MW Zimmern Lt.
for Brig Gen Commdg
125 Inf. Bde

War Diary

S E C R E T.

Copy No. 22..

125th BRIGADE OPERATION ORDER NUMBER 33. 1/9/17.

1. On Night 1/2nd September the following reliefs will take place:_

2. (a) RIGHT SUBSECTOR.

7th Lan Fus will relieve 5th Lan Fus in Front Line!

(5th Lan Fus less 2 Coys
(2 Coys 1 Manchester Regt. will relieve 7th Lan Fus in 1/1 Support.

(b) LEFT SUBSECTOR.

8th Lan Fus will relieve 6th Lan Fus in Front Line.

(6th Lan Fus less 2 coys
(2 Coys ~~Mxx~~ !... Manchester Regt ~~will~~ ~~Support.~~ will relieve 8th Lan Fus in Support

3. The 2 Coys of 5th Lan Fus and 6th Lan Fus to be withdrawn will embus at Brigade Headquarters after relief and proceed ~~the~~ to H 16 c and d.

7th and 8th Lan Fus will send one Guide per Coy Headquarters and 1 per Platoon to Brigade Headquarters at 8.15.p.m. to-night to lead the 4 Companies of the Manchesters to Right and Left Support areas.

4. All details of relief to be arranged between C.O's concerned. Intervals of 200 yards to be kept between Platoons.

5. The next inter-Battalion relief will probably take place on night 4/5th September.

6. A C K N O W L E D G E.

[signature]
Captain,
Brigade Major,
125th BRIGADE.

Issued at 10.30.a.m.
Copies to:- (6)

1. 5th Lan Fus.
2. 6th Lan Fus.
3. 7th Lan Fus.
4. 8th Lan Fus.
5. 125th M.G.Company.
6. 125th T.M.Battery.
7. 427th Field Coy R.E.
8. 428th Field Coy R.E.
9. 429th Coy A.S.C.
10. 126th Brigade.
11. 127th Brigade.
12. 142 Brigade.
13. 182 Brigade.
14. Right Sub Group Artillery.
15. Left Sub Group Artillery.
16. 42nd Division.
17. Brigade Major.
18. Staff Captain.
19. Rear Staff Captain.
20. Signalling-Officer.
(21
(22 War Diary.
23. F I L E'

1/8

CONFIDENTIAL

Vol 9

WAR DIARY of

Inf.
125 BDE –

OCTOBER 1st – 31st 1917.

VOL NO 40

Instructions regarding War Diaries and Intelligence Summaries are contained in F. S. Regs., Part II. and the Staff Manual respectively. Title Pages will be prepared in manuscript.

PAGE 1

VOL NO 20.

WAR DIARY
or
~~INTELLIGENCE SUMMARY~~

(Erase heading not required.)

of 125 BDE (INFY)

OCTOBER 1ST – 31ST. 1917

Army Form C. 2118

Place	Date	Hour		Summary of Events and Information		Remarks and references to Appendices
ST IDESBALD	OCT 1917		MAP REF		WEATHER	
"	1st		BELGIUM 19.	In camp. ST IDESBALD AREA — Training – building ranges – assault courses etc.	Fine	FC
"	2nd		"	Do Do Do Capt A.O. NEEDHAM. Staff Capt. proceeded to ENGLAND on leave.	Fine (slight rain at midnight)	FC
"	3rd		"	Major FINLAY – (North Irish Horse) – assumed duties of Staff Capt during Capt NEEDHAM's absence on leave. Do Do Do	Fine but windy	
		8pm	~~Do~~	Warning order issued re relief of 97th Bde by 125 Bde		Bde Warning order No 43 FC
"	4th		COXYDE and LOMBARTZYDE 1/20000.	Orders issued for relief of 97th Infy Bde by 125 Infy Bde. Preparations for relief:	Fine.	Bde Op order No 43 FC
"	5th		"	Preparations for relief: Night 5/6. 125 Bde H Qrs relieved 97th Bde H Qrs. 5 Lan Fus relieved 16th H L I. Right Front Battn.	Heavy Rain.	FC
NIEUPORT	6th		NIEUPORT. 1/10000	6 Lan Fus " 11th Border Regt. Left Front Battn. 7 Lan Fus " 2nd K.O.Y.L.I. Support Battn. 8 Lan Fus. " 17th H.L.I. Reserve Battn. 125 TM Batty " 97th T.M.B.	Rain	Bde Op order No 43 FC
"	7th		"	× Night 6/7. 125 M Gun Coy " 97th M G Coy. Situation Quiet.	Fine.	FC

1875 Wt. W593/826 1,000,000 4/15 J.B.C. & A. A.D.S.S./Forms/C. 2118.

Army Form C. 2118

WAR DIARY

or

~~INTELLIGENCE SUMMARY~~ of 125TH BDE

(Erase heading not required.)

PAGE 2

VOL NO 40. Oct. 1ST – 31ST 1917.

Instructions regarding War Diaries and Intelligence Summaries are contained in F. S. Regs., Part II. and the Staff Manual respectively. Title Pages will be prepared in manuscript.

Place	Date	Hour	MAP REF.	Summary of Events and Information	WEATHER.	Remarks and references to Appendices
NIEUPORT	8th		NIEUPORT. 12 SW 1. 1/10 000.	Orders issued for Inter Battn Relief to take place on 9/10th. Situation – Intell summary No 15.	Wet.	Bde op order No 44. I.S. No 15. [initials]
"	9th.		"	Situation Quiet.	Dull & showery	[initials]
				Night 9/10th. 7 Lan Fus relieved 5 Lan Fus in Right Subsector. 8 Lan Fus " " 6 " " " Left Subsector.		
"	10th		"	Situation Quiet.	Fine	[initials]
"	11th.		"	Hostile Artillery shelled Bde HQ area. Bde Office destroyed. including Office Boxes and most of the documents – 2 clerks wounded. Lt Col HOPE Commdg 1/8 Lan Fus – reported "missing, believed prisoner".	Fine	[initials]
"	12th.		"	Situation Quiet.	Fine but Cold.	[initials]
"	13th.		"	do. do.	Fine	[initials]
"	14th.		"	do. do.	Dull Showery	[initials]
"	15th.		"	do. do.	Fine	[initials]

Army Form C. 2118

Instructions regarding War Diaries and Intelligence Summaries are contained in F. S. Regs., Part II. and the Staff Manual respectively. Title Pages will be prepared in manuscript.

PAGE. 3

VOL. NO. 40

WAR DIARY or ~~INTELLIGENCE~~ SUMMARY of 125 INFY BDE

(~~Erase heading not required.~~)

OCT 1ST – 31ST 1917.

Place	Date OCT.	Hour	MAP. REF.	Summary of Events and Information	WEATHER	Remarks and references to Appendices
NIEUPORT.	16TH		NIEUPORT 12 SW1 1/10000	Bde HQs moved from M27682. to cellars in NIEUPORT, next to & opposite to ELECTRIC LIGHTING STATN in RUE LONGUE. Orders issued for Inter Battn Relief.	Fine	Bde op order No45. JC
"	17TH		"	Situation quiet. Night 17/18. 7LF relieved 5LF. 8LF relieved 6LF. 5LF moving into Support. 6LF into Reserve.	Fine.	JC.
"	18TH		"	Situation quiet.	Fine	JC
"	19TH			Situation quiet.	Fine	JC
"	20TH		1/40000 FURNES.	Night 20/21. 5 Lan Fus relieved by 7th Manchester Regt. 6 Lan Fus " " 6th " ".	Fine.	Bde op order No46 JC
LAPANNE AREA	21ST			5LF and 6LF moved to COXYDE. 5LF and 6LF (and Bde HQs) marched to LAPANNE, & billetted there. Night 21/22. 7 Lan Fus relieved by 5th Manchester Regt. 8 Lan Fus " " 8th " ".	Fine	Bde op order No46. JC
"	22ND			7 Lan Fus moved to CANADA CAMP. 8 Lan Fus " " AUSTRALIA CAMP } COXYDE. Night 22/23. 125 Light TMB and 125 MGun Coy relieved by 127 TMB & 127 MG Coy. & marched to COXYDE.	Fine	Bde op order No46. JC
"	23RD			Units: Training – Bathing – Cleaning etc. BRIG. GENL. FARGUS CMG DSO proceeded to U.K. on 10 days leave.	Very wet	JC

Army Form C. 2118

Instructions regarding War Diaries and Intelligence Summaries are contained in F. S. Regs., Part II. and the Staff Manual respectively. Title Pages will be prepared in manuscript.

WAR DIARY
or
~~INTELLIGENCE SUMMARY~~

VOL 40. PAGE 4. *(Erase heading not required.)* 125 Bde. OCT. 1st – 31st 1917.

Place	OCT 17. Date	Hour	MAP REF	Summary of Events and Information	WEATHER	Remarks and references to Appendices
LAPANNE AREA.	24th		1/40000 FURNES.	Bde Training – Working Parties found by two Battns at COXSYDE –	Showery.	FC
"	25th		"	Bde Training, Musketry etc.	Fine. Gale of wind.	FC
"	26th		"	do. do.	Fine	FC
"	27th		"	do. do.	Fine	FC
"	28th		"	do. do.	Fine very cold.	FC
"	29th		"	5 LAN FUS and 6 L Fus proceeded to COXYDE. 7 LAN FUS " 8 LAN FUS " " LAPANNE – CAPT A.O. NEEDHAM proceeded to 41st DW as acting DAQMG. MAJ. FINLAY (N.I.H) came to Bde as acting Staff Capt vice Capt NEEDHAM	Fine. Cold.	FC
"	30th		"	Bde Training.	very windy dull & cold	FC
"	31st		"	do. do.	Fine.	FC

H. Fargus [signature]
Brig. Genl
Commdg 125 Infy Bde.

23

CONFIDENTIAL

Original

Vol 10

WAR DIARY

OF

125TH INFY BDE

NOV. 1ST - 30TH 1917.

-

VOL NO. 40.

67.

Army Form C. 2118

WAR DIARY

or

~~INTELLIGENCE SUMMARY~~

~~(Erase heading not required.)~~

Instructions regarding War Diaries and Intelligence Summaries are contained in F. S. Regs., Part II. and the Staff Manual respectively. Title Pages will be prepared in manuscript.

PAGE 1.
VOL. NO: 40

125 INFY BDE
NOV. 1ST – 30TH. 1917.

Place	NOV Date 1917	Hour	MAP REF.	Summary of Events and Information	WEATHER	Remarks and references to Appendices
LA PANNE	1st		1/40000 FURNES 1/10000 SHEET 5	Bde Training. Route Marches. Musketry. Specialist Instruction	Fine	Jc
LA PANNE	2nd		Do	Bde Training – Route marches etc Bde School of Instruction.	Fine	Jc
LA PANNE	3rd		Do	Orders issued for relief of 127 Bde by 125 Bde. Bde Training. etc.	Fine	Bde Op Order No 47. Jc
LA PANNE	4th		Do	Bde Training. etc..		Jc
LA PANNE	5th		Do	Preparations for relief of 127 Bde. night 5/6 7LF marched from LAPANNE & relieved 5 M/c Regt in Support. 8LF " " " " 8 M/c Regt in Reserve.		Jc
LA PANNE	6th		Do.	Bde HQs moved by march route to NIEUPORT. 6pm. night 6/7. 8LF marched from CANADA CAMP COXSYDE & relieved 7 M/c Regt in Right Front. 6LF " " " AUSTRALIA CAMP " . " " 6/M/c Regt in Left Front	Showery	Jc
NIEUPORT	7th		Do and NIEUPORT 12 SW1.	Bde in line – situation quiet. LT REID (BLACK WATCH) O.C. Sig Sect. attd Bde HQs – wounded – CAPT. R. NEWTON MC., attd 42 Div Sig Coy assumed command No 2 Sectn. attd Bde HQs. night 7/8 125 M.Gun Coy & 125 TMB relieved 127 M.G. Coy & 127 TMB in Line.		Jc
NIEUPORT	8th		Do.	Bde School dispersed – Orders issued for inter-battalion relief.	Bde Order No 48.	Jc

1875 Wt. W593/826 1,000,000 4/15 J.B.C. & A. A.D.S.S./Forms/C. 2118.

Instructions regarding War Diaries and Intelligence Summaries are contained in F. S. Regs., Part II. and the Staff Manual respectively. Title Pages will be prepared in manuscript.

Army Form C. 2118

WAR DIARY

or

~~INTELLIGENCE SUMMARY~~ OF 125 INFY BDE

(~~Erase heading not required.~~)

PAGE 2

VOL. 40.

NOV 1ST - 30TH. 1917.

Place	Date	Hour	MAP REF:	Summary of Events and Information	WEATHER	Remarks and references to Appendices
NIEUPORT	9TH		1/40000 FURNES 1/10000 SHEET 5	Situation quiet. A certain amount of artillery activity (hostile). REDAN heavily shelled at mid-day.	Fine but showery	JC
NIEUPORT	10TH		Do	Bde HQs - TMBatty HQs. and vicinity very heavily shelled. 5.9s. Counter-battery & punishment fire brought to bear on enemy. Bde HQs much damaged but not penetrated - no casualties at Bde HQs.	Heavy Rain.	JC
NIEUPORT	11TH		Do	night 10/11. 5LF and 6LF relieved by 7LF & 8LF respectively. 5LF moved into SUPPORT. 6LF to Reserve - 7LF Right Front. 8LF Left Front. Situation quiet. Vicinity of Bde HQs shelled at intervals.	Showery	JC
NIEUPORT	12TH		Do	Orders issued for Inter-Battn Relief on 14/15 inst. Situation quiet - enemy artillery active on NIEUPORT.	Fine Sunny.	Bde Op Order No 49. JC
NIEUPORT	13TH		Do	Situation quiet. Enemy artillery active on REDAN.	Fine	JC
NIEUPORT	14TH		Do	Situation quiet. Enemy artillery less active. 14/15 Inter-battalion relief. 7LF relieved by 5LF. 8LF relieved by 6LF.	Fine	JC
NIEUPORT	15TH		Do.	Very quiet night. Situation quiet.	Fine & Sunny	JC
NIEUPORT.	16TH		Do	Orders issued for relief of 125 Bde by 2 battns 321st French Infy Regt and 1 Battn 116th Chasseurs. on nights 17/18 - 18/19. 19/20 Nov.	Fine	Bde Op Order No 50 JC

1875 Wt. W593/826 1,000,000 4/15 J.B.C. & A. A.D.S.S./Forms/C. 2118.

Instructions regarding War Diaries and Intelligence Summaries are contained in F. S. Regs., Part II. and the Staff Manual respectively. Title Pages will be prepared in manuscript.

WAR DIARY or ~~INTELLIGENCE~~ SUMMARY

(~~Erase heading not required.~~)

Army Form C. 2118

PAGE 3 VOL No 40. of 125 Infy Bde Nov 1ST – 30TH 1917.

Place	Nov Date 1917	Hour	MAP REF.	Summary of Events and Information	WEATHER	Remarks and references to Appendices
NIEUPORT	17TH		1/40000 FURNES; 1/10000 SHEET 5	Orders issued for move of 125 Bde & attached troops to TETEGHEM & WORMHOUDT 'A' areas –	Fine.	Bde op order No 51
NIEUPORT	18TH		1/100 000 Sheets 1A, 5A; 1/40000 Sheets 19, 27	Night 17/18. 8LF relieved by 6th Battn 321st French Infy Regt & marched to CANADA CAMP – night exceptionally quiet. Orders issued for continuation of march of Bde Group to WORMHOUDT 'A' AREA – night 18/19. 5LF relieved by 5 Battn 321st Fr. Inf Regt. 6LF relieved by 6th Battn 321st Fr Inf Regt. 7LF marched to CANADA CAMP. ~~[illegible] to AUSTRALIA CAMP.~~ Bde HQRS to CANADA CAMP.	Fine	Bde order No 52.
LEFFRINCOUCKE	19TH		1/100 000 Sheet 5A; 1/40000 Sheet 27.	Warning order issued for move of Bde Group to ZERMEZEELE. Bde Group marched to LEFFRINCOUCKE AREA. Bde Group billetted in LEFFRINCOUCKE AREA – night 19/20. 125 TMB moved to AUSTRALIA CAMP. 125 MG Coy relieved by Mitrailleuse 321 Fr Infy Regt –	Fine.	Bde Warning order No 53
WORMHOUDT.	20TH		1/100000 Sheet 5A. 1/40000 Sheet 27.	Orders issued for march to ZERMEZEELE – Bde Group marched to WORMHOUDT & billetted there.	Fine	Bde order No 54
ZERMEZEELE	21ST		1/100000 Sheet 5A; 1/40000 Sheet 27	Orders issued for march of Bde Group to STAPLE. Bde billetted at ZERMEZEELE.	Fine	Bde order No 55.
STAPLE	22ND		1/100.000 Sheet 5A; 1/40000 Sheets 27, 36A.	Orders issued for move of Bde Group to THIENNES AREA – Bde marched to STAPLE. Bde billetted in STAPLE AREA.	Wet.	Bde op order No 56.
THIENNES	23RD		do.	Bde Group marched to THIENNES AREA. Bde HQ – Billetted in THIENNES	Fine	
THIENNES	24TH.		do	Warning order issued for relief of 25th Div by 42nd Div in BETHUNE AREA –	Fine,	Bde warning order No 57.

1875 Wt. W593/826 1,000,000 4/15 J.B.C. & A. A.D.S.S./Forms/C. 2118.

Instructions regarding War Diaries and Intelligence Summaries are contained in F. S. Regs., Part II. and the Staff Manual respectively. Title Pages will be prepared in manuscript.

WAR DIARY
or
~~INTELLIGENCE SUMMARY~~
(Erase heading not required.)

Army Form C. 2118

PAGE 4
VOL. 40.

of 125TH INFY BDE.

Place	Nov Date 1917	Hour	MAP REF:	Summary of Events and Information	WEATHER	Remarks and references to Appendices
THIENNES	25TH		1/10.000 36 S W 3 36 C N W 1.	Bde Group in THIENNES AREA. Orders issued for march of 125 Bde Group to BETHUNE AREA –	Fine.	Bde Op order No 58 FC
THIENNES	26TH		do.	Orders issued for move of Bde by march route to relieve 75th Infy Bde in GIVENCHY – CUINCHY – CAMBRIN sector. – (74th Infy Bde on right flank – 127 Bde on left flank) Bde Group ~~marched to~~ at THIENNES.	Wet.	Bde Op order No 59. FC
BETHUNE	27TH		BETHUNE 1/10.000 36 C N.W. 1.	Bde Group ~~billetted in~~ marched to BETHUNE AREA. & billetted there.	Fine	FC
" " "	28TH		do	Bde HQs moved to F10 b. 9.1 A 7LF relieved 11th CHESHIRE REGT. D 5LF relieved 8th S. LANCS REGT. B. 8LF " " 2nd S. LANCS REGT. 125 TMB " 75th TMB. C. 6LF " " 8th BORDER REGT. A Right Front. B Left do. C Support. D Reserve.	Fine	FC
" " "	29TH		do.	125 M Gun Coy relieved 75th M. Gun Coy. Situation quiet.	Fine	FC
" " "	30TH		do.	Situation quiet:	Fine	FC.
				3/12/17. Harold Fargus		

Brigadier General
Commdg 125 Infy Bde

1875 Wt. W593/826 1,000,000 4/15 J.B.C. & A. A.D.S.S./Forms/C. 2118.

Confidential

Vol 11

WAR DIARY

of

125TH INFY BDE

VOL NO 41.

DEC: 1917.

Instructions regarding War Diaries and Intelligence Summaries are contained in F. S. Regs., Part II. and the Staff Manual respectively. Title pages will be prepared in manuscript.

WAR DIARY
or
~~INTELLIGENCE SUMMARY.~~
(Erase heading not required.)

Army Form C. 2118.

PAGE. 1. of 125TH INFY BDE. DEC 1917.
VOL No: 41

Place	1917 Date DEC	Hour	MAP REF:	Summary of Events and Information	WEATHER	Remarks and references to Appendices
CANAL SECTOR BETHUNE.	1ST		1/10000 FRANCE. 36c NW1.	Orders issued for Inter Battn Relief. Bde holding Right Sector of Divnl Front with Reserve Battn at LE PREOL (training).	Cold. Showers	Bde Op Order No 60. FC
"	2ND		do.	Situation quiet	Cold & Bright	FC
"	3RD		do	Situation quiet.	Cold & Bright	FC
"	4TH		do.	5 Lan Fus relieved 7 Lan Fus in Right Front Line. 6 Lan Fus. do . 8 Lan Fus in Left do do.	Do.	FC
"	5TH		1/40000 BETHUNE	Orders issued for relief of 125th Bde by 126th Bde.	Do.	Bde Op Order No 61. FC
"	6TH		"	Situation quiet	Misty Cold.	FC
"	7TH		"	Situation quiet.	Cold & Bright	FC
"	8TH		"	Further orders issued for relief of 125 Bde by 126 Bde.	Cold & misty	Bde Op. Order No 62. FC

1577 Wt. W10791/1773 500,000 1/15 D. D. & L. A.D.S.S./Forms/C. 2118.

Army Form C. 2118.

WAR DIARY
or
~~INTELLIGENCE SUMMARY.~~

Instructions regarding War Diaries and Intelligence Summaries are contained in F. S. Regs., Part II. and the Staff Manual respectively. Title pages will be prepared in manuscript.

PAGE 2. VOL 41. (~~Erase heading not required.~~) of 125TH INFY BDE. DEC 1917.

Place	Date DEC 1917	Hour	MAP REF.	Summary of Events and Information	WEATHER	Remarks and references to Appendices
CANAL SECTOR BETHUNE.	9TH		1/40000 BETHUNE	Bde in Line. Situation quiet.	Rain.	[initials]
BETHUNE	10TH		do.	125TH Bde relieved by 126th Bde. 5 Lan Fus relieved in Right Front by 1/9 M/c Regt. 6 Lan Fus relieved in Left Front by 1/10 M/c Regt. 1/7 Lan Fus relieved in Reserve by 4th E. Lancs. 8 LF relieved in Support by 5th E. Lancs. 125 TMB relieved by 126 TMB.	Bright & warmer	[initials]
VENDIN LEZ BETHUNE	11TH		do.	5 LF billeted at BEUVRY. Bde Hqs at VENDIN-LEZ-BETHUNE. 6 LF " " BETHUNE. 7 LF " " HINGETTE. 125 M Gun Coy relieved by 126 M Gun Coy & 8 LF " " OBLINGHEM. billeted in BETHUNE.	Cold	[initials]
"	12TH		do.	Bde in Reserve – Training.	Cold	[initials]
"	13TH		do.	Bde Training.	Bright & cold	[initials]
"	14TH		do.	Bde Training	do.	[initials]
"	15TH		do.	Bde Training	do.	[initials]
"	16TH		do.	Bde Training.	Cold & misty	[initials]

1577 Wt. W10791/1773 500,000 1/15 D. D. & L. A.D.S.S./Forms/C. 2118.

Instructions regarding War Diaries and Intelligence Summaries are contained in F. S. Regs., Part II. and the Staff Manual respectively. Title Pages will be prepared in manuscript. PAGE 3. VOL 41

WAR DIARY
or
~~INTELLIGENCE SUMMARY~~
(Erase heading not required.) of 125TH INFY BDE. DEC 1917.

Army Form C. 2118

Place	Date DEC 1917	Hour	MAP REF.	Summary of Events and Information	WEATHER	Remarks and references to Appendices
VENDIN LEZ BETHUNE	17TH		BETHUNE 1/40000.	Bde in Reserve. Training. musketry. bombing etc.	Frosty	FC
"	18TH		do	Orders issued for relief of 127 Bde by 125 Bde in Divisional Left Sector. Bde Training	do.	Bde Op Order No 63. FC
"	19TH		do and LA BASSÉE 1:10000	Orders issued for relief of 127 Bde by 125 Bde. Bde Training	do	Bde Op Order No 64. FC
"	20TH		do.	Bde Training.	do.	FC
"	21ST		do	Bde Training.	do.	FC
LOISNE	22ND		do	125 Bde relieved 127 Bde in Divnl Left Sector. 5LF relieved 8th M/c Regt in Support. 6LF relieved 5th M/c Regt. Reserve. 7LF relieved 7th M/c Regt Right Front. 8th LF relieved 6 M/c Regt. 125 TMB relieved 127 TMB. Bde HQs moved to LOISNE CHATEAU.	Bright & Frosty	FC
do	23RD		do	125 MGun Coy relieved 127 MG Coy. Bde in Line – Situation Quiet.	do	FC
do.	24TH		do.	Situation quiet	do.	FC

1875 Wt. W593/826 1,000,000 4/15 J.B.C. & A. A.D.S.S./Forms/C. 2118.

Army Form C. 2118

Instructions regarding War Diaries and Intelligence Summaries are contained in F. S. Regs., Part II. and the Staff Manual respectively. Title Pages will be prepared in manuscript.

PAGE 4.
VOL 41

WAR DIARY
or
~~INTELLIGENCE SUMMARY~~
(Erase heading not required.) of 125TH INFY BDE DEC 1917.

Place	DEC 1917 Date	Hour	MAP REF.	Summary of Events and Information	WEATHER	Remarks and references to Appendices
LOISNE	25TH		BETHUNE 1/40000 ~~LA BASSEE~~ 1/40000	Orders issued for Inter Battn Relief. Xmas Day – Holiday for Reserve Battn. Situation quiet	Snow	Bde Op Order No 65. TC
do	26TH		do	Situation Quiet Capt AE LAWRENCE (Bde Major) proceed to CAMBRIDGE (Staff Offrs Course) Major PERY (GSO 3 42 Div) assumes duties of Bde Major.	do	TC
do	27TH		do	Situation Quiet –	Frosty	TC
do	28TH		do	5th Lan Fus relieved 7th L.F. Right Front. 7LF into Support 6th Lan Fus " " 8th L.F. Left Front. 8LF into Reserve. Situation quiet	Snow	TC
do	29TH		do	Situation quiet –	Frost	TC
do	30TH		do.	Situation Quiet –	Dull morning Frost later	TC
do.	31ST.		1/40000 BETHUNE	Orders issued for Inter Battn relief. Situation quiet –	Frosty	Bde Op. Order No 66. TC
						~~Bde Op~~

7/1/18.

[signature] Lt. Col.
~~Brigadier General~~
Commanding 125th Inf. Brigade.

1875 Wt. W593/826 1,000,000 4/15 J.B.C. & A. A.D.S.S./Forms/C. 2118.

ORIGINAL COPY

CONFIDENTIAL

Vol 12

WAR DIARY

of

125 INFY BDE

JAN 1st – 31st. 1918

VOL NO: 43.

Instructions regarding War Diaries and Intelligence Summaries are contained in F. S. Regs., Part II. and the Staff Manual respectively. Title Pages will be prepared in manuscript.

WAR DIARY
or
~~INTELLIGENCE SUMMARY~~
(Erase heading not required.)

Army Form C. 2118

PAGE 1. VOL NO 43.

of 125 INFY BDE JAN 1ST - 31ST 1918.

Place	Date JAN	Hour	MAP REF.	Summary of Events and Information	WEATHER	Remarks and references to Appendices
BETHUNE AREA	1		36C NW1 LA BASSÉE 1/10000.	Bde HQs. CHATEAU LOISNE. Front line trenches of 5LF heavily bombarded with gas shells (mustard) (Portuguese on left flank of Bde - 126 Bde on right flank)	Fair + bright	
"	2		"	Situation quiet - work on trenches, Keeps etc.	Dull.	
"	3		"	6 offrs of 5LF HQs. evacuated 28 gas cases. 5LF relieved by 1/7 Lan Fus & came into Reserve. Situation quiet.	Fine + bright.	
"	4		"	Situation quiet.	Fair	
"	5		"	Situation quiet	Dull.	
"	6		"	Situation quiet.	Dull.	
BETHUNE	7		BETHUNE 1/40000. LA BASSÉE 1/10000.	Orders issued for Inter. Battn relief. 5 Lan Fus to relieve 7 LF. 6 — — 8 LF.	Cold and Damp	Bde op Order No 67
"	8.		"	Situation quiet.	Snow fall.	

Instructions regarding War Diaries and Intelligence Summaries are contained in F. S. Regs., Part II. and the Staff Manual respectively. Title Pages will be prepared in manuscript.

Army Form C. 2118

WAR DIARY
or
~~INTELLIGENCE SUMMARY~~
(Erase heading not required.)

PAGE 2. of 125 INFY BDE
VOL NO ~~2~~ 3 JAN. 1918.

Place	Date Jan	Hour	MAP REF.	Summary of Events and Information	WEATHER	Remarks and references to Appendices
BETHUNE AREA	9TH		36C NW1. LA BASSÉE 1/10000.	Situation Quiet. Bde in GIVENCHY SECTOR. Work commenced on trench improvement etc.	Fine - strong wind	FC
Do	10TH		"	Bde HdQs. (LOISNE CHATEAU) Shelled in afternoon - 14 casualties - (8 O.R. killed - 6 O.R. wounded). Signal Office destroyed & new one opened in cellar.	Dull.	FC
Do	11TH		"	Situation quiet - work on trenches etc.	Dull - Rain & wind.	FC
Do	12TH		"	Situation Quiet Bde op. order No 68 issued - re relief of 125 Bde by 126 Bde.	Dull.	Bde order No 68 FC
Do	13TH		"	Corrigendum to Bde order No 68. issued - postponing relief until further orders —	Dull.	Corrigendum to Bde order No 68. FC
Do	14TH		"	Amendment to Bde order No 68 issued. postponing Bde relief till 17th inst.	Dull. Snowfall.	Amendment No 2 to Bde order No 68. FC
Do	15TH		"	Situation Quiet.	Dull	FC
Do.	16TH		"	Situation Quiet.	Heavy Rainfall	FC

Army Form C. 2118.

WAR DIARY
~~or~~
~~INTELLIGENCE SUMMARY.~~ of 125 INFY BDE:

(Erase heading not required.)

Instructions regarding War Diaries and Intelligence Summaries are contained in F. S. Regs., Part II. and the Staff Manual respectively. Title pages will be prepared in manuscript.

PAGE 3

VOL. 43.

JANY 1918.

Place	Date Jan	Hour	MAP REF	Summary of Events and Information	WEATHER	Remarks and references to Appendices
BETHUNE (GIVENCHY SECTOR)	17TH		36C NW1. LA BASSÉE 1/10000	125 Bde relieved by 126 Bde. Bde HQs moved to CHATEAU at VENDIN-LEZ-BETHUNE. 5 LF relieved by 9th M/c Regt and marched to billets at HINGETTE. 6 LF " 10th M/c Regt " " " FERME DU ROI. 7 LF " 5th E. LANCS " " " BEUVRY. 8 LF " 4th E. LANCS " " " OBLINGHEM. 125 TM Batty relieved by 126 TMB & marched to billets in BEUVRY	Fine.	FC
"	18th		"	125 M Gun Coy (less 1 section) relieved by 126 M Gun Coy & marched to billets in ESSARS. Battns engaged in cleaning up after relief. Brig. Gen FARGUS. CMG, DSO. proceeded to England on short leave.	Fine	FC
"	19th		"	Units training & furnishing working parties. Lt P.V. HOLBERTON assumed command of Bde during absence of Brig Genl. FARGUS.	Fair	FC
"	20th		"	Bde training under unit arrangements. Working parties.	Fine	FC
"	21st		"	Training & working parties. Work on billets & horse-standings.	Mild & bright.	FC
"	22nd		"	Training & working parties. Work on billets & horse-standings.	Fine	FC
"	23rd		"	Training & working parties. General work improving billets & stables	Fine	FC
"	24th		"	Training & working parties. General work improving billets & stabling accommodation.	Dull & Cold	FC

1577 Wt. W10791/1773 500,000 1/15 D. D. & L. A.D.S.S./Forms/C. 2118.

Instructions regarding War Diaries and Intelligence Summaries are contained in F. S. Regs., Part II. and the Staff Manual respectively. Title pages will be prepared in manuscript.

PAGE 4.
VOL. 43.

WAR DIARY
or
~~INTELLIGENCE~~ SUMMARY. of 125 Infy Bde JAN 1918

(Erase heading not required.)

Army Form C. 2118.

Place	Date Jan	Hour	MAP REF	Summary of Events and Information	WEATHER	Remarks and references to Appendices
BETHUNE	25th		36c NW1. 1/40000 LA BASSÉE 1/10000	Bde training - & working parties.	Fine	FC
(CANAL SECTOR)	26th		"	Bde order No 69 issued - re relief of 127 Bde by 125 Bde in the CANAL SECTOR. Bde Training - & working parties Advance parties to CANAL SECTOR.	Fine	Bde order No 69 FC
"	27th		"	Bde Training - & working parties.	Fine	FC
"	28th		"	Bde preparing to move to CANAL SECTOR - training & working.	Fine	FC
"	29th		"	5LF relieved 6th M/c Regt in Support. 6LF relieved 7th M/c Regt in Reserve. 7LF " " 8th M/c Regt in Right Front - 8LF relieved 5th M/c Regt in Left Front - 125 TMB relieved 127 TM Batty. Bde HQs 125 Bde opened at CANAL HOUSE - junction of LA BASSÉE & BEUVRY CANALS	Fine	FC
"	30th		"	125 M Gun Coy relieved 127 M Gun Coy. Bde in CANAL SECTOR. - work commenced on improving trenches etc. Situation quiet.	Fine	FC
"	31st		"	Situation quiet - work on trenches & keeps, revetting, hurdling etc.	Frosty & Dull.	FC

MMNichols Capt for Lt Col.
a/Bde Major
~~Brigadier General~~
Commanding 125th Inf. Brigade.

1577 Wt. W10791/1773 500,000 1/15 D. D. & L. A.D.S.S./Forms/C. 2118.

SECRET.   Copy No. 23.

125th. BRIGADE ORDER NO.67.

7/1/18.

Ref Maps: BETHUNE 1:40.000. RICHEBOURG. } 1:10.000.
LA BASSEE. }

1. The following Inter-Battalion reliefs will take place on January 9th.

5th.Lan Fus will relief the 7th Lan Fus (Right Front)
6th. " " " " " 8th. " " (Left Front)

On relief 7th Lan Fus will move to Reserve and the 8th Lan Fus to Support.

2. All details of relief will be arranged direct between C.O's concerned.

3. (1). All working parties will be taken over, and arrangements made for work under 251st Tunnelling Coy to be continuous.

(2) Schemes of trench wiring and work in hand will be handed over in detail.

4. Receipted lists of all trench stores, Maps, Air photos etc handed over will be forwarded to this office within 48 hours of relief.

5. Completion of relief will be reported to this office by wiring the Code word "[illegible]".

. ACKNOWLEDGE.

[signature]
Captain,
a/Brigade Major,
125th.BRIGADE.

Issued at [illegible] by D.R..

Copy No 1 to 5th.Lan Fus.
2. 6th. " "
3. 7th. " "
4. 8th. " "
5 125th.M.G.Coy.
6. 125th.T.M.B.
7. 429th.Coy.A.S.C.
8. 1/1st.E.L.Fd.Amb.
9. 429th.Fd.Coy.R.E.
10. 211th.B'de.R.F.A.
11. Brigade Major.
12. Staff Captain,
13. Signals.
14. S.O.
15. B.T.O.
16.) 42nd Division.
17.)
18. 251st.Tunnelling Coy.R.E.
19. 127th.Brigade.
20. 2nd Portuguese Brigade.
21. Sub Area Commandant, GORRE.
22.)
23.) W.D.
24. F I L E.

WD 76

125th Brigade Order 63 — 12.1.18

Ref BETHUNE Combined Sheet [illegible]

1. The 125th Inf Bde will be relieved by the 126th Inf Bde in the GIVENCHY Sector on the 15th inst in accordance with the attached relief and March Table.

2. All details of relief will be arranged between COs concerned.

3. Units will send guides to meet following advance parties from 126th Inf Bde at ESTAMINET CORNER F.6.a.4.0 at 11 p.m. on the 14th inst.

   1 Officer per Bat HQ.
   1 " " Company
   1 NCO " Platoon
   1 Officer and 1 NCO from 126 T.M.B.

   These parties will remain until arrival of their units on 15th inst.

4. All Trench stores, RE dumps, maps, Defence Schemes, Schemes of work and mining information and Documents relating to the sector will be handed over on relief. Receipted lists of Trench Stores will be forwarded to SC [illegible] within 48 hours of Relief.

5. All permanent working parties will be handed over to incoming units. The parties being found by [illegible] will be taken over from [illegible] by [illegible] from [illegible] on the 15th inst [illegible]

[illegible]

I report that between 1 & 1.30 am this morning a raid was made by the enemy upon the trench held by the left platoon of the left Company of the Right Sector.
A barrage was fired by the enemy on, and behind the trench and on each flank of this portion of our trenches.
Our artillery responded by placing barrage on front of right & Centre Battns.
Relief of 8th Lanc. Fus. by 21st Middlesex & of 5th Lancs Fus. by 13 Yorks Regt. was in progress & was nearly completed. The last platoon of 8th L.F. on the left of this line had only left shortly before the barrage fell. This platoon was kept when it arrived at its Company HQ. Capt THORPE M.C. Commanding the Company took the platoon back over the top to Counter-attack. On reaching the front line it was found that the enemy had entered the trench & had withdrawn. The platoon advanced to the wire & found a gap some 12 yards wide. They saw no signs of the enemy. They then returned & remained for a time before withdrawing on relief.
Full details are not yet to hand. There were some casualties among the 8th & 5th L.F. from the enemy's shell fire. 1 man killed & 2 or 3 wounded in 8th L.F. & 7 men wounded in 5th L.F.

I have seen G.O.C. 121 Bde who informs me that it is believed that 1 man & a Lewis gun was captured by the enemy but this is not confirmed yet.

26.5.17.

Herbert C Frith Br. Genl
Comdg 125 Bde

They [illegible] party [illegible]
[illegible]
by similar party [illegible]
the relieving [illegible]
[illegible]

6. The [illegible] and to [illegible] with [illegible] relieve similar party of [illegible] at CAMBRIN under [illegible]. [illegible] relief to be completed by [illegible] on 15th inst. This party may be relieved [illegible] arrangements.

7. Completion of relief will be reported to this Office by wiring the [illegible] word "[illegible]".

8. Command of [illegible] will pass to [illegible] 126th [illegible] on completion of Infantry relief [illegible] with [illegible] and [illegible] at [illegible].
[illegible]

9. ACKNOWLEDGE.

[illegible]
[illegible]
[illegible]

Issued and Signed [illegible]

Copies to:–

1. [illegible]
2. 6 "
3. 7 "
4. 8 "
5. [illegible]
6. [illegible]
7. [illegible]
8. [illegible]
9. 211 [illegible]
10. [illegible]
11. 126 [illegible]
12. 127 [illegible]
13. [illegible]
14. } [illegible]
15. }
16. [illegible]
17. [illegible]
18. [illegible]
19. [illegible]
20. [illegible]
21. [illegible]
22. "
23. [illegible]
24. } W.D.
25. }
26. File.

Serial (3)	Date	Unit	Relieved By	From	To	Route	Remarks
1	2nd Jan	5 T.F.	9th Manchester Regt	Rt. Inf.	ANNEZIN	ESTAMINET CORNER – TUNING FORK S. – GORRE – LE HAMEL	Guides to be at ESTAMINET CORNER 10 a.m.
2	6th Jan	6 L.F.	10 Manchester Regt	Ct. Inf.	VERGE-DU-ROI	FESTUBERT & WEST – TUNING FORK N. – LE QUESNOY	Guides to be at ESTAMINET CORNER 11.30 a.m.
3	[illegible]	[illegible]	4th E. Lancs Regt	Supports	[illegible]	LE QUESNOY – BETHUNE	Guides to be at ESTAMINET [illegible] 1 p.m.
4	[illegible]	[illegible]	5th E. Lancs Regt	Reserve	BEUVRY	LE QUESNOY	Head of 5th E. Lancs Regt [illegible] & [illegible] GORRE [illegible] Relief to be completed by [illegible]
5	[illegible] Jan	[illegible]	126 M.G.	Coy.	BEUVRY	LE QUESNOY	Relief to be completed by 1 p.m.
6	[illegible] Jan	[illegible]	1/1 M.G.	Fire	GORRE	[illegible]	1 Section [illegible] relieving [illegible] of [illegible] in Left Battn. [illegible]

Note:– Distance of 200 yds will be maintained between [illegible] and groups of 4 vehicles East of [illegible] [illegible]. [illegible] of this line a distance of 500 yards between platoons and equivalent units; 100 yds between vehicles [illegible]

SECRET Copy No 15

GIVENCHY SECTOR.

DEFENCE SCHEME.
****

125TH. INFANTRY BRIGADE.
****

Part 1. (a) Boundaries & Dispositions.

(b) Brief description of Brigade Front including vulnerable points.

Part 2. (a) Defensive System.

(b) General Principles of Defence.

Part 3. Action in case of attack.

(1) On Brigade Front.

(2) On Front of Flanking Brigades.

APPENDICES.
****

1. Disposition of M.G's.
2. Disposition of T.M's.
3. Artillery.
4. Signal Communications.
5. KEEPS & Strong Points.
6. Administrative arrangements

Map 'A' S.O.S.Lines 125th M.G.Company.
" 'B' S.O.S.Lines 125th T.M.Battery.

Distribution:-

Copy No.1. 5th.Lan Fus.
2. 6th. " "
3. 7th. " "
4. 8th. " "
5. 125th.M.G.Coy.
6. 125th.T.M.B.
7. 429th.Fd.Coy.R.E.
8. 211th.B'de.R.F.A.
9. 126th.Brigade.
10. 127th.Brigade.
11. 2nd Portuguese Brigade.
12. 42nd Division.
13. Staff Captain.
14. B'de.Signal Officer.
15. War Diary.
16. F I L E.

SECRET.

Copy No. 25

CORRIGENDUM TO 125th.INF.BDE
ORDER NO.68.

1. The relief of the 125th.Inf.Bde. by the 126th.Bde.in the GIVENCHY Sector will not now take place on the 15th.inst, and is postponed until further orders.

2. ACKNOWLEDGE.

P.B.B.Nichols Capt.,
A/ Bde.Major,
125th.Bde.

Issued at 8.a.m. thro' Signals.
Copies to all recipients of 125th.Bde.Order No.68.

W D Howells

S E C R E T.   COPY NO. 24

No.2
AMENDMENT TO 125th, INFANTRY BRIGADE ORDER No.68

** 15/1/18.

Reference BETHUNE, Combined Sheet 1/40,000.

---

1. The relief detailed in 125th. Infantry Brigade Order No.68 will now take place on 17th. inst.

The Machine Gun Company relief will take place on the 18th. inst.

All dates in the above order and amendment No.1 will accordingly be amended by adding on 2 days in each case.

2. In addition to the advance parties notified in para.5 of above order, company commanders of the 2 front battalions of incoming Brigade will also visit the line on the 16th. inst. Guides will be sent to meet at same hour and place as detailed in Para.5.

3. ACKNOWLEDGE.

P.B.B. Nichols Capt.,
A/Bde. Major,
125th. Brigade.

Copies to all recipients of 125th. I.B. Order No.68.

SECRET.

125th Infantry Brigade Order No.69.

Copy No.....26

26/1/18.

Ref.BETHUNE Combined Sheet.1/40,000.
LA BASSEE Sheet.1/10,000.

1. The 125th Infantry Brigade will relieve the 127th Inf.Brigade in the CANAL Sector on the 29th and 30th Instant,in accordance with the attached table "A".

2. All details of relief will be arranged between C.Os concerned.

3. All Trench Stores,A.A.Lewis Gun positions,Defence Schemes,aeroplane photos,sketches,schemes of work in progress,proposed work,and working parties etc.,will be taken over on relief. Lists of Trench Stores taken over will be forwarded to the Staff Captain within 48 Hours of relief.

4. (1) Company Commanders,1 Officer from 125th M.G.Coy,and 1 Officer from 125th T.M.B. will visit line on 27th Instant.
(2) Advance parties of 1 Officer per Company,1 from Battalion H.Q., and 1 N.C.O.per platoon from all Battalions,less Reserve Battalion will proceed to line on 28th Instant,and remain until their Units come in. Guides for Company Commanders on 27th Instant,and advance parties on 28th Instant will meet at PONT FIXE, A.14.c.at 11-0 a.m.

5. (1) Attached Table "B" shows permanent working parties to be found by Battalions for work under 428th Field Company R.E. This table will come into operation at 9-0 a.m.30th Instant.
(2) Party of 1 N.C.O.and 20 men to be found by 6th L.F. will report at 6-0 p.m.28th Instant for work under R.E.KANTARA Dump F.3.c.5.2. and relieve similar party of 7th Manchester Regiment ~~XXXXXXXXXXXXX XXXXXXXXXXXXX~~. Rations for consumption 29th to be taken.
(3) Party of 1 Officer and 60 O.R.of 8th L.F. working under 3rd Australian Tunnelling Coy. at CAMBRIN will be relieved by similar party of 7th Manchester Regiment by 10/30 a.m.29th Instant.

6. In the event of the 29th Instant being a very bright day reliefs will be postponed as shown in last Column of Table "A" attached, the code word "OBJECTION" being wired to all concerned.

7. Completion of relief to be reported to Brigade Headquarters by wiring the code word "ENSERU".

8. Brigade Headquarters will close at VENDIN - les - BETHUNE at 9/30 a.m. and reopen at CANAL HOUSE, F.10.d.9.9. at 11-0 a.m.29th Instant. Command of CANAL SECTOR will pass to G.O.C.125th Inf.Brigade on completion of Infantry relief.

9. ACKNOWLEDGE.

PBBNichols
Captain,
A/Brigade Major.
125th Brigade.

ISSUED AT 8 AM THRO' SIGNALS

Copy No.1.to 5th L.F.
" " 2.to 6th L.F.
" " 3.to 7th L.F.
" " 4.to 8th L.F.
" " 5.to 125th M.G.Coy.
" " 6.to 125th T.M.B.
" " 7.to 429th Coy.A.S.C.
" " 8.to 3rd Australian Tunnelling Coy.
" " 9.to 170th Tunnelling Coy.
" " 10.to 210th B'de R.F.A.
" " 11.to 428th Fld Coy.R.E.
" " 12.to 126th Inf.Brigade.
" " 13.to 127th Inf.Brigade.
" " 14.to 32nd Inf.Brigade.
" " 15.to 42nd Division.
" " 16.to do. do.
" " 17.to C.R.E.42nd Division.
" " 18.to Staff Captain.
Copy No.19.to B'de Signal Officer.
" " 20.to Supply Officer.
" " 21.to B'de T.O.
" " 22.to Sub-Area Commandant.LOCON
" " 23.to " " BEUVRY.
" " 24.to Town Major.BETHUNE.
" " 25.W.D.
" " 26.W.D.
" " 27.F I L E.

RELIEF TABLE ISSUED WITH 125TH INFANTRY BRIGADE ORDER NO.69. TABLE "A" 26/1/18.

Serial No.	Date.	UNIT.	From.	To.	ROUTE.	To Relieve.	Guides.	Remarks.
1.	29th.	5th L.F.	HINGETTE.	SUPPORT.	LE HAMEL-GORRE Southern CANAL BANK.	6th Manchester Regiment.	WESTMINSTER BRIDGE F.18.a. 1-0 p.m.	If bright day guides meet 4/45 p.m.
2.	29th.	6th L.F.	FERME DU ROI.	RESERVE.	Southern CANAL BANK-Road loading from F.9.b.8.6.to LE PREOL.	7th Manchester Regiment.	Road junction F.10.c.5.2. 9/45 a.m.	To be clear of Drawbridg F.3.c.10/15 a.m.
3.	29th.	7th L.F.	BEUVRY	RIGHT FRONT.	ANNEQUIN.	8th Manchester Regiment.	CAMBRIN X Roads.F.20.c. 10/30 a.m.	If bright day guides meet 3/30 p.m.
4.	29th.	8th L.F.	OBLINGHEM.	LEFT FRONT.	BETHUNE RD E.5.c. 6.3.- E.11.b.4.9. Southern CANAL BANK.	5th Manchester Regiment.	WESTMINSTER BRIDGE.F.18.a. 11/30 a.m.	Not to pass Drawbridge F.3.c.before 10/15 a.m. If bright day guides meet 3/30 p.m.
5.	30th.	125 M.G.C.	ESSARS.		No restrictions.	127th M.G.C.		Relief to be complete by 2-0 p.m. All detail to be arranged between C.Os concerned.
6.	29th.	125th T.M.B.	BEUVRY.		"	127th T.M.B.		Relief to be complete by 2-0 p.m. All detail to be arranged between C.Os concerned.

NOTE. Distance of 200 yds will be maintained betweens platoons on the march.

WORKING PARTY TABLE TO ACCOMPANY 125th INFANTRY BRIGADE ORDER NO.69. TABLE "B"

Serial No.	Number Required. O.	O.R.	To report Time.	Place.	Nature of Work.	Rations to be taken.	Time at which work will probably cease.	Found by.
1.	1	28	9/15 a.m.	SPOIL BANK KEEP.	SPOIL BANK KEEP CONCRETE SHELTER.	YES.	4 p.m.	Support Battalion.
2.		21	9/0 a.m.	PONT FIXE RE DUMP.	No 1 Concrete Shelter OXFORD TERRACE.	YES.	4 p.m.	Reserve Battalion.
3.		21	9/0 a.m.	do.	No.2.Concrete Shelter OXFORD TERRACE.	YES.	4 p.m.	do. do.
4.		25	9/15 a.m.	ORCHARD KEEP.	No.4.Concrete shelter ORCHARD KEEP.	YES	4 P.m.	Support Battalion.
5.		28	9/0 a.m.	Junction of DAWSON ST & HARLEY ST.	No.5.Concrete shelter Buzzer Station A.15.c.6.3.	YES.	4 p.m.	14 O.R.Left Front Bn. 14 O.R.Support Battn.
7.	1	14	9/30 a.m.	Junction of the Lane & MARYLEBONE.	No.7.Concrete Shelter.	YES	4 p.m.	Support Battalion.
		14	5/30 p.m.	do.	do. P.B.III A.21.c.8.7.	NO.	11/30 p.m.	Support Battalion.
8.		14	9/30 a.m.	Junction of GRAFTON ST & MARYLEBONE.	No.8. do. P.B.IV	YES.	4 p.m.	Support Battalion.
		14	5/30 p.m.	do.	No.8. do. A.21R.8.7. (c 1.4)	NO.	11/30 p.m.	Support Battalion.
9.		10	9/0 a.m.	PONT FIXE R.E.Dump.	TRENCH REPAIRS.	YES.	4 p.m.	Support Battalion.
10.		5	4-0 p.m.	do.	OFF LOADING TRANSPORT.	NO.	8 p.m.	Support Battalion.
11.	1	2 N.C.Os 20 men.	9/30 a.m.	HARLEY ST R.E.Dump.	TRENCH REPAIRS.	YES.	4 P.M.	Support Battalion.
12.	1	52	5/30 p.m.	do.	do. do.	NO.	10/30 p.m.	RESERVE BATTALION.
13.	1	50	5/30 p.m.	PONT FIXE R.E.Dump.	do. do.	NO.	10/30 p.m.	RESERVE BATTALION.
14.	2	50	6/0 p.m.	do.	do. do.	NO.	11 p.m.	RESERVE BATTALION.

NOTE. 1.Serial Nos 2 and 3 are cancelled as long as Serial numbers 12,13,and 14 are found by RESERVE BATTALION.
2.Reference Serial No.5 Left Front Battalion will not find these 14 O.R.at present.
3.No tools are to be taken by any working party.
4.All parties report to an Officer or N.C.O.of 428th Fld Coy R.E.

SECRET.

125TH BRIGADE DEFENCE SCHEME.

GIVENCHY SECTOR.

Ref: BETHUNE. 1:40.000. LA BASSEE) RICHEBOURG) 1:10.000.

A. BOUNDARIES & DISPOSITIONS.

The Brigade holds the Divisional Left Sector.

(1). BOUNDARIES.

Southern. Junction of WOLFE Road and Front Line (A 9 d 7.8.) - WOLFE Road (inclusive) - PONT FIXE Road - A 8 c 80.00. - A 7 d 10.30. - F 12 c 70.00. - F 12 c 55.35. - F 11 c 15.25. - F 5 d 75.00. - F 4 d 95.00. - F 10 b 60.10. - thence along CANAL to F 3 c 50.35.

Northern (Divisional).
Junction of SHETLAND Road & Front Line (S 22 c 30.15.) - SHETLAN Road (inclusive) to its junction with O.B. Line at S 21 a 0.9. - X 23 c 00.60. - X 15 c 00.00.

Inter-Battalion Boundary.

North end of WARWICK South (A 3 c 95.90.) - A 2 d 60.70. (200 yds N of junction of FIFE Road and O.B.Line) - junction of WILLOW Road & the LE PLANTIN - FESTUBERT Road (A 2 c 40.40.)

(2). DISPOSITIONS.

The Brigade sector is held by two Battalions in the Front system, one in support (finding one company in O.B. Line, 2 Coy's in the GIVENCHY Group KEEPS) and one company at WINDY CORNER) & one ~~[illegible]~~ Battalion in Reserve.

Location of H.Q. and Companies.

Brigade H.Q.....................LOISNE. X 28 a 4.8.
Right Battalion H.Q.............A 8 d 85.47.
Right Coy H.Q...................A 9 c 57.37.
Centre Coy H.Q..................A 9 c 6.8.
Left Coy H.Q....................A 3 c 13.40. Old German Line.
Support Coy H.Q.................A 9 c 65.21.

Left Battalion H.Q..............S 26 d 45.95. In O.B. LINE.
Right Coy.H.Q...................A 3 a 55. .. BARNTONTEE.
Centre Coy H.Q..................S 27 b 29.85. RICHMOND TRENCH
Left Coy H.Q....................S 21 d 33.14. " "
Support Coy H.Q.................S 26 b 9.9. O.B.Line.

Support Battalion H.Q...........A 14 a 9.7.
Coy.O.B.Line H.Q................A 2 b 39.32.
Coy WINDY CORNER................A 8 c 86.25.
2 Coy's in KEEPS................A 8 d 8.4.

Reserve Battalion H.Q...........GORRE CHATEAU. F 3 b central.

Machine Gun.Coy.H.Q.............LE PLANTIN. A 2 c 2.8.

For dispositions & Barrage Lines see Appendix 1 and Map 'A'.

Light Trench Mortars' H.Q. .... FESTUBERT. S 25 d .5.

For disposition, arcs of fire, and barrage lines, see appendix 8 and Map 'B'.

Left Group R.F.A.H.Q. .... LOISNE. X 28 a 7.8.

Field Company R.E. The Brigade has one Field Company affiliated to it.
H.Q. .... GORRE BREWERY. F 3 c 6.4.

The 251st Tunnelling Company is working Brigade Area.

B. BRIEF DESCRIPTION OF SECTOR INCLUDING VULNERABLE POINTS.

The Right Battalion Sector contains the crest of the GIVENCHY RIDGE, the Southern Boundary falling gently to the Canal is under view from the S.E.

The Ridge which is flat topped, runs through our line in a North Easterly direction and then bending to the North, commands the whole of our breastwork up to the Left Boundary. A series of mine craters runs between our line and that of the enemy on the ridge; we command the majority of these craters.

The Left Battalion system composed entirely of breastworks.

The communications are good; roads leading forward are in good condition & of even surface, emergency routes for Infantry and Pack animals have been reconnoitred and marked with notice boards, C.T's are numerous & duckboarded.

The routes and tracks should not be used until the situation requires it.

The capture of the GIVENCHY HILL would give the enemy observation along the advanced elements of our line & also as far as BETHUNE. This is the most likely enemy objective on the Corps Front.

CANADIAN ORCHARD which is not only a pronounced salient but also the junction with the Division on our Left might be attacked without much difficulty, but the tactical advantages from the enemy's point of view are small.

DEFENCE SYSTEM

PART II.

A. Successive lines of Defence are as follows :-

(1). FRONT SYSTEM. - Consists of Saps, front, support & reserve trenches & breastworks, and communication trenches up to and inclusive of the O.B.Line. Also KEEPS, M.G. Positions & posts between these limits.

(2). INTERMEDIATE or VILLAGE LINE. - A line of posts & concrete M.G. emplacements extending from PONT FIXE through WINDY CORNER, LE PLANTIN, FESTUBERT to just East of BREWERY CORNER, thence into area of Division on Left through RUE de L'EPINETTE.

(3). SWITCH LINE. - Consists of breastworks and trenches with posts in that running through LE PREOL to TUNING FORK WEST, thence N to LE TOURET.

(4). CORPS LINE. - Consists of posts mutually supporting each other and connected by wire entanglements. Gaps have been left in the wire to facilitate counter attacks.
It runs from BEAUVRY through GORRE & MESPLAUX, thence to LACOUTURE in area of Division on Left.

The Main Line of Resistance in the defences of GIVENCHY RIDGE will be the line of KEEPS viz:-

MARIE REDOUBT.
HILDERS REDOUBT.
GIVENCHY KEEP.
MOAT FARM REDOUBT.
HERTS REDOUBT.

(c). Every soldier will know his fire position if belonging to garrison troops, and his alarm post, if belonging to Counter-attack troops.

(d). O.C. Front Battalions will have plans drawn up and known to all concerned for employment of their support Companies under varying circumstances.

(2). ACTION OF SUPPORT BATTALION.

(a). The 2 Companies garrisoning the KEEPS will hold the enemy should he succeed in breaking through the front line. The KEEPS will be held at all costs to form a pocket in, and to break up the enemy advance, until such time as our Counter-attack drives the enemy back. The garrison of these KEEPS will not, under any circumstances, leave their posts, and must be prepared to put up an all round defence.

(b). The Company in support to the Left Battalion is intended primarily as garrison of the O.B.Line.
It may be used for Counter-attack if in the opinion of the O.C. Left Front Battalion, the situation demands it.

(c). The Company at WINDY CORNER will be prepared to move up in Support of the Right Battalion. O.C. Support Battalion will at once get into communication with O.C.Right Battalion, and will order this Company to either :-

(1) Occupy the line GUNNER-SIDING - WOOD-LANE - CALEDONIAN Road - UPPER CUT.

(2) Counter-attack across the open.

(3). Form a defensive flank N or S of GIVENCHY RIDGE, as the situation demands.

(3). ACTION OF RESERVE BATTALION.

This Battalion is in Brigade Reserve and will always be ready to move at one hours notice.
It will be prepared to occupy the VILLAGE LINE moving forward in two bounds.

The first bound to SWITCH LINE between limits A.5 c 0.1. to S 29 a 0.7.

Second bound to VILLAGE LINE.

On receipt of order from Brigade H.Q. to 'Stand to', the O.C., Reserve Battalion will-

(1) Be prepared to move forward at once as above, on receipt of further orders from Brigade H.Q.

(2). Send 8 Lewis Guns to occupy positions in VILLAGE LINE as follows :-

Position	No. F 2	1 gun	A 8 c 85.35.
"	No. F 3	-	A 8 c 80.30.
"	No.LEPS 4.	-	A 8 a 88.05.
"	No.LEPS 5.	-	A 8 a 95.35.
"	No.V 7	-	A 8 a 90.95.
"	No.V 8	2 guns	A 2 c 15.87.
"	No.WEST.1.	1 gun.	A 1 b 7.6.

O.C. Reserve Battalion will ensure that all Officers and Platoon Sergeants are familiar with :-

(1). The best routes from their billets to the forward area.

(2). All C.T's and Cross country tracks forward from the VILLAGE LINE.

(4). R.E.WORKING PARTIES ETC.

These will at once occupy the nearest line of defence, and the Senior Officer present will report to the nearest Company Commander.

Personnel of ~~Tunnelling Companies will at once proceed to the~~ position previously allotted to them by the O.C. Battalion in ~~whose~~ area they are working.

and for the line N of GIVENCHY RIDGE,
the O.B.Line.

B. GENERAL PRINCIPLES OF DEFENCE.

(1). POLICY.

(a) The General policy is at present a defensive one.

(b) Every effort will, however, be made to inflict loss on the enemy by active patrolling, which affords the best protection against enemy raids, and by vigorous sniping, Lewis Gun & M.G. Fire.

(c) (1). Artillery and T.M. fire is being allowed to die down in order that the reorganisation and strengthening of our defences may proceed unhindered.
(2). At the request of Battalion Commanders, neutralizing Artillery and T.M. fire can be turned on to tender spots in the enemy's line.
(3). If heavier retaliation is required the G.O.C. Infantry Brigade has a call on Divisional H.Q. for all Field Artillery, T.M's and some Heavy Artillery to turn on to selected spots with punishment fire.

(2). DISPOSITIONS.
The disposition of the troops holding the front system is being reorganized into a series of defended localities, organized in depth.
These localities have been chosen with the idea of affording mutual support by converging fire, and will be organized for all round defence.
Detailed dispositions of the Brigade will be issued later.

(3). WORK.
The Brigade is responsible for all work in front of the VILLAGE LINE. All work in and behind the VILLAGE LINE is carried out under Divisional arrangements.
The Battalion in the line are responsible for the maintenance and improvement of defences in their area, assisted by the Field Company R.E., and such working parties as may be provided within the Brigade.

ACTION IN CASE OF HOSTILE ATTACK.

PART III

A. AGAINST BRIGADE FRONT.
(1). The general principles of defence in event of attack are as follows :-

(a). All posts and garrisons in front system will hold on at all costs. There will be no withdrawal under any circumstances.
(b). In the event of the enemy penetrating any part of our front, he will be immediately counter-attacked by the nearest Commander on the spot with all available troops.
The first counter attack troops available with exceptions of garrisons of posts and localities will be normally the support Companies of the Right & Left Battalions.
All garrison troops in Front system are , however, available for counter-attack if not actually repelling an attack themselves, with exception of garrison of the KEEPS forming the Main Line of Resistance.

5th. Lan Fus.
6th. " "
7th. " "
8th. " "
125th. M.G. Coy. "
125th. T.M.B.
429th. Fd. Coy. R.E.
211th. B'de. R.F.A.
126th. Brigade.
127th. "
2nd Portuguese Brigade.
42nd Division.
Brigade Signal Officer.

Herewith Copy No. 15 of 125th. Inf: Brigade Defence Scheme for GIVENCHY Sector. Continuation of para 2 (b) (ii) Appendices 3 and 5 will be issued later.

Please acknowledge receipt.

Captain,
a/Brigade Major,
125th. BRIGADE.

8/1/18.

B. ON FRONT OF FLANKING BRIGADES.

In the event of the enemy penetrating the front of either of the Brigades on the flank, Battalions will be prepared to form defensive flanks as follows :-

(1) FACING SOUTH

Right Battalion, with Support Company, along WOLFE Road between the junction with CAMBRIDGE TERRACE & GUNNER SIDING.
The Company of Support Battalion at WINDY CORNER will 'stand to' and be prepared to counter-attack across the open if necessary.

(2). FACING NORTH.

Left Battalion with Support Company along SHETLAND Road.
In both cases, The Reserve Battalion will, on receipt of orders from Brigade H.Q. 'stand to' and be prepared to moveat once on receipt of further orders.

P.B.A. Nicholls.
Captain,
a/Brigade Major,
125th.BRIGADE.

7/1/18.

APPENDIX.1.

DISPOSITION OF MACHINE GUNS.

1. Map Location of Guns etc.

Gun No.	Map Reference.	Group & Battery Headquarters.	Task.
1.	A 9 c 69.88.		Close Defence.
2.	A 9 c 70.90.	Right Group.	" "
A9.	A 9 c 22.66.	MOAT FARM.	" "
	A 9 c 20.71.	A 9 c 22.67.	" "
A 92.	A 9 c 15.93.		" "
3.	S 27 b 30.56.	Left Group.	" "
4.	S 27 b 27.63.	S 26 d 40.87.	" "
LEPS 3.	A 8 c 00.57.		
LEPS 6.	A 8 a 03.84.		
Right Batt'y.	A 2 a 52.67.-		
	A 2 a 49.77.		
Centre Batt'y.	S 26 c 72.30.-	S 26 c 58.34.	S.O.S. Lines A 10 c 55.25.
	S 26 c 76.40.		
Left Batt'y.	S 25 b 94.04. -		A 9 b 55.65.
	S 26 a 00.45.	S 25 b 99.70.	(See Map 'A').

BATTERY POSITIONS FOR CLOSE DEFENCE.

Right Batt'y.

REST.2 & 3.	S 25 d 58.32.
V 9.	S 26 c 00.22.
V 10.	S 25 d 99.39.
	S 26 c 67.41.

Centre Batt'y.

V 11. S 26 c 64.45. Remaining 3 Guns in Battery Positions.

Left Battery.

V 13.	S 26 a 00.67.
	S 20 c 09.03.
	S 20 c 08.10.
V 14.	S 20 c 02.18.

(2). **ANTI-AIRCRAFT MACHINE GUNS & LEWIS GUNS. MOUNTED BY DAY.**

VICKERS.	MAP REFERENCE.		MANNED BY.
	A 9 c 22.70.	1 Gun.	125th.M.G.Coy.
	S 26 c 82.41.	1 "	- do -
	S 26 c 87.37.	1 "	- do -
LEWIS.			
Position No.1.	A 9 c 5.8.	1 "	Right Battalion.
" 2.	A 3 a 20.87.	1 "	Left "
" 3.	S 21 d 40.26.	1 "	" "
" 4.	S 26 a 75.95.	1 "	" "
" 5.	A 1 b 95.00.	1 "	Support Battalion.
" 6.	X 29 b 75.70.	1 "	" "
" 7.	F 5 c 25.95.	1 "	Reserve "
" 8.	X 28 c 35.15.	1 "	" "

G U N P O S I T I O N S. APPENDIX. 2.

****

125TH.L.T.M.BATTERY.

No. of Gun.	Map Reference.	S.O.S. TARGET.	TRUE BEARING	RANGE.
1.	A 9 d 86.07.	Gaps between Crater A 9 a central.	35°	360.
2.	A 9 d 10.75.		90°	260.
4.	A 9 d 90.1[illegible].		110.	360.
4 b.	A 9 a 90.15.	(Alternative Positi n same line)		
5.	A 9 a 81.11.	Northern Craters.	45°	260.
6 a.	A 3 a 6.7.	Covering 14 & 15 Islands.	45°	680.
6 b.		Old Man's Corner.	103°	400.
6 c.		Covering WARWICK North and WARWICK South.	150°	340.
7.	S 27 b 9.8.		110°	480.
8.	S 27 b 85.88.	Covering CANADIAN ORCHARD & Road S 28 a central.	100°	480.

APPENDIX. IV.

SIGNAL COMMUNICATIONS.

Brigade H.Q. C.F.7. at X 28 a 40.60.

Brigade Test Point. C.E.7. at F 6 c 95.10.

Lines in Brigade H.Q. Signal Office.

Position Call.		Exchange.
C.I.One.	Division.	Magneto Exchange.
C.I.One.	Division.	Magneto Exchange.
C.I.One.	Division.	Sounder.
C.I.One.	'G' Division.	Brigade Major's Office.
C.D. 2.	LE QUESNOY. Adv. Div.	Magneto Exchange.
C.F. 2.	Left Group.R.F.A.	" "
C.D.14.	Right Brigade.	" "
C.G.17.	Left Brigade.	Buzzer Exchange.
C.E. 5.	428th.Fd.Coy.R.E.	Magneto Exchange.
C.D. 3.	Right Battalion.	Buzzer Exchange & Fullerphone.
C.D. 3.	- do -	- do -
C.D. 3.	- do -	- do -
C.F. 1.	Left Battalion.	- do -
C.F. 1.	- do -	- do -
C.F. 1.	- do -	- do -
C.C. 7.	Support Battalion.	- do -
C.C.7.	- do -	- do -
C.E. 4.	Reserve Battalion.	- do -
C.E. 8.)	Machine Gun Coy.	- do -
C.F.21.)	Trench Mortar Batt'y.	Buzzer Exchange.
C.E. 4.	Rear M.G.Coy.H.Q.	" "
C.E. 7.)	Brigade Test Point.	" "
C.D.31.)	Brigade Visual Station.	" "

(2). BATTALION S.O.S. LINES.

(a). Right Battalion.

Left Group Artillery..........................C.F.2.
Brewery O.P.Exchange..........................C.G.1.
4.5" Howitzer Battery.........................C.E.23.
Machine Gun H.Q...............................C.E.8.

(b) Left Battalion.

Brewery O.P.Exchange..........................C.G.1.
4.5" Howitzer Battery.........................C.E.23.
18 Pounder Battery............................C.F.5.
Machine Gun Post..............................C.F.24.

(3). VISUAL.

Visual Communication by Lamp exists between :-

(a) Right Battalion.

Left Company C.E.2. to Battalion H.Q.
Battalion H.Q. to Brigade Visual Station C.D.31.

(b) Left Battalion.

Right Company C.E.1. to Battalion H.Q.
Battalion H.Q. to O.P.Exchange C.G.1.

(c). Support Battalion.

Battalion H.Q. to Brigade Visual Station C.D.31.

RIGHT BATTALION.

There are Power Buzzers ar Right (T H G) Centre (C Z) and Left (R.E.R.) Coy which work back to an Amplifier at Battalion H.Q. (R.H.G.)

The Station at Battalion H.Q. works back to a station at (T P A) at the Brigade Test Point, which work back to station (B Z) at Brigade H.Q.

Also direct communication is possible between Centre Coy, Right Battalion to Brigade Station, and Right Battalion to Brigade Station.

Brigade Station can work both ways with station at Brigade on Right H.Q.

5. WIRELESS.

There is a Wireless Set at Brigade Headquarters which works to Brigade on Right, Division & Ist Corps.

6. PIGEONS.

Four Pifeons are sent up daily, two to the Right and to the Left Battaion H.Q..

The two at the Right Battalion are sent forward to the Left Compamy H.Q.. (C L 2.)

The Pigeon Loft is in BETHUNE, and is in touch with Division by wire.

7. DOGS.

There are two dogs at Left Battalion H.Q. One runs between the Right Company and Battalion H.Q. and the other between the Left Company and Battalion H.Q.

****

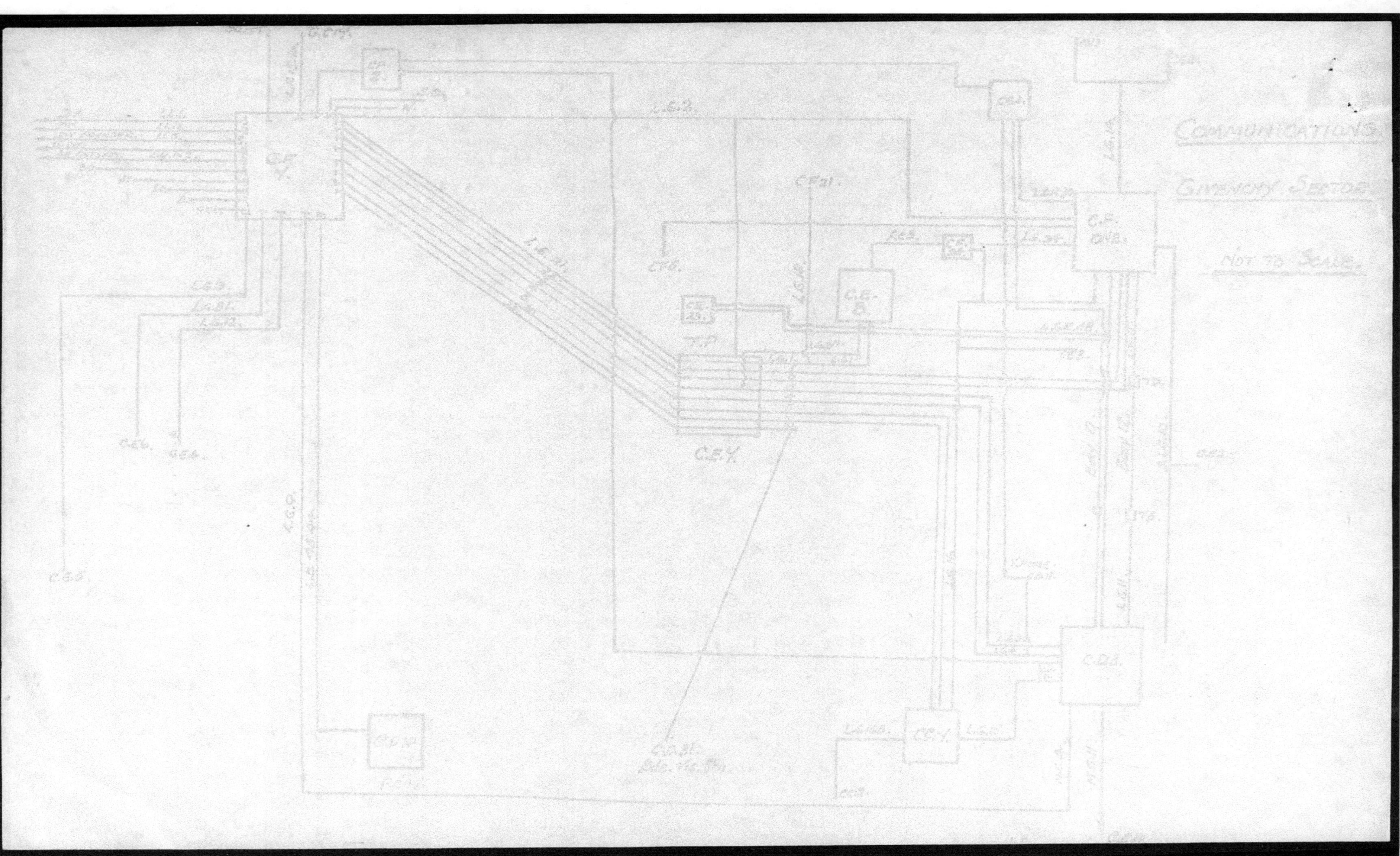
COMMUNICATIONS.
GIVENCHY SECTOR.
NOT TO SCALE.
C.F. Y.
C.F. GIVE.
C.E.Y.
C.D.3.
C.E. 8.
T.P.
L.E.2.
C.F.31.
C.F.6.
C.E.6.
C.E.4.
C.E.5.
L.G.9.
C.D.31.
Bde. Vis. Stn.

APPENDIX.6.

ADMINISTRATIVE ARRANGEMENTS.

1. AMMUNITION.

BRIGADE DUMPS.

Right Sub-Sector....................A 8 c 5.2.
Left Sub-Sector....................A 1 b 2.4.

BATTALION DUMPS.

Right Battalion.......................A 8 d 70.57.

Companies.

Right Company..........................A 9 c 60.38.
Centre Company..........................A 9 c 9.61.
Left Company..........................A 3 c 12.45.
Support Company..........................A 9 c [illegible].20.

LEFT BATTALION..........................S 26 b 8.5. & S 26 b 5.3.

Companies. S 26 b 9.05.
S 27 b 3.8.
S 27 b 75.25.
A 3 a 8.65.

SUPPORT BATTALION.	A 14 a 9.7.	Battalion.
	A 8 d 7.3.	HERTS REDOUBT.
	A 9 c 30.25.	HILDERS REDOUBT.
	A 9 c 60.44.	GIVENCHY KEEP.
	A 9 c 85.10.	MARIE REDOUBT.
	A 2 b 31.40.	P.B.Line.

2. R.E. DUMPS.

RIGHT SUB-SECTOR...........WINDY CORNER. A 14 a 9.7.
LEFT SUB-SECTOR...........ESTAMINET CORNER. F 6 c 3.9.

3. RATIONS. Rations are delivered to Right Battalion by limber to WINDY CORNER, thence by trucks to Battalion H.Q..
To Left Battalion by limber to ESTAMINET CORNER and thence by trucks to O.B.Line at BARNTON TEE - RICHMOND TERRACE.

4. WATER. In three systems.

No.1 System. - Well at Brewery RUE de CAILLOUX, supplies by pipe to COVER TRENCH.

No.2.System. - Spring A 8 a 8.8. to WILLOW ROAD A 2 b 2.5.

No.3.System. - Well A 8 d 9.4. Supplies Right Battalion & GIVENCHY KEEP.

5. GUM-BOOT STORE. RATION CORNER. A 1 a 3.3.

6. DRYING ROOM. A 14 a 85.60.

7. BATHS. GORRE & A 8 a 3.7.

8. MEDICAL ARRANGEMENTS. Advanced dressing Station on TUNING FORK at F 5 a 3.0. & at LONE FARM.

9. CEMETERY. GORRE CHATEAU.

CONFIDENTIAL.

Vol 13

WAR DIARY

of

125TH INFY BRIGADE

FEB 1918.

VOL. NO. 44.

Army Form C. 2118

WAR DIARY
or
INTELLIGENCE SUMMARY
(Erase heading not required.)

Instructions regarding War Diaries and Intelligence Summaries are contained in F. S. Regs., Part II. and the Staff Manual respectively. Title Pages will be prepared in manuscript.

Page 1. VOL NO. 44. of 125 INFY BDE FEB 1st 1918

Place	Date	Hour	MAP REF	Summary of Events and Information	WEATHER.	Remarks and references to Appendices
BETHUNE AREA	FEB 1		36cNW1. LA BASSEE 1/10000	BDE. H.Q. CANAL HOUSE. orders issued for Inter. Batt. relief 5. LF to relieve 7. LF, 6 " " " 8 L.F	Fine	BDE OP. Order No 70 MJ
"	2		"	Situation quiet	Fine	MJ
"	3		"	Interbattalion relief carried out without incident. Situation quiet	Fine	MJ
"	4		"	Situation quiet	Fine	MJ
"	5		"	orders issued for interbattalion relief 7. LF to relieve 5. L.F. 8. L.F. " " 6 L.F. situation quiet	Fine	BDE. Op order No 71 MJ
"	6		"	Amendment to Bde Op Order No 71. issued. situation quiet	Fine	amendment to O.O No 71. MJ
"	7		"	Situation quiet. Cas. for week total 1 off. missing. 1 O.R. killed.	squally.	MJ
"	8		"	Inter battalion relief carried out without incident. Situation quiet	squally	MJ.

1875 Wt. W593/826 1,000,000 4/15 J.B.C. & A. A.D.S.S./Forms/C. 2118.

Instructions regarding War Diaries and Intelligence Summaries are contained in F. S. Regs., Part II. and the Staff Manual respectively. Title Pages will be prepared in manuscript.

Page 2
Vol 44

WAR DIARY
or
~~INTELLIGENCE SUMMARY~~
(Erase heading not required.)

125 Infy Bde
Feb 1918

Army Form C. 2118

Place	Date	Hour	MAP REF	Summary of Events and Information	WEATHER	Remarks and references to Appendices
BETHUNE AREA.	FEB 1918. 9		36CNW1 LA BASSEE 1/10000	Situation quiet	fine	MB.
"	10.		"	Situation quiet	dull	MB.
"	11		"	Bde OP. Order No 72 issued re relief of 125 Bde by 164 Bde. Situation quiet.	fine	Bde Op. order No 72 MB
"	12		"	Draft of 26 O.R. posted to 5 LF. Situation quiet.	fine	MB.
"	13		"	Situation quiet. at 12.8 a.m. an enemy mineshaft, previously reconnoitred on three occasions was successfully blown up by a party of 1/7 Lancs Fus. assisted by Tunnelling Coy. R.E.	dull	MB
"	14		BETHUNE COMBINED SHEET 1/40 000.	Bde relieved in the line by 164 Inf. Bde. Bde H.Q. moved to FOUQUIERES. Bde moved into Corps & GHQ Reserve. 1/5 Lancs Fus. relieved by 1/10 L'pool Scottish & marched to HOUCHIN. 1/6 " " " 1/4 R. Lanc. Regt. " " VERQUIN. 1/7 " " " 2/5 Lancs Fus. " " FOUQUIERES. 1/8 " " " 1/4 N. Lancs Regt " " VAUDRICOURT	dull	MB.
"	15.		"	125 MG. Coy. relieved by 164 MG Coy & marched to LABEUVRIERE. 125 T.M.B. " 164 TMB. " " DROUVIN. Cas. for week 1 Off and 5 OR Wnd. 1 OR Missg. 4 O.R. Killed. Ceremonial parade. 1/6 Lancs Fus. marched past 1/5, 1/7 & 1/8 Lancs Fus, before being broken up. Divisional Commander was present. Draft of 32 OR posted to 1/7 LF.	dull	MB.
"	16.		"	Brigade in rest. Cleaning up, bathing etc. 4 offrs + 105 OR of 6 LF transferred to 1/5 Lan Fus. 8 " 139 " " " 1/7 Lan Fus. 6 " 133 " " " 1/8 Lan Fus. [illegible] proceeded " Reinforcement camp - ALLOUAGNE 1 Offr + 33 OR (Transport) remaining with 125 Infy Bde.	fine	MB.

Instructions regarding War Diaries and Intelligence Summaries are contained in F. S. Regs., Part II. and the Staff Manual respectively. Title Pages will be prepared in manuscript.

Page 3

Vol. 44.

WAR DIARY
or
~~INTELLIGENCE SUMMARY~~

(Erase heading not required.)

125 Infy Bde
Feb 1918

Army Form C. 2118

Place	Date	Hour	MAP. REF.	Summary of Events and Information	WEATHER	Remarks and references to Appendices
BETHUNE AREA.	FEB. 17/1918		BETHUNE Combined 1/40000.	Brigade in rest. Cleaning bathing etc. Drafts of 36 OR to 1/5 LF. 45 OR to 1/8 LF. Brig. Gen. H. FARGUS returned from leave & assumed command of Bde.	fine	MG.
"	18th		"	Brigade Training. Musketry. Bombing. Route marches, Lectures etc.	fine	?c
"	19th		"	Do. Do. HQs & 250 men of 1/6 Lan Fus transferred from 42 DIVN to 66 DIV & joined that Div on this date.	"	?c
"	20th		"	Draft of 26 OR to 1/5 Lan Fus and 22 to 1/8 Lan Fus. Do Do	"	?c
"	21st		"	Draft of 57 to 7 LF. 81 OR to 1/5 LF. 27 OR to 1/8 LF. Do.	"	?c
"	22nd		"	Do	"	?c
"	23rd		"	Draft of 19 to 1/7 LF. 34 OR to 1/8 LF. Do	"	?c
"	24th		"	Do	"	?c
"	25th		"	Do	"	?c
"	26th		"	Do	"	?c
"	27th		"	Do	"	?c
"	28th		"	Do.	"	?c

[illegible] Brig. Genl
Commdg 125 Infy Bde

1875 Wt. W593/826 1,000,000 4/15 J.B.C. & A. A.D.S.S./Forms/C. 2118.

42nd Division

B. H. Q.

125th INFANTRY BRIGADE

MARCH 1 9 1 8

Attached :- Situation reports etc.

Instructions regarding War Diaries and Intelligence Summaries are contained in F. S. Regs., Part II. and the Staff Manual respectively. Title pages will be prepared in manuscript.

Army Form C. 2118.

WAR DIARY
or
INTELLIGENCE SUMMARY. of 125th INFY BDE. MARCH 1918

(Erase heading not required.)

Page 1
VOL NO 45

Place	Date MAP REFERENCE	Hour	Summary of Events and Information	WEATHER	Remarks and references to Appendices
BETHUNE AREA E21 b 80	1st.	BETHUNE COMBINED SHEET 1/40000	Brigade in Corps & GHQ. Res. Training O.O.73 issued. 3/3/18 7th Lancs Fus move from FOUQUIERES to FOUQUEREUIL. 4/3/17. BDE HQ from FOUQUIERES to DROUVIN.		NB O.O.73.
"	2nd	"	Brigade Training		NB
"	3rd	"	Brigade Training		NB
K3d22 "	4th	"	Brigade Training BDE HQrs established at DROUVIN.		NB
"	5th	"	Brigade Training Reinforcements of 20 O.R received		NB
"	6th	"	Brigade Training		NB
"	7th	"	Brigade Training		NB
"	8th	"	Brigade Training		NB
"	9th	"	Brigade Training		NB
"	10th	"	Brigade Training		NB
"	11th.	"	Brigade Training		NB
"	12th	"	Brigade Training		NB

1577 Wt. W10791/1773 500,000 1/15 D. D. & L. A.D.S.S./Forms/C. 2118.

Army Form C. 2118

Instructions regarding War Diaries and Intelligence Summaries are contained in F. S. Regs., Part II. and the Staff Manual respectively. Title Pages will be prepared in manuscript.

PAGE 2

VOL. NO 45

WAR DIARY
or
~~INTELLIGENCE SUMMARY~~
(Erase heading not required.)

of 125th Inf Bde. MARCH 1918

Place	Date	MAP REF. Hour	Summary of Events and Information	Remarks and references to Appendices
BETHUNE AREA.	13th	BETHUNE COMBINED SHEE 1/40000	Brigade Training	MB
DROUVIN K3d22.	14th	"	Brigade Training	MB
"	15th	"	Brigade Training Reinforcements of 10 O.R. received.	MB
"	16th	"	Brigade Training	MB
"	17th	"	Brigade Training	MB
"	18th	"	Brigade Training	MB
"	19th	"	Brigade Training	MB
"	20th	"	Brigade Training	MB
"	21st	"	Brigade Training	MB
"	22nd	"	Brigade Training	MB
"		6pm.	Warning order received from Div, that a move might take place to BASSEUX area on 24th. Units informed by BM100	MB
"	23rd	1.30 a.m 2. a.m	Orders re embussing received by telephone from Div. orders re transport received from Div.	MB
		3 a.m. 6 a.m. noon.	Bde Operation Order No 74 issued AL 182 issued, warning units to be prepared for immediate active operations. Brigade embussed, & debussed at 9 pm at ADINFER WOOD & bivouaced night in SE side of wood.	A2 A3

1875 Wt. W593/826 1,000,000 4/15 J.B.C. & A. A.D.S.S./Forms/C. 2118.

Army Form C. 2118

WAR DIARY
or
~~INTELLIGENCE SUMMARY~~

Instructions regarding War Diaries and Intelligence Summaries are contained in F. S. Regs., Part II. and the Staff Manual respectively. Title Pages will be prepared in manuscript.

PAGE. 3
VOL. Nº 45

(Erase heading not required.)

of 125 Inf. Bde. MARCH 1918

Place	Date	Hour	Summary of Events and Information	Remarks and references to Appendices
51^c SE. ADINFER WOOD X27 b 13	23rd	9.30 pm	Brigade HQrs established in ADINFER WOOD.	
		11. pm.	Div. Order Nº 1 received giving situation on Corps front & ordering Bde to be in a state of readiness either to counter attack if required from the line ABLAINZEVELLE – COURCELLES-LE-COMTE in a S.E. direction on the general line ACHIET-LE-GRAND – GOMIECOURT, or to form a defensive flank on ABLAINZEVELLE – COURCELLES-LE-COMTE spur. Reconnaissances to be carried out at daybreak to enable moves to be made as ordered. Bde Transport billeted night at TINQUES.	
		11.30 pm	Brigadier explained situation to Battalion Commanders.	MB
	24th	7 a.m.	Reconnaissance ordered carried out.	
		10.30 a.m	Warning order received that Div would relieve 40th Div. & 125 Bde the 120 Bde. In consequence BM101 issued at 11 a.m.	A4
57C NW.		1.30 pm	Brigadier proceeded to GOMIECOURT to see Brigadier of 120th Bde.	
LOGEAST WOOD A 25 d 27		2.30. pm.	Brigade marched to LOGEAST WOOD.	
		5. pm	Brigade HQrs established in LOGEAST WOOD.	
		5. pm.	Orders re relief received from Div.	
		7.16 p.m.	In consequence BM 105 issued	A5
		7.30 pm	Special order of the day received	A6
		9 pm.	While waiting for guides at rendez-vous, Brigadier received verbal orders from Gen. Staff 40th Div. to the effect that the Bde would not relieve the 120th Bde, but would be diverted to clear up situation in BEHAGNIES & SAPIGNIES.	
		10 p.m.	Verbal orders given by Brigadier to O.C. 1/5 Lancs Fus. to send out patrols & make good these two villages before Bde. took up a position on E Side.	
57C NW. GOMIECOURT A 23 d 12		11. pm.	BM106 confirming verbal orders issued	A7
		11 pm	Bde HQrs established at GOMIECOURT CHATEAU.	MB

1875 Wt. W593/826 1,000,000 4/15 J.B.C. & A. A.D.S.S./Forms/C. 2118.

Army Form C. 2118

WAR DIARY
or
~~INTELLIGENCE SUMMARY~~ of

Instructions regarding War Diaries and Intelligence Summaries are contained in F. S. Regs., Part II. and the Staff Manual respectively. Title Pages will be prepared in manuscript.

PAGE 4
VOL No 45

(Erase heading not required.) 125 Inf. Bde. MARCH 1918.

Place	Date	Hour	Summary of Events and Information	Remarks and references to Appendices
57C NW GOMIECOURT A23d12.	25	1.15 am.	J3 timed 1255 am. recd from 1/5 L.F reporting BEHAGNIES & SAPIGNIES clear of enemy	A8
		1.35 am.	DW informed. BM107.	A9
		8.a.m.	Dispositions were now as wired in BM109	A10
		7.25 am.	1/5 L.F report being attacked from direction of FAVREUIL, but are holding on.	
		7.45 am.	Batt. on left of 1/5 L.F are reported to have beaten off attack, but nothing is known on right of 1/5 L.F.	
		8.50 am.	Adj. 1/5 L.F. reports by telephone that as far as he knows his line is holding.	
		8.40 am.	O.C. 1/5 L.F. reports by telephone enemy massing for attack N.W. of FAVREUIL.	
		9.10 am.	1/5 L.F report by phone that their right Coy state enemy are coming over ridge & getting into Sunken Road in H9c & 15a	
		9.15 am.	2 enemy guns in position on ridge 2000 yds S.E. of BEHAGNIES	
		10.5 am.	1/5 L.F report right flank being driven in as result of ~~[illegible]~~ enemy attack.	
		10.35 am.	Contact aeroplane asked for to clear up situation round SAPIGNIES.	
		10.50 am.	1/5. L.F. by telephone report that their right centre Coy report enemy advancing in mass opposite them. Their posts still holding. More artillery needed.	
		11.15 am.	120th I.Bde report they believe our right is holding.	
		11.45 am.	O.C 14th A&SH reports line runs B26 Central – H27 Central. This does not appear to be correct. At same time 1/5 L.F report by telephone that O.C. 1/5 L.F. is personally leading counter attack of 2 Coys 1/8 Lancs Fus. in direction of SAPIGNIES from BEHAGNIES	
		12 noon	O.C 1/5 L.F reports counter attack drove out the enemy who were not in great force & his line is again established S of SAPIGNIES	
		12.30 pm.	Enemy reported attacking in mass formation 1000 yds N. of BEHAGNIES	
		12.35 pm.	Reports show troops on left of 1/5 LF are holding line B26a24 – B26c42. Movements of troops on right, i.e. 1/5 L.F. unknown.	
		12.45 pm.	1/7. L.F. line holding.	

1875 Wt. W593/826 1,000,000 4/15 J.B.C. & A. A.D.S.S./Forms/C. 2118.

Army Form C. 2118

Instructions regarding War Diaries and Intelligence Summaries are contained in F. S. Regs., Part II. and the Staff Manual respectively. Title Pages will be prepared in manuscript.

PAGES.
VOL. 45.

WAR DIARY
or
~~INTELLIGENCE SUMMARY~~
(Erase heading not required.)

of 125 Inf. Bde. MARCH 1918.

Place	Date	Hour	Summary of Events and Information	Remarks and references to Appendices
57c NW GOMIECOURT A23d12.	25	12.50 pm	1/5 L.F report by telephone left is holding E bank of BEHAGNIES – BAPAUME road. Exact position not stated	
		1.15. pm	1/7 L.F report by telephone this enemy is working round their right flank.	
		1.15. pm	Message received from left Coy 1/5.L.F as follows:– Large enemy forces forming up on ridge behind MORY also large forces on our right flank. Columns of infantry marching S.E from X roads at B29c99	
		1.20 pm	In consequence BG1 sent to 127 I. Bde.	
		1.45 pm	126 I. Bde report enemy guns coming over MORY RIDGE. also enemy concentrating in H11	A11
		2.7. pm	Message by runner from 1/8 L.F. timed 1.30 pm states parties of our infantry holding BEHAGNIES, but being shelled by our own guns.	
		2.10. pm	Message received for relief of 120th I. Bde	
		2.10. pm	LT. Col. P.V HOLBERTON O.C. 1/5. LANCS FUS. rang up Brigadier & reported that enemy was in BIHUCOURT, right round his right flank, the Div. on our right having withdrawn, & that he was afraid he would have to withdraw. Brigadier concurred.	
		2.15. pm	O.C. 1/5 L.F rang up about position of his left on withdrawal. Brigadier informed him that his left should rest on ridge about B25c & his line run through G6b.	
		2.33 pm	Report received through 126 I. Bde. that enemy were 1000 yds S.W of GOMIECOURT. This proved to be incorrect.	
		3.15 pm	BM 111 sent to 1/5 L.F.	A12
		3.30. pm	Div. informed. BM112	A13
		3.38 pm	BM113 sent to Div.	A14
		3.45 pm	Bde established a line GOMIECOURT RIDGE in B25c & G6b, with 1/5 & 1/7 L.F in front & 1/8. L.F in support in touch with 4th Lincolns on left & 1/5. E Lancs on right.	
57c NW. GOMIECOURT. A22b34		4.30 pm	Bde HQrs. left GOMIECOURT CHATEAU & took up a defensive position on sunken road in A27b72 & finally on railway cutting in A22.	
			Situation quiet on Bde front, except for hostile shelling & sniping.	
		8.30 pm	G 120/1/B received from Div.	A15

1875 Wt. W593/826 1,000,000 4/15 J.B.C. & A. A.D.S.S./Forms/C. 2118.

Army Form C. 2118

Instructions regarding War Diaries and Intelligence Summaries are contained in F. S. Regs., Part II. and the Staff Manual respectively. Title Pages will be prepared in manuscript.

PAGE 6.
VOL 45

WAR DIARY
or
~~INTELLIGENCE SUMMARY~~ of 125 Inf Bde MARCH 1918.

(Erase heading not required.)

Place	Date	Hour	Summary of Events and Information	Remarks and references to Appendices
57c NW GOMIECOURT A22b34.	25	9.15pm	BM114 sent to Div.	A16
		10pm	GSO.3 Div arrived & gave verbal orders amending those contained in G 120/1/B.	
		10.45pm	In consequence BM116 was sent out	A17 WB
57D NE. ABLAINZEVELLE. F23d73	26.	1.30am	Lt Col. P.Y. Hellerton [?] 2/5 L.F. killed	
		1.45am	Bde HQrs moved to ABLAINZEVELLE	
		3.am	GSO.2. arrived with verbal orders for further withdrawal to line ABLAINZEVELLE–BUCQUOY	
		4.30am	In consequence BM117 was issued	A18
		7.30am.	The above orders not having been delivered, units being on the move, they were given verbally to C.O's by Brigadier. Withdrawal commenced at once	
57D NE. ESSARTS E24d79			Bde HQrs established at ESSARTS.	
		9.30am	Batts. in position	
		10am.	D.C. communicated verbally the fact that it was reported that HEBUTERNE was in enemy's hands & that he was advancing in a N.E. direction,	
		11.55am.	In consequence BM 120 was issued	A19
		noon	D.C. returned & stated that message re HEBUTERNE was without foundation.	
		12.18pm	BM121 issued.	A20
		2.10pm	Warning order No 2 received from Div.	
		3.40pm	In consequence BM 123 issued	A21.
		4.15pm	BM 124 sent to Div.	A22.
		4.55pm	BM 125, giving dispositions of Bde sent out.	
		10pm.	Div 120/1/C rec'd	A23
		11.55pm.	In consequence BM124a issued & reconnaissance of purple line made forthwith	A24 WB

1875 Wt. W593/826 1,000,000 4/15 J.B.C. & A. A.D.S.S./Forms/C. 2118.

Instructions regarding War Diaries and Intelligence Summaries are contained in F. S. Regs., Part II. and the Staff Manual respectively. Title Pages will be prepared in manuscript.

PAGE 7.
Vol. 45

WAR DIARY
or
~~INTELLIGENCE SUMMARY~~ of 125 Inf. Bde
(Erase heading not required.)

MARCH 1918.

Army Form C. 2118

Place	Date	Hour	Summary of Events and Information	Remarks and references to Appendices
57D NE. ESSARTS. E24d79	27	2 a.m.	GS 120/1/C cancelled. Batts informed that BM124a was cancelled	
		3.20 a.m.	GS 120/1/D. received.	
		4.15 a.m.	In consequence BM 127 was issued ordering no withdrawal	
		9.30 a.m.	BM 129 issued.	A25
			Day spent in consolidating support position & in rest. Tools, SAA sent up. The Batts were notified that continuous trench system was not to be attempted till troops had been properly disposed in depth.	A26
		noon.	Enemy attacked from direction of ABLAINZEVELLE, but made no progress on this Div. front.	
		12.55 p.m.	BM132 issued.	A27.
		3.30 p.m.	Enemy attacked again & was again broken up. In neither case was this Bde called upon.	
		4 p.m.	6 Tanks placed at disposal of Bde for use in case of counter attack.	
		7. p.m.	D.C. rang up Brigadier & informed him that there were rumours to the effect that enemy had broken through 31 Div. on our left & were in AYETTE VALLEY	
		7.15. p.m.	Hence BM133	A28
		7.30 p.m.	Message received from Div that 42 Div. Composite Batt. were moving up to old reserve line in E24a at once & on arrival coming under orders of 125 I. Bde, not to be used for operations unless ordered by D.H.Q. or in grave emergency.	
		8. p.m.	Comp. M.G. Squadron att. 125 Bde were ordered to alter their dispositions to cover LE COTEUL valley if required.	
		9.15 p.m.	Div. G 596 received	A30
		9.20 p.m.	BM135 issued.	A31
		10.35 p.m.	2 Coys 1/7 L.F. placed at disposal of 127 I.B. in event of S.O.S. or attack. BM138 issued	A32

1875 Wt. W593/826 1,000,000 4/15 J.B.C. & A. A.D.S.S./Forms/C. 2118.

Instructions regarding War Diaries and Intelligence Summaries are contained in F. S. Regs., Part II. and the Staff Manual respectively. Title Pages will be prepared in manuscript.

WAR DIARY
or
INTELLIGENCE ~~SUMMARY~~ of 125 Inf Bde.

(*Erase heading not required.*)

Army Form C. 2118

page 8
Vol 45.

MARCH 1918.

Place	Date	Hour	Summary of Events and Information	Remarks and references to Appendices
57D N.E ESSARTS E24d79.	28.	12.15am.	G603 received from Div. This was not understood & no action was taken. Div. informed.	A33
		12.15am.	Liaison officer from Guards Bde. 31 Div. came & stated situation on left clear, 126 I.B. having filled any gaps between themselves & Guards Bde.	
		12.45am.	BM139 issued, warning 2 Coys of 1/8 L.F to be in readiness to support 126 I. Bde.	A34
		1.35am.	Patrol reports received from 1/8 L.F. & forwarded to Div. They shewed there was no cause for alarm, the AYETTE VALLEY being clear of enemy & our Bdes in touch.	
		1.0am.	BM 141 issued	
		1.30am	BM142 issued.	A35
		4.45am.	Situation unchanged.	A36
		9.45am.	BM148 issued.	
		11.25am.	BM 149	A37
		11.45am.	1/7 N.F. pioneers moved forward. BM150.	A38.
		12.45pm.	BM 152 issued.	A39
		2.30pm.	1/7 L.F. report all 4 Coys in position in sunken road, 2 in E27b85 & 2 in F27c67. Reinforcements carried out without casualties.	A40
		6.50pm.	Div. O. No3 received.	
		8.30pm.	Hence BM156 issued, ordering relief of 127 & part of 185 I Bde by this Bde tonight.	A41.
			approx casualties up to date 26 off. 597 O.R.	

MB

MB

1875 Wt. W593/826 1,000,000 4/15 J.B.C. & A. A.D.S.S./Forms/C. 2118.

Instructions regarding War Diaries and Intelligence Summaries are contained in F. S. Regs., Part II. and the Staff Manual respectively. Title Pages will be prepared in manuscript.

page 9
Vol 45.

WAR DIARY
or
~~INTELLIGENCE SUMMARY~~

(Erase heading not required.)

125 Inf. Bde — MARCH 1918.

Army Form C. 2118

Place	Date	Hour	Summary of Events and Information	Remarks and references to Appendices
57 D N E ESSARTS. E24d79	29.	5 am	relief complete.	
		5.30 am.	Situation report. a quiet night.	
			a quiet day, with little hostile artillery activity	
		4 pm.	Div. O. 4 received.	
		8 pm.	Hence BM 163 issued ordering relief of Bde by 124 I. Bde.	A 42. MB
57 D.N.E. GOMMECOURT E28d66.	30	3.15 am	relief reported complete.	
		6 am.	Bde Hqrs. established in GOMMECOURT WOOD. Dispositions as in BM163. Day was spent in rest & sleep. 500 men found at night for carrying up material for use in Purple line, for part of which Bde is now responsible.	MB.
——	31.		Day spent in refitting & resting	
			D.C. visited Bde.	
			Trench strength of Bde 38. off. 117 O.R. 49 L.G.S.	
		11. pm.	Div O. No 5 received.	
		11.30 pm.	Hence BM 175 issued notifying relief would take place to-morrow.	A 43 MB

Harold Fargus
Brig. Gen.
Cmdg. 125 Inf. Bde

1875 Wt. W593/826 1,000,000 4/15 J.B.C. & A. A.D.S.S./Forms/C. 2118.

A P P E N D I C E S

A.1 to A.28

and

A.30 to A.43

SECRET.   Copy No.......9

125TH, INFANTRY BRIGADE ORDER NO.73.

Ref Map: BETHUNE Combined Sheet.   1/3/18.

1. 46th.Division commence moving from the BOHY Area on the 1st March to take over the centre sector of I Corps Front from the 11th & 55th Divisions.

2. Consequent thereon the following moves will take place :-

Date.	UNIT	From	To	Remarks.
Mar:3rd.	7th.Lan Fus.	FOUQUIERES.	FOUQUEREUIL.	Move to be completed by 4.p.m. and completion to be reported to these H.Qrs.
Mar:4th.	125th.B'de. H.Qrs.	FOUQUIERES	DROUVIN	B'de.H.Qrs. will close at FOUQUIERES at 4.p.m. & open at DROUVIN at same hour.

3. An interval of 100 yards will be maintained between companies and an interval of 100 yards between units and its transport.

4. ACKNOWLEDGE.

E.W. Sartin, Captain,
a/Brigade Major,
125th.BRIGADE.

Issued at 8.p.m. thro' Signals.

Copies to :-

1.5th.Lan Fus.
2.7th.Lan Fus.
3.8th.Lan Fus.
4.125th.T.M.B.
5.)
6.)42nd Division.
7.B'de.I.O.
8.)
9.)W.D.
10.F I L E.

[illegible]
7th L.F.
8th L.F.
125th T.M.Bty.
429 Coy A.S.C.
1/1st E.L.Field Amb.
429 Field Coy R.E.

B.M. 100.

The Division may be required to move to BASSEUX on 24th inst. by bus.
[illegible] D.A. and all transport will move by road on 23rd instant and be billetted night 23rd/24th by 13th Corps and will be fed by lorries.

Captain,
A/Brigade Major,
125th Inf. Brigade.

22/3/18.
D.

A2.   8

SECRET.   COPY NO......

125th.BRIGADE ORDER NO.74.

23/3/18.

Ref Map. BETHUNE Combined Sheet 1:.40.000.
LENS Sheet. 1.100.000.

1. Moves will take place as follows today :-

(a). Transport by Road.
(b). Dismounted personnel by Bus.

2. Transport of the Brigade Group will march under Orders of the B'de.T.O., to the MONCHY - BRETON Area (N of ARRAS - St.POL Road). Route ~~[illegible]~~ via HAILLICOURT - HOUDAIN, to pass starting point, Cross Roads, HAILLICOURT, J.18.d.4.3. as follows :-

5th.Lan Fus..................8.15.a.m.
8th. " " ....8.20.a.m.
7th. " " ....8.25.a.m.
B'de.H.Qrs...................8.30.a.m.
429th.Coy.A.S.C..............8.32.a.m.
1/1st.E.L.Field Amb..........8.37.a.m.

Interval of 100 yards between transport of units.

3. Dismounted personnel will embuss, destination to be notified later, as follows :-

Embussing point, FOUQUIERES - LABUISSIERE Road, with head of column at J.5.d.3.2.
Units will be drawn up on the North Side of road, and be in position as follows by 10.30.a.m. :-

7th.Lan Fus from J.5.d.3.2. N.E. along road for 400 yds.

5th.Lan Fus from end of 7th.Lan Fus N.E. along Rd for 400 yds.
8th. " " " " " 5th. " " " " " " " "
125th.T.M.B. }
B'de.H.Qrs. }from end of 8th.Lan Fus N.E. along Rd for 100 yds.
dismounted personnel }
of 429th.Coy.A.S.C. }
1/1st.E.L.Field Amb.) " " " B'de.H.Qrs.Group N.E. along Rd for 100 yds.
42nd M.G.Bn. from end of 1/1st E.L.Fd.Amb. N.E.along Rd for 400 yds

Troops will be drawn up in groups of 25, 4 groups to each 50 yds of Road space.

4. Lorries for transport of baggage, blankets etc, will be allotted as follows : -

5th.,7th.,8th.Lan Fus ... 3 Lorries each.
125th.T.M.B. ... 1 Lorry.
1/1st.Field Amb. ... 1 Lorry.
42nd M.G.Bn. ... 2 Lorries.

Guides to meet will be at B'de.H.Qrs. at 7.45.a.m. On being loaded lorries will return to B'de.H.Qrs. and move ~~with the~~ as a convoy.

5. Billeting parties not to exceed 4 men per Bn, 1 T.M.B. & Field Amb, will be at B'de.H.Qrs. at 8.0.a.m.

6. Rations for consumption 24th inst will be drawn from refilling point forthwith, and ill be carried on the man, in the busses in addition to those for consumption 23rd instant.

7. ACKNOWLEDGE.

Issued at 7.0 AM.

Captain,
B/Brigade Major, 125th.Brigade.

Prefix........Code........m. | Words | Charge
Office of Origin and Service Instructions. Mist

Sent At........m. To........ By........

This message is on a/c of: ....Service. (Signature of "Franking Officer.")

Recd. at........m. Date A3 From........ By........

TO 5 / 2 / 8 L7 125 T M B.

Sender's Number.	Day of Month.	In reply to Number.	AAA
* AL182.	23		

First Corps will begins
aaa All units moving
South will be prepared
to take part in
active operations at an
early date. aaa All
superfluous Kit & Stores will
consequently be left behind
and stored locally under
Corps arrangements aaa All
Echelons other than M.T's.
will proceed full. aaa
Latter will receive special
Instructions if required to
move full aaa ends
Addsd all concerned

From 125 Bde
Place
Time

The above may be forwarded as now corrected. (Z)

Censor. Signature of Addressor or person authorised to telegraph in his name. [illegible] Capt

* This line should be erased if not required.

(3198.) Wt. W 12952/M1294. 375,000 Pads. 1/17. H. W. & V., Ld. (E. 818.)

"A" Form. Army Form C. 2121.

MESSAGES AND SIGNALS. No. of Message

Prefix........Code........m | Words | Charge
Office of Origin and Service Instructions

Sent At........m. To........ By........

This message is on a/c of: ....Service. (Signature of "Franking Officer.")

Recd. at........m. Date........ From A4 By........

TO 3 Bdes / 1?? T[illegible] / 1?? F[illegible] Amb.

Sender's Number.	Day of Month.	In reply to Number.	AAA
* BM 101	24		

Division less artillery is relieving
49th Div. in the line tonight aaa
Units will be prepared to move to
vicinity of LOGEAST WOOD or further
forward if possible by daylight &
[illegible] by night aaa Detailed
orders follow aaa acknowledge
aaa addressed 3 Bdes, T[illegible] & F[illegible]
[illegible].

From 125th Inf Bde
Place 11.0
Time [illegible] AM

The above may be forwarded as now corrected. (Z)

Censor. Signature of Addressor or person authorised to telegraph in his name.

* This line should be erased if not required.

Printed and supplied by Hugh Rees, Ltd., 5, Regent Street, London, in blocks of 60, 9d. per block.

93.

MESSAGES AND SIGNALS.

No. of Message

Prefix ...... Code ...... m. | Words | Charge

Office of Origin and Service Instructions: Ref. 57C NW 1/20,000

Sent At ...... m. To ...... By ......

This message is on a/c of: ...... Service. (Signature of "Franking Officer.")

Recd. at ...... m. Date ...... From A5 By ......

TO: 5th L.F. — 125 T.M.B. — 7th L.F. — Bde Signal Officer — 8th L.F. — Staff Capt.

Sender's Number.	Day of Month.	In reply to Number.	AAA
* BM 105	24.		

The Bde will relieve the 120th
Inf Bde in the line tonight 24th/25th
inst as follows aaa 1/5th L.F. on right
will relieve 14th A&S.H. from about
B.30.c.8.6 to B.29.c.8.9 with
HQ probably about H.4.b.8.3 aaa
1/9th L.F. on left Bn will relieve
portions of 13th 11th & 14th H.L.I. &
20th Middlesex from B.29.c.8.9 thro
B.29.a.4.8 to 0.9. B.23.b.04 to
B.28.a.04 with HQ probably
about H.4.a.1.3 aaa 1/8th L.F. in
support will relieve 7th C. Surrey
& be disposed in dugouts H.3.c,
H.3.d H.4.a & B.27.d aaa
Bns will in all cases be
disposed as far as possible in

From
Place
Time

The above may be forwarded as now corrected. (Z)

Censor. Signature of Addressor or person authorised to telegraph in his name.

* This line should be erased if not required.

Printed and supplied by HUGH REES, LTD., 5, Regent Street, London, in blocks of 60, 9d. per block.

MESSAGES AND SIGNALS.

No. of Message

Prefix ...... Code ...... m. | Words | Charge

Office of Origin and Service Instructions

Sent At ...... m. To ...... By ......

This message is on a/c of: ...... Service. (Signature of "Franking Officer.")

Recd. at ...... m. Date ...... From ...... By ......

TO: (2)

Sender's Number.	Day of Month.	In reply to Number.	AAA
* BM 105			

depth aaa Bde HQ CHATEAU
GOMIECOURT B.23.a.2.2 aaa Guides
will be met in first instance at
FOREST LODGE G.2.a.3.9. aaa Bns
will move off from present bivouacs
as follows: 1/5th L.F. 7.50 PM followed
by 1/7th L.F. & then 1/8th L.F. aaa Distances
to be kept 100 yds between Bns
50 yds between Coys aaa 125th
T.M.B. will move from ADINFER
WOOD to GOMIECOURT as soon
as transport is available aaa
Completion of relief will be
wired to Bde HQ by the code
word "AMIENS" aaa All tools
& ammunition will be taken
over aaa ACKNOWLEDGE

From 125th Inf Bde
Place
Time 7.16 PM

The above may be forwarded as now corrected. (Z) [illegible signature]

Censor. Signature of Addressor or person authorised to telegraph in his name.

* This line should be erased if not required.

Printed and supplied by HUGH REES, LTD., 5, Regent Street, London, in blocks of 60, 9d. per block.

A6

S P E C I A L   O R D E R   O F   T H E   D A Y.

By Major-General A. SOLLY-FLOOD, C.M.G.,D.S.O.
Commanding 42nd (East Lancs.) Division.

On this, the first occasion on which the Major-General has had the honour of leading the Division into action, he desires to wish all ranks the best of luck. When the enemy attacks, the Divisional Commander is convinced that the Division will give such an account of itself as to make the enemy regret that they tried conclusions with East Lancashire.

This is the opportunity we want to "GO ONE BETTER"

[signature]
Lt. Colonel,
General Staff,
42nd Division.

24th March 1918.

Prefix........ Code........m. | Words | Charge | This message is on a/c of: ....Service. | Recd. at........m.

Office of Origin and Service Instructions

Sent At........m. To........ By........

(Signature of "Franking Officer.") | Date A7 | From........ | By........

TO 1/5th L.F.

Sender's Number.	Day of Month.	In reply to Number.	
* B M 106	24.		AAA

Your J.2. received aaa If BEHAGNIES + SAPIGNIES found to be clear establish line E of 2 villages forming defensive flanks to N + S. aaa Please take charge of Bde + form above line with 1/5th + 1/7th L.F with 1/8th L.F. in support aaa Establish double HQrs with 1/7th L.F in BEHAGNIES if possible aaa If these villages are not clear please notify me at once.

From 125 Bde.
Place CHATEAU GOMMIECOURT.
Time 11.0 PM

The above may be forwarded as now corrected. (Z)

Censor. | Signature of Addressor or person authorised to telegraph in his name. [signature] Capt

* This line should be erased if not required.

Printed and supplied by HUGH REES, LTD., 5, Regent Street, London, in blocks of 60, 9d. per block.

MESSAGES AND SIGNALS. No. of Message........

Prefix ...... Code ...... m.	Words.	Charge.	This message is on a/c of:	Recd. at ...... m.
Office of Origin and Service Instructions.	Sent At ......m. To ...... By		...... Service. (Signature of "Franking Officer.")	Date A8 From ...... By ......

TO 125 Bde

Sender's Number.	Day of Month.	In reply to Number.	AAA
* J3			

Bihucourt & Sapignies reported clear by Major Hitchcock RFA who has seen our patrol and Have told 127 Bde, aaa Now moving to carry out instructions in your BM106

Both our patrols have now returned

1.15 pm

From	~~12.35~~ 5LF
Place	Achiet-le-Grand
Time	12.55 am

The above may be forwarded as now corrected. (Z) [signature] Capt.

Censor. Signature of Addressor or person authorised to telegraph in his name.

* This line should be erased if not required.

"A" Form. Army Form C. 2121. (In pads of 100.)

MESSAGES AND SIGNALS. No. of Message........

Prefix ...... Code ...... m.	Words.	Charge.	This message is on a/c of:	Recd. at ...... m.
Office of Origin and Service Instructions.	Sent At ......m. To ...... By		...... Service. (Signature of "Franking Officer.")	Date A9 From ...... By ......

TO 40th Divn. 42nd Divn.

Sender's Number.	Day of Month.	In reply to Number.	AAA
* BM 107	25.		

Our patrols ~~[illegible]~~ have reported SAPIGNIES + BEHAGNIES clear of Enemy aaa We are therefore establishing line E. of two villages in touch with 120th Inf Bde on left + 127th Inf Bde on right aaa addressed 40th Divn rptd 42nd Divn.

From	125th Inf Bde
Place	Chateau Grevillers
Time	1.35 AM

The above may be forwarded as now corrected. (Z) MMNicholls Capt

Censor. Signature of Addressor or person authorised to telegraph in his name.

Prefix........ Code........ m | Words. | Charge. | *This message is on a/c of:* ....Service. | Recd. at ....m. Date A10 From .... By ....

Office of Origin and Service Instructions. Sent At ....m. To .... By .... (Signature of "Franking Officer.")

TO

Sender's Number.	Day of Month.	In reply to Number.	AAA
BM 119	25		

1 Bn (5th L.F.) on line about 500 yds E of ARRAS – BAPAUME RD with flanks on road on North at B 26 c 5 0 in touch with E SURREYS on South at H 8 d 5 7 where in touch with [illegible] Bn (7th L.F.) [illegible] S of SAPIGNIES up to H 7 b 3 6 thence along road running SW to G 12 c 0 3. Third Bn (8th L.F.) in Support in trenches [illegible] from H 7 a 0 5 to H 1 b 4 7 aaa

From ? E Surreys

Place ?125th Bde

Time

The above may be forwarded as now corrected. (Z) [signature]

Censor. Signature of Addressor or person authorised to telegraph in his name.

* This line should be erased if not required.

Wt. W 12952/M1294. 375,000 Pads. 1/17. H. W. & V., Ld. (E. 818.)

Prefix........ Code........ m. | Words | Charge. | *This message is on a/c of* ....Service. | Recd. at ....m. Date A11 From .... By ....

Office of Origin and Service Instructions. Sent At ....m. To .... By .... (Signature of "Franking Officer.")

TO 127 Brigade

Sender's Number.	Day of Month.	In reply to Number.	AAA
B G 1	25th		

Enemy reported working round night flank of 7th Lan Fus on right side of BIHUCOURT con[illegible] help

From 125 Inf Bde

Place

Time 1.20 pm

The above may be forwarded as now corrected. (Z) [signature]

Censor. Signature of Addressor or person authorised to telegraph in his name

* This line should be erased if not required.

Wt. W492/M1647 100,000 pads. 4/17. W. & Co., Ltd. (E. 1137.)

Prefix........ Code........ m | Words. | Charge.

Office of Origin and Service Instructions.

Very Urgent

Sent At........m. To........ By........

This message is on a/c of: ....Service.

(Signature of "Franking Officer.")

Recd. at........m. Date A 12 From........ By........

TO 1/5th L F

Sender's Number.	Day of Month.	In reply to Number.	AAA
BM 111	25		

The 127th Inf Bde are holding a line through G.6. central G.5. central facing South aaa Collect what you can of 1/5, 1/7 + 1/8 L Fs + establish a line from G.6. central through G.6.c. + B 25 C. forming with 126th Inf Bde on North

From 125th Inf Bde
Place
Time 3.15 PM.

The above may be forwarded as now corrected. (Z)

Censor. MMcNicholls Capt
Signature of Addressor or person authorised to telegraph in his name.

* This line should be erased if not required.

(3198.) Wt. W 12952/M1294. 375,000 Pads. 1/17. H. W. & V., Ld. (E. 818.)

MESSAGES AND SIGNALS. No. of Message........

Prefix........ Code........ m | Words. | Charge.

Office of Origin and Service Instructions.

Very Urgent

Sent At........m. To........ By........

This message is on a/c of: ....Service.

(Signature of "Franking Officer.")

Recd. at........m. Date........ From A 13 By........

TO 42nd Divn

Sender's Number.	Day of Month.	In reply to Number.	AAA
BM 112	25		

OC 1/5th L.F. reports he has had to retire from BEHAGNIES Enemy having worked round SAPIGNIES + SW of BEHAGNIES aaa He has retired in direction of GOMIECOURT aaa Am endeavouring to get what is left of 3 Bns established between left of 127th Inf Bde at G.6. central + right of ~~[illegible]~~ 126th Inf Bde about B.25. central

From 125th Inf Bde
Place
Time 3.30 PM

The above may be forwarded as now corrected. (Z)

Censor. MMcNicholls Capt
Signature of Addressor or person authorised to telegraph in his name.

* This line should be erased if not required.

(3198.) Wt. W 12952/M1294. 375,000 Pads. 1/17. H. W. & V., Ld. (E. 818.)

"A" Form. Army Form C. 2121. (In pads of 100.)

MESSAGES AND SIGNALS. No. of Message..........

Prefix.......... Code.......... m | Words. | Charge. | This message is on a/c of: | Recd. at .... m.

Office of Origin and Service Instructions. Very Urgent

Sent At..........m. To.......... By..........

.... Service. (Signature of "Franking Officer.")

Date.......... From A14 By..........

TO 4th Div.

Sender's Number.	Day of Month.	In reply to Number.	AAA
* BM 113	25		

Ref	telephone	conversation	with
G.S.O.1	can	can you	give
me	any	further	information
with	regard	to	Bde of
62nd	Div.	~~[illegible]~~	+ Tanks
stated	to	be	going to advance
towards	BIHUCOURT		

From 125th Inf Bde.
Place GOMIECOURT
Time 3.35 PM

The above may be forwarded as now corrected. (Z) [signature] Capt

Censor. Signature of Addressor or person authorised to telegraph in his name.

* This line should be erased if not required.

(3198.) Wt. W 12952/M1294. 375,000 Pads. 1/17. H. W. & V., Ld. (E. 818.)

A15

Copy No. 1

SECRET & URGENT. G.S.130/1/B.

42nd DIVISION (~~Warning~~) ORDER.

25th March 1918.

1. It is not the intention of the Divisional Commander to order a withdrawal from present positions unless the action of the flanking troops necessitates it.

2. In this eventuality, the 126th Inf. Bde. will get into touch with the 92nd Inf. Bde. and will make the movements of his left Battn. to conform to those of the 92nd Inf. Bde. All possible precautions will be taken to ensure the Left Battn., 126th Inf. Bde., do not lose touch with Right Battn., 92nd Inf. Bde.

3. 92nd Inf. Bde. is to hold from A.23.a.5.5. to A.11.a.7.0.

4. 4th Guards Brigade is to withdraw through 92nd and 93rd Inf. Brigades and is to take up a line running along the ridge A.5.a.9.9. to A.19.b.0.0.

5. B.G.C. 126th Inf. Bde. will at once send an officer to get into touch with 92nd Inf. Brigade to arrange all details.

6. In the event of a retirement being ordered, the withdrawal will be made by bounds as follows:-

1st Bound.	Line of railway.
2nd "	High ground E. of LOGEAST WOOD.
3rd "	ABLAINZEVILLE - BUCQUOY Line.
4th "	ESSARS - GOMMECOURT (prepared position known as PURPLE LINE).

B.G's.C. Inf. Bdes. will have these lines reconnoitred by an officer if possible.

7. D.H.Q. will move to FONQUEVILLERS.

R.F. Guy

8.30 pm.

Lt. Colonel,
General Staff,
42nd Division.

Issued at 5 p.m., 25/3/18.
Distribution as follows:-

Copy No.1. 125th Inf. Bde.	6. 42nd M.G. Battn.	10. 40th Divn.
2. 126th Inf. Bde.	7. 1/7th N. Fus.	11. 62nd Divn.
3. 127th Inf. Bde.	8. Signal Coy.	12. 31st Divn.
4. C.R.A.	9. 'Q'.	13. IV Corps.
5. C.R.E.	10. 41st Division.	

Reference attached ~~Warning~~ Order, the withdrawal mentioned in para 6 will commence as soon as practicable.

R.F. Guy

Lt.Col.G.S.

101.

Prefix ...... Code ...... m | Words | Charge

Office of Origin and Service Instructions.

Urgent

This message is on a/c of: ...... Service.

Recd. at ...... m. Date A16 From ...... By ......

TO 42nd Divn

Sender's Number. BM 114 | Day of Month. 25 | In reply to Number. | A A A

Reference your G.S. 120/11/B of today's date aaa It is proposed to make first bound to line of Railway at 2.0 AM 26th inst aaa This has been arranged in conjunction with 126th Inf Bde aaa Is it proposed to make more than one bound tonight if so how many as the question of hours of darkness is important.

From 125th Inf Bde

Place A.22.b.3.4 Railway Cutting

Time 9.15 PM

The above may be forwarded as now corrected. (Z)

Censor. Signature of Addressor or person authorised to telegraph in his name.

* This line should be erased if not required.

(3198.) Wt. W 12952/M1294. 375,000 Pads. 1/17. H. W. & V., Ld. (E. 818.)

MESSAGES AND SIGNALS.

Prefix ...... Code ...... m | Words | Charge

Office of Origin and Service Instructions.

This message is on a/c of: ...... Service.

Recd. at ...... m. Date ...... From A17 By ......

TO 1/5 L F, 1/7 L F, 1/8 L F, [illegible]

Sender's Number. BM 116 (?) | Day of Month. 25 | In reply to Number. | A A A

Divn to withdraw tonight to line to be held by 126 + 127 Inf Bdes between LEVEL CROSSING A.16.d.3.0 + FOREST LODGE G.2.b.2.0 aaa 125 Inf Bde will be in support distributed as follows aaa 1/5th L F square A.19.d 1/7th L.F square A.25.b 1/8 L F squares F24c + F30a aaa Bns will in all cases be distributed in depth aaa withdrawal tonight will commence at 2.0 AM under C.O's arrangements aaa 1/8 L F will move first aaa Rations water tools + SAA will all be dumped ready for Bns in new positions at F.24.a.8.2 aaa ACKNOWLEDGE

From 125 Inf Bde

Place Railway Cutting A.22.b.3.4

Time 10.45 pm

The above may be forwarded as now corrected. (Z)

Censor. Signature of Addressor or person authorised to telegraph in his name.

* This line should be erased if not required.

(3198.) Wt. W 12952/M1294. 375,000 Pads. 1/17. H. W. & V., Ld. (E. 818.)

and one of the 9th Infantry Brigade by

MESSAGES AND SIGNALS. No. of Message

Office of Origin and Service Instructions: Urgent

Recd. at ... m. Date A18

TO: 1/5 L.F. / 1/7 L.F. / 1/8 L.F. — Staff Capt.

Sender's Number: BM 117 | Day of Month: 26 | In reply to Number: | AAA

A further withdrawal will take place as follows AAA The Div^n will hold the line BUCQUOY – ABLAINZEVELLE with the 127 & 126 Bdes & between South of CRUCIFIX in L.4.a & grid line between squares F.18 & 24 AAA 125th Inf Bde is in support AAA 1/5 L.F will take up position in F.20.b AAA 1/7 L.F F.20.d AAA 1/8 L.F F.20.a & c AAA All positions to be organized in depth AAA Bde H.Q. will be in ESSARTS AAA Withdrawal will commence at once on receipt of these orders.

From: 125th Inf Bde
Place: ABLAINZEVELLE
Time: 4.45 am

The above may be forwarded as now corrected. (Z)

Censor. — Signature of Addressor or person authorised to telegraph in his name: [signature] Capt

* This line should be erased if not required.

(3198.) Wt. W 12952/M1294. 375,000 Pads. 1/17. H. W. & V., Ld. (E. 818.)

MESSAGES AND SIGNALS. (In pads of 100.) No. of Message

Recd. at ... m. From A19

TO: 1/5 L.F. / 1/7 " / 1/8 " — 126 MGC / 178 Bde RFA.

Sender's Number: BM 120 | Day of Month: 26 | In reply to Number: | AAA

125th Inf Bde will take up position covering ESSARS from S.W at once AAA 1/7 L.F. will move across E.30.a & b where they will establish themselves AAA 1/8 L.F will move in & take up position in F.25 a & b AAA 1/5 L.F will take up position in close defence of ESSARS in F.19.c & E.24.d AAA 126 MGC will place his guns in suitable position south of ESSARS AAA Addressed 3 Bns, 126 MGC & 178 Bde, RFA.

From: 125th Inf Bde
Place: E.24. b 8.0.
Time: 11.55 AM.

The above may be forwarded as now corrected. (Z)

Censor. — Signature of Addressor or person authorised to telegraph in his name: [signature] Capt

* This line should be erased if not required.

(3198.) Wt. W 12952/M1294. 375,000 Pads. 1/17. H. W. & V., Ld. (E. 818.)

MESSAGES AND SIGNALS.

No. of Message ....

Prefix ...... Code ...... m. | Words. | Charge.

Office of Origin and Service Instructions.

Sent At ...... m. To ...... By ......

This message is on a/c of: ...... Service.

(Signature of "Franking Officer.")

Recd. at ...... m. Date A 20 From ...... By ......

TO 3 Bns / 126 MGC / 178 Bde RFA.

Sender's Number.	Day of Month.	In reply to Number.	AAA
* BM 121	26		

Ref my BM 120 of today aaa Stand-by in whatever position you now occupy facing South & East as far as possible aaa 126 MGC will carry out instructions as in BM 120 aaa addressed 3 Bns 126 MGC repd 178 Bde RFA.

From 125 Inf Bde

Place ESTAIRS

Time 12.18 PM

The above may be forwarded as now corrected. (Z)

Censor. Signature of Addressor or person authorised to telegraph in his name. [signature illegible]

* This line should be erased if not required.

(3198.) Wt. W 12952/M1294. 375,000 Pads. 1/17. H. W. & V., Ld. (E. 818.)

MESSAGES AND SIGNALS.

No. of Message ....

Prefix ...... Code ...... m. | Words. | Charge.

Office of Origin and Service Instructions. URGENT.

Ref Sheet 57a NE. 1.20 000

Sent At ...... m. By ......

This message is on a/c of: ...... Service.

(Signature of "Franking Officer.")

Recd. at A21 m. Date [illegible] From [illegible] By ......

TO 1/8 L.F. / 1/7 L.F. / 1/5 L.F. / 126 M.G. Coy. / 178 Bde R.F.A. (File)

Sender's Number.	Day of Month.	In reply to Number.	AAA
* BM 123.	26.		

Warning Order aaa Retirement on Divn Front to a line E.29.c.6.0 - LA BRAVELLE FARM inclusive may be made necessary by operations South aaa In this case new line will be held by 127th Bde on Right + 126th Bde on left this retirement to this line being covered by 125 Bde aaa When these Bdes are in position in new line 125 Bde will withdraw through them to positions about E.28.a. in support aaa The withdrawal of 125 Bde will be ~~covered~~ by fire, if necessary, from 126 M.G. Coy. aaa 1/5 + 1/7 L.F.s will withdraw through 1/8 L.F. who after covering the ~~withdrawal~~ retirement of these 2 Bns will withdraw themselves aaa The 126th M.G. Coy. will withdraw after the 1/5 + 1/7 + before the 1/8 L.F. aaa Disposition of Bde after

From

Place

Time

The above may be forwarded as now corrected. (Z)

Censor. Signature of Addressor or person authorised to telegraph in his name.

* This line should be erased if not required.

(3796.) Wt. W 492/M1647. 650,000 Pads. 5/17. H. W. & V., Ld. (E. 1187.)

MESSAGES AND SIGNALS.

No. of Message.

TO (2)

Sender's Number. Day of Month. In reply to Number. AAA

withdrawal to new line as follows:- 1/5 LF on Left Front 1/7 LF on Right Front in old German System aaa D Riding Line between Bns E.29.a.2.5 - E.29.a.0.7 aaa 1/8 LF in support in Old British System in about Squares E.22.d + E.28.a aaa Bde H Qrs will be disposed as near as possible behind the 1/8 LF. aaa Exact location will be notified on arrival aaa

Reference time of retirement of 1/5 + 1/7th LFs aaa This will be ½ hour after last troops of 126 + 127 Bdes have passed unless anything unforeseen occurs aaa addressed 3 Bns, 126 MGC + 178 Bde RFA.

Bns informed the same. Above communicated verbally by BGC in afternoon.

From 125 Inf Bde.
Place ESSARTS.
Time 3.40 pm.

The above may be forwarded as now corrected. (Z) Censor.
Signature of Addressor or person authorised to telegraph in his name. M.W. Nichols Capt.

* This line should be erased if not required.

(3796.) Wt. W492/M1647. 650,000 Pads. 5/17. H. W. & V., Ld. (E. 1187.)

"A" Form. Army Form C. 2121. (In pads of 100.)

MESSAGES AND SIGNALS.

No. of Message.

From A22

TO (RANDOM) 42 Div.

Sender's Number: BM 174. Day of Month: 26. In reply to Number. AAA

Approximate fighting strength of Bde in line including details 34 officers + 880 ORs aaa Situation unchanged

From RAZOR
Place
Time 4.15 PM

The above may be forwarded as now corrected. (Z) Censor.
Signature of Addressor or person authorised to telegraph in his name. M.W. Nichols Capt.

* This line should be erased if not required.

(3198.) Wt. W12952/M1294. 375,000 Pads. 1/17. H. W. & V., Ld. (E. 818.)

MESSAGES AND SIGNALS. No. of Message

Prefix Code m | Words | Charge | This message is on a/c of: | Recd. at m.

Office of Origin and Service Instructions. J.C.L.S.

Sent At m. To By

Service.

(Signature of "Franking Officer.")

Date A23

From

By

TO 126 Inf Bde
127 Inf Bde.

Sender's Number.	Day of Month.	In reply to Number.	AAA
* BM 125	26		

Dispositions of this B/e are as follows aaa Bde HQrs E.24.b.8.0 ESSARTS aaa 1/5th L.F. F.20.b 1/7th L.F. F.20.d 1/8th L.F. F.20.a + c aaa 126 M.G.C. disposed South of ESSARTS in E.24.a + F.19.c aaa addressed 126 + 127 Inf Bde for information

From 125 Inf Bde
Place
Time 4.55 PM

The above may be forwarded as now corrected. (Z) [illegible] Capt

Censor. Signature of Addressor or person authorised to telegraph in his name.

* This line should be erased if not required.

(3198.) Wt. W 12952/M1294. 375,000 Pads. 1/17. H. W. & V., Ld. (E. 818.)

"A" Form.

MESSAGES AND SIGNALS.

Army Form C. 2121. (In pads of 100.)

No. of Message

Prefix Code m | Words | Charge | This message is on a/c of: | Recd. at m.

Office of Origin and Service Instructions.

Sent At m. To By

Service.

(Sig. of "Franking Officer.")

Date

From A24

By

TO

Sender's Number	Day of Month	In reply to Number	AAA
*			

From
Place
Time

The above may be forwarded as now corrected. (Z)

Censor. Sig. of Addressor or person authorised to telegraph in his name.

* This line should be erased if not required.

(27964) Wt. W492/M1647. [E 1187]

187

"A" Form. (In pads of 100.)

MESSAGES AND SIGNALS.

No. of Message

Prefix / Code / m.	Words.	Charge.	This message is on a/c of:	Recd. at ____ m.
Office of Origin and Service Instructions.	Sent		____ Service.	Date
	At ____ m.			From
	To			
	By		(Sig. of "Franking Officer.")	By

TO (2)

* Sender's Number	Day of Month	In reply to Number	AAA

Battalion will occupy the line in depth
Bn. H.Q. will probably be situated in
F.7.b. [illegible] Front line will be not less
than [illegible] 120 [illegible] F.7.6 [illegible] will
[illegible] from [illegible] direction [illegible]
F.7.c.7.7./F.8.c.1.5 and on [illegible]
[illegible] the line [illegible] South [illegible]
A reconnaissance of the line is being made
by [illegible] with the Battalion
[illegible] will [illegible]
[illegible] at 27/[illegible]
[illegible] orders [illegible]
will move [illegible] from present positions in [illegible]
[illegible] will
[illegible] to report to
[illegible] will [illegible]

From
Place
Time

The above may be forwarded as now corrected. (Z)

Censor. Sig. of Addressor or person authorised to telegraph in his name.

* This line should be erased if not required.

(27964) Wt. W492/M1647. [E 1187]. 130,000 Pads—5/17. M.R.Co.,Ltd. Forms/C.2121.

"A" Form. Army Form C. 2121. (In pads of 100.)

MESSAGES AND SIGNALS.

No. of Message

Prefix / Code / m.	Words.	Charge.	This message is on a/c of:	Recd. at ____ m.
Office of Origin and Service Instructions.	Sent		____ Service.	Date
	At ____ m.			From
	To			
	By		(Sig. of "Franking Officer.")	By

TO (3)

* Sender's Number	Day of Month	In reply to Number	AAA

[illegible]
[illegible] O.C. [illegible]
[illegible]
[illegible] front [illegible]
[illegible] responsible [illegible] position
[illegible] The [illegible]
[illegible]
[illegible]
[illegible] Each battalion
[illegible]
[illegible]
to be [illegible] [illegible] 3
[illegible] 123 [illegible]

From 123 I.B.
Place [illegible]
Time [illegible]

The above may be forwarded as now corrected. (Z) [illegible] Capt

Censor. Sig. of Addressor or person authorised to telegraph in his name.

* This line should be erased if not required.

(27964) Wt. W492/M1647. [E 1187]. 130,000 Pads—5/17. M.R.Co.,Ltd. Forms/C.2121.

"A" Form.

MESSAGES AND SIGNALS.

Army Form C. 2121. (In pads of 100.)

No. of Message.

Prefix ... Code ... m. | Words. | Charge.

Office of Origin and Service Instructions.

URGENT
SECRET

Sent At ... m. To ... By ...

This message is on a/c of: ... Service.

(Signature of "Franking Officer.")

Recd. at ... m. Date ... From A25 By ...

TO Lyle

Sender's Number.	Day of Month.	In reply to Number.	AAA
* BM 127	27		

Rd my BM 123 & 124 of yesterday aaa If the following had been received from 3RD Army aaa The situation demands that the line of 2nd Army be maintained at all costs aaa There must be NO withdrawal aaa If breaks occur the line must be linked up again on the line of our present positions with the aid of any fresh troops as can be made available and which are now beginning to arrive aaa Any local withdrawal owing to enemy infiltration will be in the general direction East & West & Not N.W. and must be temporary only pending restoration of the line

From

Place

Time

The above may be forwarded as now corrected. (Z)

Censor. Signature of Addressor or person authorised to telegraph in his name.

* This line should be erased if not required.

(3796.) Wt. W 492/M1647. 650,000 Pads. 5/17. H. W. & V., Ld. (E. 1187.)

"A" Form.

MESSAGES AND SIGNALS.

Army Form C. 2121. (In pads of 100.)

No. of Message.

Prefix ... Code ... m. | Words. | Charge.

Office of Origin and Service Instructions.

Sent At ... m. To ... By ...

This message is on a/c of: ... Service.

(Signature of "Franking Officer.")

Recd. at ... m. Date ... From ... By ...

TO

Sender's Number.	Day of Month.	In reply to Number.	AAA
* Contn			

New boundaries between Divns and consequently between BDES and BATTS will be issued as soon as possible running generally E & W instead of NW & SE. aaa ends aaa The following is latest news with regard to Army Front (A) A N.Z. BDE has come into position on right of 62 Divn at HEBUTERNE (B) 3RD Aust Divn is approaching SAILLY AU BOIS (C) situation on left of front reported satisfactory (D) N.Z Div is now advancing on PUSIEUX (E) 4th Aust BDE occupies HEBUTERNE Acknowledge

From 1st BDE

Place

Time 4.15 PM

Add 3 Batts 2 M.G Coys Bde R.F.A.

The above may be forwarded as now corrected. (Z)

Censor. Signature of Addressor or person authorised to telegraph in his name. [signature illegible] Capt

MESSAGES AND SIGNALS.

No. of Message

Prefix — Code — m. Words. Charge.

Office of Origin and Service Instructions.

Sent At — m. To — By —

This message is on a/c of: — Service. (Sig. of "Franking Officer.")

Recd. at — m. Date — From A26 By —

TO: 5 LF, 7 LF, 8 LF, 126 MGC

Sender's Number	Day of Month	In reply to Number	AAA
BM 129	27		

Information has been received from prisoners to effect that German Guards Divn have been ordered to take BUCQUOY today aaa addressed 3 Bns + 126 MGC.

From: 125th Inf Bde

Place:

Time: 9.30 AM

The above may be forwarded as now corrected. (Z)

Censor. — [illegible] Capt

Sig. of Addressor or person authorised to telegraph in his name.

* This line should be erased if not required.

Wt. W492/M1647. [E 1187]. 130,000 Pads—5/17. M.R.Co.,Ltd. Forms/C.2121.

MESSAGES AND SIGNALS.

No. of Message

Prefix — Code — m. Words. Charge.

Office of Origin and Service Instructions.

Sent At — m. To — By —

This message is on a/c of: — Service. (Sig. of "Franking Officer.")

Recd. at — m. Date — From A27 By —

TO: OC 125 T.M.B.

Sender's Number	Day of Month	In reply to Number	AAA
BM 132	27.		

The 125th T.M.B will move forward today + report to Bde HQrs at ESSARTS at 7.0 P.M aaa Guns will be left behind with a small party to act as guard at the Transport lines aaa The remainder will parade in fighting order + if possible 2 days rations in addition to emergency rations aaa Those without [illegible] will carry great coats [illegible] aaa The T.M.B. will be accommodated near ESSARTS + act as a carrying + loading party etc or alternatively as reinforcements

From: 125th Inf Bde.

Place: Dugout E.24.b.6.0.

Time: 12.55 PM

The above may be forwarded as now corrected. (Z)

Censor. — [illegible] Capt

Sig. of Addressor or person authorised to telegraph in his name.

* This line should be erased if not required.

(27964) Wt. W492/M1647. [E 1187]. 130,000 Pads—5/17. M.R.Co.,Ltd. Forms/C.2121.

MESSAGES AND SIGNALS. No. of Message

Prefix Code m. Words. Charge.

Office of Origin and Service Instructions. Very urgent

Sent At m. To By

This message is on a/c of: Service.

(Sig. of "Franking Officer.")

Recd. at m. Date From A28 By

TO 1/8th L.F.

Sender's Number KM 135 | Day of Month 27 | In reply to Number | AAA

It is reported that the enemy has broken through East of AYETTE into AYETTE Valley aaa 1/8th L.F. will immediately send out patrols towards AYETTE to clear up situation aaa Further instructions follow re forming a defensive flank facing NE if necessary aaa Patrol reports to be forwarded as soon as received

From 125 Inf Bde.
Place
Time 7.15 PM

The above may be forwarded as now corrected. (Z)

Censor. Sig. of Addressor or person authorised to telegraph in his name.

* This line should be erased if not required.

(27964) Wt. W492/M1647. [E 1187]. 130,000 Pads—5/17. M.R.Co.,Ltd. Forms/C.2121.

MESSAGES AND SIGNALS. No. of Message

Prefix XB Code Words 49 £ s. d.

Charges to Collect

Service Instructions Priority

Received. From By

Sent, or sent out. At m. To By

Office Stamp. A30

Handed in at Office 7.40 m. Received 8.46 m.

TO 125 Bde. 126 127

*Sender's Number. G596 | Day of Month. 27 | In reply to Number. | AAA

Ref 31st divn G470 aaa my front intact at present do not intend to alter my dispositions as ordered in my G591 unless you fall back when left Bde will form a defensive flank facing NE aaa Added 31 divn repeated all concerned

9.45 PM

FROM 42 Divn

PLACE & TIME

* This line should be erased if not required.

(3856.) Wt. W528/M1970. 100,000 Pads. 5/17. H. W. & V., Ld. (E. 1213.)

MESSAGES AND SIGNALS. No. of Message

Prefix Code m. | Words. Charge. | This message is on a/c of: Service. | Recd. at m. Date From A 30

Office of Origin and Service Instructions. Sent At m. To By (Sig. of "Franking Officer.") By

TO 1/5th L F

Sender's Number	Day of Month	In reply to Number	AAA
BM 135	27		

It is reported that the enemy has broken through E of AYETTE in AYETTE VALLEY aaa 1/8th L F have sent out patrols to try & clear up situation aaa If necessary defensive flank will be formed but you will not move aaa you will receive further orders later

From 125th Inf Bde
Place
Time 9 20 PM

The above may be forwarded as now corrected. (Z) Censor. MMcNab[illegible] Capt
Sig. of Addressor or person authorised to telegraph in his name.
* This line should be erased if not required.
(27964) Wt. W492/M1647. [E 1187]. 130,000 Pads—5/17. M.R.Co.,Ltd. Forms/C.2121.

"A" Form
MESSAGES AND SIGNALS.
Army Form C.2121 (In pads of 100.)
No. of Message

Prefix Code m. | Words. Charge. | This message is on a/c of: Service. | Recd. at m. Date From A 32

Office of Origin and Service Instructions Sent At m. To By (Signature of "Franking Officer.") By

TO 7th L F
127 I B
42 Div.

Sender's Number.	Day of Month.	In reply to Number.	AAA
BM 138	27		

In the event of an SOS or attack on the 127th I B front you will send forward without further orders two Coys. to occupy Sunken Road from F 27 b 8 5 northwards aaa These Coys. will come under orders of OC Support Bn 127 I B [illegible] [illegible] HQ F 28 a 0 9 [illegible] where you should direct officer from each of the two Coys. concerned to get in touch at once aaa Addsd 7th L F rptd 127 I B + 42 Div.

From 125 Inf Bde
Place
Time 10 35 PM

The above may be forwarded as now corrected. (Z) Censor. MMcNab[illegible] Capt
Signature of Addressor or person authorised to telegraph in his name.
* This line should be erased if not required.
(7981) Wt. W492/M1647 130,000 Pads 5/17 D. D. & L. E1187

sector of his attack from

MESSAGES AND SIGNALS.

This message is on a/c of:	PRIORITY Service.
Date	A33
TO	125th - ~~126th - 127th~~ Inf. Bdes. 31st Divn. 62nd Divn.
Sender's Number	G.603
Day of Month	27
In reply to Number	AAA

Liason Officer with Division on left reports that their line now runs from F.19.d. - F.14.central. East of LITTLE FARM - F.3.central with a line of posts in trench in F.9. and 10 central to original line at F.16.b.10.9. AAA Counter attack will be made from line of posts in S.W. direction towards BUCQUOY - AYETTE Road to join up gap between left of this Divn. and F.16.b.10.9. AAA 125th and 126th Inf.Bdes. will co-operate with counter attack and will be ready to cut off any retreating enemy AAA Addsd 125th and 126th Inf. Bdes. reptd 127th Bde. 31st Divn. and 62nd Divn.

Recd 12.15 am

From: 42nd Divn.

Time: 11.50 pm

R. Ray[illegible]

Lt.Col.G.S.

The above may be forwarded as now corrected. (Z)

* This line should be erased if not required.

(3795.) Wt. W 492/M1647. 650,000 Pads. 5/17. H.W.&V., Ld. (E. 1187.)

Army Form C. 2121 (In pads of 100)

"A" Form
MESSAGES AND SIGNALS.

Date	A34
TO	1/8 L.F. 1/5 L.F 1/7 L.F 126 I.B.
Sender's Number	BM 139
Day of Month	28
In reply to Number	AAA

The situation on left flank of 126 Bde is now quite satisfactory aaa The enemy is not in the LE COJEUL valley aaa The 1/8th L.F will hold 2 Coys in immediate readiness to move forward to reinforce 1/5th E. Lancs 126 I.B aaa Guides will report to HQ 1/8th L.F provided by HQ 126 I.B aaa Coys will not move until confirming order is received from this office aaa Added 1/8 L.F repd 1/5 & 1/7 L.F.s & 126 I.B.

From: 125 I.B.

Time: 12.45 AM

[illegible] Capt

The above may be forwarded as now corrected. (Z)

* This line should be erased if not required.

(7981) Wt. W492/M1647 130,000 Pads 5/17 D. D. & L. E1187

Army Form C. 2121
(In pads of 100.)

MESSAGES AND SIGNALS.

No. of Message..........

Prefix.......... Code..........m. | Words. | Charge.
Office of Origin and Service Instructions.

Sent
At..........m.
To..........
By..........

This message is on a/c of:
..........Service.
(Signature of "Franking Officer.")

Recd. at..........m.
Date..........
From A35
By..........

TO { 1/8 L.F.
126 I.B.

Sender's Number.	Day of Month.	In reply to Number.	AAA
* BM 141	28		

Ref my BM 139 of today aaa Orders is confirmed aaa There 2 Coys will move off at once on arrival of guides aaa 1/8 L.F. [illegible] 126 I.B.

From 125 I.B.
Place
Time 1.0 AM

The above may be forwarded as now corrected. (Z)
Censor. [illegible] Capt
Signature of Addressor or person authorised to telegraph in his name.
* This line should be erased if not required.

(7981) Wt. W492/M1647 130,000 Pads 5/17 D. D. & L. E1187

"A" Form
MESSAGES AND SIGNALS.

Army Form C. 2121
(In pads of 100.)

No. of Message..........

Prefix.......... Code..........m. | Words. | Charge.
Office of Origin and Service Instructions.

Sent
At..........m.
To..........
By..........

This message is on a/c of:
..........Service.
(Signature of "Franking Officer.")

Recd. at..........m.
Date..........
From A36
By..........

TO { Composite M G Squadron
1/7 N.F. Pioneers.

Sender's Number.	Day of Month.	In reply to Number.	AAA
* BM 142	28		

The situation on left flank of 126 I.B. now appears to be clear & there are no enemy in the [illegible] valley aaa Composite MG Squadron will however remain in their present positions & 1/7 N.F. Pioneers will be prepared to move immediately should necessity arise aaa Addsd Composite MG Squadron & 1/7 N.F. Pioneers.

From 125 I.B.
Place
Time 1.30 AM

The above may be forwarded as now corrected. (Z)
Censor. [illegible] Capt
Signature of Addressor or person authorised to telegraph in his name.
* This line should be erased if not required.

(7981) Wt. W492/M1647 130,000 Pads 5/17 D. D. & L. E1187

within a hundred yards of the British trenches.

"A" Form
MESSAGES AND SIGNALS.

Army Form C. 2121 (In pads of 100)

No. of Message.............

Prefix........ Code........m. | Words. | Charge.

Office of Origin and Service Instructions

Sent At........m. To........ By........

This message is on a/c of: ....Service.

(Signature of "Franking Officer.")

Recd. at........m. Date........ From A37 By........

TO: 1/7th L F / 127 I B

Sender's Number.	Day of Month.	In reply to Number.	AAA
BM 148	28		

Ref BM 138 of yesterday [illegible] Move the 2 Coys forward at once to reinforce as arranged [illegible] addsd. 1/7th L F repeated 127 I B.

From 125 I B
Place
Time 9.45 AM

The above may be forwarded as now corrected. (Z) .... Censor.

[signature] Signature of Addressor or person authorised to telegraph in his name.

* This line should be erased if not required.

(7981) Wt. W492/M1647 130,000 Pads 5/17 D. D. & L. E1187

"A" Form
MESSAGES AND SIGNALS.

Army Form C. 2121 (In pads of 100)

No. of Message.............

Prefix........ Code........m. | Words. | Charge.

Office of Origin and Service Instructions

Sent At........m. To........ By........

This message is on a/c of: ....Service.

(Signature of "Franking Officer.")

Recd. at........m. Date........ From A38 By........

TO: 1/7 L F / ~~[illegible]~~ / 127 I B

Sender's Number.	Day of Month.	In reply to Number.	AAA
BM 149	28		

~~[illegible]~~ Send up remaining 2 Coys at once to reinforce 127 I B [illegible] They should report to O C Bn 127 I B to be in support HQ F.28 a 0.9, [illegible] occupy BEATHCRWN [illegible] road from F 27 b 8.5 Northward [illegible] addsd. 1/7th L F [illegible] 127 I B

From 125 I B
Place
Time 11.25 AM

The above may be forwarded as now corrected. (Z) .... Censor.

[signature] Signature of Addressor or person authorised to telegraph in his name.

* This line should be erased if not required.

(7981) Wt. W492/M1647 130,000 Pads 5/17 D. D. & L. E1187

of men of the

Infantry Regiment (both belonging to the

Reinforcements of A Squadron of the 5th Dragoon Guards

MESSAGES AND SIGNALS.

No. of Message........

Prefix........ Code........m. | Words. | Charge. | This message is on a/c of: ....Service. | Recd. at........m. | Date........ | From A39 | By........

Office of Origin and Service Instructions. Sent At........m. To........ By........ (Signature of "Franking Officer.")

TO 1/7th N.F Pioneers

Sender's Number.	Day of Month.	In reply to Number.	AAA
* BM 150	28		

Your Battn will move forward at once to occupy the position vacated by the 1/7th L.F who have advanced to reinforce the 127th I.B. This position consists of support trenches in F.20 with HQrs at F.20 b 6.3 where OC 1/7 L.F will be waiting [on your arrival] to help put your Bn in these trenches. Please call at Bde HQrs on the way up.

From 125th Inf Bde

Place

Time 11.45 AM

The above may be forwarded as now corrected. (Z)

Censor. [illegible] Col. Signature of Addressor or person authorised to telegraph in his name.

* This line should be erased if not required.

(7981) Wt. W492/M1647 130,000 Pads 5/17 D. D. & L. E1187

MESSAGES AND SIGNALS.

(In pads of 100) No. of Message........

Prefix........ Code........m. | Words. | Charge. | This message is on a/c of: ....Service. | Recd. at........m. | Date........ | From AFO | By........

Office of Origin and Service Instructions. Sent At........m. To........ By........ (Signature of "Franking Officer.")

TO 42nd Divn, 5th L.F, 8th L.F, Comp. M.G. Squadron

Sender's Number.	Day of Month.	In reply to Number.	AAA
* BM 152	28		

Operations & situation report AAA In response to request from 127 I.B 2 Coys of 7th L.F were moved up to reinforce 127 I.B at 9.45 AM & remaining 2 Coys at 11.25 AM AAA 1/7 N.F. Pioneers have been moved up to replace 7th L.F in support trenches in F.20 AAA The 127 I.B report that they were attacked at 10.30 AM & that they met the attack in the open & drove the enemy back AAA The 127 I.B also report that at 11.15 AM the enemy appeared to be advancing again from LOSGAIT [?] WOOD AAA An officer of the 7th N.F. Pioneers reports

From

Place

Time

The above may be forwarded as now corrected. (Z)

Censor. Signature of Addressor or person authorised to telegraph in his name.

* This line should be erased if not required.

(7981) Wt. W492/M1647 130,000 Pads 5/17 D. D. & L. E1187

A Form
MESSAGES AND SIGNALS.

(In pads of 100.) No. of Message........

Prefix........ Code........ m. | Words. | Charge. | This message is on a/c of: | Recd. at........ m.
Office of Origin and Service Instructions | Sent At........ m. To........ By........ | .... Service. (Signature of "Franking Officer.") | Date........ From........ By........

TO (2)

Sender's Number. | Day of Month. | In reply to Number. | AAA

from forward at 11.25 AM a dense smoke barrage has been placed in the valley between COURCELETTE - ABLAINZEVELLE RIDGE + the AYETTE - ABLAINZEVELLE Road At 11.30 AM he reports this smoke barrage has extended further N towards aerodrome between AYETTE + MOYENVILLE [illegible] Phosphorus shells being used in the ground line AYETTE - ABLAINZEVELLE [illegible] Shelling behind ABLAINZEVELLE - BUCQUOY ridge still severe [illegible] 126, 127 Bdes + gunners have been informed of smoke barrage and also 42 Div. [illegible] 5th + 8th C. [illegible] for information.

From 125 I.B.
Place
Time 12.45 PM

The above may be forwarded as now corrected. (Z)
Censor. [illegible] Capt.
Signature of Addressor or person authorised to telegraph in his name.

* This line should be erased if not required.

(7981) Wt. W492/M1647 130,000 Pads 5/17 D. D. & L. E1187

An attack against the 9th

MESSAGES AND SIGNALS.

(In pads of 100.) No. of Message........

Code........ m. | Words. | Charge. | This message is on a/c of: | Recd. at........ m.
Office of Origin and Service Instructions | Sent At........ m. To........ By........ | .... Service. (Signature of "Franking Officer.") | Date A40 From........ By........

TO 1/5 L F, 1/7 L F, 1/8 L F, 1/7 N F Pioneers, 427 Field Coy R E, 126 I B, 127 I B, 185 I B, 42 Division

Sender's Number. B M 156 | Day of Month. 28 | In reply to Number. | AAA

Relief orders

(1) The 125 I B together with two companies 1/7 N F Pioneers and 427 Field Coy R E will relieve the 185 I B and part of the 127 I B on the line tonight

(2) The 7 L F will relieve 1/5 + 1/7 Manchesters between the limits F 28 c 75 and F 28 b 35 starting at 9 p.m. All details will be arranged between C.O.s concerned. H.Q. 7 L F will be at F 28 a 08. 7 L F will [illegible] 2 guides for support locality at F 20 d + F 26 b for 1/7 Manchesters to report at once to 127 I B report centre F 28 a 08

(3) [illegible] 1/5 L F will relieve 2 coys 2/7th W Yorks and A Coy of 1/5th W Yorks in the southern sub sector of the 185 I B front from L 3 a 9 1 to BUCQUOY - ACHIET-LE-PETIT road L 4 a 4 0 inclusive with dispositions as follows

From
Place
Time

The above may be forwarded as now corrected. (Z)
Censor.
Signature of Addressor or person authorised to telegraph in his name.

* This line should be erased if not required.

(7981) Wt. W492/M1647 130,000 Pads 5/17 D. D. & L. E1187

MESSAGES AND SIGNALS.

No. of Message........

Prefix ... Code ... m. Office of Origin and Service Instructions	Words. Charge.	This message is on a/c of: ... Service. (Signature of "Franking Officer.")	Recd. at ... m. Date ... From ... By ...
	Sent At ... m. To ... By ...		

TO 2

Sender's Number.	Day of Month.	In reply to Number.	AAA

1 Coy in front line, 1 Coy in support 1 Coy in reserve H^d Q^rs at F 26. d 0 0.
The 18th L F will supply two guides for support locality in F 20 a for 1/5 Manchesters to report at once to 127 I B report centre at F 28 a 08
3 (b) Two companies 1/7th N F Pioneers and the 427 Field Company R E will relieve two companies 2/7 W Yorks and 1 Coy 2/5th W Yorks in the Northern sub-sector of the 185 I B front from the BUCQUOY – ACHIET-LE-PETIT road L 4 a 40 excl to F 28 c 75
disposition 1½ Coys in front line ½ Coy in support
headquarters F 27 d 35
3 (c) 18th L F will relieve 2 Coys of 2/5th W Yorks and 2 Coys 8 W Yorks in squares F 26 c + d H^d Q^rs at F 26 d 99.

From
Place
Time

The above may be forwarded as now corrected. (Z)
Censor. Signature of Addressor or person authorised to telegraph in his name.

* This line should be erased if not required.

(7981) Wt. W493/M1647 130,000 Pads 5/17 D. D. & L. E1187

MESSAGES AND SIGNALS.

(In pads of 100)

No. of Message........

Prefix ... Code ... m. Office of Origin and Service Instructions	Words. Charge.	This message is on a/c of: ... Service. (Signature of "Franking Officer.")	Recd. at ... m. Date ... From ... By ...
	Sent At ... m. To ... By ...		

TO 3

Sender's Number.	Day of Month.	In reply to Number.	AAA

18 L F will provide two guides for [illegible] area for 1/6 Manchesters to report at once to 127 I B report centre F 28 a 08
3 (d) Guides for relief of units of 185 I B will be met as follows
Rendezvous junction of light railway and trench F 26 d 99
45 L F 7 pm
47 N F Pioneers + 427 Field Coy R E 9.30 pm
48 L F 10 pm
The 427 Field Coy R E will meet the 1/7 N F Pioneers at time stated at above rendezvous
(4) All tools and S O S signals in possession will be carried into the trenches
5 Bde H Q will remain in present position F 24 d 77
(6) Completion of relief to be reported by code word BINGE

From 7. Acknowledge
Place 125 I B
Time 8.30 pm

The above may be forwarded as now corrected. (Z) [signature] Col.
Censor. Signature of Addressor or person authorised to telegraph in his name.

* This line should be erased if not required.

(7981) Wt. W493/M1647 130,000 Pads 5/17 D. D. & L. E1187

were the first to get into Messines at its north-eastern corner at 10 a.m. "Ypres 1914" p.80. The Regimental History of the 122nd

MESSAGES AND SIGNALS. (In pads of 100.) No. of Message........

Prefix........ Code........ m. | Words. | Charge. | This message is on a/c of: .... Service. | Recd. at .... m. | Date........ | From A42 | By........

Office of Origin and Service Instructions. Sheet 57 D. N.E. 1/20000

Sent At........m. To........ By........ (Signature of "Franking Officer.")

TO 1/5 L.F. 125 T.M.B. 124 I.B.
1/7 L.F. 1/1 N.F. Pioneers 126 I.B.
1/8 L.F. 427 Field Co. 186 I.B. 42 Div. D. Grp R.F.A.

Sender's Number.	Day of Month.	In reply to Number.	AAA
B.M.163	29		

Relief orders.

(1) The 126 I.B. will be relieved in the line tonight by the 124 I.B. and on relief will occupy positions in GOMMECOURT line.

(2)(a) 1/5 L.F. 427 Field Coy R.E. and B. Coy 1/7 N.F. Pioneers will be relieved by the 20th D.L.I. in the right subsector from right boundary L.3.d.9.1 – front line trench square L.4 and F.28.

(2)(b) 'C' Coy 1/7 N.F. Pioneers and 1/7 L.F. will be relieved by 26th Royal Fusiliers in the left sub-sector from front line as above to left boundary F.28.b.3.5.

(2)(c) 1/8 L.F. in support will be relieved by the 10th Queens.

(3) Guides will be provided 1 per coy and 1 per headquarters of units as

From
Place
Time
The above may be forwarded as now corrected. (Z)
Censor. Signature of Addressor or person authorised to telegraph in his name.
* This line should be erased if not required.
(3796.) Wt. W492/M1647. 650,000 Pads. 5/17. H. W. & V., Ld. (E. 1187.)

General Briggs, and received authority to
withdraw the 9th Lancers from the eastern

"A" Form. Army Form C. 2121. **MESSAGES AND SIGNALS.** (In pads of 100.) No. of Message........

Prefix........ Code........ m. | Words. | Charge. | This message is on a/c of: .... Service. | Recd. at .... m. | Date........ | From........ | By........

Office of Origin and Service Instructions.

Sent At........m. To........ By........ (Signature of "Franking Officer.")

TO

Sender's Number.	Day of Month.	In reply to Number.	AAA

follows.

Rendezvous: Junction of road and light railway F.27.c.1.9. for 20 D.L.I. at 10 p.m. for 26 Royal Fusiliers at 10.30 p.m. for 10 Queens at 11 p.m.

(4) On relief units will be disposed as follows

427 Field Coy R.E. will move independently and rejoin Div. Engineers at N.W. corner of GOMMECOURT WOOD E.28.b.6.2

Infantry Battns & Pioneer Batt will occupy positions in GOMMECOURT line in depth with line of posts in front.

8th L.F. Right front from L.5.d.8.7 – road E.29 to 2.1. Headquarters E.29.c.5.1.

7th L.F. Left front from road as above to about E.24.c.4.6. H.Q. E.29.a.7.5

From
Place
Time
The above may be forwarded as now corrected. (Z)
Censor. Signature of Addressor or person authorised to telegraph in his name.
* This line should be erased if not required.
(3796.) Wt. W492/M1647. 650,000 Pads. 5/17. H. W. & V., Ld. (E. 1187.)

MESSAGES AND SIGNALS.

No. of Message..............

Prefix........ Code........ m. | Words. | Charge.
Office of Origin and Service Instructions.
Sent At........ m. To........ By........
This message is on a/c of: .... Service. (Signature of "Franking Officer.")
Recd. at .... m. Date........ From........ By........

TO 3

Sender's Number.	Day of Month.	In reply to Number.	A A A

5th L.F. support trenches square E 28 d. Hd Qrs E 28 d 73.

1/7 N.F. Pioneers. Reserve. Trenches about Gird line between squares E 27 b and E 28 a. Hd Qrs E 27 b 79.

(5) Route out: BUCQUOY – ESSARTS road – cross roads F 19 c 82 – GOMMECOURT road.

Guides to conduct Battns to their respective areas as above will be waiting at corner of wood E 30 a 03.

(6) S.O.S. signals and a certain proportion of Tools will be handed over on relief.

(7) Bde Hd Qrs will move to position in E 28 d central on completion of relief. exact location will be notified later. 125th T.M.B. will move off with Bde Hd Qrs.

From
Place
Time

The above may be forwarded as now corrected. (Z)
Censor. Signature of Addressor or person authorised to telegraph in his name.

* This line should be erased if not required.

(3796.) Wt. W 492/M1647. 650,000 Pads. 5/17. H. W. & V., Ld. (E. 1187.)

was

MESSAGES AND SIGNALS.

No. of Message..............

Prefix........ Code........ m. | Words. | Charge.
Office of Origin and Service Instructions.
Sent At........ m. To........ By........
This message is on a/c of: .... Service. (Signature of "Franking Officer.")
Recd. at .... m. Date........ From........ By........

TO 4

Sender's Number.	Day of Month.	In reply to Number.	A A A

(8) Completion of relief will be reported to these Hd Qrs by code word BLIND.

(9) Acknowledge.

From 125 I.B.
Place
Time 8 p. m.

The above may be forwarded as now corrected. (Z) [illegible] Capt
Censor. Signature of Addressor or person authorised to telegraph in his name.

* This line should be erased if not required.

(3796.) Wt. W 492/M1647. 650,000 Pads. 5/17. H. W. & V., Ld. (E. 1187.)

Own Scottish Borderers and the 2/King's Own
Yorkshire Light Infantry of the 13th Infantry

"A" Form.

Army Form C. 2121.
(In pads of 100.)

MESSAGES AND SIGNALS.

No. of Message..........

Prefix..... Code..... m	Words.	Charge.	This message is on a/c of:	Recd. at ..... m.
Office of Origin and Service Instructions.	Sent		File ..... Service.	Date.....
	At..... m.			From 1143
	To.....			
	By.....		(Signature of "Franking Officer.")	By.....

TO
5 & 7 — 125. T.M.B.
7 & 7. — 126. M.G. Coy.
8 & 7. — 1/7 N.F. PIONEERS.

Sender's Number.	Day of Month.	In reply to Number.	AAA
* BM. 175	31		

WARNING ORDER.

The 125 Infy Bde together with the 126th M.G. Co + 1/7 N.F. PIONEERS will relieve the 124th Infy Bde + 19th Middlesex PIONEERS + 1 M.G. Coy 41st Div in the Right Sub sector of the 41st Div front tomorrow night April 1/2nd aaa First Bn will ~~[illegible]~~ probably meet guides at 9.0 pm. aaa Detailed orders will follow.

From 125 I/Bde
Place
Time 11-30 Am.

The above may be forwarded as now corrected. (Z) ..... Censor.

AMcNicholas Capt.
Signature of Addressor or person authorised to telegraph in his name.

* This line should be erased if not required.

(5198.) Wt. W 12952/M1294. 375,000 Pads. 1/17. H. W. & V., Ld. (E. 818.)

42nd Div.
IV.Corps.

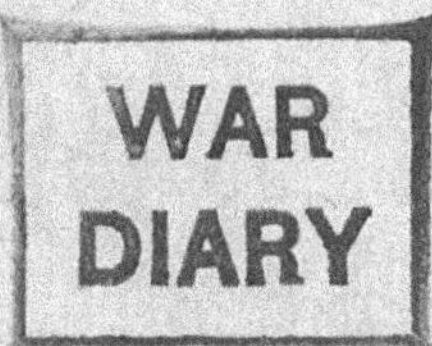

Headquarters,

125th INFANTRY BRIGADE.

A P R I L

1 9 1 8

Attached:

Appendices 1 to 31.

21

Vol 15

CONFIDENTIAL

125 Inf. Bde.

WAR DIARY

VOL. 46.

1st - 30 APRIL 1918.

Instructions regarding War Diaries and Intelligence Summaries are contained in F. S. Regs., Part II. and the Staff Manual respectively. Title Pages will be prepared in manuscript.

PAGE 1.

Vol. No 46.

WAR DIARY
or
~~INTELLIGENCE SUMMARY~~ of

(Erase heading not required.)

125 Inf. Bde.

APRIL 1918.

Army Form C. 2118

Place	Date	Hour	Summary of Events and Information	Remarks and references to Appendices
57D N.E. GOMMECOURT E 28d 66	1	2.15pm	BM 178 issued ordering relief	A 1
ESSARTS E24d79		11. pm	Bde HQrs moved to ESSARTS.	MB
—"—	2.	1.45 am	relief complete	
		4.0 am	Situation unchanged & quiet	
		10. am	Situation unchanged & quiet.	
		3 pm.	GS 120/4/E received & sent out to Batts, re organisation of defences in depth. This warned 1/7 & 1/8 LFs to be prepared to take over further portion of front with grid line between F28 & L4 as boundary & to organize their defences in depth on that basis.	
		4.30 pm	Situation unchanged.	
		10 pm.	Situation unchanged. Bde HQrs heavily shelled from 4.45 pm – 9 pm. with bursts of 4.2s. Front areas quiet.	
		10. pm	Wounded prisoner of 90 Fus Regt. 17 Div captured in F 28C by 1/7 N.F. Pioneers during an offensive patrol on new enemy work in F28d. Patrol reported work as consisting of at least 6 slit trenches, occupied by enemy in strength. Trench strength of Bde.	MB
—"—	3	4.55 am	Situation unchanged & quiet	
		10.10 am	Situation unchanged & quiet. BUCQUOY bombed by EA at 8 am	
		1.45 pm	BM 198 issued regarding relief of 1/7 N.F.	A2
		4.30 pm	Situation unchanged. Some shelling of front line from direction of LOGEAST WOOD. Spasmodic shelling of BUCQUOY.	
		10. pm.	Situation unchanged & quiet. Enemy dump at ACHIET-LE-GRAND exploded at 8.30 pm still burning.	MB

1875 Wt. W593/826 1,000,000 4/15 J.B.C. & A. A.D.S.S./Forms/C. 2118.

Army Form C. 2118

Instructions regarding War Diaries and Intelligence Summaries are contained in F. S. Regs., Part II. and the Staff Manual respectively. Title Pages will be prepared in manuscript.

PAGE 2.

WAR DIARY
or
~~INTELLIGENCE SUMMARY~~

(Erase heading not required.)

125 Inf Bde

APRIL 1918.

Place	Date	Hour	Summary of Events and Information	Remarks and references to Appendices
57D NE ESSARTS E24d79	4	4.30a.m.	Situation unchanged & quiet	
		6 a.m.	Brigadier & Bde. Major went round the trenches in front of BUCQUOY & gave personal instructions to C.O's that further reorganisation in depth should take place	
		7 a.m.	Examination of 2 prisoners of 90 Fus. Regt. 17 Div, captured at 4.45 a.m by 1/7 L.F in F28d. They knew nothing of impending operations but confirmed Div relief on night of 1/2 nd April.	
		10.20a.m.	Situation unchanged. Few heavy shells at intervals in BUCQUOY	
		4.50p.m.	Situation quiet & unchanged. Batt. H.Qrs. F27d35 shelled during afternoon. A 6" How shoot on new enemy work in F28d had been arranged for this day, but had to be postponed owing to lack of communication by RGA, due to scarcity of cable.	
		10.20p.m.	Situation unchanged & quiet. Some shelling of BUCQUOY - ESSARTS - HANNESCAMPS RD.	MJ
— " —	5	5.a.m.	Heavy shelling on Bde front, gas & H.E in valley between ESSARTS & BUCQUOY & in ESSARTS. Heavy shelling with 5.9's on BUCQUOY – HANNESCAMPS RD. at 5.30a.m. right Bde of 37th Div. on our right attacked.	
		9a.m	Verbal message received from right group RFA that S.O.S had been sent up.	
		10.30a.m	Situation:- No reports received from forward. Heavy shelling, including gas, of ESSARTS & main road. all lines down. Message sent by wireless.	
		10.30a.m.	Message by runner timed 9.8a.m received from 1/7 L.F. Stating situation unchanged since 5.30a.m. Heavy hostile shelling of wood near batt H.Qrs. at F27d53. At same hour, untimed message received by runner from 1/7 LF, stating enemy are in 1/8 L.F left Coy's front trenches Am forming a right defensive flank.	
		11.a.m.	BM254 sent to Div. by D.R.	A 3
		~~11.50a.m.~~	~~Message received from 1/5 L.F Coys are being extended in battle positions in support of~~ 1/8 L.F.	
		~~12.10p.m.~~	~~BM 251. sent to Div.~~	

1875 Wt. W593/826 1,000,000 4/15 J.B.C. & A. A.D.S.S./Forms/C. 2118.

Army Form C. 2118

Instructions regarding War Diaries and Intelligence Summaries are contained in F. S. Regs., Part II. and the Staff Manual respectively. Title Pages will be prepared in manuscript.

page 3
Vol. 46

WAR DIARY or ~~INTELLIGENCE~~ SUMMARY

(Erase heading not required.)

125 Inf. Bde. APRIL 1918.

Place	Date	Hour	Summary of Events and Information	Remarks and references to Appendices
57D N.E. ESSARTS. E24d79.	5	11.30 a.m.	Message received by runner from A Coy 42 Div M.G. Batt. reporting that his left Battery at F26d95 report enemy had broken through left flank of 1/8 L.F.	
		11.40 a.m.	Right Liaison officer reported to his group that he had been sent back by O.C 1/8 L.F as all lines were down. He reports line about L4a broken. i.e. left of right batt.	
		11.40 a.m.	BM 256 sent out	A 4
		11.45 a.m.	Message received from 1/5. L.F. Coy are being extended in battle positions in support of 1/8. L.F.	
		12.18 p.m.	BM 251 sent to Div.	A5
		12.30 p.m.	234. received by runner from 1/8. L.F	A6
		12.30 p.m.	In consequence BM 258 sent out	A7.
		12.45 p.m.	Message received by power buzzer from 1/5 L.F. to say that 2 platoons had been sent up to reinforce 1/8 L.F. at their request.	
		12.50 p.m.	BM 259 Situation report sent to Div.	
		1.30 p.m.	237, timed 12.50 p.m. received from 1/8 L.F	A8.
		1.40 p.m.	1/8 L.F informed that 2 MGs. had been ordered to report to their Hqrs from B. Coy 42 MG batt.	A9
		1.55 p.m.	241. timed 1.26 p.m. received from 1/8 L.F	A10
		2.5. p.m.	Message from 1/7 L.F. timed 1.10 p.m received:- My right quite all right. Have formed defensive flank with Support Coy from my original right to Batt HQ. F27d53. 1/8th L.F have not yet got in touch with my right.	
		2.20 p.m.	BM 261. sent to Div.	A11
		2.27. p.m.	Situation explained to 1/7. L.F.	
		2.55 p.m.	Telephone message from 1/5 L.F to effect that 2 Coy moved off to counterattack with 1/8 L.F at 2 p.m. LT. Col. O.St.L. DAVIES. OC. 1/8. L.F. badly wounded.	
		3.30 p.m.	244. timed 2.15 p.m. received from 1/8 L.F.	A12
		3.30 p.m.	Adj. 1/8 L.F telephones that 1/5 L.F are assembling for counter attack after a preliminary reconnaissance by Major CASTLE MC. LT. Col. O.St.L. DAVIES O.C 1/8 L.F. died of wounds.	

1875 Wt. W593/826 1,000,000 4/15 J.B.C. & A. A.D.S.S./Forms/C. 2118.

Instructions regarding War Diaries and Intelligence Summaries are contained in F. S. Regs., Part II. and the Staff Manual respectively. Title Pages will be prepared in manuscript.

Army Form C. 2118

WAR DIARY
or
~~INTELLIGENCE SUMMARY~~
(Erase heading not required.)

PAGE 4
VOL. 46.

of 125 Inf. Bde.

APRIL 1918.

Place	Date	Hour	Summary of Events and Information	Remarks and references to Appendices
57D N.E. ESSARTS E24d79.	5	4 p.m.	B 20. timed 3.5 p.m. received from 1/7. L.F.	A13
		4.30 p.m.	Message received from 1/5 L.F. stating counterattack would be at 4.30 p.m., C.O.s of 1/5. 1/8 L.F.s & 13 R.F. having arranged this in conjunction.	
		4.30 p.m.	42 Div. Warning O. No 7. ordering relief on nights of 7/8. 8/9th April. Batts informed	
		4.45 p.m.	BM 265 sent to Div.	A14
		5. p.m.	Telephone message from 1/7. L.F. stating they were unable to get touch with 1/5 & 1/8 L.F. Patrols had pushed down to main X roads in BUCQUOY.	
		6.15 p.m.	Enemy reported by R.F.A. to be massing on ridge S. of LOGEAST WOOD.	
		6.30 p.m.	246 received from 1/8 L.F. timed 5.45 p.m. Counterattack going well so far. Little opposition. Line advanced to X roads. 1/7 L.F. in touch with 1/5 L.F.	
		7.15 p.m.	B.20 received from 1/7. L.F. timed 6.30 p.m.	A15
		7.15 p.m.	In consequence, Div. asked for reinforcements.	
		7.30 p.m.	250 timed 7. p.m. received from 1/8 L.F.	
		7.45 p.m.	Batt. of 126 I Bde. placed at disposal of 125 Bde by Div. Hence BM 268 sent to Batts	A16
		7.45 p.m.	Situation as follows reported by 1/7. L.F. timed 7. p.m. - 1/5 L.F. in touch with my right. Major Castle R.E. is moving up remaining Coy to form a right defensive flank & will send out patrols to get touch with 37 Div. Lt Col. Clive, C.O. 1/5. L.F. has been killed. 1/8 L.F. have only one remaining combatant officer.	A17
		8.10 p.m.	W. 33 received from 1/5. L.F. Div. & flanking Bdes informed.	
		8.25 p.m.	126 I. Bde informed us 1/5. E. Lancs. Regt. standing to, ready to move under our orders, but not to be employed forward of F26d, unless urgent necessity compelled it.	A18
		9.0 p.m.	B29 received from 1/7 L.F.	A19
		9.30 p.m.	Message timed 8.50 p.m. from 1/7 L.F. reporting situation quiet.	

1875 Wt. W593/826 1,000,000 4/15 J.B.C. & A. A.D.S.S./Forms/C. 2118.

Army Form C. 2118

Instructions regarding War Diaries and Intelligence Summaries are contained in F. S. Regs., Part II. and the Staff Manual respectively. Title Pages will be prepared in manuscript.

PAGE 6.
Vol 46

WAR DIARY
or
~~INTELLIGENCE SUMMARY~~
(Erase heading not required.)

of 125 Inf. Bde APRIL 1918

Place	Date	Hour	Summary of Events and Information	Remarks and references to Appendices
57D NE. ESSARTS F24d79.	6	8.pm.	1/5. L.F. report capture of 1 prisoner by patrol in L3C at 6. p.m. He belonged to Sharpshooter Detachment. M.G. Coy. 17 Div.	
		8.30pm.	Congratulations from Lord Mayor of Manchester received	A25
		11.55pm.	1/5. L.F. report front line from L3b47 – L3a84, where touch is gained with A Coy. Bedfords, held by 2 Coys. 3rd Coy in yellow line in F26d.	MB
—"—	7	2.25am.	relief complete	
		3.2am.	Batts told that our artillery would bombard likely places of assembly & lines of approach opposite Bde front from 4.40am – 5.a.m.	
		4.45am.	Situation unchanged & quiet.	
		7.35am.	Artillery opened on S.O.S lines in response to signal on 1/5th L.F front. Enemy reported assembling in 3 waves with scouts in front in L10a & L16b.	
		8.30am.	Our guns reported firing a little too long & too far N. Left group of Div. on right cooperated. No infantry attack developed.	
		9.40am.	Enemy reported thick in our old trenches in L4a & b. Artillery dealt with this. No infantry attack developed.	
		2.45pm.	Bde O. 75 issued	A26
		4.30pm.	Situation unchanged & quiet.	
		6.45pm.	Addendum No1. to O. No 75 issued.	A27.
		10.15.pm.	Situation unchanged & quiet	
		11.45pm.	all battalions except 1/8 Manch Regt reported relief complete.	MB

1875 Wt. W593/826 1,000,000 4/15 J.B.C. & A. A.D.S.S./Forms/C. 2118.

Army Form C. 2118

WAR DIARY
or
~~INTELLIGENCE SUMMARY~~ of 125 Inf. Bde.

Instructions regarding War Diaries and Intelligence Summaries are contained in F. S. Regs., Part II. and the Staff Manual respectively. Title Pages will be prepared in manuscript.

page 7.
Vol 46.

(Erase heading not required.)

APRIL 1918.

Place	Date	Hour	Summary of Events and Information	Remarks and references to Appendices
57D N.E. ESSARTS E24d79. 57D. VAUCHELLES I 32b87	8	2.a.m	Message received timed 12.35a.m. from 185 I. Bde stating relief complete. This was not accepted no message having been received from 1/8 Manch. Regt. On enquiry it was found that 185 I. Bde had refused to relieve left Centre Coy of 1/8 Manch. Regt, as apparently they had not brought up enough men. This was confirmed by 1/8 Manch. Regt. by wire timed 5.50a.m. Bde HQ. closed at ESSARTS at 4a.m. & reopened at VAUCHELLES at 6.30.a.m.	
		4p.m.	1/7 L.F moved from billets in MARIEUX to VAUCHELLES.	
—"—	9		Brigade in rest, in IV Corps Reserve.	
—"—	10	3.a.m	Brigade received orders to be ready to move at half an hours notice between 5 am & 9.a.m. Brigade in rest.	
—"— 57D. VAUCHELLES. I 32b 19	11.	4.p.m.	Bde Hqrs moved to School Camp. Brigade in rest.	
—"—	12.		Div. Order No 9 received.	
		2.p.m.	In consequence Bde.O. 76 was issued, ordering move of Bde. group to WARNIMONT WOOD & ST LEGER. Brigade in rest.	A28
—"— ST. LEGER. I 12c17	13.	6a.m.	Bde Hqrs opened at ST LEGER.	

1875 Wt. W593/826 1,000,000 4/15 J.B.C. & A. A.D.S.S./Forms/C. 2118.

Army Form C. 2118

WAR DIARY
or
INTELLIGENCE ~~SUMMARY~~
(Erase heading not required.)

Instructions regarding War Diaries and Intelligence Summaries are contained in F. S. Regs., Part II. and the Staff Manual respectively. Title Pages will be prepared in manuscript.

Vol 46 page 8 of 125 Inf Bde APRIL 1918,

Place	Date	Hour	Summary of Events and Information	Remarks and references to Appendices
57D. ST. LEGER. I12c17	14.		Bde in rest.	
— " —	15.	8.p.m.	Order No10 received from Div. ordering Bde to relieve 112 Bde in line. In consequence Bde O. No 77 was issued	A29
— " — 57D. N.E. GOMMECOURT. E28d89	16	8.30.pm	Bde Hqrs opened in GOMMECOURT WOOD.	
— " —	17.		Situation quiet.	
57DNE. E27c96	18.	6.pm	Bde Hqrs moved to FONQUEVILLERS. Situation quiet.	
— " —	19		Situation unchanged & quiet.	
— " —	20		— " —	
— " —	21		— " —	
— " —	22		— " — Div. O. No 12 received	
— " —	23	8pm	In consequence. Bde O. No 78	A 30
— " —	24		Situation unchanged & quiet.	

1875 Wt. W593/826 1,000,000 4/15 J.B.C. & A. A.D.S.S./Forms/C. 2118.

Army Form C. 2118.

WAR DIARY
or
~~INTELLIGENCE SUMMARY.~~

(*Erase heading not required.*)

Instructions regarding War Diaries and Intelligence Summaries are contained in F. S. Regs., Part II. and the Staff Manual respectively. Title pages will be prepared in manuscript.

page 9
Vol. 46.

125 Inf Bde.

APRIL.

Place	Date	Hour	Summary of Events and Information	Remarks and references to Appendices
57D NE E27C96 FONQUEVILLERS	25.		Bde in line on right. Situation quiet.	
	26.		Situation quiet.	
	27.		Situation quiet. Order No 14 received from Div. In consequence Bde O. No 79 issued	A31.
57D NE COUIN. J1d65	28.		Situation quiet. Bde H.Q.'s opened at COUIN. Total casualties 16/4/18 – 28/4/18 Killed 3. O.R. Wounded 2 OFF. 51 O.R.	
	29.		Bde in Div. Reserve.	
	30.		Bde in Div. Reserve.	
				MB.

Hanna Forgus [signature]

Brig. Gen

Comdg 125. Inf Bde

2/5/18.

A P P E N D I C E S

1 to 31 .

SECRET & URGENT.

FILE

B.M. 178
1-4-18.

A1

Ref 57 D.N.E. 1:20.000.

1/5 L.F.	1/7 N.F. Pioneers	Rt Group R.F.A.
1/7 L.F.	C Coy 42 M.G. Bn.	42 Division
1/8 L.F.	112th I.B.	
	124th I.B.	
125 T.M.B.	126th I.B.	

RELIEF ORDER

1. The 125th I.B. together with the 1/7 N.F. Pioneers will relieve the 124th I.B. + 1 Bn of the 122nd I.B in the line tonight, between the limits L 3 d. 9 1 Right Boundary to F 28. b 3.5. Left Boundary.

2 (a) The 1/8 L.F. will relieve the 20th D.L.I. from Rt Boundary to Road inclusive L 4 a 66 - H.Qrs F 26. d 0.0.

(b) The 1/7 N.F. Pioneers will relieve the 10th Queens from Road exclusive L 4 a. 66. to F 28. c 8.4. H.Qrs. F 27. d. 3.5.

(c) The 1/7 L.F. will relieve the 26 R.F.s from F. 28. c 8.4. to Left Boundary - H.Qrs with 1/7 N.F. Pioneers at F. 27. d 3.5

(d) The 1/5 L.F. will relieve the 12th E. Surreys, 122nd I.B. in Support in Squares F 26 c + d. H.Qrs. F. 26 d 8.9.

All details of relief will be arranged between C.O.s concerned.

3 Guides will be met as follows:—
Rendezvous junction of Light Railway & Road. F 27. c. 1.9.

(2)

for 1/5 L.F. — 9-0 pm.
1/7 L.F. — 9-30 pm.
1/8 N.F. Pioneers — 10-0 pm.
1/8 L.F. — 10-30 pm.

4. 125 T.M.B. will relieve the 124 T.M.B. in the line under arrangements to be made between C.Os concerned.
5. 'B' Coy 42nd M.G. Bn will support the Bde & is relieving one Coy of the 41st M.G. Bn. in the line tonight.
6. The troops on our flanks with whom touch will be maintained are - On our Rt 112th I.B., 37 Divn & on our left 126th I.B.
7. All maps, programmes of work, S.O.S. Signals, Tools, Petrol Tins etc. will be taken over from relieved units.
8. Bde H.Qrs will close in GOMMECOURT Wood at 11-0 pm & reopen at ESSARTS E.24.d.7.9. at same hour.
9. Completion of relief will be reported to these H.Qrs by Code Word "MACDONALD"
10. ACKNOWLEDGE

1-4/18

[signature] Capt.
a/Bde Major
125 Bde.

Issued by orderly at 2.15 pm.

(A2)

SECRET + URGENT.

Ref 57 D.N.E. 1:20.000. FILE. B.M. 198
3-4-18.

1/5 L.F.
1/7 L.F.
1/8 L.F.
125 T.M.B.
1/7 N.F. Pioneers
427 F. Coy R.E.

A Coy } 42 Bn M.G.C.
B Coy }
112th F.B.
126th I.B.
Rt Group R.F.A.
42 Division

Inter Bn. Relief order

1 The 1/7 N.F. Pioneers will be relieved in the line tonight by the 1/8 L.F. + 1/7 L.F. who will extend their fronts N + S respectively.
(a) The 1/8 L.F. will relieve 5 platoons of the 1/7 N.F. Pioneers between limits L.4.a.6.6 + the grid line between Squares F.28 + L.4.
(b). The 1/7 L.F. will relieve 5 platoons of the 1/7th N.F. Pioneers between limits grid line between Squares F.28. + L.4 + F.28.c.8.4.
(c) All details of relief will be arranged between C.Os concerned.
2. On relief the 3 Coys of the 1/7 N.F. Pioneers will be attached as follows:- 1 Coy to each Bde. The Coy being attached to this Bde will report to O.C. 1/5 L.F. H.Qrs F.26.d.8.9. for accommodation in Support trenches.
3. 427 Fld Coy R.E. is being attached to this Bde & will also report to O.C. 1/5 L.F. for

(2)

accommodation in Support trenches.
4. Completion of reliefs as in Para 1 above will be reported to this Office by the Code Word "MACHUFFLE".

5 ACKNOWLEDGE.

[signature]
Captain
a/Bde Major
125 Brigade

3-4-18

Issued at 1.45pm by D.R.

Prefix........ Code........ m | Words. | Charge.

Office of Origin and Service Instructions.

D.R.

Sent

At........ m.

To........

By........

This message is on a/c of:

.... Service.

(Signature of "Franking Officer.")

Recd. at .... m.

Date........

From A3

By........

TO RANDOM.

Sender's Number.	Day of Month.	In reply to Number.	AAA
* BM 254.	5		

Left Battn reported situation unchanged 9.8 AM ~~aaa~~ aaa Heavy shelling of BUCQUOY village & wood from 5.30 AM onwards aaa Unconfirmed message from left Battn (1/7 L F) states the enemy are in the left Coy trench of the Right Battn (1/8 L F) & that a defensive flank is being formed aaa This is not confirmed through any other source & there appears to have been practically complete absence of MG & rifle fire aaa Situation now sounds much quieter ~~[illegible]~~ ~~[illegible]~~

From RAZOR.

Place

Time 11.0 AM.

The above may be forwarded as now corrected. (Z) [illegible] Capt

Censor. Signature of Addressor or person authorised to telegraph in his name.

* This line should be erased if not required.

(3796.) Wt. W492/M1647. 650,000 Pads. 5/17. H.W. & V., Ld. (E. 1187.)

Prefix..........Code..........m | Words. | Charge.

Office of Origin and Service Instructions.

Sent
At..........m.
To..........
By..........

This message is on a/c of:
.... Service.
(Signature of "Franking Officer.")

Recd. at
Date..........
From A 4
By..........

TO { 1/8 LF
1/5

Sender's Number.	Day of Month.	In reply to Number.	AAA
* BM 256	5		

Ref report received that enemy have broken through your left Coy aaa Immediate steps will be taken to eject them aaa If necessary you can call on 1/5 LF for support up to 2 Coys aaa.
Addsd 1/8 LF rptd 1/5 L.F.

From 125 I B.
Place
Time 11.40 a.m.

The above may be forwarded as now corrected. (Z)

Censor.

M W Nichols Capt.
Signature of Addressor or person authorised to telegraph in his name.

* This line should be erased if not required.

(3796.) Wt. W 492/M1647. 650,000 Pads. 5/17. H.W.&V., Ld. (E. 1187.)

Prefix........ Code........ m Office of Origin and Service Instructions. DR	Words.	Charge.	*This message is on a/c of:* .... *Service.* (Signature of "Franking Officer.")	Recd. at .... m. Date A5 From .... By ....
	Sent At........m. To........ By........			

TO 42 Div.
112 Inf Bde

Sender's Number.	Day of Month.	In reply to Number.	AAA
* BM 257	5		

Reports of wounded tend to confirm fact that enemy attacked & captured left Coy front line of 1/8 LF for about Road L.4.a.45.55 to grid line between F.28 & L.4 aaa Time of attack unknown aaa OC 1/8 LF has been instructed to eject enemy immediately aaa 2 Coys support Bn 1/5 LF have been placed at his disposal aaa Addsd 42 Div. Rptd 112 Inf Bde

From 125 Inf Bde
Place
Time 12.18 pm

The above may be forwarded as now corrected.
(Z)
.... Censor. [illegible] Capt
Signature of Addressor or person authorised to telegraph in his name.

* This line should be erased if not required.

(3796.) Wt. W 492/M1647. 650,000 Pads. 5/17. H.W. & V., Ld. (E. 1187.)

Prefix .... Code .... m.	Words.	Charge.	*This message is on a/c of:*	Recd. at .... m.
Office of Origin and Service Instructions.	Sent		.... Service.	Date
	At .... m.			From A6
	To			
	By		(Sig. of "Franking Officer.")	By

TO { 175 Bde.

Sender's Number	Day of Month	In reply to Number	AAA
* 234	5	–	

Enemy have broken through ~~my left flank~~ on my front Am holding a line from main X rds in village of Bocavor to the 13th R.F. on my right aaa 7 Lanc. fus. line intact defensive flank formed by 7 L.F. from their right to Batt HQ. aaa Have asked 5 L.F. for 2 platoons to reinforce my right aaa Reinforcements required to fill gap from my left at main X rds. to right of 7 Lancs fus. aaa Reported only few enemy in village

From
Place
Time

The above may be forwarded as now corrected. (Z)
.... Censor. Sig. of Addressor or person authorised to telegraph in his name.

* This line should be erased if not required.

(27964) Wt. W492/M1647. [E 1187]. 130,000 Pads—5/17. M.R.Co.,Ltd. Forms/C.2121.

Prefix .... Code .... m	Words.	Charge.	*This message is on a/c of:*	Recd. at .... m.
Office of Origin and Service Instructions.	Sent		.... *Service.*	Date
	At .... m.			From
	To			
	By		(Sig. of "Franking Officer.")	By

TO

Sender's Number	Day of Month	In reply to Number	AAA
*			

Have counter attacked but am held up on line now held

Recd. 12.30 PM

From	Slane · fr	
Place		
Time	12 noon	

The above may be forwarded as now corrected. (Z)

.... Censor. [illegible] Capt

Sig. of Addressor or person authorised to telegraph in his name.

* This line should be erased if not required.

(27964) Wt. W492/M1647. [E 1187]. 130,000 Pads—5/17. M.R.Co.,Ltd. Forms/C.2121.

Prefix.......... Code.............. m | Words. | Charge.

Office of Origin and Service Instructions.

~~V. Urgent~~ ~~Priority~~

Sent At..............m. To.............. By..............

This message is on a/c of: .... Service.

(Signature of "Franking Officer.")

Recd. at .... m. Date .... From A7 By ....

TO 1/8th L F
1/5th L F

Sender's Number.	Day of Month.	In reply to Number.	AAA
* BM 258	5.	234.	

You should ~~[illegible]~~ have received my BM 256 by now aaa This placed 2 Coys of the 1/5th L F at your disposal for counter-attack aaa Village should be cleared as soon as possible aaa 1/8th L F relieve 1/5th L F aaa Position of HQs of 1/8th L F as shown at the same place F.16.d.0.0.

From 125 Inf Bde.

Place

Time 12.30 PM

The above may be forwarded as now corrected. (Z) [illegible signature]

Censor. Signature of Addressor or person authorised to telegraph in his name.

* This line should be erased if not required.

(3796.) Wt. W 492/M1647. 650,000 Pads. 5/17. H.W. & V., Ld. (E. 1187.)

Prefix.......... Code.......... m	Words.	Charge.	This message is on a/c of:	Recd. at .... m.
Office of Origin and Service Instructions.			.... Service.	Date
SDR	Sent			From A8
	At.......... m.			
	To..........			
	By..........		(Signature of "Franking Officer.")	By..........

TO 42nd Divn. 127 Inf Bde. 112 Inf Bde.

Sender's Number.	Day of Month.	In reply to Number.	AAA
* BM 259.	5.		

Message received from 1/8th L.F.
timed 12 noon as follows aaa
Begins aaa Enemy has broken through on
my front aaa Am holding a line from
main X roads in village of BUCQUOY to the
13th R.F. on my right aaa 1/7th L.F. line
intact defensive flank formed by 1/7 L.F.
from their right 5 Bn HQ aaa Have
asked 1/5th L.F. for 2 platoons to reinforce
my right aaa Reinforcements required to
fill gap from my left at main X roads
to right of 1/7 L.F. aaa Reported only
few enemy in village aaa Have counter-
-attacked but are held up on line now
held aaa Ends aaa 2 Coys of
1/5th L.F. have been placed at disposal
of 1/8 L.F. for counter attack aaa

From
Place
Time

The above may be forwarded as now corrected. (Z)

Censor. Signature of Addressor or person authorised to telegraph in his name.

* This line should be erased if not required.

(3796.) Wt. W492/M1647. 650,000 Pads. 5/17. H.W. & V., Ld. (E. 1187.)

Prefix............Code..............m | Words. | Charge. | *This message is on a/c of:* .... Service. (Signature of "Franking Officer.") | Recd. at ....m. Date............... From............... By...............

Office of Origin and Service Instructions.

Sent At..............m. To.............. By..............

TO ②

Sender's Number. *	Day of Month.	In reply to Number.	AAA

Barrage on original right lines is being thickened on Southern sector aaa 'C' Coy 7th N.F. Pioneers have taken up position 200x behind Light Railway in F.27. central aaa Add'd 42 Div. rep'd 127 & 126 Inf Bdes.

From 125 Inf Bde
Place
Time 12.52 pm.

The above may be forwarded as now corrected. (Z) [illegible] Capt

Censor. Signature of Addressor or person authorised to telegraph in his name.

* This line should be erased if not required.

(3796.) Wt. W492/M1647. 650,000 Pads. 5/17. H.W. & V., Ld. (E. 1187.)

Prefix .... Code .... m	Words.	Charge.	This message is on a/c of:	Recd. at .... m.
Office of Origin and Service Instructions.	Sent		.... Service.	Date
	At .... m.			From A 9
	To			
	By		(Sig. of "Franking Officer.")	By

TO		135	Bde.	

Sender's Number	Day of Month	In reply to Number	AAA
* 237	5	–	

Situation aaa following report received from A. coy. aaa 12 noon 5. 4. 18 The enemy has broken through on our left and is bringing up reinforcements into the village A Coy. on our left have been captured We still hold our original positions save working on way up A Coy trench The enemy is in the wood to our rear On the right the R.F. hold the line intact. We are in touch with them but with nobody else. The enemy is

From
Place
Time

The above may be forwarded as now corrected. .... Censor.

(Z) .... Sig. of Addressor or person authorised to telegraph in his name.

* This line should be erased if not required.

(37964) Wt. W492/M1647. [E 1187]. 130,000 Pads—5/17. M.R.Co.,Ltd. Forms/C.2121.

Prefix	Code	m	Words.	Charge.	This message is on a/c of:	Recd. at m.
Office of Origin and Service Instructions.			Sent		Service.	Date
			At m.			From
			To			
			By		(Sig. of "Franking Officer.")	By

TO

Sender's Number *	Day of Month	In reply to Number	AAA

fairly quiet to my front aaa ends

Following report received from OC in village timed 12 noon aaa Enemy holding a line astride the main BUCQUOY road through the village just below the Aid Post. Bombs Machine Guns & men are urgently wanted. I cannot counter attack with my small force aaa ends

Recd 1.30 pm

From 8 Lan. Fus

Place

Time 12.50 pm

The above may be forwarded as now corrected. (Z) [illegible] Capt [illegible]

Censor. Sig. of Addressor or person authorised to telegraph in his name.*

* This line should be erased if not required.

(27964) Wt. W492/M1647. [E 1187]. 130.000 Pads—5/17. M.R.Co.,Ltd. Forms/C.2121.

G.41.

Recd. 1.55 pm

A10

125 Bde.

Have called on 2 Coy.
5 L.F. to counter attack and
clear village and occupy
old line aaa Have. ...
contact with defensive flank from
their right to their Batt. H.Q.
aaa Line held by the batt.
lies across Bucquoy Rd just
W. of X rds. L3 b 3.3. 150x N.
200x S. in touch with 13th R.F.
who have withdrawn their left flank
to conform with ours. 1.26 pm. [illegible]

5.4.18 Capt. [illegible]

Prefix ... Code ..... m.

Office of Origin and Service Instructions. F.D.R.

Words

Received At.............. m. From................ By ....

Sent At................ m. To..................... By ....

Office Stamp: File A11

TO: 42 Div^n. 127 I.B. 112 I.B. | Rt Group RFA.

* Sender's Number.	Day of Month.	In reply to Number.	AAA
BM 261	5		

Following message received from 1/8th L.F. timed 1.26 PM aaa Begins aaa 2 Coys 1/5 L.F. called on to counter-attack & clear village & occupy old front line aaa 1/7 L.F. extend with defensive flank from their right to their Bn HQrs aaa Line held by these Bns lies across BUCQUOY Rd. just W. of X roads L.3.b.3.3. 150x N. 200x S. in touch with 13th R.F. who have withdrawn their left flank to conform with ours aaa Ends aaa

From 125 Inf Bde

Place

Time 2.20 pm

* This line should be erased if not required.

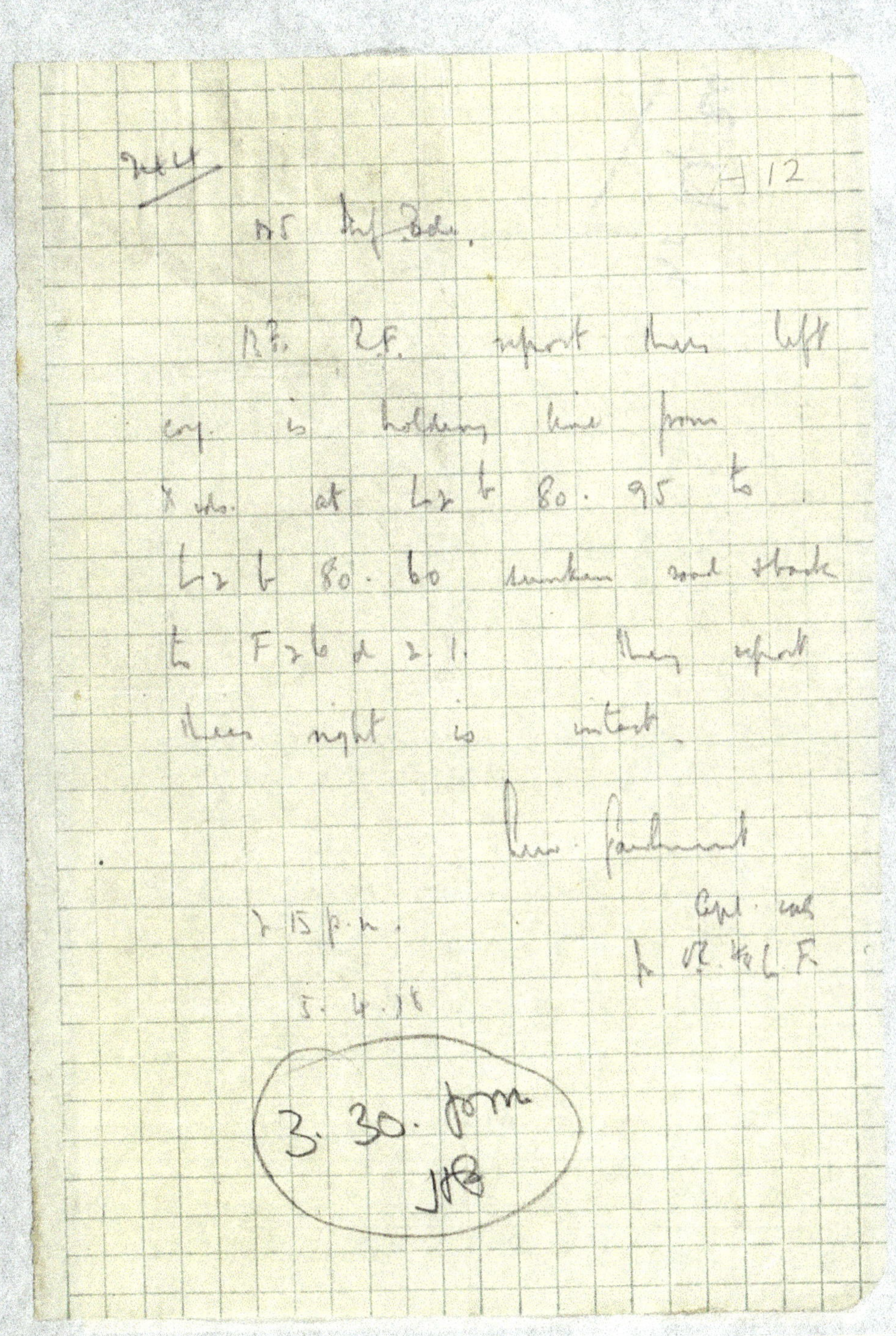

[illegible]

412

125 Inf Bde.

LF. 2F. report their left coy. is holding line from X rds. at L2 b 80.95 to L2 b 80.60 sunken road & track to F2b d 2.1. They report their right is intact.

[illegible]

Capt. cmdg [illegible] L.F.

2.15 p.m.

5.4.18

3.30 pm

JHB

Prefix............ Code............ m	Words.	Charge.	This message is on a/c of:	Recd. at .... m.
Office of Origin and Service Instructions.	Sent		......................Service.	Date...........
	At...............m.			From A13
	To...............			
	By...............		(Signature of "Franking Officer.")	By...............

TO RAZOR

Sender's Number.	Day of Month.	In reply to Number.	AAA
* B 20	5.		

My	right	coy	reports
snipers	active	on	his
front	and	has	asked
for	artillery	to	be
put	on	ridge	300
yds	to	his	front
aaa	he	further	reports
enemy	still	on	the
ridge	and	I	have
directed	guns	on	to
it	aaa	My	defensive
flank	now	runs	F 28 c 4 1
to	cemetery	– L 4 a 0 5.	– L 3 b 35.80.
Battn	HQ	holding	trench
50 yds	either	side	of
Battn.	HQ on	edge	of
wood.	We	are	quite

From

Place

Time

The above may be forwarded as now corrected. (Z)

Censor. Signature of Addressor or person authorised to telegraph in his name.

* This line should be erased if not required.

(3796.) Wt. W 492/M1647. 650,000 Pads. 5/17. H.W. & V., Ld. (E. 1187.)

Prefix .... Code .... m	Words.	Charge.	This message is on a/c of:	Recd. at .... m.
Office of Origin and Service Instructions.	Sent		.... Service.	Date ....
	At .... m.			From ....
	To			
	By		(Signature of "Franking Officer.")	By ....

TO 2 (contd)

Sender's Number.	Day of Month.	In reply to Number.	AAA
*	5		

ready	to	support	counter
attack	of	5th & 8th	L.F.
when	it	comes	off
aaa	Lateral	communication	
re-established	between	5th & 8th	L.F.
Right	coy	reports	about
15	casualties	aaa	defensive
flank	coy	about	6
aaa	What	enemy	have
been	seen	by	the
defensive	flank	coy	have
appeared	very	frightened	and
have	retired	very	quickly

Recd 4.0 pm

From RASP

Place

Time 3.5 p.m.

The above may be forwarded as now corrected. (Z) A.A. Lewis Lieut Adjt

Censor. Signature of Addressor or person authorised to telegraph in his name.

* This line should be erased if not required.

(3796.) Wt. W 492/M1647. 650,000 Pads. 5/17. H.W. & V., Ld. (E. 1187.)

Prefix.........Code.........m.	Words.	Charge.	This message is on a/c of:	Recd. at ....m.
Office of Origin and Service Instructions. DR	Sent At.........m. To......... By.........		.........Service. (Signature of "Franking Officer.")	Date......... From A46 By.........

TO 42nd Divn.

Sender's Number.	Day of Month.	In reply to Number.	AAA
* BM 265	5		

In confirmation of telephone conversation aaa Defensive flank of 7th L.F runs as follows :– F.28.c.4.1. – CEMETRY – L.4.a.0.5 – L.3.b.35.80 aaa Batn HQrs (F.27.d.3.5) are holding trench on either side of Batn HQrs on edge of wood aaa

Counter-attack took place at 4.30 PM after consultation between O.C. 5th, 8th L Fs + 13 R.Fs.

From 125 Inf Bde
Place
Time 4.45 PM

The above may be forwarded as now corrected. (Z) [illegible] Capt

Censor. Signature of Addressor or person authorised to telegraph in his name.

* This line should be erased if not required.

(3796.) Wt. W492/M1647. 600,000 Pads. 5/17. H.W. & V., Ld. (E. 1151.)

Prefix..........Code..........m | Words. | Charge. | This message is on a/c of: | Recd. at..........m.

Office of Origin and Service Instructions.

Sent At..........m. To.......... By..........

..........Service.

ved 7.15 PM

(Signature of "Franking Officer.")

Date A15

From

By

TO RAZOR

Dvn 112 Inf

Sender's Number.	Day of Month.	In reply to Number.	AAA
B 20	5.		

Counterattack	seems	to	be
Tardy	Held	up	on
BUCQUOY	AYETTE	Road	and
right	flank	of	5th L F
is	open	from	X-roads
Southwards AAA	Reinforcements	appear	to
be	vital	on the	left of
the	37	Division.	NO
liaison	is	in	progress with them
Major	Castle	has	first
been	to	see	me
and	we	agree	that
troops	are	wanted	forward.
a	reinforcement	of	one
Batt:	should	clear up	the
situation	but	it	ought
to	come	before	dark AAA.

From RASP

Place

Time 6.30 pm.

The above may be forwarded as now corrected. (Z) E L Bond Lt Col

Censor. Signature of Addressor or person authorised to telegraph in his name.

* This line should be erased if not required.

(3796.) Wt. W492/M1647. 650,000 Pads. 5/17. H.W. & V., Ld. (E. 1187.)

Prefix..........Code..........m. | Words. | Charge. | *This message is on a/c of:* ....Service. | Recd. at..........m.

Office of Origin and Service Instructions.

Sent At..........m. To.......... By..........

(Signature of "Franking Officer.")

Date

From

By

A16

recd 7.30 pm

TO 115 Inf. Bde.

Sender's Number.	Day of Month.	In reply to Number.	AAA
* 250	5	–	

Remainder of Batt ~~[illegible]~~ counter attacked through village at 4.30 p.m between roads Main Road through BUCQUOY and road to south running parallel aaa Badly cut up with M.G. fire about L3a62 aaa About 12 men under Lyt. now on BUCQUOY–AYETTE road just S. of X roads L3b22 aaa Am only officer left in battalion aaa Can reinforcements be sent up to fill gap from X roads to 13th R.F. on our right? aaa Position of left flank of 13th R.F. obscure.

From 96. F.

Place

Time 7p. m.

The above may be forwarded as now corrected. (Z) [illegible] Capt

Censor.

Signature of Addressor or person authorised to telegraph in his name.

* This line should be erased if not required.

(18965.) Wt. W12952/M1294. 187,500 Pads. 1/17 McC. & Co., Ltd. (E. 818.)

Prefix.......... Code.......... m.	Words.	Charge.	This message is on a/c of:	Recd. at .... m.
Office of Origin and Service Instructions.	Sent		.... Service.	Date..........
	At..........m.			From A17
	To..........			
	By..........		(Signature of "Franking Officer.")	By..........

TO { 5 L.F. / 7 L.F. / 8 L.F.

Sender's Number.	Day of Month.	In reply to Number.	AAA
* BM 118	5		

The 37th Div: are filling up gap between right of 5 L.F. & left of 112 Inf Bde aaa A fresh Battn has been moved up to occupy the YELLOW LINE from about L.2.b.0.5. through F.26.d. the [illegible] the F.27.c aaa [illegible] 8th L.Fs. 4 Machine Guns are being put in position in L.2.b.2.8 and [illegible] 5th 7th & 8th L.Fs.

From 125 Inf Bde
Place
Time 8 15 PM

The above may be forwarded as now corrected. (Z) [illegible] Capt

Censor. Signature of Addressor or person authorised to telegraph in his name.

* This line should be erased if not required.

(3796.) Wt. W492/M1647. 6?0,000 Pads. 5/17. H.W. & V., Ld. (E. 1187.)

Prefix SM Code AS Words

£ s. d.

Charges to Collect

Service Instructions.

Received. From MR6 By Reeve

Sent, or sent out. At ....m. To .... By ....

Office Stamp. rec. A18

Handed in at MR6 Office [illegible] m. Received 8.1[illegible] m.

TO Major. Repld Rasf. Raul

*Sender's Number.	Day of Month.	In reply to Number.	AAA
1033	5		

Taking	up	defensive	flank
with	my	3	Coys
along	the	line	L3D3.8
[illegible]	left	where	touch
is	gained	with	7/67
due	west	to	ESSARTS
– BUCQUOY	Road	thence to	L2B0.5
where	I hope	to get	touch with

63 RF aaa Will report as soon as line is established

FROM

TIME & PLACE (8.10 pm) Rolt Y. 50PM

*This line should be erased if not required.

Prefix .... Code .... m	Words.	Charge.	This message is on a/c of:	Recd. at .... m.
Office of Origin and Service Instructions.	Sent		.... Service.	Date ....
	At .... m.			From A1G
	To			
	By		(Signature of "Franking Officer.")	By ....

TO RAZOR (Rec 9.0 pm)

Sender's Number.	Day of Month.	In reply to Number.	AAA
* B 29	5		

We are now readjusting line as follows AAA F28C41 L3648 then westward to L2605 where we hope to touch up with 13 R.F. AAA Everything seems quiet at present, Getting on to cleaning rifles. Major Castle's headquarters still at original place. Capt Fairhurst still at original place. AAA All 3 headquarters' details being used as strong posts ~~for~~ at their respective headquarters AAA lateral communication still holds AAA My Artillery liaison OK. My 2 left Coys report situation normal on my left front

(margin: all 3 Bns being used)

From RACP.

Place

Time 8.15 pm.

The above may be forwarded as now corrected. (Z) E S Brown Lt Col

Censor. Signature of Addressor or person authorised to telegraph in his name.

* This line should be erased if not required.

(3796.) Wt. W 492/M1647. 650,000 Pads. 5/17. H.W. & V., Ld. (E. 1187.)

Prefix............Code..............m	Words.	Charge.	This message is on a/c of:	Recd. at ....m.
Office of Origin and Service Instructions.	Sent		......................Service.	Date..............
	At..............m.			From A.20
	To..................			
	By..................		(Signature of "Franking Officer.")	By..................

TO 5 L.F.
7 L.F.
8 L.F.

Sender's Number.	Day of Month.	In reply to Number.	AAA
* G.M. 269	8th		

Reference my G.M. 268 The four battalions [illegible] moving on to Yellow line at present. If all ready to move up should occasion demand [illegible] 1 Battalion in support [illegible] (2) [illegible] on F 21.a and [illegible] help as necessary.

From 125 Bde

Place

Time 10.45 p.m.

The above may be forwarded as now corrected. (Z) [illegible]

Censor. Signature of Addressor or person authorised to telegraph in his name.

* This line should be erased if not required.

(3796.) Wt. W492/M1647. 600,000 Pads. 5/17. H.W. & V., Ld. (E. 1187.)

951

A 21

135 Bde.

I 13th R.F. report. timed 1.10 am

"A defensive flank is being formed by A Coy. 6th Bedfordshire Regt. from L 2 b 95.35 to ORCHARD at about L 3 b 1.4 gaining touch with 5th L.F. at the latter point.

At L 2 b 95.35 A Coy. of the 6th Bedfords will be in touch with No: 1 Coy. of the 13th R. Fusiliers who are lining the road southwards from this point."

II Am in touch with Royal Fusiliers and Bedfords on my right.
Enemy shelling this Hd.
heavily at frequent intervals, otherwise everything quiet, nothing to report.

[illegible]
3 am. Capt [illegible]
6. 4. 18. 3.50 [illegible]

Hd

25 Inf. Bde.

A 22. (Recd. 8.30 AM)

Situation on this front unchanged and quiet, occasional shelling of Batt. HQ.

Have established strong post round these HQ.

13th R.F. report timed 5.55 am.

"Right coy. in touch with batt. on right at L 2 a 1.2. Line runs thence to L 2 d 5.7 – L 3 c ~~0.5~~ 05. 85 – L 3 a 05. 40 – L 3 a 3.4. – L 3 a 7.5

Coy. Bedford Regt. on our left in touch with 5 L.F.

Support coy. from L 2 d 5 7 – L 3 a 0.5.

7.30 am

6. 4. 18.

[illegible]

Capt. [illegible]

8 L.F.

SECRET + URGENT   A23

Ref. 57D N.E. 1:20.000.   B.M. 278.

6-4-18.

Inter Battalion Relief Order.

1. (a) The 1/8 Manchester Regt 126th I. Bde will relieve the 1/7 L.F. in the line tonight, between the limits L.3.b.40.70 to F.28.b.4.5. with H.Qrs at F.27.d.3.5.

(b) Time of relief is dependent on the relief of the 1/8th Manchester Regt in their present position F.21.c. with H.Qrs F.20.d.30.45. by the 42nd Div Composite Battalion.

On Completion of this relief the 1/8 Manchester Regt will be free to relieve the 1/7 L.F.

(c) All details of relief, including guides etc. will be arranged between C.O's Concerned.

2. On Completion of relief the 1/7 L.F. will move into Support in the YELLOW LINE, and in depth behind as required, with H.Qrs. at F.27.c.3.8. YELLOW LINE will be occupied from left of Support Company of 1/5 L.F. who will close up to the right in touch with the 1/8 L.F. whose right will be on the ESSARTS BUCQUOY Road.

'C' Coy 1/7 N.F. Pioneers will remain under the order of the O.C. 1/7 L.F.

(2).

3. Completion of relief will be reported to these H. Qrs by the Code Word "MACROGER".

4. ACKNOWLEDGE.

[signature]
Captain
a/Bde Major.
125 Brigade

Issued at 4.45 pm by D.R.
Copies to:-
1/5 L.F.
1/7 L.F.
1/8 L.F.
125 T.M.B.
1/8 Manchester Regt
A Coy } 42 Div M.G.C.
B Coy }
C Coy 1/7 N.F. Pioneers
427 Fld Coy R.E.
126 I.B
127 I.B.
112 I.B.
42 Division
✓ Rt Group R.F.A.

A24

1/5th. L.F. 1/7th L.F. 1/8th Manchester

B.M. 279.

(1) Corps are very anxious to secure an identification of division which attacked Bucquoy yesterday; endeavour to capture a Boche by patrolling.

(2) Avoid having one line of defence utilize shell holes to get depth. The enemy barrage fell on our front line yesterday morning where the bulk of the men were and he was able to get through in consequence. If posts had been out in front they would have escaped the barrage and held up the enemy attack.

6/4/18 Harold Fargus. B.G.
6.15 p.m. comdg 125th I.B.

S P E C I A L   T E L E G R A M.

To

Major-General A. SOLLY-FLOOD, C.M.G., D.S.O.,
Commanding 42ND DIVISION.

Bravo East Lancashires. Hearty congratulations to you and the gallant lads who have fought so bravely. MANCHESTER is proud of you all.

Lord Mayor, MANCHESTER.

-*-*-*-*-*-*-*-*-*-

SECRET & URGENT

A26

Copy No 16

7-4-18

125th Infy Bde Order No 75.

REF. 57D NE 1:20,000
LENS sheet 11 1:100,000

1. The 125th I.B. together with the 1/8 Manchester Regt will be relieved in the line tonight by the 185 I.B. & part of the 186. I.B. as follows:–

(a) The 1/5 L.F., 3 Coys of 1/8 Manchester Regt & the 1/7 L.F. in Support will be relieved by the 2/5 W. Yorks between the limits L.3.a.7.5. (main BUCQUOY – ACHIET-LE-PETIT Rd) to F.28.c.8.7. with H.Qrs at F.26.a.8.9.

(b) The left Coy of the 1/8 Man/r Regt will be relieved by the 5th Duke of Wellingtons, 186th I.B. between the limits F.28.c.8.7. to F.28.b.4.5. Four Guides from this Coy, 1 per incoming platoon, will report with orders in writing to H.Qrs 127 I.B. F.24.d.95.65 at 7-30pm tonight.

(c) 1/8 L.F. in Support in the YELLOW LINE immediately N of ESSARTS – BUCQUOY Rd will be relieved by part of the 2/7th W. Yorks who are taking over the line between limits L.2.d.3.3. to L.3.a.7.5.

2. All details of relief including guides, except as in para 1(b) above will be arranged between C.O's concerned.

(2)

The 2/5 W Yorks are not moving off from area round PIGEON WOOD before 8-0. pm.

3. The 125 T.M.B. will be relieved by the 185. T.M.B. under arrangements to be made between C.Os concerned.

4. All programmes of work, maps etc together with Tools, S.O.S Signals & Petrol tins will be handed over on relief. All Tools, S.O.S Signals not in the Front Line & all lists of trench stores & maps will be collected & dumped, by all Battalions except 1/8 L.F. at 1/5 L.F. H.Qrs F 26. d 8.9. & by 1/8 L.F. at H.Qrs 13 R.F.

5. The 427 Field Coy R.E. & C Coy 1/7 N.F. Pioneers will stand fast in their present position & be relieved night 8/9th under orders of C.R.E.

6. On relief the Bde will go into Corps Reserve. Details of route & transport will be notified later.

7. Completion of relief will be notified to this Office by Code Word "MACDART".

8. Command of Right Brigade 9 [illegible] of Left Sector IV Corps will pass to G.O.C. 185 I.Bde on completion of Infy relief.

9. Brigade H Qrs. will close at ESSARTS on completion of relief & reopen at the CHATEAU VAUCHELLES on arrival.

10. ACKNOWLEDGE.

[signature]
Captain
a/Bde Major
125 I Bde.

Issued at 2.45 pm by orderly.

Copies to:-
5 L F
7 L F.
8 L F.
125 T.M.B
1/8 Manchester Reg't
427 Field Coy R.E.
'C' Coy 1/7 N.F. Pioneers
127 I.B
126 I.B
112 I.B
185 I.B
42 DW
R.[illegible] Group. R.F.A.
Bde Sigs
W.D
FILE.

SECRET AND URGENT Copy No. 6

Addendum No 1 Apr 7/1918 A27

to 125 Inf Bde Order No 75.

Ref Para 6.

1. Brigade will be disposed in Corps Reserve as follows:-
Bde HQ 5 LF 6 LF 125 TMB VAUCHELLES
7 LF [illegible] x

(a) Battalion [illegible] are marching to HENU [illegible] relief will march to [illegible] and proceed thence to their destinations by bus.

(b) Busses will be parked on SOUASTRE HENU Rd from D 22 c 1.8 to D 21 d 5.9. An Officer from Bde HQ will supervise embussing.

(c) Tea will be ready for troops before embussing as follows:-
2 cookers 8 LF N of Road at D 21 a 5.46 [illegible] 5 LF 6 LF Bde HQ 125 TMB
2 cookers 7 LF S of road at above point for 7 LF

(d) Breakfast will be ready for troops on arrival at destination.

3. Route - SOUASTRE as follows -
X Roads S of ESSARTS - GOMMECOURT - FONQUEVILLERS. PTO

2

4 Acknowledge.

Issued at 6.45 by orderly.

[signature]
Capt
a/ Bde Major
125 Bde.

7/4/18

Copies to:-
1/5 L.F.
1/7 L.F.
1/8 L.F.
125 T.M.B.
1/8 Manchester Regt

SECRET. Copy No. 16.

A 28

125TH.INFANTRY BRIGADE ORDER NO.76.

Map Ref:Sheet 57.D. 1:40.000. 12/4/18.

1. VAUCHELLES is to be cleared by 5.0.a.m. tomorrow to provide accommodation for other troops.

2. The Brigade Group will move tomorrow via AUTHIE into bivouacs in WARNIMONT WOOD and Billets in St.LEGER (7th.Lan Fus) as under :-

U N I T.	Starting Point.	Time.
427th.Fd.Coy.R.E.	Cross Roads I.27.c.	4.0.a.m.
429th.Coy.A.S.C.	- do -	4.10.a.m.
8th.Lan Fus.	- do -	4.16.a.m.
5th.Lan Fus.	Railway Crossing I.33.c.	4.16.a.m.
7th.Lan Fus.	- do -	4.26.a.m.
125th.T.M.B.	- do -	4.36.a.m.
125th.B'de.H.Qrs.	- do -	4.39.a.m.
1st.Line T & Baggage Wagons of Bns & B'de.H.Qrs. in same order as units.	Cross Roads I.27.c.	4.50.a.m.

A distance of 100 yds will be maintained between Companies & Transport of equivalent road space. There will not be the usual halts at 10 minutes to the clock hour.

3. The Staff Captain will allot areas this afternoon, about 100 tents are available.

4. Units will report their arrival in new areas.

5. Brigade H.Qrs. will close at VAUCHELLES at 4.30.a.m. & open at St.LEGER-les-AUTHIE at 6.a.m.

6. ACKNOWLEDGE.

A R Lawrence
Captain,
Brigade Major,
125th.Brigade.

Issued at 2 pm thro' Signals.

Copies to :-

1. 5th.Lan Fus.
2. 7th. " "
3. 8th. " "
4. 125th.T.M.B.
5. 429th.Coy.A.S.C.
6. 427th.Field Coy.R.E.
7. 125th.B'de.T.O.
8. Brigade Major.
9. Staff Captain.
10. Signals.
11. Capt.BARTON.
12.) 42nd Division.
13.)
14. 126th.Inf'y.Brigade.
15. 127th.Inf'y.Brigade.
16.) W.D.
17.)
18. F I L E.

S E C R E T.
****

Copy No.......23

125TH.INFANTRY BRIGADE ORDER NO.77. 15/4/18.

A29

Map Ref: Sheet 57.D. 1:40,000.

1. The 42nd Division (less Artillery) is relieving the 37th Division (less Artillery) in the Centre Sector IV Corps Front.

2. (a). The 125th.Inf'y.Brigade & 427th.Field Coy.R.E. less 1 Section (under arrangements of C.R.E.) will relieve the 112th Inf'y Brigade in the Centre of the Divisional Sector on nights 16/17th & 17/18th April as in para 3.
268th.M.G.Co is taking over in Centre Subsector on night 17/18th.
(b). The 126th.Inf'y Brigade ~~are~~ is to be on the Left & 127th Inf'y Brigade on the Right.

3. (a). 5th.Lan Fus will relieve 13th.R.Fus on Right (H.Q. K.4.b.6.2.) Guides at junction of O.G.Line & GOMMECOURT - FONQUEVILLERS Road E.28.c.6.4. at 9.15.p.m.

(b). 8th.Lan Fus. will relieve 6th.Beds.Reg't. on Left (H.Q. K.5.d.9.8.) Guides as for 3 (a) at 8.30.p.m.

(c). 7th.Lan Fus will relieve 1st Essex Reg't in Support (H.Q.K.3.d.9.9.) Guides as for 3 (a) 10.0.p.m.

(d). 125th.L.T.M.B. will relieve 112th.L.T.M.B. on night 17/18th arrangements to be made between C.O's concerned.

4. Battalions will move via St.LEGER - COIGNEUX - Road junction J.10.c. - BAYENCOURT - CHATEAU de la HAIE - FONQUEVILLERS as follows :-
There will be a halt for teas at BAYENCOURT.

(a). First Phase.

U N I T.	Starting Point.	Time.	Halt Position.
8th.Lan Fus.	Road Junction I.11.d.5.2.	4.p.m.	N of Road in J.5.c.
5th.Lan Fus.	- do - do -	4.45.p.m.	S of Road in J.5.c.
7th.Lan Fus.	X Roads I.12.c.6.6.	5.40.p.m.	- do - do -

(b). Second PHASE.

U N I T.	Starting Point.	Time.
8th.Lan Fus.	Cross Roads, J.5.d.	7.30.p.m.
5th.Lan Fus.	- do -	8.15.p.m.
7th.Lan Fus.	- do -	9.0.p.m.

(c). If at 7.30.p.m. visibility should be very clear, O.C. 8th.Lan Fus will delay his departure from BAYENCOURT.

(d). 200 yards distance will be maintained between platoons throughout the march.

5. All maps, photographs & Defence Schemes will be taken over on relief. Existing Defence Orders will remain in use for the present.

6. Completion of relief will be reported by wire "GOB".

7. 42nd Division H.Q. are closing at PAS at 4.0.p.m. 16th inst and reopening at COUIN at same hour.

(2).

8. 125th.Inf'y.Brigade H.Qrs. will close at St.LEGER les AUTHIE at 8.30.p.m. and open at GOMMECOURT WOOD L.28.d.8.9. at same hour. G.O.C., 125th.Inf'y Brigade will assume Command of the Centre Brigade Sector on Completion of Infantry relief.

9. ACKNOWLEDGE.

A.L. Lawrence.
Captain,
Brigade Major,
125th.Brigade.

Issued at 8 p.m. thro' Signals.

Copies to :-

1. 5th.Lan Fus.
2. 7th.Lan Fus.
3. 8th.Lan Fus.
4. 125th.T.M.Battery.
5. 427th.Fd.Coy.R.E.
6. 428th.Coy.A.S.C.
7. 268th.Coy.M.G.C.
8. 126th.Inf'y.Brigade.
9. 127th.Inf'y.Brigade.
10. 112th.Inf'y.Brigade.
11. 63rd.Inf'y.Brigade.
12. }
13. } 42nd Division.
14.
15. 42nd Bn.M.G.C.
16. A.P.M., 42nd Division.
17. Brigade Major.
18. Staff Captain.
19. Signals.
20. 125th.B'de.T.O.
21. 125th.B'de.S.O.
22. Lt.BARTON.
23. }
24. } W.D.
25. }
26.) F I L E.

SECRET. Copy No 12

A 29 30

125 Inf Bde Order No. 78

23.4.18

Maps Ref 57 D NE $\frac{1}{20000}$

1a. Night 24/25 April N.Z. Div are extending their left to K 10 d 4 3. (approx)

b. At the same time 125 Inf Bde will extend their right to this point, 5 LAN Fus taking over approx 1 Coy front from 1/5 MAN Regt.

c. Night 24/25 8 LAN Fus will take over down to K 11 b 10 65 from 5 LAN Fus.

d. All details of relief to be arranged between C.O.s concerned.

e. Relief complete to be reported by wire ROOT.

2a. After relief 127 Inf Bde are being withdrawn into reserve at COLINEUX with 1 batn ROSSIGNOL Farm
1 [illegible] J 12 [illegible]
1 [illegible] K 3 & 8.

b. After relief Bde front will be covered by 1 Group R.A.

3 After relief boundaries will run as follows –

Divl boundary.

South K 10 d 4 0 – K 4 c 0 0 – K 3 d 0 0

J 12 a 4 0 – J 11 c 4 0 – J 16 a 0 0

North L 2 c 9 1 – S corner of BIEZ WOOD thence along present boundary.

Inter Bde boundary

K 11 b 10 65 – K 5 c 60 70 – K 5 c 30 45

NE end of Cemetery – K 4 d 55 50.

4 G O C 125 Inf Bde will assume Command as far South as K 10 d 4 3 on Completion of relief

5 ACK

[signature]

Captain

Bde Major

125 Bde

Issued at 8 pm by DR

Copy No 1 5 Lan Fus

2 7 Lan Fus

3 8 Lan Fus

4 125 T M B

5 No 3 Group M G (C Coy) 42 Bn M G C

6 126 Inf Bde.

7 127 Inf Bde.

8 + 9 42 Div

10 [illegible] Group RA

11 R Group RA

12 + 13 W D

14 F I L E

WD 17 [illegible]

125 Inf Bde Order No 79 A31

27. 4. 18

Map 1/20,000 57 D.NE

1. 125 Inf Bde is being relieved by 127 Inf Bde night 28/29 Ap as under.-

a. 5 L F by 5 MAN
guides junction of MULE Track and FONQUEVILLERS-HEBUTERNE Road E 27 C 8.4
8.30 pm.

b. 8 L F by 6 MAN
guides 9.15 pm
rendezvous same

c. 7 L F by 7 MAN
guides 10 pm
rendezvous same

One guide per platoon will be provided.

2 On relief units will move as under:–

.1 5 L F COIGNEUX relieving 6 MAN

7 L F J 6 d " 7 MAN

8 L F ROSSIGNOL Fm " 5 MAN

.2. T M B will move tomorrow night after relief to BAYENCOURT.

.3 .1 All maps defence schemes work policies will be handed over.

2 All posts are to be very carefully handed over.

.4 Relief complete by wire "NINON NICKERS"

.5 Bde HQ will close at E 27 C 85.70 after relief is complete. ~~[illegible]~~
Rear HQ will open at COUIN at 4 pm 25th inst.

Issued at 8pm by DR

6 Ack

A J Lawrence
Capt
Bm 125 Inf Bde

PTO.

Copy No 1 5 L 7
2 7 L 7
3 8 L 7
4 125 TMB
5 C Coy [illegible] 42 Bn MGC.
6 126 Inf Bde
7 127 " "
8 1 NZ Rif Bde
9 S. C
10 Sig Officer
11 Rear S. Capt
12 427 Fd Coy RE
13 B T O
14 428 Co ASC
15/16 42 Div
17/18 WD
19 File

166 [illegible]

CONFIDENTIAL

125 INF BDE

Vol 16

WAR DIARY

VOL 47

MAY 1st – 31st 1918

Army Form C. 2118.

WAR DIARY
or
~~INTELLIGENCE SUMMARY.~~ 125 Inf. Bde.
(Erase heading not required.)

May 1918.

Instructions regarding War Diaries and Intelligence Summaries are contained in F. S. Regs., Part II. and the Staff Manual respectively. Title pages will be prepared in manuscript.

PAGE 1. Vol. 47.

Place	Date	Hour	Summary of Events and Information	Remarks and references to Appendices
57.D.N.E. COUIN. J1d65	1.		Orders to relieve 126. I. Bde in left sector of Div. Front received & Bde O.O. 80 issued. Relief to take place night 2/3rd. Brigade in Div. Reserve.	1.
57.D.N.E. GOMMECOURT E28d16.	2.	8pm	Bde HQ opened at GOMMECOURT.	
	3		Bde in line. Situation quiet.	
	4.		— " — — " — Bde on right advanced their line slightly. Bde front not affected.	2
	5.		— " — — " — Orders for relief of Div. by 57th Div & of Bde by 171 Bde on night 6/7th received & Bde OO No 82 issued.	3
COUIN J1d65.	6.	4pm	Total casualties 3/5/18 – 6/5/18. Killed: OFF. –, O.R. 3; Wounded: OFF. –, O.R. 14; Sick: OFF. –, O.R. 15. Bde HQ opened at COUIN.	
	7.		Bde in Army Reserve, ready to move at 1 hours notice from 9pm – 9am & 2 hours notice from 9am – 9pm.	
	8.		Bde in Army Reserve.	
	9.		In conjunction with 126 & 127 Bde. Bde practised moving into battle positions.	
	10		Bde in Army Reserve. Training	
	11.		Battle positions manned for practise	

MB

1577 Wt. W10791/1773 500,000 1/15 D. D. & L. A.D.S.S./Forms/C. 2118.

Instructions regarding War Diaries and Intelligence Summaries are contained in F. S. Regs., Part II. and the Staff Manual respectively. Title pages will be prepared in manuscript.

Army Form C. 2118.

Page 2
Vol 47.

WAR DIARY
or
~~INTELLIGENCE SUMMARY.~~
(Erase heading not required.)

125 Inf Bde MAY 1918.

Place	Date	Hour	Summary of Events and Information	Remarks and references to Appendices
COUIN. 57D NE J1D6S.	12		Bde in Army Reserve. Training	
	13		— . — — . —	
	14.		1 Batt. 307. Regt. USA. joined Bde. — . —	
	15		Bde in Army Reserve. Training	
	16		— . — — . —	
	17		— . — — . —	
	18		— . — — . —	
	19		— . — — . —	
	20		— . — — . —	
	21		— . — — . —	
	22		— . — — . —	
	23		— . — — . —	
	24		— . — — . —	
	25		— . — — . —	
	26		Practice manning of battle positions — . —	
	27		Bde in Army Res. — . —	
	28		— . — — . —	
	29		— . — — . —	
	30		— . — — . — Presentation of medals by D.C.	
	31		— . — — . —	

31/5/18. Harold Fargus Brig. Gen. Cmdg 125 Inf Bde.

MB

SECRET.

Copy No...19.

125TH. INFANTRY BRIGADE ORDER NO. 8.

****

1/5/18.

(1)

Map Ref: 1:20.000.57.D.N.E.

1. 125 Inf Bde will relieve 126th Inf Bde in Left Sector night 2/3rd May as under :-

(a). 7 Lan Fus will relieve 8 Man Regt (Left Front)
H.Q. K.?.c.90.66.
Guides at junction of O.G. Line. & GOMMECOURT - FONQUEVILLERS Road 8.45.p.m.

(b). 8 Lan Fus will relieve 5 E.Lancs (Right Front).
H.Q. K.6.a.2.2.
Guides 9.30.p.m.
Rendezvous as for (a).

(c). 5 Lan Fus will relieve 10 Man Regt (permanent garrison of ~~GOMMECOURT WOOD~~) Purple System in Brigade Area.
Guides 11.15.p.m.
Rendezvous as for (a).

(d). 125 L.T.M.B. will relieve 126 L.T.M.B., all details to be arranged between C.O's concerned.

(e). Distance of 200 yds to be maintained between platoons.

2. Relief complete to be reported by wire "VENNS UNDIES".

3. Bde.H.Q. will close at COUIN at 8.p.m. tomorrow and open at same hour at E.28.d.1.6.

4. ACKNOWLEDGE.

A. Lawrence

Captain,
Brigade Major,
125th.Brigade.

Issued at...6...p.m. thro' Signals.

Copy No.		Copy No.	
1.	5th.Lan Fus.	11.)	
2.	7th. " "	12.)	42nd Division.
3.	8th. " "	13.	42nd.Bn.M.G.C.
4.	125th.T.M.B.	14.	Staff Captain.
5.	429 Coy.A.S.C.	15.	Rear S.O.
6.	S.O.	16.	Bde.T.O.
7.	1st N.Z.Bde.	17.	Signals.
8.	63 Inf Bde.	18.)	
9.	126 Inf.Bde.	19.)	W.D.
10.	127 Inf Bde.	20.	F I L E.

SECRET Copy No 13

(2)

125 Inf Bde Order No 81.

Map Ref 1/20000 57 D N E 3-5-18.

1. (a) Night 4/5 May 1st N Z. Bde are advancing their line from K.16 b 55.00 - K.16.b.85.25 - K 17 a 0.5.40 - thence along O.B line - K 11 c 15.30.

(b) 127 Inf Bde & 42 D.A. are co-operating.

(c) 42 D.A. are bombarding ROSSIGNOL WOOD at Zero - 2'.

2 (a) 125 L.T.M.B will bombard ROSSIGNOL WOOD from Zero - 5' to Zero

(b) An officer 125 L.T.M.B will report at 127 Inf Bde HQ at 2 pm 4th May to synchronize watches.

3 After operation Divl. S Boundary will run K17 a 10.75 - K 10 d 45.05 to present boundary.

4. Zero hour later.

5 ACKNOWLEDGE.

A. Lawrence.
Captain
Brigade Major
125 Brigade.

Issued at 8 pm thro' Signals

Copy No 1. 5 Lan Fus
2. 7 —"—
3. 8 —"—
4. 125 T.M.B.
5. 428 Fd Coy R.E.
6. 112 Inf Bde
7. 127 Inf Bde
8 & 9 42 Div.
10. Left Group R.A.
11. A Coy 42 M.G Bn
12 & 13 W. D.
14 FILE.

SECRET

Copy 18
W.D

(3)

125 Inf Bde Order No 82

5.5.18.

Map Ref $\frac{1}{20.000}$ 57 D. NE.

1. 42 Div (less Arty) is being relieved by 57 Div (less Arty).

2. ~~on nt~~ 125 Inf Bde will be relieved night 6/7 May by 171 Inf Bde as follows:-

.1. 7 L. Fus by 2/6 Kings Liv Regt
guides 8.45 p.m.
junction of O G line and GOMMECOURT - FONQUEVILLERS Road.

.2. 8 L Fus by 2/7 K. L. Regt
guides 9.30 p.m.
rendezvous same.

.3. 5 L. Fus by 8 K. L. Regt
guides @ 10.15 pm rendezvous same.

.4. 125 L T M B by 171 L T M B, details to be arranged by C.Os concerned.

3. Defence schemes & maps marked with information concerning the Sector will be handed over. All other maps will be retained.

(2)

4\. 1. After relief the Division passes into Army Reserve.

2\. 125 Inf Bde will relieve 170 Inf Bde at COUIN, units will take over as under:-

5 L Fus	from	1/5 L North Lancs.
7 L Fus	–	1/5 Kings Own Regt
8 L Fus	–	2/4 L North Lancs.
125 L.T.M.B.	–	170 L T M B.

5\. While in Army Reserve ~~units~~ the Brigade will be ready to move at 1 hours notice from 9 pm – 9 a.m & at 2 hrs notice from 9 a.m – 9 p.m. Pending further instructions the orders for action in case of attack of 170 Inf Bde will remain in force.

6\. Relief complete will be reported by wire "KIDNEY WIPER".

7 Bde HQ will close at E 28 d 1.6 after relief ~~of~~ is complete. Rear HQ will open at COUIN at J1d 6.4 at 4pm tomorrow.

8 Acknowledge ×

Issued at 8pm thro Sigs. A E Lawrence
Captain
Bde Major
125 Inf Bde

Copy No 1. 5 L Fus ×
2. 6 L Fus ×
3. 8 L Fus ×
4. 125 L T M B ×
5. 428 Fd Co RE.
6. 429 Co ASC
7. A by 42 BN M.G.C.
8 Left group RA
9 & 10 42 Div
11 170 Inf Bde
12 171 "
13 172 "
14 112 "
15 S. Capt
16 Rear S.C. ×
17 S. O.
18 & 19 ~~R.D. B.T.O.~~ W D
20 & 21 File

CONFIDENTIAL.

Vol 17

WAR DIARY.

125 INF. BDE.

JUNE 1918.

VOL. 48.

Army Form C. 2118.

Instructions regarding War Diaries and Intelligence Summaries are contained in F. S. Regs., Part II. and the Staff Manual respectively. Title pages will be prepared in manuscript.

WAR DIARY
or
~~INTELLIGENCE SUMMARY~~.
(Erase heading not required.)

PAGE 1. 125 Inf. Bde. VOL 48 JUNE 1918.

Place	Date	Hour	Summary of Events and Information	Remarks and references to Appendices
57D NE COUIN J1d65	1		Brigade in Army Reserve Training	
"	2-3		— " — — " —	
"	4.		— " — — " — Bde OO 83 issued. Div. relieving New Zealand Div in right sector IV Corps front. Bde in reserve, with one batt. attached to each Bde in line	1
"	5-6		— " — Training	
"	7-12		Brigade in Div. Reserve.	
"	12		Bde O.O. 84. issued, ordering relief of 127 Bde in left sector of Div. Front, by this Bde.	2
"	13.		Bde. in Div. Reserve.	
57D N.E. J18.b.1.9	14	9p.m.	Bde H.Q.s moved to SAILLY AU BOIS.	
	15-27.		Bde in line. Nothing of importance took place. Situation unchanged & quiet.	
	19.		Bde O.O. 85, ordering inter batt. relief issued.	3
	28.		Warning order issued, re relief of Bde partly by 126 Inf. Bde & partly by 3 W.N.Z.R.B.	4
	29		Situation unchanged and quiet	
	30.		Bde O.O 86 issued.	5

H. Fargus [signature]
Brig. Gen.
Cmdg. 125 Inf Bde.

1/7/18.

1577 Wt. W10791/1773 500,000 1/15 D. D. & L. A.D.S.S./Forms/C. 2118.

(1)

SECRET.

Copy No......16

125TH.INFANTRY BRIGADE ORDER NO.83.

Ref Map 1:40.000. 57.D. 4/6/18.

1. 42nd Division (less Artillery) is relieving N.Z.Division (less Artillery) in Right Sector, IV Corps Front on nights 6/7th & 7/8th June.

2. Orders to 5th & 8th Lan Fus have already been issued. 5th & 8th Lan Fus will come under tactical command of G.O's.C. 126th & 127th Inf Brigades respectively on leaving present camps.

3. 7th.Lan Fus & 125th.L.T.M.B. will clear present camps at 4.p.m. 7th instant.

4. Present Camps are being taken over by 63rd Inf Brigade.

5. 1/307th.Regt, U.S.Army will move to PAS, orders later.

6. Completion of reliefs to be reported to Brigade H.Q. by wire "47.000".

7. Divl H.Q. move to BUS les ARTOIS at 4.p.m. June 7th.

8. Brigade H.Q. will close at COUIN and reopen at St LEGER les AUTHIE at 4.p.m. June 7th.

9. ACKNOWLEDGE (125th.Inf Bde units only).

A R Lawrence
Captain,
Brigade Major,
125th.Brigade.

Issued at 8.p.m. thro' Signals.

Copies to :-

1. 5th.Lan Fus.
2. 7th.Lan Fus.
3. 8th.Lan Fus.
4. 125th.L.T.M.B.
5. 1/307th.Regt.
6. 429th.Coy.A.S.C.
7. 126th.Inf Brigade.
8. 127th.Inf Brigade.
9. 3rd N.Z. (R) Bde.
10.)
11.) 42nd Division.
12. Staff Captain.
13. Signal Officer.
14. Bde.T.O.
15. S.O.
16.)
17.) W.D.
18. F I L E.

90.

ADDENDUM TO 125TH INFANTRY BRIGADE ORDER NO.83.

****

5/6/18.

Delete para 3.4

2 Battalions 3rd N.Z. (Rifle) Brigade are taking over our present camps.

Lawrence

Captain,
Brigade Major,
125th.Brigade.

5th.Lan Fus.
7th.Lan Fus.
8th.Lan Fus.
1/307th.Regt.
125th.T.M.B.
429th.Coy.A.S.C.
Staff Captain.

CORRIGENDUM TO 125TH INFANTRY BRIGADE ORDER NO.83.
****

6/6/18.

Delete para 8.

Brigade H.Q. will not move from COUIN at present.

Captain,
Brigade Major,
125th.Brigade.

Distribution as for 125th.Inf Bde Order No.83.

(2)

S E C R E T.

Copy No......14

125TH. INFANTRY BRIGADE ORDER NO. 84.

12/6/18.

Map Ref: 57.D. N.E. & S.E. 1:20.000.

1. 125th. Inf Bde will relieve 127th Inf Bde in Left Sector of Divisional Front night 14/15th June as per attached Table.

2. Battalions going in to Front Line will send up advance parties 24 hours prior to relief.

3. 127th. Inf Bde are issuing all orders for working parties up to 7.a.m. 15th inst.

4. Relief complete to be reported by wire "TUPPER".

5. 125th. Inf Brigade H.Q. will close at COUIN at 9.p.m. 14th inst and open at J.18.b.1.9. at the same hour.

6. ACKNOWLEDGE. (units of 125th. Inf Bde. only).

A. Lawrence
Captain,
Brigade Major,
125th. Brigade.

Issued at 6.30.p.m. thro' Signals.

Copies to :-

1. 5th. Lan Fus.
2. 7th. Lan Fus.
3. 8th. Lan Fus.
4. 125th. L.T.M.B.
5. 429th. Coy. A.S.C.
6. 126th. Inf. Bde.
7. 127th. Inf. Bde.
8.)
9.) 42nd Division.
10. Staff Captain.
11. Bde. T.O.
12. Bde. S.O.
13. Signals.
14.)
15.) W.D.
16. F I L E.

P.T.O.

TABLE ISSUED WITH 125th INFANTRY BRIGADE ORDER NO.84.
****

Serial. No.	U N I T.	Relieving.	Relieved by.	Remarks.
1.	5th.Lan Fus.	5th.MAN Regt. Right Front. H.Q. K.14.b.8.0.	6th.MAN Regt.	Relief to be carried out in small parties between 12.noon and 9.p.m. 14th inst.
2.	7th.Lan Fus.	7th.MAN Regt. Left Front. H.Q. K.9.d.1.2.	5th.MAN Regt.	Guides at CAT LODGE K.8.b.90. 10.p.m.
3.	8th.Lan Fus.	6th.MAN Regt. Support. H.Q. K.9.a.6.7.	7th.MAN Regt.	Relief to be complete by 9.p.m.
4.	125th.L.T.M.B.	127th.L.T.M.B.	127th.L.T.M.B.	Daylight relief.

SECRET.

Copy No.....15.

ADDENDUM TO

125TH. INFANTRY BRIGADE ORDER NO.84.

12/6/18.

1. Cancel para 5.

2. 7th.Lan Fus & 125th.L.T.M.B. will move tomorrow to BUS Woods J.20.c.9.4. & J.20.[illegible].9.7. respectively.

3. Brigade H.Q. will close at COUIN at 3.p.m. and open at BUS Les ARTOIS on arrival.

4. Brigade H.Q. will close at BUS Les ARTOIS at 9.p.m. 14th inst and open at J.18.b.1.9. at same hour.

A. R. Lawrence
Captain,
Brigade Major,
125th.Brigade.

Distribution as for 125th.Inf Bde Order No.84.

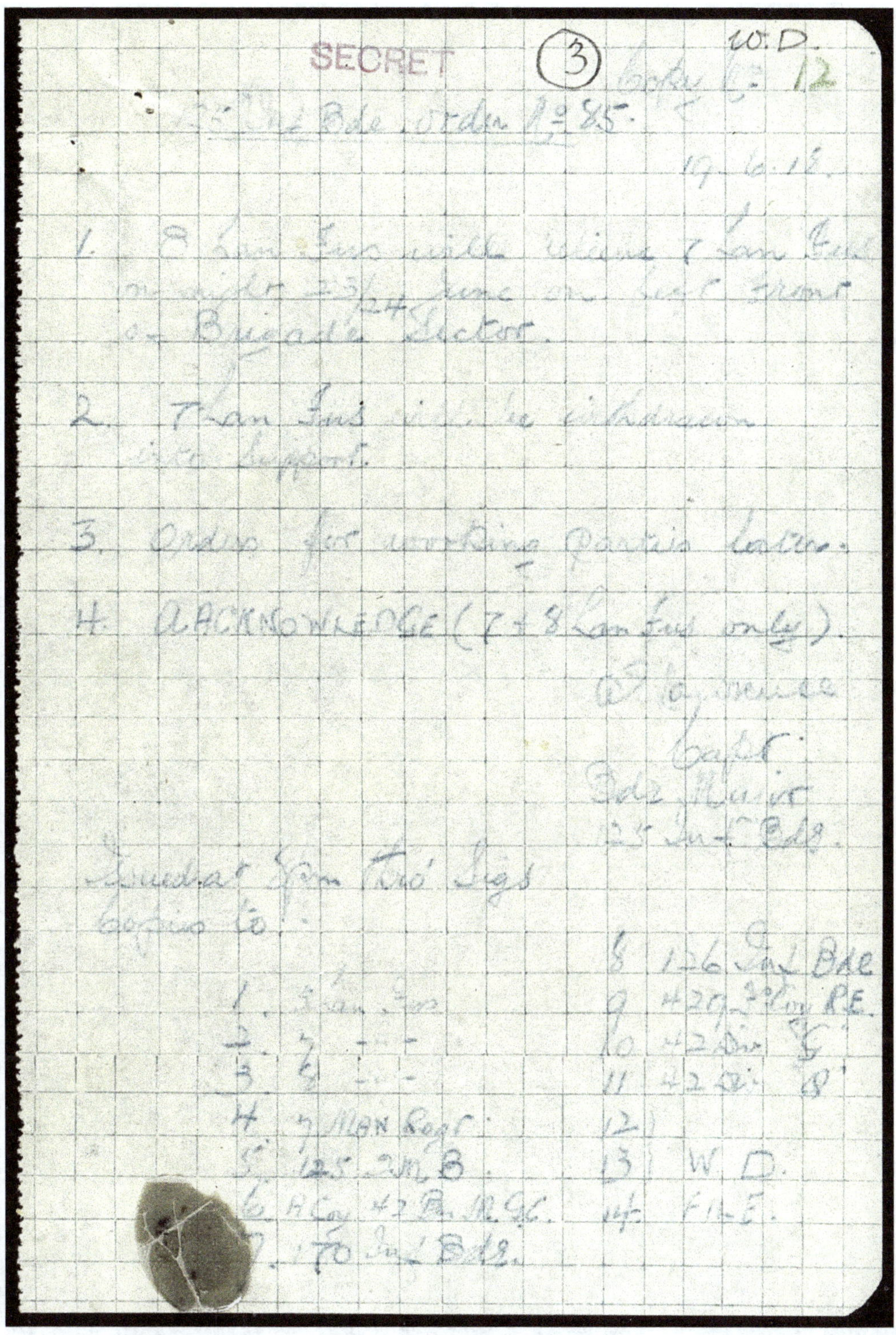

SECRET (3) W.D.

Copy No. 12

125 Inf Bde Order No 85.

19. 6. 18.

1. 8 Lan Fus will relieve 7 Lan Fus on night 23/24 June in left front of Brigade Sector.

2. 7 Lan Fus will be withdrawn into support.

3. Orders for working parties later.

4. ACKNOWLEDGE (7 + 8 Lan Fus only).

[illegible]
Capt.
Bde Major
125 Inf Bde.

Issued at 5 pm thro' Sigs

Copies to:

1. 5 Lan Fus	8. 126 Inf Bde
2. 7 —	9. 427 Fd Coy R.E.
3. 8 —	10. 42 Div "G"
4. 7 Man Regt	11. 42 Div "Q"
5. 125 T.M.B.	12.
6. A Coy 42 Bn M.G.C.	13. W.D.
7. 170 Inf Bde.	14. FILE.

SECRET W.D.

125 Inf. Bde. Order No. 85.

Copy No.- 13

1. 8 Lan. Fus. will relieve 7 Lan. Fus. on night 23/24 th June, on Left front of Bde Sector.

2. 7 Lan. Fus. will be withdrawn into support.

3. Orders for working parties later.

4. ACKNOWLEDGE. (7 & 8th L.F. only).

A R Lawrence
Captain,
Brigade Major,
125 Inf Bde.

19-6-18.

Issued at 8 p.m thro' Sigs.

COPIES TO.

1.	5 Lan Fus.	8.	126 Inf Bde.
2.	7 – –	9.	429 Fd Coy. R.E.
3.	8 – –	10.	42 Div. "G"
4.	7 Man. Regt.	11.	– – "Q"
5.	125. T.M.B.	12. }	W.D.
6.	"A" Coy. 42 Bn. M.G.C.	13. }	
7.	170 Inf. Bde.	14.	File.

(4)

3 Lan Fus Y. 142
7 " "
8 " "
125 T.M. Bty

SECRET

WD

WARNING ORDER.

1. The N. Z. Divn (less Arty) will relieve 57 Divn (less Arty) and will extend its right to the Southern end of HEBUTERNE, on nights 1/2nd + 2/3rd July.

2. Boundary between 42 Divn and N. Z. Divn will then run as follows:- Road at K/6 c. 2.2. (inclusive to 42 Divn) Southern end of FORT HAROLD (inclusive to N. Z. Divn) Road Junction K. 14 a. 95.30 (inclusive to 42 Divn) thence along road to K. 13. c. 0.0. (inclusive to 42 Divn) thence due West.

Inter Brigade Boundary. K.27 d 45.90. - c. 85.85. - K. 26. b. 00.35. - thence along road to K. 25. d. 15.75. - a. 6.0. - thence due West.

3. On the night July 2/3rd, 125 Infy Bde will be relieved by the 3rd N.Z.R. Bde. and 126 Inf Bde. as follows:-

5 Lan Fus will be relieved by a Battn. of the 126 Inf Bde & on relief will proceed to BUS WOOD

7 Lan Fus. will be relieved by a Battn of the 3rd N.Z.R. Bde and on relief will take over from the Battn of the 2 N.Z.R Bde in the PURPLE System South of the Inter Brigade Boundary.

8 Lan Fus will be relieved by a Battn of the 3 N.Z.R. Bde. and on relief will take over from the Battn of the 2nd N.Z.R. Bde, in the PURPLE System North of the Inter Brigade Boundary.

4. 125 T.M.B. North of the New Divn Boundary will be relieved by 3 N.Z.R. Bde and South of the Boundary by 126 Inf Bde.

5. Detailed orders will be issued later.

6. Acknowledge.

[illegible signature] Capt.
for Bde Major
125 Inf Bde.

28.6.18.

Secret.

Copy No. 16

(5)

125' Bde Order No. 86.

Map Ref 57 C N.E 1/20,000.

29/6/18.

1. The 125' Inf. Bde will be relieved by the 126' Inf. Bde and 3rd N.Z.R.B. on the night July 2nd/3rd in accordance with attached table.

2. All Defence Schemes will be handed over. No maps with a scale smaller than 1/10,000 will be handed over, unless they contain important information of the front.

3. Intelligence personnel of the 2 Battns, 3rd N.Z.R.B. will report to 8' Lan. Fus. 48 hours previous to relief. Advanced parties from the 8 Bn. Manchester Regt (1 officer per Coy and 1 N.C.O per Platoon) will report to the 5 Bn. Lan. Fus 24 hours previous to relief. All possible assistance will be given to these parties in studying our own and the enemy's trenches and accurate maps handed over.

4. 125' Inf Bde. will find Working Parties up to 4 P.M. 2nd July. Tunnelling Parties will be relieved by 126' Inf. Bde at the 4 p.m. Shift on July 2nd.

5. On completion of relief Brigade Sector will be handed over to G.O.C. 126' Inf. Bde and G.O.C. 3rd N.Z.R.B. respectively. 125 Bde H.Q will move to BUS.

6. Units of 125 Inf. Bde. to acknowledge ~~by code word POPPY~~.

7. Completion of relief to be reported by code word "POPPY".

E.G. Sacton Lieut
A/Brigade Major
125 Inf. Bde.

Issued at 9 a.m. thro' Signals

Copies to:-

1. 5' L.F.
2. 7 L.F.
3. 8 L.F.
4. 125 T.M.B.
5. 429 Coy A.S.C.
6. 429 Field Coy R.E.
7. 126 Inf. Bde.
8. 2nd N.Z.R.B.
9. 3rd -do-
10. } 42nd Division
11. }
12. Staff Capt
13. Bde T.O
14. " S.O
15. Signals
16. } W.D.
17. }
18. File.

UNIT to be RELIEVED	RELIEVING UNIT	GUIDES	DISPOSITION on RELIEF	REMARKS
5 Lan Fus	8 Manc Regt	1 per Bn HQ 1 per Coy HQ 1 per PLATOON at FORK ROADS K 13 a 4 4 at 9 30 pm.	BUS WOOD	Take over camp of 1/10 MANCHESTERS
7 Lan Fus	2nd Battn 3 N Z R B	Commanding Officers concerned to arrange.	Bn HQ + 2 Coys - WINDMILL J 34 b 2 6 2 Coys in PURPLE RESERVE LINE - from J 28 b 65 00 - Divisional Southern bdy.	2nd OTAGO REGT 2 NZRB will be relieved in this area. but their disposition not taken over
8 Lan Fus	2nd Battn 3 N Z R B.	do	Bn HQ + 2 Coys in bivouacs in J 22 c 2 Coys in PURPLE RESERVE LINE from J 28 b 65.00 - J 24 b 30 95	1 CANTERBURY REGT 2 NZRB will be relieved in this area but their dispositions not taken over
5 E Lancs 2 Coys in K 8 c & d, K 13 b & K 14 a & c.	4th Battn 3 NZ R B	do	Under orders of 126 Inf Bde.	Daylight relief.
5 E Lancs 2 Coys in SAILLY district	1st Battn 3 N Z R B	do	do	do
125 T M Bty	3 NZ R B 126 Inf Bde	do	BUS WOOD	Daylight relief. O.C. 125 T M Bty will hand over 7 guns to O.C. T M Bty 3. N.Z. R.B. and 1 gun to O.C. 126 T M B. Corresponding number of guns will be taken over from relieving units.

"A" Form
Army Form C. 2121
(In pads of 100.)

MESSAGES AND SIGNALS.

No. of Message............

Prefix..........Code..............m.	Words	Charge.	This message is on a/c of:	Recd. at......m.
Office of Origin and Service Instructions	Sent At ....m. To .... By		War Diary Service.	Date......... From .... By.........
			(Signature of "Franking Officer")	(10)

TO MOLA DURI N.Z. DIVN.
MOWE PIRI
MOKU VAVU

Sender's Number.	Day of Month.	In reply to Number.	AAA
BM28	23.		

JUNE Order No 123. aaa JUNE will withdraw from present positions to billets in VIESLY as follows aaa Times are those at which Units will start withdrawing aaa MOLA 1000 MOKU 1100 MOWE 1200 DURI from receipt of this order aaa Any enemy left W of BLUE LINE will be dealt with vigorously by Bns before withdrawing aaa A Echelon Transport will join rear H.Qrs. aaa Addsd MOLA MOWE MOKU DURI to A C.S. reptd VAVU N Z Divn & PIRI.

From JUNE
Place
Time 0930

The above may be forwarded as now corrected. (Z)

Censor. Signature of Addressor or person authorised to telegraph in his name

Capt.

* This line should be erased if not required.

Order No. 1625 Wt. W3253/ P 511 27/2 H. & K.. Ltd. (E. 2634).

VOL. No. 48 (14)

HQ 125 Infy Bde

Vol 18

WAR DIARY

FOR

JULY 1918

5 Lancs Fus. Y. 174.
7 Lancs Fus.
8 Lancs Fus. SECRET.
125 T.M. Battery
"C" Coy. 42 M.G. Battn.
42 Division
188 Inf. Bde.
Right Group.
War Diary (2 copies)

---

1. On 24th July Corps Heavy Artillery will cooperate with 42 Divisional Artillery in a bombardment of VALLADE TRENCH, WATLING STREET and occupied enemy trenches in K.34, and LEGEND TRENCH.

2. OC. 1/7 Lancs Fus will clear from his front line between ROMAN ROAD and Q.4.a 80.80. all troops by zero−10. Every precaution will be taken to prevent the enemy observing that the front line has been evacuated.

3. 42 Divisional Artillery will put down a Shrapnel barrage in NO MAN'S LAND from K.34. c. 90.10 to K.34. a. 00.00 from zero hour to zero plus 15 minutes and afterwards at intervals. A shrapnel barrage will also be put down at intervals behind WATLING STREET to prevent the enemy escaping.

4. Zero hour will be 12 noon.

2

5. At 2 pm. OC. 7 Lancs. Fus. will send out Search Parties to examine WATLING STREET opposite MOUNT JOY road (K. 34. c. 90. 35) and BORDEN AVENUE K. 34. c. 45. 80

These parties will be covered by a protective barrage for 1 hour put down by the Divisional Artillery as follows – K 34. d. 15. 30. – K. 34. d. 30. 30 along VALLADE TRENCH to K. 34. b. 05. 00 – K. 34. e. 70. 90.

Detailed artillery programme will be forwarded to O.C. 7 Lan. Fus. as soon as received.

6. If the search parties return to our lines within an hour, smoke bombs No. 27 will be fired from our front line and the Artillery will cease fire.

7. OC. 7 Lan. Fus. will detail a Lewis Gun to take up a position in SIXTH AVENUE at about K. 34. c. 65. 39 at 2 p.m. This gun will only fire in the event of emergency and then sweep NO MANS LAND.

8. ACKNOWLEDGE.

[signature] Captain.
Brigade Major,
125 Inf Brigade

23-7-18.

S E C R E T.

COPY NO.... 15

125th.INFANTRY BRIGADE ORDER NO.88.

Ref.Maps, 57 D., N.E., and 57 D., S.E. 24/7/18.

---

1. The 125th.Infantry Brigade will be relieved by the 126th.Infantry Brigade on the 26th.July, and night 26/27th. July, in accordance with the attached table.

2. On relief, the 125th.Infantry Brigade will be in Divisional Reserve, and Battalions will take over positions vacated by Battalions of the 126th.Infantry Brigade.

3. Maps, Plans, Air Photographs, work programmes and new proposed work will be handed over.

4. An advance party of 1 Officer, and 4 N.C.O's.per Company of the relieving battalions will arrive during the afternoon of the 26th.inst. Every facility will be given to these parties to reconnoitre, especially any new posts which have been established.

5. Arrangements for relief of Tunnelling parties will be notified later.

6. The relief of the 5th.Bn.Lancashire Fusiliers will take place by daylight with the exception of the three new posts around LA SIGNY FARM, which will not be relieved until dark. The relief of the 5th.Bn.Lancashire Fusiliers less these three posts will be notified to this Office by the Code Word "HALF TIME".

7. On completion of relief, the 125th.Infantry Brigade Headquarters will move to BUS CHATEAU.

8. Completion of relief will be reported to this Office by the Code Word "JOST".

9. Units of 125th.Infantry Brigade to A C K N O W L E D G E.

[signature] Capt.,
Brigade Major,
125th.Inf.Brigade.

Issued at.......thro'Signals.

Copies to:-

1. 5th.L.F.
2. 7th.L.F.
3. 8th.L.F.
4. 125th.T.M.B.
5. 427 Fd.Coy.R.E.
6. 'C'Coy., 42nd.M.G.Bn.
7. 126th.Inf.Bde.
8. 127th.Inf.Bde.
9. 62nd.Inf.Bde.
10. 42nd.Div.
11. Signals.
12. Staff Capt.
13. Gas Officer.
14. Rear H.Q.
15.) W.D.
16.)
17. File.

RELIEF TABLE TO ACCOMPANY BDE.ORDER 88.

UNIT.	RELIEVED BY.	GUIDES AT.	ON RELIEF, TAKE OVER FROM	REMARKS.
5th.Lan.Fus.	8th.Manchester Regt.	Road Junction K.25.a.5.0 at 2.30.p.m.	8th.Manchester Regt. H.Q., J.22.c.	400 yds.to be maintained between platoons.
7th.Lan.Fus.	5th.E.Lancs.Regt.	J.36.a.2.7., 2.30.p.m.) for two rear coys.) J.36.a.2.7, 9.30.p.m.) for two front line) coys.	10th.Manchester Regt.H.Q., Windmill-BERTRANCOURT.	Do.
8th.Lan.Fus.	10th.Manchester Regt.	6.0.p.m., Place to be arranged between C.O's. concerned.	5th.E.Lancs.Regt., BUS WOOD	Do.
125th.T.M.Battery.	126th.T.M.Battery.		126th.T.M.Battery.	Details of relief to be arranged between C.O's.concerned.

N.B. 5 guides per company and 1 guide per battalion for Battalion Headquarters.

6

Instructions regarding War Diaries and Intelligence Summaries are contained in F. S. Regs., Part II. and the Staff Manual respectively. Title pages will be prepared in manuscript.

WAR DIARY

or

~~INTELLIGENCE SUMMARY.~~

(Erase heading not required.)

Army Form C. 2118.

Vol 19

Place	Date	Hour	Summary of Events and Information	Remarks and references to Appendices

125 INFANTRY BRIGADE

FROM - 1ST AUGUST 1918

TO - 31ST AUGUST 1918

VOLUME No. 49

CONFIDENTIAL

D. D. & L., London, E.C.
(A8004) Wt. W1771/M2331 750,000 5/17 Sch. 52 Forms/C2118/14

Army Form C. 2118.

Instructions regarding War Diaries and Intelligence Summaries are contained in F. S. Regs., Part II. and the Staff Manual respectively. Title pages will be prepared in manuscript.

WAR DIARY
or
~~INTELLIGENCE SUMMARY.~~

(Erase heading not required.)

AUGUST. 1918
SHEET No1.
125 INFANTRY BDE

Place	Date	Hour	Summary of Events and Information	Remarks and references to Appendices
REF. SHEET 57D 1/40000	AUGUST 1918			
J26a95	1		Brigade in Divisional Reserve - H.Q. at Chateau BUS-les-ARTOIS.	
	2		—— do ——	
	3.		125 INF BDE relieved 127 INF. BDE in left Sector Divisional Front	
J17c31	3	9.0PM	Bde H.Q. established at J17c31	
	4th to 10th		Brigade held line. Work was done on defences & patrols were active.	
	11th		1/7th LAN. FUS. relieved 5th LAN. FUS in left subsector.	
	12th		Situation quiet.	
	13th		—— do ——	
	14th		Enemy retired in front of 125 Inf. BDE - Patrol pushed forward to keep in touch with enemy & following line established 1/7th LAN. FUS. - WALTER TRENCH from K24c41 to K29d43 1/8 LAN FUS - MUNICH TRENCH from K30d10 to K36a44 Touch maintained with flank brigade.	

D. D. & L., London, E.C. (A8004) Wt. W1771/M2 31 750,000 5/17 Sch. 52 Forms/C2118/14

Army Form C. 2118.

Instructions regarding War Diaries and Intelligence Summaries are contained in F. S. Regs., Part II. and the Staff Manual respectively. Title pages will be prepared in manuscript.

WAR DIARY
or
~~INTELLIGENCE SUMMARY.~~
(Erase heading not required.)

AUGUST 1918
125 INF BDE
SHEET No 2

Place	Date	Hour	Summary of Events and Information	Remarks and references to Appendices
REF SHEET 57c 1/40000	AUGUST			
BDE H.Q. J17c31	15	1.15AM	Bde. O.O. No 90 issued ordering pursuit of enemy & consolidation of new line.	(1)
			Enemy retired - our patrols followed - line established as follows.	
			L26a 23 - L26a 20 - L26c 07 - L25 d 50 - L31b 06 - L31a 86	
			Enemy on high ground E. of sunken road in L31b & L26c.	
	16.	1.30PM	Bde O.O. No 91 issued giving new disposition of Bde.	(2)
		11-0PM	Bde O.O. No 92 issued giving disposition of flank division & stating policy to be pursued	(3)
		4.0AM	Enemy attacked two of our posts - driven from one - our men succeeded in withdrawing from other post after, all were wounded	
	17th	10.10AM	Bde O.O. No 93 issued ordering artillery preparation on given targets	(4)
			Consolidation of line.	
	18	5.30AM	Enemy raided two posts - driven from one but succeeded in entering post at L26c07 - we attacked this post shortly afterwards & retook it. The 184 IR was identified	
	19		Consolidation of line.	

D. D. & L., London, E.C.
(A8004) Wt. W1771/M2031 750,000 5/17 Sch. 52 Forms/C2118/14

Army Form C. 2118.

Instructions regarding War Diaries and Intelligence Summaries are contained in F. S. Regs., Part II. and the Staff Manual respectively. Title pages will be prepared in manuscript.

WAR DIARY
or
~~INTELLIGENCE SUMMARY.~~
(Erase heading not required.)

AUGUST 1918
125 INF BDE
SHEET No 3.

Place	Date	Hour	Summary of Events and Information	Remarks and references to Appendices
REF SHEETS 57D & 57C 1/40000	AUGUST 1918			
K31b48	20	3.0pm	Bde H.Q. established at K31b48	
		4.45pm	Bde O.O. No 95 issued ordering brigade attack - objectives as follows:-	(5)
			1. ZERO - Red line L27a26 - L32b98	
			2. ZERO+120 - Blue line L27b78 - L27b30 - L27c63 - L32b98	
			3. ZERO+240 - Brown line L28a49 - L28a80 - L28d00 (BEAUREGARD DOVECOTE)	
			Patrols to be pushed forward to L29 central & toward MIRAUMONT.	
		9.0pm	HQ 1/5 LAN. FUS. established K36a76	
	21	3.0am	H.Q. 1/7 LAN. FUS. established K29b70	
		4.0am	H.Q. 1/8 LAN. FUS. established K21b10.	
		4.55am	1/5 LAN. FUS. less 1 coy: attacked 1st objective (Red line) under cover of Field & Heavy Artillery Barrage	
		6.38am	CO. 1/5 LAN. FUS. reported by wire 1st objective believed taken.	
		6.55am	1 coy 1/5 LAN. FUS. attacked 2nd objective successfully	
		8.55am	1/7 LAN. FUS. less 2 coys. attacked 3rd objective & took it with exception of BEAUREGARD DOVECOTE which was strongly held by enemy M.Gs.	

D. D. & L., London, E.C. (A8004) Wt. W1771/M2·31 750,000 5/17 Sch. 52 Forms/C2118/14

Instructions regarding War Diaries and Intelligence Summaries are contained in F. S. Regs., Part II. and the Staff Manual respectively. Title pages will be prepared in manuscript.

WAR DIARY
or
~~INTELLIGENCE SUMMARY.~~ AUGUST. 125 INF. BDE. SHEET No 4.

(*Erase heading not required.*)

Army Form C. 2118.

Place	Date	Hour	Summary of Events and Information	Remarks and references to Appendices
REF SHEETS 57D & 57C 1/40000	AUGUST 21st (cont.)			
K31b & 8 (Bde H.Q.)		11.25 am	Wire from 1/5 LAN FUS. stating 2nd objective captured & being consolidated	
		11.31 am	Wire from 1/5 LAN. FUS. confirming capture of 1st objective	
		11.50 am	Wire from 1/5 LAN. FUS. giving dispositions	
		12.40 pm	Warning Order No 37 received from Division	
		1.25 pm	Wire from 1/7 LAN FUS. reporting 3rd objective gained & an officers patrol out in L29 central	
		2.5 pm	Warning Order no. 38 received from Division - 21st Div. to attack when IRLES falls; 126 Inf. Bde to take MIRAUMONT & exploit success in R17-R23-R35; 125 Bde to become Divnl. Reserve	

D. D. & L., London, E.C.
(A8004) Wt. W1771/M2 31 750,000 5/17 Sch. 52 Forms/C2118/14

Instructions regarding War Diaries and Intelligence Summaries are contained in F. S. Regs., Part II. and the Staff Manual respectively. Title pages will be prepared in manuscript.

WAR DIARY
or
~~INTELLIGENCE SUMMARY.~~
(Erase heading not required.)

Army Form C. 2118.

AUGUST
125 INF. BDE.
SHEET No 5.

Place	Date	Hour	Summary of Events and Information	Remarks and references to Appendices
REF. 57D N.W. 57C N.W.	AUGUST			
K31 b 4 8 (Bde HQ)	22	2.0am	1 coy. 1/7 LAN.FUS. attacked & captured BEAUREGARD DOVECOTE	
		4.45am	Enemy counter-attacked - was beaten off with heavy casualties - owing to enemy M.G. fire our line was withdrawn & following line taken up:- L27 b 78 - along sunken road to L28 c 73 - L28 c 00	
		9.25am	Pigeon message from 'A' Coy 1/7 LAN.FUS. asking for barrage on DOVECOTE	
		9.30am	1/7 LAN.FUS. repeated message	
		12.25pm	R.A.F. reconnaissance - failed to see any enemy movement in DOVECOTE area - our men seen on BEAUCOURT - PUISIEUX road	
		1?pm	R.A.F. report no movement IRLES - MIRAUMONT Rd. Troops observed in MIRAUMONT. No movement in L22, 23, 24, 28 29 30. Our troops recognised	
		2.57pm	Div. wire stating 1/10 Manchester Regt placed at disposal of 125 Inf. Bde	
		7.50pm	Div order no. [illegible] received and in consequence	
		8.30pm	Bde. O.O. No 96 issued ordering attack by 2 coys. 1/8 LAN.FUS.	(6)

D. D. & L., London, E.C.
(A8004) Wt. W1771/M2 31 750,000 5/17 Sch. 52 Forms/C2118/14

Army Form C. 2118.

Instructions regarding War Diaries and Intelligence Summaries are contained in F. S. Regs., Part II. and the Staff Manual respectively. Title pages will be prepared in manuscript.

WAR DIARY
or
~~INTELLIGENCE SUMMARY.~~
(Erase heading not required.)

AUGUST
125 INF. BDE. SHEET 6.

Place	Date	Hour	Summary of Events and Information	Remarks and references to Appendices
REF 57D & 57C 1/40000	AUGUST 1918			
K31 b 48 (Bde. H.Q.)	23	2.40am	Assaulting troops attacked & captured 1st objective	
		2.56am	" " " 2nd objective.	
		5.40pm	Order from Div. – 1/8 LAN. FUS. left at disposal of 126 INF. BDE. only to be used in case of grave emergency.	
			Brigade ordered to withdraw into reserve (Divisional).	
K25a85	24		– Brigade in Divnl. Reserve	
		2.0am	– Bde. H.Q. established at K25a85	
		8.0am	Bde. moved forward in accordance with Divnl. Order No. 46	
K36a76			Bde. H.Q. established in MUNICH TRENCH at K36a76	
		3.30pm	Divnl. Order No. 48 received ordering 3 Inf. Bdes. to concentrate near LOUPART WOOD and Division to come into reserve hence Bde. O.O. No. 97 issued	(7)
		5.0pm	Brigade started to move by march route.	
		5.50pm	Divnl. Order 49 received cancelling 48 & ordering Bde. to concentrate in MIRAUMONT	
		7.30pm	Bde. H.Q. established at R5a29	

D. D. & L., London, E.C. (A8004) Wt. W1771/M2-31 750,000 5/17 Sch. 52 Forms/C2118/14

Instructions regarding War Diaries and Intelligence Summaries are contained in F. S. Regs., Part II. and the Staff Manual respectively. Title pages will be prepared in manuscript.

WAR DIARY
or
~~INTELLIGENCE SUMMARY.~~
(Erase heading not required.)

Army Form C. 2118.

AUGUST.
125 INF. BDE
SHEET No 7

Place	Date	Hour	Summary of Events and Information	Remarks and references to Appendices
REF SHEETS 57D & 57C	AUGUST 1918			
R5d78	26	10.0am	Bde. H. Q. established at R5d78	
		4.0pm	Warning Order No. 50 from Div. - 125 Bde. to be prepared to take over from Reserve Brigade 63rd Div.	
	27	5.30pm	Bde. O.O. No 98 issued ordering Div relief of 63rd Div with 125 Bde. in Div. Reserve	
M2d24		9.0pm	Bde H.Q. established at PYS CEMETERY	
	28		Line of resistance reconnoitred for occupation in case of enemy attack.	
	29		Bde. refitted & rested	
	30	9.45pm	Bde O.O. issued placing 1/8 LAN. FUS. at disposal of 126 INF. BDE.	(9)
			Divnl. wire G 949 warning Bde. to be prepared to relieve 126 INF. BDE. in support on 31st August	
	31	10.50AM	Divnl. wire G 917 received ordering Bde. to relieve 126 INF. BDE. at 7.0pm. Hence	
		1.0pm	Bde O.O. No. 100. issued	(10)
M12a59		5.0pm	Bde H.Q. established at M12a59	
		8.0pm	Bde. O.O. No. 101 issued giving line of resistance	

1577 Wt. W10791/1773 500,000 1/15 D. D. & L. A.D.S.S./Forms/C. 2118.

Army Form C. 2118.

Instructions regarding War Diaries and Intelligence Summaries are contained in F. S. Regs., Part II. and the Staff Manual respectively. Title pages will be prepared in manuscript.

~~WAR DIARY~~ AUGUST.
or
INTELLIGENCE SUMMARY. 125 INF BDE
(Erase heading not required.) SHEET No 8

Place	Date	Hour	Summary of Events and Information	Remarks and references to Appendices
			Casualties, Prisoners etc ~~during~~ August 1918	
			1. Trench Strength 125 INF BDE. on 21·8·18	
			65 offrs. 1886 O.R.	
			2. Casualties from 1st to 31st August 1918.	
			19 off. 403 O.R.	
			3. Prisoners taken during August. 1918	
			356 all ranks.	
			Henry Fagan[?]	
			Brig-Gen.	
			Cdg. 125 Infty. Bde	

D. D. & L., London, E.C.
(A8004) Wt. W1771/M2·31 750,000 5/17 Sch. 52 Forms/C2118/14

W.D.

S E C R E T.

Copy No....17..

125TH.INFANTRY BRIGADE ORDER NO.89.

2/8/18.

Ref Map: 57.D.N.E.

1. The 125th.Inf Brigade will relieve the 127th.Inf Brigade in the Left Sector of the Divisional Front on the 3rd inst and night 3rd/4th inst, in accordance with table overleaf.

2. Maps, plans, air photographs, work programmes etc, will be handed over. Battalions will take over the working parties at present found by the Battalions they relieve, commencing 7.0.a.m. 4th August.

3. An advance party of 1 Officer and 4 N.C.O's per Company will report to their new respective Battn Headquarters at 7.30 p.m. tonight, rations will be carried. In addition to these advance parties, front line Companies will each send 10 men per Company, to reconnoitre the forward posts.

4. Tunnelling parties will be found up to and including the morning shift tomorrow 3rd inst; other working parties will not be found after tonight.

5. Brigade Headquarters will close at BUS at 6.0.p.m. 3rd inst, and reopen at J.17.c.4.3. at the same hour.

6. Completion of relief to be reported to this office by Code Word "THUMBS UP".

7. ACKNOWLEDGE. (Units of 125th.Inf Bde only).

E.C.Sarton Captain,
Brigade Major,
125th.Inf Bde.

Issued at 3.0.p.m. thro' Signals.

Copies to :-

1. 5th.Lan Fus.
2. 7th.Lan Fus.
3. 8th.Lan Fus.
4. 125th.T.M.Battery.
5. 428th.Fd.Coy.R.E.
6. 429th.Fd.Coy.R.E.
7. 126th.Inf Bde.
8. 127th.Inf Bde.
9. Rt..N.Z.Bde.
10.) 42nd Division.
11.)
12. Signals.
13. Staff Capt.
14. Gas Officer.
15. Bde.T.O.
16.) W.D.
17.)
18. F I L E.
19. 252 Tunn..Coy.R.E.
20. ~~1??.Tunn. Coy.R.E.~~

TABLE TO ACCOMPANY 125TH INFANTRY BRIGADE ORDER.No.89.

U N I T.	Position.	To relieve.	Guides 1 per platoon. & 1 per Coy.H.Q.	Remarks.
5th.Lan Fus.	Left Sub Sector.	1/6th.Manchesters.	Battn.H.Q. FORT STEWART. K.20.b.1.8. 7.0.p.m.	Rear Companies to be relieved first. Front Coys will not be relieved until dark.
7th.Lan Fus.	Support.	1/5th.Manchesters.	Junction of COUNTRY Trench & COURCELLES - COLINCAMPS Road. J.30.a.7.0. 3.0.p.m	Battn.H.Q. J.24.d.6.9.
8th.Lan Fus.	Right Sub Sector.	1/7th.Manchesters.	Dugout on Roadside K.25.b.9.4. 6.0.p.m.	Rear Coys to be relieved first. Front line Coy will not be relieved until Dark. Battn.H.Q.K.19.c.6.0.
125th.T.M.Battery.	-	127th.T.M.Battery.	-	All arrangements to be made between C.O's concerned, relief to be complete by 6.0.p.m.

N.B. Interval of 400 yards to be maintained between platoons.

(1)

SECRET.

Copy No. 15

125TH.INFANTRY BRIGADE ORDER. NO.90.

****

Ref Map : Sheet 57.D.N.E. 1:20.000   15/8/18.

1. No information is available of how far the enemy is withdrawing his troops.

2. The IV Corps will not leave its present defensive positions to pursue, but reconnoitring patrols will be pushed forward to get and maintain touch with the enemy.

3. 125th.Infantry Brigade will make good their present line of advanced posts, and, unless serious enemy resistance is encountered, reconnoitring patrols will resume the advance at 3.30.a.m. today 15th instant.
The advance will be carried out by bounds. The objectives of each bound are shown on attached traces (issued down to Companies).
The 7th.Lan Fus will continue the advance in the Left Subsector of the Brigade Front, and the 8th.Lan Fus in the Right Subsector.

4.(a). Supports must be provided in rear of advanced troops.

(b). Relay posts and visual signalling stations, to enable information to be rapidly communicated, will be established in each Battalion area.

(c). The Brigade Signal Officer will establish a runner post and visual station in the Old Front Line at K.21.d.2.0. connected by wire to Brigade Headquarters by 3.30.a.m.
When possible a forward relay and visual station will be established at SERRE, at approximately K.30.a.6.1.

5. The Divisional, Inter Brigade, and Inter Battalion boundaries are marked on the attached traces.
Battalion Commanders will ensure that liaison is established with flanking troops at liaison posts before the first and subsequent "Bounds" are carried out.

6. The reconnoitring patrols will each be a Platoon strong (not less than 20 men) and should as far as possible be the same for all bounds, fresh troops being sent forward to maintain the positions gained.

7. The 429th Fd.Coy.R.E. will detail one N.C.O. and two Sappers to report forthwith to each Battalion Headquarters, the R.E. personnel will accompany the Infantry Patrols to search for "BOOBY TRAPS" and clear obstacles.

8. Two Batteries R.F.A. in each Brigade Sector have moved into forward positions about COLINCAMPS and FORT STEWART.

9. Battalions will notify this office immediately each bound is reached.

10 ACKNOWLEDGE.

[signature]
Captain,
Brigade Major,
125th.Inf Bde.

Issued at 1.15.a.m. thro' Signals.
Copies to :-

1. 5th.Lan Fus.
2. 7th.Lan Fus.
3. 8th.Lan Fus.
4. 125th.T.M.B.
5. Signals.
6. 429th.Fd.Coy.R.E.
7. Left Group.
8. 'B' Coy., 42nd.M.G.Bn.
9. 127th.Inf Bdo.
10. 2nd.N.Z.Bde.
11. Staff Captain.
12. S.C.
13.)
14.) 42nd Division.
15. W.D.
16. W.D.
17. F I L E.

(2)

SECRET. Copy.No....16.....

125th.INFNATRY BRIGADE ORDER.NO.91.
****

Ref Map: Sheet 57.D.N.E. 1:20.000 15/8/18.

1. 126th.Infantry Brigade are placing 1/5th.Bn.E.Lancs. at the disposal of this Brigade from 6.0.p.m. tonight. They will take over the positions of the three rear Companies of the 5th.Lan Fus and the Company area in FORT CHARLES vacated by 8th.Lan Fus.Battn Headquarters, will be at K.24.d.60.90.

2. The Battalions of the 125th.Inf Brigade will be disposed tonight as follows :-

5th.Lan Fus.- Battn Headquarters PIONEER TRENCH K.25.b.00.45
1 Company FORT STEWART.
1 Company FORT HOD.
1 Company in FORBES TRENCH (Support Coy of 7th.Lan Fus)
1 Company around NORTHERN AVENUE and CENTRAL AVENUE.
(Third Company of 8th.Lan Fus)

7th.Lan Fus.- Battn Headquarters FORT STEWART.
2 Companies occupying original front line positions, remaining 2 Companies will be distributed in depth from advanced posts established today, back to original front line.

8th.Lan Fus.- Battn Headquarters K.19.c.70.00.
1 Company occupying original front line positions.
1 Company occupying positions of present second Company.
Remaining two Companies will be distributed in depth from advanced posts established today, back to original front line.

3. All moves West of the line K.15.central - K.21.central - K.27.central- to be complete by 7.0.p.m. tonight.

4. O.C., 5th.Lan Fus will detail a guide from each of the three rear Companies to be at his Headquarters at 7.0.p.m. to guide the Companies of the 5th.East Lancs into position.

O.C., 8th Lan Fus will detail a guide from the Company which vacated FORT CHARLES to be at the 5th.Lan Fus Headquarters at 7.0.p.m., to guide the incoming Company to FORT CHARLES and show the Platoon dispositions.

5. ACKNOWLEDGE. (Units of 125th.Inf Bde Only)

E.C.Sartin
Captain,
Brigade Major, 125th.Inf Bde.

Issued at 1-30pm thro' Signals.
Copies to :-

1.	5th.Lan Fus.	9.	126th.Inf Bde.
2.	7th.Lan Fus.	10.	127th.Inf Bde.
3.	8th.Lan Fus.	11.	2nd N.Z.Inf Bde.
4.	125th.T.M.B.	12.	Staff Captain.
5.	'B' Coy., 42nd.M.G.Bn.	13.	I.O.
6.	Left Group.	14.)	
7.	429th.Fd.Coy.R.E.	15.)	42nd Division.
8.	1/5th.E.Lancs.	16.)	
		17.)	W.D.
		18.	F I L E.

WO 16

SECRET. Copy No......

125th.INFANTRY BRIGADE ORDER NO.92.
\# 15/8/18.

Ref Map : Sheet 57.D.N.E.

1. Our troops are disposed as follows :-

21st.DIVISION, are holding a line R.7. central - Artillery Lane - R.I.a.0.3. where they join with 127th.Inf Brigade.
During the morning their troops endeavouring to advance in R.2.b. and d, encountered considerable opposition.
21st Division do not intend moving further forward than R.1.b. central tonight.

N.Z.DIVISION are holding the line K.30.b.3.0. to L.25.a.52. - 70.46. along Tramline to L.26.a.1.5. N.E. along trench to L.20.c.8.0. and L.20.c.55.85. North along road to L.20.a.45.80. to L.14.c.0.0. - L.14.a.1.3. - 10.95. - L.8.d.1.8.

2. (a). 7th.Lan Fus & 8th.Lan Fus will continue to work forward as far East as the high ground in L.26 - 27 - 32 - 33, i.e., The RED LINE marked on trace issued with 125th.Inf Brigade Order No.91.

(b). No general advance will be made beyond the RED LINE mentioned above until further orders, but as soon as the RED LINE has been made good reconnoitring patrols will be pushed forward EAST of it. It is of great importance that the Hill in K.26.d. - K.27.c. - K.32.d. - K.33.d. be occupied. Any information will be immediately reported to this office. Scouts will be left out to observe.

3. Certain Batteries of Field and Heavy Artillery have been ordered to prepare to move forward tonight to closer support of the Infantry.

4. A visual Signal Station and Telephone Post have been established in K.29.c.8.7. Full use of the station will be made.

5. ACKNOWLEDGE. (Units of the 125th.Inf Bde.Only).

E.C. Sartin. Captain,
Brigade Major,
125th.Inf Bde.

Issued at 11.0am thro' Signals.
Copies to :-

1. 5th.Lan Fus. (6 Topo Maps)
2. 7th.Lan Fus. (6 " ")
3. 8th.Lan Fus. (6 " ")
4. 125th.T.M.B. (1 " Map)
5. 1/5th.E.Lancs.1 " ")
6. 'B' Coy., 42nd.M.G.Bn.
7. Left Group. (1 Topo Map).
8. 429th.Fd.Coy.R.E.
9. 126th.Inf Bde.
10. 127th.Inf Bde.
11. 2nd N.Z.Inf Bde.
12. Staff Captain.
13. I.O.
14.)
15.)42nd Division.
16.)
17.) W.D.
18. F I L E.

Secret (7) Copy No 9.

125 Inf Bde Order No 97.

Ref Maps: 57°N.E + S.E. 25-8-18.
57c N.W + S.W.

1. 125 Inf Bde will concentrate in the vicinity of LOUPART WOOD tonight.

2. Battns will march as soon as rations arrive by the following routes:-

5 Lan Fus via Light Rly. - PUISIEUX-MIRAUMONT Rd - DOVECOTE - MIRAUMONT - thence via PYS. Transport via PUISIEUX + MIRAUMONT.

7 Lan Fus via Track across MUNICH TRENCH K36.a.88 to MIRAUMONT thence via PYS.

8 Lan Fus via Road in L.33.a to MIRAUMONT thence via PYS.

C Coy 42 M.G.Bn. via BEAUREGARD via DOVECOT - MIRAUMONT thence via PYS.

125 T.M.B. - via track across Munich Trench K36.a.88. to MIRAUMONT thence via PYS, to follow Bde H.Q. which will start from present Bde H.Q. at 5.0.pm.

3. Staff Capt will arrange areas & will notify the mounted Officers detailed to meet him at PYS, of the areas allotted.

4 ACKNOWLEDGE

Capt.
Bde Major
125 Inf Bde.

Issued at 2-45 pm thro' Sigs

Copies to:–

1 5 Lan Fus
2 7 " "
3 8 " "
4 125 T.M.B.
5 C Coy M.G.C.
6 }
7 } 42 Division
8 }
9 } W.D.
10 File.

(8)

Secret

Copy No 11

125th Inf Bde Order No 98.

27-8-18.

Ref Map Sheets 57D NE & SE.
57C NW & SW.

1. 42 Division will relieve 63 Divn in the Right Sector of the IV Corps front tonight. 125 Inf Bde Group will be in Support & disposed as follows:-

Bde HQ.	PYS Cemetery M2.d.2.5.
5 Lan Fus	G34.c. & G35.d.
8 "	M.4.a. & M.3.b.
7 "	G33.c. & M.3.a.
C Coy 42 M.G.C.	M.3.c.
125 TMB.	M.2.d.

2. Units will send representatives to reconnoitre the above areas at once.

3. Units will march from their present areas as follows:-

5 Lan Fus	leave present camp	7.30 pm
8 "	" " "	7.50 pm
7 "	" " "	8.10 pm
C Coy 42 M G C.	" " "	8.30 pm
125 TMB	" " "	9.0 pm.

4. Completion of move to be notified to this office.

5. Bde H.Q. will close at 9.30pm at R.5 d 7.7. & reopen at Q.4.S Cemetery at same hour.

6 ACKNOWLEDGE. (Units 125 Inf Bde

[signature] Capt.
Bde Major
125 Inf Bde.

Issued at 5.30pm thro' Sigs.

Copies to:-

1 5 Lan Fus
2 7 —"—
3 8 —"—
4 125 T.M.B.
5 C Coy M.G.C.
6 1/1st E L Fd Amb.
7 S.C.
8 Signals
9 } H.Q. Division
10 }
11 } W.D.
12 }
13. File.

Secret. (9) Copy No: 7

125 Inf Bde Order No: 99.

30-8-18

Ref Map Sheet 57c NE + N.W.

1. 126 Inf Bde are carrying out an operation on RIENCOURT tonight. After this operation 127 Inf Bde will take over from 126 Inf Bde less 1 Battalion.

2. 4 Lan Fus will be at the disposal of 126 Inf Bde from midnight 30/31st August.

3. In the event of an enemy counter attack the lines of resistance will be as follows:-

First Line - Road Junction N.9.b.8.0. N.E. along road to H.34.c.8.0. thence to H.35.d.45.55. when touch will be kept with N.Z. Division. An outpost system will be pushed out.

Second Line - LIGNY-THILLOY high ground N.2 central & 32.c. + d.

Third Line LOUPART ROAD within Divisional Boundaries.

Advance Brigade will occupy First Line of Resistance. Support Brigade will the Second Line. Reserve Brigade the Third Line of Resistance.

4. 125 Inf Bde less 8 Lan Fus is in Reserve. In the event of an hostile counter-attack the 5 Lan Fus will take over the BATTLE dispositions of the 8 Lan Fus & will arrange to reconnoitre these positions at once. All other Battle dispositions will be as previously arranged.

5. 125 Inf Bde Group will be prepared to take over from 126 Inf Bde Group tomorrow at a time to be notified later.

6 Acknowledge.

R. M. Sutton Capt.
Bde Major
125 Inf Bde.

Issued at 9.48pm Div Sigs.

Copies to:-

1 5 Lan Fus	6 Staff Capt.
2 7 -"-	7 } War Diary
3 8 -"-	8 }
4 125 T.M.B.	9 } 42 Division
5 C Coy 42 M.G.Bn.	10 }
	11 File.

Secret. (10) Copy No 11.

125 Inf Bde order No 100. 31-8-18.

Ref Map 57c N.E. & N.W.

1. 125 Inf Bde will relieve 126 Inf Bde less 1 Battn today 31st Aug: also 1 Battn 127 Inf Bde.

2. 8 Lan Fus will relieve 7 Man Regt & be at disposal of the 127 Inf Bde but will only be used in the event of tactical emergency.

3. 125 Inf Bde on completion of relief will be the Brigade in Support:-

UNIT	To relieve	Guides	Remarks.
5 Lan Fus	8 Manchesters	5 L.F. will send advance parties at once.	8 Manchesters situated in LOUPART Road. Relief to be complete by 7 pm
7 Lan Fus	5 E Lancs.	1 per platoon X Roads M11b. at 4.0. pm.	
8 Lan Fus	7 Manchesters	1 per platoon Time & place to be notified later	H.Q. 7 Manchrs Brickfield M.2.a.
125 T.M.B.	126 T.M.B.		all arrangements to be made by C.O.s concerned. H.Q. M.12.b.0.6.

C Coy 42 M G Bn. All arrangements will be notified later.

4 Brigade Headquarters will close at PYS Cemetery at 5.0 pm. & re-open at M 12 a 6 8 at the same hour.

5 Completion of relief to be notified to this office.

6 ACKNOWLEDGE.

E.S. Sartin? Capt.
Brigade Major
125 Inf Bde.

Issued at 1.0 pm thro' Sigs
Copies to:-

1 5 Lan Fus
2 7 " "
3 8 " "
4 125 T.M.B.
5 C Coy M G Bn
6 126 Inf Bde
7. 127 " "
8 Staff Capt.
9, 10 42 Division
11, 12 W. D.
13 FILE.

SECRET

11

Copy No 9.

125 Inf. Bde. Order No 101.

Ref. Map 57c N.E. and N.W. 31-8-18

1. 125 Inf. Bde. being in support is responsible for the Second Line of Resistance which runs as follows:-
LIGNY - THILLOY - high ground N 2 central - N 31 c central.

2.(a) In the event of an enemy counter attack the 7 Lan. Fus. will take up position on this line, one company being distributed in depth from the Southern outskirts of THILLOY to the Southern Divisional Boundary, the remaining three companies being distributed in depth from the Northern outskirts of THILLOY to the Northern Divisional Boundary.

(b) 5 Lan. Fus. will send two companies to take up position on the high ground about N 1 a and b, the remaining two companies will take up positions on the high ground immediately West of the BAPAUME - LE SARS road, M 6 b a and c and M 11 b.

(c) O.C. "C" Coy. 42nd Bn. M.G. Bn. will detail 1 section (4 guns) to report to the 7 Lan. Fus. and 5 Lan. Fus. O.C. "C" Coy. will reconnoitre positions for these guns in consultation with the O.C. Battalion concerned.

3. Above positions will be reconnoitred

tonight.

4. ACKNOWLEDGE.

[illegible]
Captain.
Brigade Major
125 Inf. Brigade.

Issued at 8 pm. thro' Signals.

Copies to:

1. 5 Lan Fus
2. 7 Lan Fus
3. 125 T.M. Bty
4. C Coy 42nd Bn M.G.C.
5. 127 Inf. Bde.
6. }
7. } 42nd Division
8. }
9. War Diary
10. File

WS

SECRET. Copy No. 15

125th. INFANTRY BRIGADE ORDER NO.93.

17/8/18.

Ref Map : Sheet 57.D.N.E.

1. Heavy Artillery will bombard the Hill in L.26.d. - 27.c. - 33.a. - 32.b. from 11.30.a.m. to 1.0.p.m. today.

2. Field Artillery and Machine Guns will harass the forward slope of the hill between those hours, but not West of the line L.26.a. 60.30. - L.26.c.40.20. - L.32.a.10.70.
   Field Artillery will fire heavy bursts at intervals.

3. Reconnoitring patrols should be pushed forward on completion of the bombardment.

4. Units of 125th.Inf Bde. to ACKNOWLEDGE.

E.H. Saxton, Captain,
Brigade Major,
125th.Inf Bde.

Issued at 10.0.a.m. thro' Signal.
Copies to :-

1. 5th.Lan Fus.
2. 7th.Lan Fus.
3. 8th.Lan Fus.
4. 125th.T.M.B.
5. 'B' Coy., 42nd M.G.Bn.
6. Left Group.
7. 429th.Fd.Coy.R.E.
8. 127th.Inf Bde.
9. 2nd.N.Z.Inf Bde.
10. I.O.
11. Staff Captain.
12.)
13.) 42nd Division.
14. W.D.
15. W.D.
16. F I L E.

wp

SECRET. Copy No.......15

125th.INFANTRY BRIGADE ORDER NO.94.

****

Ref Map:Sheet 57.D.N.E. 17 8/18.

1. Heavy Artillery will bombard the Hill in L.26.d. - 27.c. - 33.a. - 32.b. from 11.0.p.m. - 12.midnight and again from 3.0.a.m. - 4.0.a.m. tomorrow 18th instant.

2. Field Artillery and 'B' Company 42nd M.G.Bn. will harass the forward slope of this hill at intervals during the night, especially during the hours mentioned in para 1, with heavy bursts.

3. Reconnoitring patrols should be pushed forward at 4.0.a.m. on completion of bombardment.

4. Units of 125th.Inf Bde to acknowledge.

[signature] Captain,
Brigade Major,
125th.Inf Bde.

Issued at 10.... thro' Signals.

Distribution as for Order No.93.

(5)

W D.

Z.13.

SECRET.

Copy No....15

20/8/18.

Reference 125th.Infantry Brigade Order No.95.

****

1. ZERO HOUR will be 4.55.a.m. 21st August 1918.

2. Brigade Headquarters will close at J.17.c.4.2. at 3.0.p.m. today and reopen at K.31.b.4.8. at the same hour.

3. ACKNOWLEDGE.

Distribution as for 125th.Inf Bde. Order No.95.

E.L. Saxton. Captain,
Brigade Major, 125th.Inf Bde.

SECRET. Copy No. 15

125th. INFANTRY BRIGADE ORDER NO. 95.

20/8/18.

Ref Map: Sheet 57.D.N.E.

1. The Third Army has been ordered to press the enemy back towards BAPAUME without delay, and to make every effort to prevent the enemy from destroying Road and Rail Communication.

2. The following operations will take place tomorrow 21st August:-

(a). The 37th Division has been ordered to attack and capture the high ground East of BUCQUOY and ABLAINZEVELLE.

(b). Following preliminary operation (a), the 5th. Division (on right) and 63rd (R.N.) Division on left with the 10th Battn. Tanks have been ordered to be ready to push forward to the line IRLES - BIHUCOURT.

3. 42nd Division in conjunction with N.Z. Division on left and 21st Division on Right will co-operate as follows :-

(a). With the operation detailed in para 2 (a) by advancing and securing general line R.2.central and High Ground in L.32.b. and L.36.d. - Eastern outskirts of PUISIEUX - and to keep touch with enemy by patrols.

(b). With the operation detailed in para 2 (b) by advancing to the general line L.29.b.central - BEAUREGARD DOVECOTE - R.2.b.central.

4. 125th. Infantry Brigade will attack on the left of the Divisional Front in co-operation with the N.Z. Division, as follows :-

At ZERO - 5th. Lan Fus, less 1 Company, will attack the first Objective, the RED LINE on attached map 'A', under cover of a Field and Heavy Artillery Barrage, the Barrage will lift at the rate of 100 yards every 4 minutes.

At ZERO + 120. - 1 Company 5th. Lan Fus will attack the Second objective, the BLUE LINE on attached map 'A'. The advance of the N.Z. Division has been arranged to take place at the same hour.

At ZERO + 240. - 7th. Lan Fus, less two Companies, will attack the Third objective, BROWN LINE on attached map 'A'. 127th. Infantry Brigade will depart for their final objective at the same hour. The 125th. Infantry Brigade will be supported by N.Z. Divisional Artillery. When the Third objective has been captured and protective barrage lifted, O.C., 7th. Lan Fus will arrange to push fighting patrols forward to L.29. central and in the direction of MIRAUMONT.

5. Hostile counter-attacks may be expected from the direction of:-

MIRAUMONT, BEAUCOURT and GRANDCOURT.

In the event of counter-attack, lines of resistance will be held as under :-

(a). OUTPOST LINE.

(b). First line resistance :-

L.28.a. - BEAUREGARD DOVECOTE - L.33.b.2.2.

(c). Second line resistance :-

First objective, RED LINE on attached Map.

6. 59th Squadron R.A.F. have been ordered to arrange for a contact Aeroplane to call for flares at the following times ;-

ZERO +1 hour. ZERO+5 hours
ZERO +3 hours ZERO+7 hours.

The signal to denote the assembly of enemy to counter - attack is the dropping of a RED Smoke Bomb over the place the enemy is seen.

7. O.C., 'B' Coy., 42nd M.G.Battn. will push forward four Machine Guns to the RED LINE when it is captured, two guns being sited on each flank and another four guns to the Third Objective when it is captured.

8. Attached maps 'B', 'C' and 'D', show signal communications within the Brigade Area, sufficient copies are issued for distribution down to Companies.

9. Attached Time Table 'E', shows dispositions of troops up to ZERO+240.

10. Artillery Arrangements will be notified later.

11. Acknowledge.

[signature] Captain,
Brigade Major,
125th. Inf Bde.

Issued at 4.45pm thro' Signal.
Copies to :-

1. 5th. Lan Fus.
2. 7th. Lan Fus.
3. 8th. Lan Fus.
4. 125th. T.M.B.
5. 'B' Coy., 42nd M.G.Bn.
6. Left Group.
7. 429th. Fd. Coy. R.E.
8. 127th. Inf Bde.
9. 3rd N.Z. Inf Bde.
10. I.O.
11. Staff Captain,
12.-13. 42nd Division.
14. 125th. Inf Bde. Rear H.Q.
15.-16. W.D.
17. F I L E.

N.B. Maps "A", "B", "C", "D". issued only with Copies 1, 2, 3, 5.

TIME TABLE 'E'.

DISPOSITIONS OF BATTALIONS OF 125TH INFANTRY BRIGADE.

5TH.LANCS FUSILIERS.

Night 20th/21st.- 3 Companies in assembly positions in present front line.
1 Company in Trench K.36.a.70.80. - L.25.a.45.00.

ZERO. - 3 Companies will attack 1st Objective.
1 Company will move forward to positions vacated by assaulting troops.

ZERO + 120. - 1 Company 'Leap Frog' 3 Companies in 1st Objective and assaults 2nd Objective.

H.Q., 5th.Lan Fus will close at K.25.b.5.5. at 7.30.p.m. tonight, and reopen at K.30.c.6.2. at the same hour.

7th. LANCS FUSILIERS.

Night 20th/21st. - 2 Companies East of the Broad Guage Railway running through K.29.
1 Company in present front line.
1 Company in WALTER TRENCH.

ZERO + 120. - 2 Companies will move forward from the Railway to Second Objective.

ZERO + 240. - 2 Companies will attack the Third Objective.
1 Company will move forward from WALTER TRENCH to trench K.36.a.70.80. - L.25.a.45.00.
1 Company will remain in present front Line.

H.Q., 7th.Lan Fus will close at FORT STEWART at 3.0.a.m. 21st and reopen at K.29.b.7.0. at the same hour, and move to K.30.c.6.2. when Second Objective has been captured.

8TH. LANCS FUSILIERS.

Night 20th/21st. - Company in present front line will withdraw to trenches West of WALTER TRENCH, when assaulting troops of 5th.Lan Fus are in position, remaining 3 Companies as at present.

ZERO + 120. - 1 Company will move to ROB ROY TRENCH.
1 Company will move to NORTHERN AVENUE extension about K.22.d.
1 Company will move to CETORIX.

H.Q., 8th.Lan Fus will close at K.19.c.6.0. at 4.a.m. 21st and reopen at K.21.b.1.0. at the same hour.

WD 15

SECRET. Copy No.....

ARTILLERY PROGRAMME.

1. The advance will be made under a Field Artillery 'CREEPING' Barrage and will be divided into four phases, as shown on attached tracing, (Battalions & M.G.Coy only).

PHASE 'A' in RED - ZERO to ZERO plus 45.

PHASE 'B'.in BLUE - - ZERO plus 50 - ZERO plus 110.

PHASE 'C' in YELLOW - ZERO plus 120 - ZERO plus 152.

PHASE 'D' in GREEN - ZERO plus 240 - ZERO plus 302.

The attached trace shews the initial and final barrage line for each phase.

In Phases 'A', 'B', and 'C', 42nd Div'l Artillery will provide all the Field Artillery Fire; in Phase 'D' the 125th.Inf Brigade will be covered by N.Z., Divisional Artillery.

2. In all four phases the barrage will lift at the rate of 100 yds every four minutes. The first lift taking place [illegible] four minutes after opening fire on each initial barrage line.

3. 4.5" Hows will be used in the creeping barrage with the 18 pdrs, their fire, however, will be placed 50 yards further in advance of the fire of the 18 pdrs.

4. In phase 'D' the 'Creeping' Barrage will arrive at its final barrage line at ZERO plus 272. It will remain on this barrage line until ZERO plus 302 thus forming a PROTECTIVE Barrage for 30 minutes.

5. Heavy Artillery will be co-operating and in the event of an enemy counter-attack on the first objective all Heavy Guns firing on the Brigade front, will fire rapid.

6. ACKNOWLEDGE.

E.H. Carter Captain,
Brigade Major,
125th.Inf Bde.

20/8/18.

Distribution as for 125th.Inf Bde. Order No.95.

(6)

SECRET. Copy No.......

125TH. INFANTRY BRIGADE ORDER NO.96.
*** 22/8/18.

Ref Map : Sheet 57.D.N.E.

1. O.C., 8th.Lan Fus will place two Companies at the disposal of O.C., 7th.Lan Fus to carry out the following attacks :-

FIRST OBJECTIVE.- L.28.c.45.65. - L.28.a.85.10. thence due East - L.28.b.85.10. which will be consolidated & held.

SECOND OBJECTIVE.- L.34.a.50.70. - L.34.b.30.75. - L.29.c.00.00. - L.29.c.50.55.

2. TIME TABLE.

ZERO - 4 hours. - O.C., 7th.Lan Fus will detail 8 guides under an Officer to meet 2 Companies 8th.Lan Fus at 'T' Roads L.25.a.35.90.

ZERO - 2 hours. - Officer 8th.Lan Fus will meet Officer 3rd N.Z.Bde at L.22.c.6.5.

ZERO - 90 minutes.- Assaulting troops will move ~~in~~ to their assembly positions along Railway from L.27.b.7.8. - L.22.c.6.5.

ZERO - 45 minutes. Assaulting troops move to their assaulting positions, a line parallel to, and 300 yards ~~from~~ NORTH of the First Objective.

ZERO - Artillery Barrage drops on the First Objective. 125th.T.M.Battery opens fire on BEAUREGARD DOVECOTE. Assaulting troops move towards the Barrage.

ZERO plus 10. - Artillery Barrage creeps to second objective at the rate of 100 yds in four minutes, assaulting troops following. First Objective assaulted. 125th.T.M. Battery ceases fire.

ZERO plus 26. - Assaulting troops enter Second Objective. Artillery Barrage continues creeping at the same rate down to the Valley. Assaulting troops push out patrols.

3. Assaulting troops will carry 200 rounds S.A.A. and two Bombs per man.

4. Officer in charge of the guides will inform all Officers of the Companies of 8th.Lan Fus the position of the forward Headquarters of 7th.Lan Fus.

5. The Artillery Barrage between the First and Second Objectives will come close to the Right Company of the 7th.Lan Fus, the Company Commander will be warned and if necessary he will withdraw his troops in the front line but will immediately occupy the vacated positions when the barrage has passed.

6. When Second Objective has been gained O.C., 'B' Coy 42nd M.G.Battn. will send forward two Machine guns.

7. NORTHERN Divisional Boundary is as follows :-

L.29.c.5.5. - L.29.a.0.0. - L.22.d.0.0.

8. ZERO Hour 2.30.a.m. 23rd August 1918.

9. ACKNOWLEDGE. (Units of 125th.Inf Bde. only).

[signature]
Captain,
Brigade Major,
125th.Inf Bde.

Issued at 8.30 p.m. thro' Signals.
Distribution as for 125th.Inf Bde.Order No.95.

7

Vol 20

WAR DIARY

125 Inf BDE HQ

SEPT 1918

VOL 50.

Instructions regarding War Diaries and Intelligence Summaries are contained in F. S. Regs., Part II. and the Staff Manual respectively. Title pages will be prepared in manuscript.

WAR DIARY or ~~INTELLIGENCE SUMMARY~~.

SEPTEMBER

(Erase heading not required.)

125 INF. BDE

SHEET No 1. VOL 50

Army Form C. 2118.

Place	Date	Hour	Summary of Events and Information	Remarks and references to Appendices
REF 57c 1/40000	SEPTEMBER.			
M12a 59	1		Brigade in Divisional Support. - Situation quiet	
	2	4.20pm	G14 received from Div - Be prepared to relieve 127 INF.BDE. to-morrow night.	
		6.5pm	S.C.20 issued placing 1/5 LAN. FUS. at disposal of 127 INF.BDE. from 6.0 pm.	
		6.10pm	Div. wire G17 received - 1/8 LAN.FUS. at disposal of 127 INF.BDE. will be put into line to-night aaa 125 INF.BDE. to put another battalion at disposal of 127 INF.BDE. in case of emergency.	
		2.47pm	1/5 LAN. FUS. report 3 coys. established in area N2b & N3c	
		7.12pm	1/5 LAN. FUS. wires 4th coy. in area N2b & N3C.	
		7.45pm	127 INF.BDE. O.O. No 29 despatched ordering 1/8 LAN. FUS. to relieve 1/6 MANCHESTERS & 1/5 LAN. FUS. to be in support	
		11.0pm	Bde O.O. No 102 issued ordering Bde to relieve 127 INF. BDE on night 3/4th	(1)
		11.0pm	Bde. O.O. No 103 issued given lines of resistance in case of enemy attack	(2)
	3	9.15am	Div. Wire G 28 states 125 Bde will move up & leap-frog through 127 Bde; become advance Bde. of Division	
N3C26		9.30am	Bde H.Q. established at N3c26	
		8.0am	1/8 LAN. FUS. ordered to move forward as adv. guard to Div. - final objective trenches 500yds E. of YTRES.	

D. D. & L., London, E.C. (A8004) Wt. W1771/M2-31 750,000 5/17 Sch. 52 Forms/C2118/14

Instructions regarding War Diaries and Intelligence Summaries are contained in F. S. Regs., Part II. and the Staff Manual respectively. Title pages will be prepared in manuscript.

WAR DIARY
or
~~INTELLIGENCE SUMMARY.~~
(Erase heading not required.)

Army Form C. 2118.

SEPTEMBER
125 INF. BDE.
SHEET No 2.

Place	Date	Hour	Summary of Events and Information	Remarks and references to Appendices
Ref. 57c 1/40000	SEPTEMBER.			
O 7 b 95	3	2.0 pm	Bde H.Q. established at O 7 b 95	
O 15 b 99		5.0 pm	Bde. H.Q. established at O 15 b 99	
		8.15 pm	Div. Order No 54 despatched - Advance will be resumed to-morrow at 7.0 am. Div will be prepared to make good ~~trench~~ line E. of METZ en COUTURE. Advance to be made by bounds. 125 Bde. forming advance guard.	
		9.0 pm	1/8 LAN. FUS. reached final objective & halted for the night	
		9.15 pm	Bde O.O. No 104 issued giving disposition of Bde.	(3)
	4	1.0 AM	Bde. O.O. No 105. issued ordering advance to continue at 7.0 AM.	(4)
		12.30 AM	Div. wire G.57 received giving liaison points with flanks during advance	
		7.0 AM	1/5 LAN. FUS. advanced to line 300 Yds E. of CANAL DU NORD in P21 b & d & in trenches in P27 b & d where they were held up by M.G. fire	
		7.0 AM	2 coys 1/8 LAN. FUS. attacked behind barrage & captured NEUVILLE-BOURJONVAL in the N. The coy in the S. was held up by M.Gs & unable to advance.	
		10.30 pm	Bde OO no 106 issued giving disposition & line of resistance for night	(5)
	5.	4.17 pm	Div. wires - 125 I.B. with N.Z. Div. will attack under Arty. barrage & establish line from road junction P29 b 1060 - NW. along POWER TR. to N.Z. boundary - Zero hour 5.30 pm	
		4.15 pm	Bde O.O. No 107 issued ordering attack by 1/7 LAN. FUS.	(6)
		5.30 pm	1 coy 1/7 LAN. FUS. attacked & secured objectives except in S. where a defensive flank was formed in P22c. 6 offrs & 111 O.R. were captured.	
		8.0 pm	Div. Order No 56 received ordering relief of Div by N.Z. Div - 125 I.B. to be in P Y S area	
		11.15 pm	Bde O.O. No 108 issued ordering relief	(7)

D. D. & L., London, E.C. Wt. W771/M2 350,000 5/17 Sch. 52 Forms/C2118/14

Army Form C. 2118.

Instructions regarding War Diaries and Intelligence Summaries are contained in F. S. Regs., Part II. and the Staff Manual respectively. Title pages will be prepared in manuscript.

WAR DIARY
or
~~INTELLIGENCE SUMMARY.~~

(*Erase heading not required.*)

September 125 Inf. Bde
PAGE 3. VOL 50

Place	Date	Hour	Summary of Events and Information	Remarks and references to Appendices
57c M2d54.	6.	10 a.m.	Bde HQ. opened at PYS.	
	6 - 19		Div in rest. Training & refitting.	
		7.30 pm	Bde O.O No 110 issued, ordering relief by 125 Bde of 63 Bde in BEUGNY - LEBUCQUIERE Area.	8
	20/21.		Bde in rest. Training etc	
I 30 a 98.	22.	2.30 p.m.	Bde HQ. moved to LEBUCQUIERE. Bde in Div. Reserve	
	23.	9.30 a.m.	Conference of COs to discuss forthcoming operations	
	24.		Bde in reserve. Reconnaissances of front made	
	25.	9 a.m.	Conference of C.O.S. to give them arrangements etc for the operations.	
	26.	2 p.m.	Bde O.O No. 111. issued, ordering attack on morning of 27th The objectives were	9
			1st from S. Div boundary Q11 d 87 - Q5 d 72 - STAFFORD TR - DERBY TR. - CHAPEL WOOD SWITCH	
			2nd Obj (BROWN LINE) YORK AV. - ARGYLE RD.	
			3rd Obj (YELLOW LINE) VILLERS PLOUICH - RIBECOURT RD.	
			4th Obj HIGHLAND RIDGE. (BLUE LINE)	
			with 7th L.F on right, 8th LF on left & 5th LF in support.	
Q10 Central		5 pm	Bde HQ. established at Q10 Central.	
	27th	2.30 a.m	All batts reported in assembly positions. 5th LF area Q10 Central. 7th LF trenches in Q11 a & c. 8th LF trenches in Q4 d & Q5 c. TMB in trenches in Q 4d.	
		5.20 a.m	Zero hour.	

D. D. & L., London, E.C.
(A8004) Wt. W1771/M2-31 750,000 5/17 Sch. 52 Forms/C2118/14

Instructions regarding War Diaries and Intelligence Summaries are contained in F. S. Regs., Part II. and the Staff Manual respectively. Title pages will be prepared in manuscript.

WAR DIARY
or
INTELLIGENCE ~~SUMMARY.~~

(Erase heading not required.)

Army Form C. 2118.

125 Inf Bde HQ. PAGE 4. Vol. 50. SEPT 1918.

Place	Date	Hour	Summary of Events and Information	Remarks and references to Appendices
57^c Q10 Central	27	8.20am	Attack launched under creeping barrage, & proceeded satisfactorily on right where first objective was taken, but heavy MG fire was encountered at Q12 a 55 from guns located at Q12 a 82 & 86. Various subsequent attempts to outflank these guns were frustrated by further MG fire from right flank, but an enemy counter attack with bombs was successfully repulsed. The right batt finally withdrew to first objective, where it reformed, ready for a new assault in conjunction with Bdes on right & left, timed for 6.30 pm. This was subsequently postponed till 2.30 am 28th inst. The 8th LF on left encountered very heavy MG fire from 1st objective & their right flank. After suffering fairly heavy casualties, they got 1st objective by noon, Sunken road in Q6 a & c by 2 pm & BROWN LINE was reached by patrols in the ~~afternoon~~ evening. This was evacuated before the new assault commenced. About 200 prisoners were taken.	
		2-3 pm	Both 7th & 8th in Sunken Rd in Q6 c & a.	
		9.30pm	BM 100 issued, ordered attack on BROWN, YELLOW & BLUE LINES in conjunction with 5th Div on right & 127 Bde on left. Zero hour subsequently altered to 2.30 a.m.	10.
	28	2.30am	Attack launched. BROWN LINE & about 200 prisoners captured. YELLOW LINE was also captured.	
		12.40pm	Blue line taken & consolidated & posts established in valley at R2 b 73 & R2 d 48.	

(A9175) Wt W2358/P360 600,000 12/17 D. D. & L. Sch. 52a. Forms/C2118/15

Instructions regarding War Diaries and Intelligence Summaries are contained in F. S. Regs., Part II. and the Staff Manual respectively. Title pages will be prepared in manuscript.

WAR DIARY
or
~~INTELLIGENCE SUMMARY.~~
(Erase heading not required.)

Army Form C. 2118.

125 Inf Bde HQ.

PAGE 5 Vol 50. Sept 1918

Place	Date	Hour	Summary of Events and Information	Remarks and references to Appendices
57c Q10 Central	28.	1pm.	2 Coys 1/8 LF passed through 1/5 LF & occupied SUNKEN RD in R8b & R3c with fighting	
		5pm.	patrols pushed forward on to WELSH RIDGE, touch being maintained on both flanks.	
			During these operations the Bde suffered total casualties of 18 OFF & 375 O.R. It captured	
			600-700 prisoners, & large numbers of MGs & TMs & some field guns.	
	29.		2nd NZ Bde passed through 125 Bde to resume the attack at 3.30 am. Units of 125 Bde	
			on relief, moved to areas just E of HAVRINCOURT WOOD.	
Q3b32		2pm	BDE HQ. established at Q3b32. Div in reserve.	
	30.		Bde in Reserve. Rest & reorganisation.	

Hamilton Fergus[?] Brig. Gen.
Cmdg 125 Inf Bde.

2/10/18.

(A9175) Wt W2358/P360 600,000 12/17 D. D. & L. Sch 52a. Forms/C2118/15

(10)

SECRET. B.M.100.

5 Lan Fus. 127 Bde File
7 " " 15 "
8 " " War Diary.
C Coy 42 M.G. Bn

1) In conjunction with 127 Inf Bde on the left and 85 Div Inf Bde on the right, the attack will be resumed tomorrow morning, 28th inst. Zero hour 1.30 a.m.

2) Time Table Barrage will move at rate of 100 yds in 5 mins

Zero Initial barrage will fall on line
Q6a85 – Q6c85 – Q6c60 – Q12a20

Z + 10. One Coy 7 Lan Fus on the right & one Coy 8 Lan Fus on the left will advance & occupy the BROWN LINE under a rolling barrage.

Z + 45 Barrage becomes protective to BROWN LINE, 300 yds E. of it.

Z + 55 Two first Coys 1/5 Lan Fus will leap frog 7 & 8 Lan Fus & capture YELLOW LINE.

(2)

2 + ~~100~~ 95 Barrage becomes protective to YELLOW LINE, 300 yds E of it.

2 + ~~115~~ 105 2 Second Coys of 5 Lan Fus will leap frog 2 first Coys 1/5 Lan Fus & advance to the BLUE LINE.

2 + ~~155~~ 145 Barrage becomes protective to BLUE LINE (final objective)

2 + ~~185~~ 175 Protective barrage dies away. Patrols pushed forward to Sunken Road in R2b, R2d, R8 ~~a~~ c.

3) In advancing to yellow line, a party to be detailed to mop up PLUSH TRENCH.

~~4) 5th Div are co~~

E. Clarke? Capt.
Bde Major 125 Bde.

Issued thro. S.D.R. at 9.30 p.m.
27/9/18.

SECRET (1) Copy No. 11. W.D.

125 Inf Bde Order No 102.

Ref Map. 57c N.E. & N.W. 2-9-18

1. The 125 Inf Bde Group will be prepared to relieve 127 Inf Bde Group tomorrow night 3/4th September.

2. The 8 Lan Fus have taken over the Front Line of the Left Sector of the Divisional Front.
The 5 Lan Fus were placed at the disposal of the 127 Inf Bde from 6-0 pm tonight & have been moved into Support.

3. The 7 Lan Fus will be prepared to relieve the 7 Manch Regt in Right Sector of the Divisional Front tomorrow night 3/4th Sept. Details of relief to be arranged by Commanding officers concerned. Relief to be complete by midnight. Battn H.Q. 7 Manch Regt are situated in RIENCOURT N.5.d.7.2.

4. 'C' Coy 42 M.G. Bn. will be prepared to relieve 'A' Coy 42 M.G. Bn. tomorrow night 3/4th September. H.Q. 'A' Coy are at N.5.c.4.3.
Relief to be complete by midnight.

5. 125 T.M. Bty will be prepared to relieve 127th T.M. Bty, all arrangements for relief to be

arranged between Commanding Officers Concerned. H.Q. at H.34.c.5.1.

6. Units will render a disposition map within 12 hours of relief.
Completion of relief to be notified to these Headquarters.

7. ACKNOWLEDGE (Units of 125 Inf Bde Group only).

E.H. Carter. Capt.
Bde Major
125 Inf Bde

Issued at 11 pm 2/3 Sept
Copies to:-

1	5 Lan Fus	8	42 Div.
2	7 -"-	9	
3	8 -"-	10	W.D.
4	125 T.M. Bty	11	
5	'C' Coy 42 M.G. Bn.	12	Rear H.Q.
6	127 Inf Bde	13.	File.
7	S.C.	14	S.O.

WD

SECRET

(2)

Copy No. 8

125 Inf Bde Order No. 103

Ref. Map 57 C N.E. & N.W. [illegible].7.18

1. The 1st line of resistance is the Front line which runs as follows –

O 8 a 6 7 – O 14 b 6 7 – O 14 d 3 5.

The Second line of resistance for which the 125 Inf Bde Group is responsible runs as follows –

SUNKEN ROAD in N 12 – N 6 d – O 1 a within the Divisional Boundaries.

2. In the event of an enemy counter attack the 7 Lan Fus will immediately man the Second line of resistance.

"C" Coy 42nd M. G. Battn will detail one section to proceed at once to take up positions on the high ground in N 6 b

3. ACKNOWLEDGE (Units of 125 Inf Bde)

[signature] Capt.
Bde Major,
125 Inf Bde

Issued thro' Signals
at 11 p.m.

Copies to

1 7 Lan Fus
2 "C" Coy 42 M.G.Bn
3 127 Inf Bde
4 S.C.
5 } 42nd Division
6 }
7 } War Diary
8 }
9 File

SECRET

(3)

W.D.
Copy No: 8.

125 Infy Bde Order No: 104
Ref Map 57C SW + SE 2-9-18

1. 125 Inf Bde will be disposed tonight as follows + the necessary moves will take place forthwith.

(a) 8 Lan Fus will hold an outpost line East of YTRES in P14 d – P20 b – P21 c – P27 a and d.
Battalion Headquarters will be in YTRES

(b) 5 Lan Fus will be on the first line of resistance along the Railway line in P13 d – P19 b – P20 c – P26 a

(c) 7 Lan Fus will be on the Second Line of resistance East of BUS running through O18 d – O24 b and d.

2. 8 Lan Fus will get touch with the 2 N Z Bde at crossing of Railway and road in P15 c and with the 50 Inf Bde on the right at VALLULART WOOD P23 a

3. Completion of move will be reported to these Headquarters, also map reference of Battalion H Qrs

4. ACKNOWLEDGE

G. S. Horton? Captain
Bde Major
125 Inf Bde

Issued at 9.15 pm Div Sigs
Copies to:–

1 5 Lan Fus
2 7 Lan Fus
3 8 Lan Fus
4 210 Bde RFA
5 2 NZ Bde
6 50 Inf Bde
7 War Diary
8 — " —
9 File

SECRET

4 Copy No: 15

125 Inf Bde Order No: 105.

Ref. Map 57c N.E + S.W. 4-9-18.

1. The advance will be resumed at 7.0 am today.

2 (a) 42 Divn will be prepared to make good Trench line East of METZ-en-COUTURE

(b) The advance will be made by four bounds as follows:-

1st Bound High ground in P.21.d and P 27 b

2nd Bound High ground in P23.b + d 29. b and d.

3rd Bound High ground in Q19 b + d. + Q 25 d.

4th Bound Final objective – Trench line East of METZ-en-COUTURE.

3. The Divl boundaries Eastwards will be as follows:-

(a) Southern Boundary between 42nd Divn and 17th Divn – grid line East + West between P.36 and P.30.

(b) Northern Boundary between N.Z. Divn and 42nd Divn – grid line running East + West between P18 and P.24.

4 5 Lan Fus will form the advance guard, passing through the 8 Lan Fus at 7.0 am. 7 Lan Fus will follow the 5 Lan Fus at a distance of 1000 yards. 8 Lan Fus will follow 7 Lan Fus at a similar interval.

5 (a) O.C. 210 Bde RFA will detail one battery and a liaison officer to move forward with the advance guard under orders of OC 5 Lan Fus.

(b) OC 'C' Coy 42 M.G. Bn will detail two sections to report to OC 5 Lan Fus by 5.0 am today Sept 4th.

(c) OC 429 Fd Coy RE will detail one section to report to OC 5 Lan Fus by 5.0 am today. This section will go forward with the advance guard and look for BOOBY TRAPS and examine roads etc.

(d) OC two troops, 3rd Hussars will order these troops to report to OC 5 Lan Fus by 6.0 am today. These troops will not be used until the situation warrants the use of Cavalry.

6. Headquarters 5 Lan Fus are at O.23 d 6 7

7. Division are establishing visual report centres at P 21 d 8 6. P.23 d 4 3. and Q 19 central

8. ACKNOWLEDGE

[signature] Captain
Bde Major
125 Inf Bde.

Issued at 12.45 am thro' Signals.
Copies to:-

1 5 Lan Fus
2 7 " "
3 8 " "
4 125 T M Bty.
5 'C' Coy 42 M G Bn.
6 210 Bde RFA
7 3rd Hussars
8 429 Fd Coy RE
9 42 Division
10. 42 Division
11. 50 Inf Bde.
12 2 N. Z Bde
13. Signals
14 SE.
15 } War Diary
16 }
17 FILE

SECRET

5

W.D.

Copy. No. 16

125 Infantry Brigade Order No. 106.

Ref Map. 57c S.E. and S.W. 4-9-18

1. 125 Infantry Brigade will be disposed tonight as under :.
5 Lan. Fus. will hold their advance positions as and outpost line with the remainder of the battalion in close support.
8 Lan Fus. will man the first line of resistance, the trench system immediately east of YTRES running through P.14.d – P.20.b. P.21.c – P.27.b.
7 Lan. Fus will be in support to the First Line of Resistance and occupy positions on the railway in P.13.d – P.19.b – P.20.c – P.26.a and c.

2. 125 Infantry Brigade will follow up the enemy tomorrow, keeping touch with him when he retires. The objective for the 125 Inf. Brigade for 5th September is the trench system east of NEUVILLE – BOURJONVAL, if not already captured. 5 Lan. Fus. will push out patrols tomorrow morning and if the enemy has retired will occupy the trench: if the trench is found to be occupied a report will be rendered to this office, not later than 10am when 7 Lan Fus. will be prepared to leap [illegible] the 5 Lan. Fus. and 8 Lan. Fus. and [illegible]

the trench under cover of a barrage.
Detailed orders will be issued from this office.

3. 42nd Division will be prepared to hand over to N.Z. Division tomorrow night 5th/6th September.

4. ACKNOWLEDGE.

[signature] Captain,
Brigade Major,
125 Inf. Brigade

Issued at 10.30 p.m. thro Signals

Copies to:

1.	5 Lan Fus.	10.	2nd N.Z. Bde.
2.	7 Lan Fus.	11. }	
3.	8 Lan Fus.	12. }	42nd Division
4.	125 T M Bty	13.	S.C.
5.	"C" Coy 42 M.G. Bn.	14.	Signals
6.	429 Fd. Coy R.E.	15. }	
7.	210 Bde R.F.A.	16. }	War Diary
8.	126 Inf. Bde	17.	File
9.	50 Inf. Bde.		

Secret

Copy No 16

25th Inf Bde Order No. 104

6

5/9/18

Ref Map 57c SE & SW

1. 7 Lan Fus less 3 Coys will attack and occupy the trench system P.17 b 4.0 - P 23 c 8.0 P 29 b 2 4 with a defensive flank thrown back from P 29 b 2 4 to get touch with 51st Inf Bde on the right. One additional platoon will be detailed to form this defensive flank by OC 7 Lan Fus.

2 The artillery will put down a barrage on the line P 28 a 5.0 - P. 23 b 4 9 at zero and will remain on this line till zero plus 12

At zero +12 the barrage will proceed S.E at the rate of 100 yards in 3 minutes to objective becoming protective on the zone P 23 b and d central - P 29 b 5 2. P 29 c 5 2, remaining protective for a maximum time of 30 minutes

3. B Coy 42nd Bn MGC will take up positions on Kings Hill in P 16 c & P 22 a and fire on the trench system on P 24 a P 24 c - P 30 a and P 30 c from Zero - Zero +64

4. 125 L.T.M.B. will take up a position

– PONDER RESERVE at approximately P 27 l 3 4 and fire on the objective from Zero – Zero + 12

5. An Officer of 125 Inf Bde Headquarters will report to the O 7 L F, 210 Bde RFA & B Coy 42nd Inf Bn by 4/0 pm to synchronize watches

6 Zero hour will be 5/30 pm 5 Sept

7 ACKNOWLEDGE

Issued at 4/15 thro' Signals

[signature illegible]
Capt
Brigade Major
125 Inf Bde

Copy No 1 5 L F
2 7 L F
3 8 L F
4 125 TMB
5 B Coy 42nd Inf Bn
6 L " "
7 210 Bde RFA
8 51 Inf Bde
9 2 NZ Bde
10 126 Inf Bde
11 } 42nd Div
12 }
13 Signals
14 Staff Capt
15 }
16 } WD
17 File

Secret 7 Copy No 4

125 Inf Bde Order No 108.

Ref Map 57c S.E. & S.W. 5-9-18.

1. 42 Div (less Arty) will be relieved by N.Z. Div tonight.

2. 125 Inf Bde will be relieved by 2 N.Z. Bde. Relief to be complete by 4.0 am. On relief 125 Inf Bde will move to PYS area. Areas have been allotted by the Staff Capt.

3. The front line posts will be handed over with great care especially flank posts.

4. No troops will move from the front line which have not been directly relieved by troops of 2 N.Z. Bde.

5. As soon as the front line posts of the 5 Lan Fus & 7 Lan Fus have been relieved this office will be immediately informed by wire.

6. Orders will be issued from this office when troops not directly relieved may withdraw.

G.S.B. Capt.
Bde Major
125 Inf Bde

Issued at 11.15 am this day

Copies to	1	5 Lan Fus	4 } W.D
	2	7 ---	5 }
	3	8 ---	6. File

8

WD

12

S E C R E T.
****

Copy No.........

125th. INFANTRY BRIGADE ORDER NO.110.

19/9/18.

Ref Map: 57.c. 1:40.000.

1. 42nd Division (less Artillery) will relieve 37th Division (less Artillery) on September 20th, 21st, and 22nd, and will become Left Division IV Corps.

2. The Boundaries of the 42nd Division will be :-

Southern Boundary - Q.7.central - Q.9.c.0.0. thence due East.

Northern Boundary - K.33.central - K.28.d.0.0. thence due East.

3. The 125th.Infantry Brigade Group will relieve the 63rd Infantry Brigade Group in the BEUGNY - LEBUCQUIERE Area on the 22nd inst, and become the Brigade in Divisional Reserve.

4. Units will march with transport complete.

5. All plans, Defence Schemes, etc, will be handed over by the 63rd Infantry Brigade.

6. Complation of relief will be reported to these Headquarters.

7. Brigade Headquarters will close at FYS at 2.30.p.m. 22nd inst and reopen at the same hour at I.30.a.9.8.

8. ACKNOWLEDGE. (Units of 125th.Infantry Brigade Group only).

E.U. Sarton
Captain,
Brigade Major,
125th.Inf Bde.

Issued at 7-30pm thro' Signals.
Copies to :-

1. 5th.Lan Fus.
2. 7th.Lan Fus.
3. 8th.Lan Fus.
4. 125th.T.M.Battery.
5. 'C' Coy.,42nd M.G.Bn.
6. 429th.Fd.Coy.R.E.
7.)
8.) 42nd Division.
9. 63rd Inf Brigade.
10. Staff Captain.
11. Signals.
12.)
13.) W.D.
14. F I L E.

MARCH TABLE TO ACCOMPANY 125TH.INFANTRY BRIGADE ORDER NO.110.

UNIT.	TO relieve.	Location.	Head of column to pass starting point M.10.a.2.6. at :-	Route.	Remarks.
5th.Lan Fus.	8 LINCOLNS.	BEUGNY.	11.15.a.m.	WARLENCOURT - BAPAUME FREMICOURT thence by shortest route to area.	Battn will halt at 12.50.p.m., men given midday meal & march continued at 2.0.p.m., Suitable ground clear of road to be reconnoitred. Ground to be left clean and clear of paper before Battn marches off.
7th.Lan Fus.	8 SOMERSETS.	LEBUCQUIERE I.30.a.9.8.	9.15.a.m.	- do -	March direct to new area.
8th.Lan Fus.	4 MIDDLESEX.	I.29.central.	10.15.a.m.	- do -	Battn will halt at 12.50.p.m., men given midday meal & march continued at 2.0.p.m. Suitable ground clear of road to be reconnoitred. Ground to be left clean and clear of papers before Battn marches off.
125th.T.M.Bty.	63rd.T.M.Bty.	I.29.b.2.3.	12.40.p.m.	- do -	March direct to new area.
'C' Coy, 42nd M.G.Bn.	'C' Coy 37th.M.G.Bn.	I.24.d.1.1.	8.30.a.m.	- do -	- do -
429th.Fd. Coy.R.E.	153rd.Fd. Coy.R.E.	I.28.b.7.0.	8.0.a.m.	- do -	- do -
Brigade H.Q.		I.30.a.9.8.	12.30.p.m.	- do -	- do -

N.B. - Above Areas are now occupied by units of 111th Infantry Brigade Group.

(9)

mp

SECRET.

Copy No. 15

125TH. INFANTRY BRIGADE ORDER NO.111. 26/9/18.

Ref Map; Sheet. 57.c.N.E. & S.E.

1. In conjunction with operations by the First Army, the Third Army is resuming the advance.

2. The IV Corps is to capture BEAUCAMP RIDGE and HIGHLAND RIDGE and is to clear the HINDENBURG LINE as far as the COUILLET VALLEY. If the advance of the VI Corps on MARCOING is successful the IV Corps is to advance to WELSH RIDGE to cover the flank of the VII Corps.

3. The 5th. Division will be on the right of the 42nd Division and the 3rd Division on the Left.

4. The attack on the 42nd Divisional Front will be carried out by the 125th. Infantry Brigade on the Right, and the 127th. Infantry Brigade on the Left.
Objectives, Divisional, Brigade and Battalion boundaries are shown on the attached Map.

5. The attack on the 125th. Infantry Brigade Front will be carried out by the 7th. Lancs. Fus on the Right and the 8th. Lancs. Fus on the Left, in accordance with Table 'A'.

6. The attack will be commenced by a hurricane bombardment of Artillery and Trench Mortars on the enemy's forward position, and the Infantry advance will be covered by a creeping barrage arranged in depth in accordance with Table 'A' and attached Map.

7. On the night 26th/27th September, the 126th. Infantry Brigade will withdraw from the line, leaving a screen of outposts to hold the line and to patrol the Divisional Front. Under cover of these outposts the 125th. Infantry Brigade will move into their assembly positions in accordance with Table 'B'.

8. Two Tanks will be detailed by O.C., 'C' Coy 11th Battn Tanks, to deal with BILHEM FARM and BOAR COPSE locality. All ranks will be made acquainted with the signals to be used between Tanks and Infantry.

9. The 59th. Squadron R.A.F. are sending a contact Aeroplane to call for Flares at the following hours :-

ZERO plus 220. on RED Objective.
ZERO plus 300, on BROWN and BROWN Dotted objectives.
ZERO plus 420, on BLUE Objective.

In addition special reconnaissances have been arranged.

The signal to denote the assembly of the enemy to counter-attack will be the dropping of a RED Smoke Bomb over the place where the enemy is seen.
Code Letters for communicating to the Plane will be the Four Letter Code Calls at present in use by the Division.

10. All means of communication will be employed; a Brigade Forward Station will be established in the vicinity of R.7.a.
The Forward Station will accept messages from all units whether Infantry, Artillery or Machine Guns, and will be marked by a BLUE and WHITE Flag.
Visual will be established between the Brigade Forward Station and Brigade Headquarters. Battalions will arrange for Flapper Communication between Companies and Battalions and the Brigade Forward Station.

11. P. of W. Cage will be P.11.central.

Any subsequent Forward move of cage will be notified by 'Q' to all concerned.

12. Battle Headquarters will be established as follows :-

42nd Division........	I.36.d.8.1.
125th.Inf Bde.........	Q.10.central.
126th.Inf Bde.........	Q.8.d.2.5.
127th.Inf Bde.........	Q.3.b 5.2.
15th.Inf Bde. Left Bde. 5th.Division.	BATTERY POST. Q.22.a.6.2.

13. All troops are again to be warned against entering Dug-outs before they have been examined and passed as safe by R.E.

14. 'C' Coy., 42nd M.G.Bn. is co-operating with the 125th.Infantry Brigade and will go forward to consolidate the four objectives in accordance with reports received. The following points will be consolidated by 'C' Coy., 42nd M.G.Bn.:-

(i). About Q.12.central.
(ii). About R.1.c.8.5.
(iii). About Q.6.b.0.6.
(iv). About R.8.a.1.9.

15. 'Handshakes' have been arranged with the 15th. Infantry Brigade at the following points :-

SUNKEN ROAD ..... BLACK Dotted Line.
YORK AVENUE...... RED Line.
HIGHLAND ROAD)... BLUE Line.
R.8.a.1.7.)

16. Brigade Headquarters will close at LEBUCQUIERE at 5.0.p.m. on 'Y' Day and re-open at the same hour at Q.10.central.

17. 'Z' Day and ZERO Hour will be notified later.

18. Watches will be synchronised by an Officer of 125th.Infantry Brigade Headquarters at the Headquarters of Units on 'Y' night.

19. ACKNOWLEDGE.

E.C. Sarton [signature] Captain,
Brigade Major,
125th.Inf Bde.

Issued at 2.a.m.thro' Signals.
Copies to :-

1. 5th.Lan Fus. *	8.127th.Inf Bde.
2. 7th.Lan Fus. *	9.15th.Inf Bdo.
3. 8th.Lan Fus. *	10.Right Group.
4. 125th.T.M.Battery.	11.Signals.
5. 'C' Coy, 42nd.M.G. Bn.	12.Staff Captain.
6. 'C' Coy., 11th.Tank Bn.	13.) 14.) 42nd Division. 15.)
7. 126th.Inf Bde.	16.) War Diary.
	17. F I L E.

* Map only.

TABLE 'A' - TO ACCOMPANY

125TH. INFANTRY BRIGADE ORDER NO. 111.
****

NOTE. ZERO Hour is the hour at which the Corps to the North of us start their attack.

ZERO plus 152. - Initial Barrage commences and stands for 10 minutes.

ZERO plus 162. - Leading Companies of 7th and 8th. Lancs. Fus advance to 1st Objective under rolling barrage.

ZERO plus 190. - Barrage reaches protective line for 1st Objective and stands for 8 minutes.

ZERO plus 198 - Second Companies of 7th and 8th. Lancs. Fus having leap-frogged leading Companies, advance to 2nd Objective under rolling barrage, the Company of the 8th. Lancs. Fus after reaching Second Objective makes a swing pivoted on their Right and still under rolling barrage, so as to get onthe BROWN Line; at the same time the first Company of the 8th. Lancs. Fus swing pivoted on their right so as to get on line of road running North and South in Q.6.a & b. and in time with 1st Company of 7th. Lancs. Fus.

ZERO plus 222. - Barrage reaches protective line for BROWN Line and stands for 8 minutes.

ZERO plus 230. - Third Companies of 7th. Lancs. Fus and 8th. Lancs. Fus having leap-frogged second Companies in BROWN Line advance under rolling barrage to 3rd Objective.

5th. Lancs. Fus occupy SNAP Trench, SHERWOOD AVENUE, DERBY Support, DERBY TRENCH, and Southern portion of CHAPEL WOOD Switch.

ZERO plus 236. - Barrage reaches protective line for 3rd Objective and stands for 54 minutes.

ZERO plus 270. - Right Flank of 7th. Lancs. Fus Company in 3rd Objective advances under rolling barrage to PLOWGH Trench to join up with 5th. Division on South.

ZERO plus 320. - Fourth Companies of 7th and 8th. Lancs. Fus having leap-frogged third Companies, advance under rolling barrage to final objective.

ZERO plus 324. - Barrage reaches protective line on South.

ZERO plus 348. - Barrage reaches protective line on North.

TABLE 'B'. - TO ACCOMPANY
125TH. INFANTRY BRIGADE ORDER NO.111
****

The 125th.Infantry Brigade will proceed to assembly positions by BUS to RUYALCOURT thence by route march via MATHESON Road and tracks South of Inter Brigade Boundary prolonged South Westwards through CLAYTON CROSS as follows :-

UNIT.	Embussing point & time.	Remarks.
8th.Lan Fus.	I.29.central. 1.0.p.m.	Battalion after debussing will rendezvous in P.9.b. where hot food will be given to troops under Battn arrangements. Guides from 126th.Inf Bde will be at ammunition dump, junction of Road and Light Railway Q.15.a.1.9. at 9.15.p.m.
7th.Lan Fus.	3.0.p.m.	Battalion after debussing will rendezvous in P.9.d. where hot food will be given to troops under Battn arrangements. Guides from 126th.Inf Bde will be at ammunition dump, junction of Road and Light Railway Q.15.a.1.9. at 10.15.p.m..
5th.Lan Fus.	BEUGNY. 5.0.p.m.	Battalion after debussing will rendezvous in P.10.a. where hot food will be given to troops under Battn arrangements. Battalion will march to assembly positions so as to reach ammunition dump junction of Road and Light Railway Q.15.a.1.9. at 11.15.p.m
125th.T.M.Battery.	I.29.central. 1.0.p.m.	Unit after debussing will proceed in two parties to Headquarters 126th.Inf Bde where a carrying party will be ready to carry ammunition from the Dump to the Tanks at Q.14.d.5.4. on completion of which it will proceed to assembly positions.

All units will report completion of moves.

7th.Lan Fus and 8th.Lan Fus will each send a mounted Officer to reconnoitre the route from the debussing point to the rendezvous for guides, an interval of 200 yards to be mainteined between platoons.

All ranks will carry Greatcoats to the assembly positions where they will be dumped by Companies by ZERO plus 100 and one man per Company left to take charge of them.

During the halt after debussing, battalions will draw Bombs and S.O.S.Rockets.

All units will be assembled EAST of TRESCAULT VALLEY in the following reconnoitred areas :-

5th.Lan Fus... Trenches arounf Q.10.central.
7th.Lan Fus... Trenches in Q.11.a & c.
8th.Lan Fus... Trenches in Q.4.d & Q.5.c.
125th.T.M.Bty. Trenches in Q.4.d.

TIAL

Vol 21

WAR DIARY

125 Inf. Bde. H.Q.

OCT. 1918

VOL 51.

Instructions regarding War Diaries and Intelligence Summaries are contained in F. S. Regs., Part II. and the Staff Manual respectively. Title pages will be prepared in manuscript.

WAR DIARY or INTELLIGENCE SUMMARY.

(Erase heading not required.)

Army Form C. 2118.

125 Inf Bde. October 1918.

PAGE 1. VOL. 51.

Place	Date	Hour	Summary of Events and Information	Remarks and references to Appendices
57c Q 3 b 32.	1–7		Div. in Reserve IV. Corps. Bde training & reorganising.	
	7.	15.00	D.O. No 65 states Division will be prepared to move forward at 0700 hours on the 8th inst.	
			125 Inf Bde will be prepared to move forward at 0730 hours on the 8th inst.	
		1920	Bde order No 113 states: Bde will be prepared to move forward at 0730 hours on the 8th inst.	1
R 13 d. 9.5	8	13.00	Bde H.Q. established at R 13. d 9 5. Move complete at 13.15.	
		18.00	Div. order No 66 states Div. will resume advance at 0800 on 9th inst. to areas about	
			M11. & if situation permits, further to areas between ESNES & GUILLEMIN.	
		2130	Bde order 114 states Bde will move to M11 tomorrow 9th inst.	2
M 11 c 2.7	9		Move complete at 10.50. Bde HQ established at M11. c. 2. 7.	
		10.00	D.O. 68 states Bde group will move forthwith to area between GUILLEMIN & ESNES.	
		13.15	B.M 90. States, in continuation of Bde order No 114, move of Bde group will be	
			continued this afternoon to square N4.	
N 4 b. 4.0			Move complete at 17.10. Bde H.Q. located at N4. b 4.0.	
	10	13.00	D.O. No 69 states Bde group will march to area I 15. 16. 17. 21 & 22 today.	
	10	13.15	Bde order No 115 states Bde group will move this afternoon to squares I 15. 16. 17	3
I 15. c. 8.8			21 & 22. Move complete by 18.30 Bde HQ established at I 15. c. 88	
		2045	D.O. No 70 States Bde will be ordered by NZ Div: B.G.C. 125 Bde will keep close touch	
			with B.G.C. 1st NZ Bde & be prepared to take over the line tomorrow night.	
		2000	G 682 NZ Div. order states, Bde group will move tomorrow 11th to squares J 1 & D 25.	
		23.45	Bde order No 116 states, Bde group is now under tactical orders of NZ Division &	4

(A9175) Wt W2358/P360 600,000 12/17 D. D. & L. Sch 52a. Forms/C2118/15

Army Form C. 2118.

Instructions regarding War Diaries and Intelligence Summaries are contained in F. S. Regs., Part II. and the Staff Manual respectively. Title pages will be prepared in manuscript.

WAR DIARY
or
~~INTELLIGENCE SUMMARY.~~
(Erase heading not required.)

125 Inf Bde
Page 2

Place	Date	Hour	Summary of Events and Information	Remarks and references to Appendices
57 B.	10	2345	will move tomorrow to squares J1 & D25.	
J1 a. 5.5			Move complete by 1500. Bde H.Q. established at J1. a. 5.5	
	11.	1800	Div order No 71 states that the Div. less artillery will relieve NZ Div. in the line on the night of the 12th/13th Oct. in accordance with march table attached, which directs that 125 Bde plus 1 Bn of 126 Bde will relieve 1st NZ Bde in the line which runs as follows: E19.c 7.9 through copse in E19.a. N to D18.d 5.1 thence along W bank of river to D18.b 4.7 then due N.	
	12	10.30	Bde order No 117 states 125 Bde plus 1 Bn of 126 Bde (1/8 Manch Regt) will relieve the 1st NZ Bde in the line today & tonight 12/13 Oct. in accordance with attached relief table & on completion of relief will hold Div. Front.	5
			8th Lan Fus. relieve 1st Bn. Wellington Regt on Rt. Front. B.H.Q. D28 a 8.2	
			5th Lan Fus relieve 2nd Bn Auckland Regt on Left Front B.H.Q. D22.a 7.2	
			1/8th Manc Regt. relieve 1st Bn Auckland Regt. in Right Support B.H.Q. D28 a. 8.1	
			7th Lan Fus relieve 2nd Bn Wellington Regt. in Left Support B.H.Q. D26 a. 6.2	
			125 LTM By. relieve 1st NZ LTM By.	
			'C' Coy 42 M.G Bn relieve 'W' Coy NZ MG Bn H.Q J3. c 5.8	
J3. c. 5.8	13		Relief complete by 00.35 (13th) Bde H.Q. located at J3. c. 58	
			7 Lan Fus reported relief complete at 15.30 ([illegible]) 125 LTM By at 17.00	

(A9475) Wt W2358/P360 600,000 12/17 D. D. & L. Sch 52a. Forms/C2118/15

Instructions regarding War Diaries and Intelligence Summaries are contained in F. S. Regs., Part II. and the Staff Manual respectively. Title pages will be prepared in manuscript.

WAR DIARY
or
~~INTELLIGENCE SUMMARY.~~
(*Erase heading not required.*)

125 Inf. Bde.
Page 3.

Army Form C. 2118.

Place	Date	Hour	Summary of Events and Information	Remarks and references to Appendices
X			Right Coy. post reported attacked during the night. Enemy driven off by L.G. fire leaving 1 prisoner in our hands.	
13.c.5.8	12		1/8 M/c Regt. at 18.30. 5th Lan Fus at 2050. 8 Lan Fus. 00.31 (13th).	
Bde. H.Q.			C. Coy 1/4 E Lan at 0230 (13th).	
	13	16.12	Provisional Defence Scheme issued to units. Heavy barrage put down on front line of Right Bn. 8th Lancs Fus.	
		16.30	C.O. reported to Bde H.Q. & our barrage was opened on S.O.S. lines.	5 (a)
		17.00	Enemy movement reported on right flank, but none opposite Bn. front.	
		17.15	Heavy attack developed & right front posts of Bn were driven in, left front posts holding good. Casualties heavy owing to enfilade fire from right. Two platoons sent forward to reinforce	
		17.20	Intelligence Officer sent forward to ascertain position & report	
		17.40	Situation unchanged. By this time all available men at Coy H.Qrs had been pushed forward to re-establish right flank of Bn. & if necessary form defensive flank to the South, having touch with Div. on right. Report that left front Coy. was holding its original position confirmed.	
		18.00	Situation in Copse E19.a.c.4 acute, severe fighting, casualties heavy. Wounded men report line withdrawn from BELLE-VUE.	
		18.15	Situation explained to Bde.	
		18.20	Information received states Right Coy strength. 27. Left Coy. 50	

(A9173) Wt W2358/P360 600,000 12/17 D. D. & L. Sch. 52a. Forms/C2118/15

Instructions regarding War Diaries and Intelligence Summaries are contained in F. S. Regs., Part II. and the Staff Manual respectively. Title pages will be prepared in manuscript.

WAR DIARY
or
~~INTELLIGENCE SUMMARY.~~
(Erase heading not required.)

125 Inf. Bde.
Page 4.

Army Form C. 2118.

Place	Date	Hour	Summary of Events and Information	Remarks and references to Appendices
13.c.5.8 Bde. H.Q.	13	1900	Line now runs along East of river in D24.b & a. Heavy artillery & M.G. fire directed on forward areas.	
		1920	Patrols sent out to find out situation & keep touch with enemy encounter heavy M.G. fire	
		2100	Enemy M.G. posts reported at E19.c.4.7 E19.a.4.2 & E19.c.2.6. Reliable communication established with Divn. on right. Liaison Post at D24.d.75.20. Situation now quiet, with intermittent shelling of BRIASTRE & forward areas. Enemy M.G. posts are being harried with LTMs & Field artillery during the night.	
			Casualties. 2 officers. 34 other ranks.	
			Line now runs as follows:- D24.d.9.8 – D24.b.7.4 – D18.d.5.1 & thence along road east of river to point west of factory in E13.a.	
	14		D.O. No 74 directs that 125 Bde will improve its position towards E13 cent. & E18 cent. to enable more bridges to be thrown over River SELLE & gives instructions should enemy withdraw. Situation unchanged.	
		1800	BM146 instructs that if enemy withdraws, patrols will be sent forward by 5th L.F. and 8th L.F. to keep in touch giving bounds as follows. Road W. of railway in E13.a. Railway in E13. & E19.a. High ground in E14 & E8.c. E15.b. & E9. central. Cavalry patrols will go forward after 4th bound. 7th L.F. & 8th Manc. Regt. will conform to above. One section M.G. & one section F.A. will go forward with front Bns.	

Instructions regarding War Diaries and Intelligence Summaries are contained in F. S. Regs., Part II, and the Staff Manual respectively. Title pages will be prepared in manuscript.

WAR DIARY
or
~~INTELLIGENCE SUMMARY~~.
(Erase heading not required.)

125 Inf. Bde.
Page 5

Army Form C. 2118.

Place	Date	Hour	Summary of Events and Information	Remarks and references to Appendices
J3.c.5.8	14	1800	Adv. Bde HQ will be established at E19.a.2.3.	
Bde HQ		2000	Above order was amended by BM149 as follows. If enemy withdraw & no opposition experienced, outpost line will be established along 2nd bound with patrols sent out to Sundur road in E14. 5th Div. on right are conforming to this movement.	
	15		Situation unchanged.	
		1330	Bde order No 118 directs that the 9th LF will relieve the 8th LF on night of 15/16 oct. Relief was completed by 19.50	6
	16		Right Bn established a post at E19.c.25.60.	
		1600	Div. Order No 75. States 125 Bde (less one Battn) will be relieved by 126 Bde on night 18/19 oct. Remaining Battn to be at disposal of 126 Inf Bde.	
	17	1500	Bde order No 119 states Bde, less one Battn will be relieved in line on night of 18/19 oct by 126 Bde. On relief 125 Bde less one Battn will become reserve Bde & will be located in BEAUVOIS-en-CAMBRESIS.	7
I10.a.5.9	18.	~~2330~~	Relief was complete by 21.25. and Bde HQ established at BEAUVOIS I10.a.5.9. Bde reported in billets by 05.20 19th oct.	
		2330	Div. order No 76. states 125 Bde being in Divisional Reserve & will be prepared to	

(A9175) Wt W2358/P360 600,000 12/17 D. D. & L. Sch. 52a. Forms/C2118/15

Instructions regarding War Diaries and Intelligence Summaries are contained in F. S. Regs., Part II. and the Staff Manual respectively. Title pages will be prepared in manuscript.

WAR DIARY
or
~~INTELLIGENCE SUMMARY.~~
(*Erase heading not required.*)

Army Form C. 2118.

125 Inf. Bde.
Page 6

Place	Date	Hour	Summary of Events and Information	Remarks and references to Appendices
I.10.a.5.9	18	2330	at 0800 hours on the 20th to AULICOURT and HERPIGNY FARMS & move further east if situation permits.	
	19	1052	Div. Wire G.752 directs that Bde less one Bn at D26.a will move to AULICOURT area to ~~night~~ day & will be clear of BEAUVOIS by 1900 hours.	
		1145	Bde order No 120 states advance being resumed on 20th ZERO hour 0200. 125 Bde group is in Div. Reserve & will move this evening, (less 8th LF at D36.d.) to AULICOURT & HERPIGNY FMS area.	8
J.1.a.5.5			Move complete by 20.45 Bde H.Q. located at J.1.a.5.5.	
	20	11.40	BM 197. Moved 8th LF to D17.c under command of G.O.C. 127 Bde.	
	20	14.25	Div. Wire G.792 states 125 Bde will be prepared to take over line of Divl front on night of 21/22 Oct. & to continue advance on the 22nd Oct.	
		1455	BM 199. Bde prepared to take over line night of 21/22 Oct. & continue advance 22nd.	
		17.30	Div. Wire G.795 says 125 Bde will remain in Div. reserve in present locations, prepared to move at one hours notice. Advance will not be resumed to morrow unless enemy withdraws.	
		18.15	BM 201. Bde remains in present position, ready to move at one hours notice	
		2210	G.O.C. attends conference at 126 Bde H.Q. 33.c of Inf. Bdes.	
		2230	Div order No 80. In event of enemy withdrawing, following bounds will be made good within Div. Boundaries. (1.) E10 central – W28.c0.7 (2) Railway W29.d – W28.a (3) Chapelle de 6 Chemins W26.d – Cross roads W17.c.	

(A9175) W1 W2358/P360 600,000 12/17 D. D. & L. Sch. 52a. Forms/C2118/15

Instructions regarding War Diaries and Intelligence Summaries are contained in F. S. Regs., Part II. and the Staff Manual respectively. Title pages will be prepared in manuscript.

WAR DIARY
or
~~INTELLIGENCE SUMMARY~~.
(Erase heading not required.)

Army Form C. 2118.

125 Inf. Bde.
Page 7

Place	Date	Hour	Summary of Events and Information	Remarks and references to Appendices
J1a. 5.5	20	2220	First bound by 127 Bde. 125 Bde to close up behind Advanced Bde & leap frog it on	
Bde HQ			first bound. When first Bde has cleared this bound 125 Bde becomes advanced	
			Bde, taking over attached Cavalry, Artillery & RE units	
	21	0900	Bde 282. Warning order. States above & gives order of advance 8th LF 7 LF & 5 LF	
		1000	BM.1 States Bde will relieve 127 Bde in the line tonight. Details later.	
		1200	Div. order No 81: 125 Bde group will relieve 127 Bde group tonight. Command	
			of front passes to B.G.C. 125 Bde on completion of relief.	
E19.a.3.2			Relief complete by 0115. 22nd. Bde HQ. established at E19.a.3.2.	
			Bde 2 States 7th LF will be on the right & the 8 LF on the left with the 5th LF	
			in support. H.Q.s as follows 7th LF E14a.4.1. 8th LF E14a.2.4 & the 5th LF E20a.6.5.	
	22	0900	G.O.C. Div. holds conference at 125 Bde HQ.	
		1330	do do.	
		1630	Div. order No 93: 125 Bde will carry out attack at Zero plus 86.	
		1840	Bde order 122 issued ordering Bde attack. objectives as follows	9
			Red Line E16.b.1.1 - E16.a.9.5 - E16.a.5.9. E4.c.4.4 E4a.0.3	
			Black Line E4 d.95.00 - E4 b 4.0 E4 b.0.6 - W28 c 6.0 W28 c 0.9	
			Blue Line E5c 8.7 - E5a 0.3 E4 b 5.6 W28 d 35.00 W28.b 3.0	
			W28 b 35.50 - W22 d 3.1	

(A9175) Wt W2358/P360 600,000 12/17 D. D. & L. Sch 52a. Forms/C2118/15

Instructions regarding War Diaries and Intelligence Summaries are contained in F. S. Regs., Part II, and the Staff Manual respectively. Title pages will be prepared in manuscript.

WAR DIARY
or
~~INTELLIGENCE SUMMARY.~~
(Erase heading not required.)

Army Form C. 2118.

125 Inf Bde
Page 8

Place	Date	Hour	Summary of Events and Information	Remarks and references to Appendices
E19.a.7.2	23	0336	3 Coy' 8 LF & 2 Coys 7 LF attacked under heavy barrage	
Bde HQ		0615	E10 central reported held by the 7th LF at 0515.	
		0645	Right flank coy reported to reach Black Line at 0530	
		0700	Tank in action in vicinity of E10 central, cleared M.G.s that were holding advance on the right. Black Line now reported held.	
		0745	Left flank coy (8 LF) reported to have reached final objective, in touch on both flanks.	
		0800	Final objective reached along whole front. In touch with both flank Divisions.	
		0840	~~[illegible]~~ N.Z. Div. took over line & continued advance.	
		0920	Bde order 123 issued states Bde will withdraw from present positions to	10
D28.a.5.1			VIESLY. Move was complete by 16.45 & Bde H.Q. established at D28.a.5.1	
		1600	Bde order 124. Bde group moves from VIESLY to ~~[illegible]~~ FONTAINE tomorrow 24th	11
I.15.d.2.6	24	1450	Move complete by 14.20 & Bde H.Q. established at I.15.d.2.6. Div. in	
	31		reserve. reorganisation & training.	

(A9175) Wt W2358/P360 600,000 12/17 D. D. & L. Sch 52a. Forms/C2118/15

Army Form C. 2118.

Instructions regarding War Diaries and Intelligence Summaries are contained in F. S. Regs., Part II. and the Staff Manual respectively. Title pages will be prepared in manuscript.

WAR DIARY
or
~~INTELLIGENCE SUMMARY~~.
(Erase heading not required.)

125 Inf Bde
Page 9

Place	Date	Hour	Summary of Events and Information	Remarks and references to Appendices
			Casualties & Prisoners 23rd Oct. 1918.	
			Off. OR	
			1 Trench Strength 23rd Oct. 61 1233.	
			2 Casualties. 7 Officers 161 other ranks.	
			3 Prisoners. 4 Officers 286 other ranks.	
			Harold Fargus Brig. Gen. Cdg. 125. Inf Bde.	

(A9175) Wt W2358/P360 600,000 12/17 D. D. & L. Sch. 52a. Forms/C2118/15

"A" Form.
MESSAGES AND SIGNALS.

Army Form C. 2121.
(In pads of 100.)
No. of Message..........

Prefix........ Code........ m. | Words. | Charge.

Office of Origin and Service Instructions.

URGENT

Ref 57b 1/40,000

Sent
At........ m.
To........
By........

This message is on a/c of:
.... Service.
War Diary
(Signature of "Franking Officer.")

Recd. at .... m.
Date........
From........
By........

TO			
MOLA	DURI	VAVU.	(2)
MOWE	PIRI		
MOHU	1 sect. LOVU		

Sender's Number.	Day of Month.	In reply to Number.	
* BM 90	9.		AAA

In continuation of JUNE order No 114 aaa Move of the Bde Group will be continued this afternoon to square N.4. aaa Starting Point X roads M.5.c.7.1. aaa Units pass S.P. at following times aaa Bde HQs + 1 sect LOVU 1400 MOLA 1405 MOHU 1420 MOWE 1435 DURI 1500 PIRI 1505 aaa Route LE BOSQUET - RAPERIE - LESDAIN - LE GRAND PONT - ESNES aaa Transport + distances as this morning aaa Bde HQs close present location 1400 + reopen N.4.b.4.0. on arrival aaa ACKNOWLEDGE aaa Addsd All Units of Bde Group plus 1 sect LOVU rptd VAVU

From JUNE
Place
Time 1315

The above may be forwarded as now corrected. (Z) R.H.Nichols Capt
Censor. Signature of Addresser or person authorised to telegraph in his name.

* This line, except AAA, should be erased if not required.

Wt. W 3253/P511. 500,000 Pads. 1/18. R. & S. Ltd. (E2389.)

SECRET. COPY NO......11 WD

(1)

125TH.INFANTRY BRIGADE ORDER NO.113. 7/10/18.

Ref Map 57.B.N.W. & S.W.

1. The Third and Fourth Armies are resuming the advance on the 8th instant.

2. The IV Corps is attacking with the 37th Division on the Right and the N.Z.Division on the Left.

<u>First objective of IV Corps</u> is the line BONNE ENFANCE FARM - N.13.b.3.0. - Road N.1.b.1.4. - H.35.a.4.0. - trench to H.20.c.6.1.

<u>Second objective</u> is the line N.13.b.2.4. - N.14.central - N.15.a.3.6. - Road to H.33.d.3.1. - East of ESNES MILL - Road in H.21.d,c & a.

If the attack is successful, exploitation will be carried out East of ESNES.

Boundary between 37th Division and N.Z.Division will be M.8.c.0.0. due East to M.10.d.0.0. - N.2.c.0.0. - N.2.d.0.4. due East to N.4.c.0.4. to N.5.central.

3. 42nd Division (less Artillery) will be prepared to move forward at 0700 hours on the 8th instant.
125th.Infantry Brigade Group will be prepared to move forward at 0730 hours on the 8th instant.

4. 125th.Infantry Brigade Group will march in the following order, regulation intervals between Companies, Units, Sections of Transport will be maintained :-

H.Q., 125th.Inf Brigade.
5th.Lancs.Fus.
8th.Lancs.Fus.
7th.Lancs.Fus.
125th.T.M.Battery.
'C' Coy., 42nd M.G.Battn.

Strict March Discipline will be maintained.

5. Units will march in Fighting Order with 1st Line Transport.

6. March Table will be issued later.

7. ACKNOWLEDGE.

E.K. Sarton [signature]
Captain,
Brigade Major,
125th.Inf Bde.

Issued at 1930 thro' Signals.
Copies to :-

1. 5th.Lan Fus.
2. 7th.Lan Fus.
3. 8th.Lan Fus.
4. 125th.T.M.Battery.
5. 'C' Coy., 42nd M.G.Bn.
6. Staff Captain.
7. 126th.Inf Brigade.
8. 127th.Inf Brigade.
9.)
10.) 42nd Division.
11. War Diary.
12. War Diary.
13. F I L E.

SECRET.   COPY NO.......15

(3)

125th.INFANTRY BRIGADE ORDER NO.115.

10/10/18.

Ref Sheet 57.B.1:40.000.

1. The 125th.Inf Brigade Group will move this afternoon to Squares I.15, 16, 17, 21 and 22.

2. Starting point on LONGSART ROAD at H.34.b.8.6.

3. Units will pass starting point at following times:-

125th.Inf Bde.H.Q. &
1 Sec.427th.Fd.Coy.R.E.)......... 1500.
1/5th.Lan Fus.................... 1505.
1/8th.Lan Fus.................... 1520.
1/7th.Lan Fus.................... 1535.
125th.T.M.B...................... 1600.
'C' Coy.42nd M.G.C............... 1605.

4. ROUTE - Along side of road to LONGSART - LONGSART - along side of road to road junction H.30.b.5.9. - track I.19.c & d and beside railway to I.20.c.6.0. - track I.20.c & b - thence along road to FONTAINE-AU-PIRE.

5. 1st Line transport and baggage wagons will accompany units. Baggage wagons will ~~xxxxxxx~~ not however leave main road.

6. Distances of 200 yards between companies, Section of transport, and units, will be maintained.

7. Mounted Officers or representatives of each Units will meet Staff Captain at Brigade H.Q. at 1330, and go forward to reconnoitre new areas.

8. O.C., No.2.Coy, 42nd Div Train, on his arrival in FONTAINE-AU-PIRE, will report to Staff Captain, to be allotted accommodation.

9. Brigade H.Q. will close at N.4.d.5.8. at 1430 and reopen at FONTAINE-AU-PIRE on arrival.

10. ACKNOWLEDGE (Units of Bde group only).

[signature]
Captain,
Brigade Major,
125th.Inf Bde.

Issued thro Signals at......1315

Copies to :-

1. 5th.Lan Fus.
2. 7th.Lan Fus.
3. 8th.Lan Fus.
4. 125th.T.M.B.
5. 'C' Coy., 42nd M.G.Bn.
6. 1 Sec, 427th.Fd.Coy.R.E.
7. No.2.Coy. 42nd Div Train.
8. Bde Signal Officer.
9. Staff Captain.
10. 126th.Inf Bde.
11. 127th.Inf Bde.
12.)
13.) 42nd Division(for information)
14. W.D.
15. W.D.
16. F I L E.

(4)

10 D

SECRET.

125TH.INFANTRY BRIGADE ORDER NO.118.

Copy No. 15

Map Ref: 57.B. 1/40,000.

10/10/18.

1. The 125th.Inf Bde Group is now under the tactical orders of the N.Z.Division, and will move tomorrow 11th inst to squares J.1 and D.25.

2. Starting Point on Road at I.15.d.8.4.

3. Units will pass starting point at following times :-

125th.Inf Bde.H.Q. & 1 Sect 427th.Fd.Coy.R.E.	1030.
1/5th.Lan Fus	1035.
1/8th.Lan Fus	1100.
1/7th.Lan Fus	1115.
125th.T.M.Battery	1130.
'C' Coy,42nd M.G.Bn	1135.

4. ROUTE - Most convenient cross-country tracks as reconnoitred by advance party (see para 6 (a)).

5. 1st Line Transport & baggage wagons will accompany units. Baggage wagons will not leave roads. Usual distances will be observed.

6. One Mounted Officer per Battn and 1 from C Coy, 42nd M.G.Bn. will report to Bde.H.Qrs. at following times :-

(a). At 0630 to go forward with Bde Intelligence Officer to reconnoitre cross-country routes.
(b). At 0900 to go forward with Staff Captain to reconnoitre new Area.

7. No.2 Coy,42nd Div Train will not move from their present location until further orders.

8. Bde H.Qrs. will close at I.15.c.8.8. at 0930 and reopen in new Area on arrival.

9. ACKNOWLEDGE.(Units of Bde Group only).

P.B.B. Nichols
Captain.,
Brigade Major,
125th.Inf Bde.

Issued at 2345 thro' Signals.
Copies to :-

1. 5th.Lan Fus.
2. 7th.Lan Fus.
3. 8th.Lan Fus.
4. 125th.T.M.B.
5. 'C' Coy,42nd.M.G.Bn.
6. 1 Sect,427th.Fd.Coy.R.E.
7. No.2 Coy.42nd Div:Train.
8. Staff Captain.
9. Bde.Signal Officer.
10. 126th.Inf Bde.
11. 127th.Inf Bde.
12. 42nd Division.) For information.
13. N.Z.Division.)
14.) War Diary.
15.)
16. F I L E.

(5)

S E C R E T.

Copy No...... 20

Oct 12th/1918.

125TH. INFANTRY BRIGADE ORDER NO. 117.

Ref 57.B. 1/40.000.

1. (a). The 42nd Division (less Artillery) is relieving the N.Z. Division in the line tonight 12/13th October.
   (b). Boundaries of 42nd Division will be :-
   Southern Boundary - BRIASTRE CHURCH - BELLEVUE (incl.) - E.20.a. - E.15.c.0.0. - E.15.b.6.0.
   Northern Boundary - QUIEVY (excl.) - SOLESMES (excl.)

2. The 125th. Inf Bde plus 1 Bn of 126th Inf Bde (1/8th. Manchester Regt) will relieve the 1st N.Z. Inf Bde in the line today and tonight 12/13th October, in accordance with attached relief table, and on completion of relief will hold the Divisional Front.

3. All details of relief which are not mentioned in this order will be arranged direct by C.O's concerned.

4. O.C, 125th. L.T.M.B. will attach 1 Section of his Battery to each of the 2 front line Bns. The remaining four guns will be in reserve.

5. The Section of 427th Fd. Coy. R.E. at present attached to the Brigade will move with Brigade Headquarters.

6. Administrative Instructions will be issued separately.

7. Completion of relief will be notified to this office by wiring the name of the Commanding Officer concerned.

8. Command of Sector will pass to G.O.C, 125th. Inf Bde at 1830.

9. (a). Brigade H.Qrs. will close at AULICOURT FARM at 1630 and reopen at PRAYELLE J.3.c.5.8. at same hour.
   (b). Bde Advanced Report Centre will be established on relief at D.28.a.8.2.

10. ACKNOWLEDGE. (Units of Bde Group only).

P.B.B. Nichols.
Captain.,
Brigade Major,
125th. Inf Bde.

Issued at 10.30 thro' Signals.
Copies to :-

1. 5th. Lan Fus.
2. 7th. Lan Fus.
3. 8th. Lan Fus.
4. 125th. T.M. Battery.
5. 'C' Coy., 42nd M.G. Bn.
6. 1 Sect. 427th. Fd. Coy. R.E.
7. No. 2. Coy., 42nd Div Train.
8. 1/8th. Manch. Regt.
9. Staff Captain.
10. Bde. Sig. Officer.
11. 126th. Inf Bde.
12. 127th. Inf Bde.
13. 1st. N.Z. Inf Bde.
14. 3rd Guards Bde.
15. 63rd Inf Bde.
16. 1st Group N.Z.F.A.
17. 42nd Division.) For information.
18. N.Z. Division.)
19.)
20.) War Diary.
21. F I L E.

RELIEF TABLE TO ACCOMPANY 125TH.INF BDE ORDER NO.117.

12/10/18.

SERIAL. No.	Date.	U N I T.	From.	To.	In relief of.	H.Qrs. at.	Remarks.
1.	12th.Oct.	8th.Lan Fus.	HERPIGNY Fm. AULICOURT Fm. Area.	Line Rt Front.	1st Bn.Wellington Regt.	D.28.a.8.2.	Not to leave present area before 1630. Assemble in D.21.d. Guides meet on Railway D.21.d.central 1700. Route - Any.
2.	12th Oct.	5th.Lan Fus.	- do -	Line Left Front.	2nd Bn.Auckland Regt.	D.22.a.7.2.	To be clear of present area by 1620. Assemble in D.21.b. Guides meet at D.22.a.7.2. at 1700. Route - Any.
3.	12th Oct.	1/8th.Manch. Regt.	- do -	Line Right Support.	1st Bn Auckland Regt.	D.28.a.8.1.	Daylight relief. To be complete by 1700. Route - when East of CAUDRY - QUIEVY Rd - J.1, J.2, J.3.a., D.27.c & d.
4.	12th Oct.	7th.Lan Fus.	- do -	Line Left Support.	2nd Bn Wellington Regt.	D.28.a.6.2.	Daylight relief. To be complete by 1630. Route - Any N.of Track HERPIGNY Farm - VIESLY.
5.	12th Oct.	125th.L.T.M.B.	- do -	Line.	1st N.Z.L.T.M.B.	-	All details arranged by C.O's.concerned.
6.	12th Oct.	'C' Coy., 42nd M.G.Bn.	- do -	Line.	'W'Coy, N.Z.M.G.Bn.	J.3.c.5.8.	- do - do -

NOTE :- All movements EAST of Road CAUDRY - QUIEVY to be in Artillery Formation.

Secret.

13 Inf Bde.
Bde on Left
Group RFA.
26 Inf Bde.

W.D. 247.

Herewith account of yesterdays operations for information in connection with Bde Intelligence Summary to be forwarded later.

14-10-18.

Brig - Genl
Comdg 13th Inf Bde.

42nd Division Z.46.

Attached report from [illegible] forwarded herewith.

What happened is as follows: the troops on our right were forced to withdraw, the enemy occupied the positions they were holding & then enfiladed the men holding BELLE VUE and COPSE in E.19.a. These were then obliged to conform to the movement and take up the line of the road just East of the river.

Harold [illegible]
Brig-Genl.
14/10/18. Cmdg 125 Inf Bde.

W.D. (5.a)

8th.LANCS. FUS.

SUMMARY OF OPERATIONS - OCTOBER 13TH.1918.

4 p.m. - Intermittent shelling of support Company front, BRIASTRE and VIESLY.

4.12 p.m.- A very heavy barrage was put down on our front line, BRIASTRE and VIESLY.

4.30 p.m.- Commanding Officer reported to Brigade and our Barrage was opened on S.O.S.Lines.

5.0 p.m. - Intelligence Officer reported that Infantry & retrograde movement was seen on Right Flank, but none opposite Bn Front.

5.15 p.m.- Officer Commanding forward Coys reported heavy attack, and right front posts of Bn driven in. Left Coy front holding good. Casualties heavy. (owing to enfilade fire from their right).

5.15 p.m.- Two platoons sent forward to reinforce.

5.20 p.m.- Intelligence Officer sent forward to ascertain situation and report.

5.30 p.m.- Officer Commanding forward Coys confirmed 5.15 p.m. information and reported stating that he was going forward to ascertain situation.

5.40 p.m.- Situation unchanged. By this time all available men at Coy H.Qrs. had been pushed forward by Orders of Capt.H.D. CUMMING. M.C. to re-establish right flank of Bn. Not in touch with Division on Right. Again confirmed information that Left Coy Front was holding its original position.

6 p.m. - O.C., Front Line Companies reported that all available men had been sent forward to re-establish situation around BELLE-VUE and if necessary to form a defensive flank to the South.

6 p.m. - Situation in COPSE E.19.a.4.4. acute. Severe fighting, casualties heavy. Wounded men report line withdrawn from BELLE-VUE.

6.15 p.m.- Situation explained to Brigade.

6.30 p.m.- Information received - Right Flank Coy Strength 27, Left Flank Coy Strength 50.

7 p.m. - Line now runs along road East of river in D.24.b & d. Heavy Artillery and M.G.Fire directed on forward areas.

7.30 p.m.- Patrols sent forward to find out situation and keep touch with enemy. Heavy M.G. fire encountered.

9 p.m. - Patrols report enemy M.G. Posts at E.19.c.4.7. E.19.a.4.3. & E.19.c.2.6.
Reliable communication established with Division on Right.
Liaison post established at D.24.d.75.30.
The situation is now quiet with intermittant shelling of BRIASTRE and forward areas.
Enemy M.G.Posts are being harried by L.T.M's. and Field Artillery during the night.
Casualties are roughly estimated as follows:-
1 Officer killed 2 Officers wounded.
80 Other Ranks killed and wounded.

(sd) JAMES.S.MAC LEOD.Lt Col.,
Commanding 1/8th.Lan Fus.

G 238.
13/10/18.

(6)

SECRET.

wp
16

125TH.INFANTRY BRIGADE ORDER NO.118.

Copy No.......

Ref 57.B.N.E.1/20,000.

Oct:15th 1918.

1. The 7th.Lan Fus will relieve the 8th.Lan Fus in the Right Sub-sector of the Brigade Front tonight 15th/16th instant.

2. On relief the 8th.Lan Fus will move into Support and occupy accommodation vacated by 7th.Lan Fus in squares D.20, 21, 22 and 26.

3. Guides provided by 8th.Lan Fus will meet 7th.Lan Fus at junction of road and Railway D.22.c.7.0. at 1730.

4. All other details of relief will be arranged direct by C.O's. concerned.

5. All Aeroplane photos, Schemes of Defence, Liaison Posts, etc, will be handed over on relief.

6. Completion of relief to be notified to this office by wiring the name of the Adjutant concerned.

7. ACKNOWLEDGE. (Units of Bde Group only).

P.B.B. Nichols
Captain.,
Brigade Major,
125th.Inf Bde.

Issued thro' Signals at ....1330.

Copies to :-

1. 5th.Lan Fus.
2. 7th.Lan Fus.
3. 8th.Lan Fus.
4. 125th.T.M.Battery.
5. 'C' Coy, 42nd M.G.Bn.
6. 427th.Fd.Coy.R.E.
7. Group R.F.A.
8. 90th Bde H.A.
9. Staff Captain.
10. Bde Signal Officer.
11. 126th.Inf Bde.
12. 127th.Inf Bde.
13. 1st Guards Bde.
14. 13th Inf Bde.
15. 42nd Division (for information.)
16. War Diary.
17. War Diary.
18. F I L E.
19. 1/8 Manch Regt.

(7)

WD

SECRET.

20

Copy No........

125TH INFANTRY BRIGADE ORDER NO. 119.

Ref: 57.B. 1/40,000.

17th.Oct:1918.

1. The 125th.Inf Bde less 1 Bn, will be relieved in the line by the 126th.Inf Bde on the night 18th/19th October, in accordance with relief table overleaf.

2. On relief the 125th.Inf Bde less 1 Bn. will become Reserve Bde, and will be located in BEAUVOIS-en-CAMBRESIS.

3. All details of relief will be arranged direct by Commanding Officers concerned.

4. Advance parties will be sent on to BEAUVOIS on the morning of the 18th inst to take over billets.

5. The 1 Section, 427th.Fd.Coy.R.E. at present attached to Bde.H.Qrs. will return to their unit as from 1200 18th October.

6. Completion of relief will be notified to this Office by wiring the words "No.119".

7. Command of Sector will pass to G.O.C. 126th.Inf Bde. on conclusion of Infantry relief, at which hour Bde.H.Qrs. will close at LA PRAYELLE and reopen at BEAUVOIS-en-CAMBRESIS at same hour,

8. Units of 125th.Inf Bde to ACKNOWLEDGE.

F B B Mitchell,
Captain.,
Brigade Major,
125th.Inf Bde.

Issued thro' Signals at 1500.

Copies to :-

1. 5th.Lan Fus.
2. 7th.Lan Fus.
3. 8th.Lan Fus.
4. 125th.T.M.Battery.
5. 'C' Coy., 42nd M.G.Bn.
6. No.2 Coy, 42nd Div Train.
7. 1/8th.Manch.Regt.
8. 427th.Fd.Coy.R.E.
9. R.F.A.Group, 42nd Division.
10. 90 Bde H.A.
11. 126th.Inf Bde.
12. 127th.Inf Bde.
13. 13th.Inf Bde.
14. 186th.Inf Bde.
15. 42nd Division.(For information).
16. Town Major, BEAUVOIS-en-CAMBRESIS.
17. Staff Captain.
18. Bde.Transport Officer.
19. Bde Signal Officer.
20. War Diary.
21. War Diary.
22. F I L E.

RELIEF TABLE ISSUED WITH 125TH. INFANTRY BRIGADE ORDER NO.119.

18th.Oct 1918.

Serial. No.	UNIT.	From.	Relieved by.	To.	Route.	Remarks.
1.	5th.Lan Fus.	Left Front.	(a) 2 Front Coys by 1 Coy 1/8th.Lanch.Regt, who are putting 1 Platoon only East of River SELLE. (b) H.Qrs.Support & Reserve Coys by H.Qrs. & 2 Coys of 1/5th.E.Lancs Regt.	BEAUVOIS-en CAMBRESIS.	Track D.27, 26, 25. J.1, 6, to JENLAIN BOIS.	Relief to be complete as follows:- Front Coys 2230. Support and Reserve Coys 1900. Take over billets and Transport lines vacated by 1/7th. Lanch.Regt.
2.	7th.Lan Fus.	Right Front.	1/10th.Lanch.Regt.	- do -	- do -	Relief to be complete by 2200. Take over billets and transport lines vacated by 1/6th.Lanch. Regt.
3.	8th.Lan Fus.	-	-	-	-	Will stand fast in present position and take over role of Reserve Bn to Front Line Bdes under tactical orders of B.G.C. 1 6th.Inf Bde, on completion of relief.
4.	125th.L.T.M.B.	Line.	126th.L.T.M.B.	BEAUVOIS en CAMBRESIS.	As in Serial No.1.	4 Gun positions in BRIASTRE only to be handed over. All details to be arranged between C.O's. Take over billets from 127th.L.T.M.B.

NOTE. - 200 yards distance between platoons on march back.

(8) WD

SECRET.

125TH. INFANTRY BRIGADE ORDER NO. 120.

Copy No......

Ref Sheets. 57B.N.E.)
51A.S.E.) 1/20,000.
57b. 1/40,000.

Oct 19th 1918.

1. The Third Army is resuming the advance on 20th October. ZERO Hour will be at 0200 hours.

2. Trace showing boundaries and objectives of attack of :-

   (a). 42nd Division.
   (b). Flanking Divisions.

   will be forwarded later to units of 125th. Inf Bde Group only.

3. The 5th. Division is attacking on the right of the 42nd Division, and the 62nd Division on the Left.

4. The attack on the 42nd Division Front will be carried out in two phases :-

<u>PHASE 'A'</u>. - By 126th. Inf Bde Group, who are advancing to the GREEN LINE.

<u>PHASE 'B'</u>. - By 127th. Inf Bde Group, who are leapfrogging the 126th Inf Bde Group in the GREEN LINE, and advancing to the BROWN LINE.

5. The attack of the Division is being supported by six Brigades of Field Artillery, one Brigade Heavy Artillery, M.T.M's. and L.T.M's.

6. (a). The 125th. Inf Bde Group is in Divisional Reserve.
   (b). The Group, less 8th. Lan Fus, will move this evening to AULICOURT and HERPIGNY FARMS Area, and will be prepared to move further East when situation permits.
   (c). Starting Point :- I.4.c.5.4.
   (d). <u>ROUTE</u> - Track through I.4.a., I.5.a., I.6.b.
   (e). Order of march, times of passing starting point and location as follows :-

125th. Inf Bde. H.Qrs.	1820.	AULICOURT FARM Area.
5th. Lan Fus.	1825.	HERPIGNY FARM Area.
7th. Lan Fus.	1840.	AULICOURT FARM Area.
125th. L.T.M.B. (less 1 Sect. in line)	1855.	AULICOURT FARM Area.

   (f). 1st Line Transport and Baggage wagons will accompany units. Baggage wagons by road.
   (g). Units will be prepared to bivouac outside Farms until these are cleared by 127th. Inf Bde.

7. If necessary the N.Z. Division is prepared to pass through the 42nd Division on the night 20th/21st October, and continue operations on 21st October.

8. The strictest measure must be taken to maintain secrecy.

9. Each unit of Bde Group will send a watch to Bde H.Qrs. to be synchronised at 1500 hours today.

10. <u>Distinguishing badges.</u>
   The 13th Inf Bde, 5th. Division, will wear a white tape over the Left shoulder under the right arm.
   The 95th Inf Bde will wear a white tape tied on to the left shoulder strap.
   The 62nd Division will wear a white band on the left arm.

P.T.O.

11. The watchward for 42nd Division will be "WON BETTER".

12. ACKNOWLEDGE.

F.B.B. Nichols
Captain.,
Brigade Major,
125th.Inf Bde.

Issued at 1145 thro' Signals.

Copies to:-

1. 5th.Lan Fus. 9. C.R.E., 42nd Division.
2. 7th.Lan Fus.. 10. 42nd Division. (For information).
3. 8th.Lan Fus. 11. Staff Captain.
4. 125th.T.M.Battery. 12. Bde Signal Officer.
5. 126th.Inf Bde. 13. Bde.T.O.
6. 127th.Inf Bde. 14. War Diary.
7. 42nd Bn.M.G.C. 15. War Diary.
8. C.R.A., 42nd Division. 16. F I L E.
17. No 2 Coy 42 Div. Train

W.D (9)

SECRET.
****

125TH. INFANTRY BRIGADE ORDER NO. 182.
****

Copy No..... 18

Ref: 57B.N.E. } 1/20,000.
51A.S.E. }
& Special Map issued to Units.

22/10/18.

1. The advance will be resumed by Third Army on 23rd inst. Fourth and First Armies are co-operating. ZERO Hour will be 0200, at which hour the V Corps will attack.

2. (a). The boundaries and objectives of attack of the 42nd Division are shown on map already issued.
(b). The 5th.Division is attacking on the Right of the 42nd Division, and the 3rd Division on the Left.

3. (a). The 125th.Inf Bde will carry out the attack being made by the 42nd Division.
(b). On conclusion of this attack the 2nd N.Z.Bde will go through the 125th.Inf Bde, and continue the advance.

4. (a). The Brigade will attack with the 7th.Lan Fus on the Right, and the 8th.Lan Fus on the Left and the 5th.Lan Fus in support.
(b). The Inter Bn boundary will be E.3.D.9.2. - E.4.B.0.6. - W.28.D.3.0.
(c). The attack will be made in four bounds viz:- to the GREEN Dotted Line, the RED Dotted Line, The BLACK Dotted Line, and BLUE Line. (final objective of Brigade).
(d). 7th.Lan Fus are attacking with 2 Companies, advancing to furthest objective, and 1 Company in close support to BLACK Dotted Line; in addition 1 Platoon is being detailed to mop up each of the following areas :-

(1). E.10.Central.
(2). Quarry E.11.A.3.8.
(3). Cross Roads in E.4.B.

(e). 8th.Lan Fus are attacking with 3 Companies advancing to furthest objective. In addition 1 Platoon is being detailed to mop up each of the following areas :-

(1). Cross Roads W.27.D.9.8. & COPSE W.27.D.
(2). Railway in W.28.D. and W.28.B. as shown in ringed point in Special Map.

(f). The 5th.Lan Fus will support the attack of the Right Bn with 2 Companies and the attack of the Left Bn with 2 Companies. These Companies will be under orders of Right and Left Bn Commander without reference to Brigade H.Qrs.
In the normal event 1 Company supporting Right Bn will move to GREEN Dotted Line, 1 to BROWN Line in Right Bn Area. Similarly the 2 Companies supporting Left Bn will move to BROWN Line in that Bn Area.
Companies of 5th.Lan Fus will be prepared to assist attack or to form defensive flanks or otherwise mop up, hold tactical points, as required.

(g). Time table of attack is attached.

5. Forward Bns will form up as follows :-

7th.Lan Fus - Track in E.15.B. and E.9.D. and Road in E.9.B. and E.3.D.
8th.Lan Fus - Along Road in E.3.D. and E.3.B.

Forming up will be complete by 0200 hours.

6. 22 Machine Guns of 'C' and 'D' Companies, 42nd M.G.Bn. are available for purposes of consolidation of the BLUE Line and also for covering the advance of the 2nd N.Z. Inf Bde when it goes through.

7. 125th.L.T.M.B. will arrange for 6 guns to fire during initial barrage as follows :-

(a). 2 Guns from positions in E.9.B. to fire on targets in E.10.A.
(b). 4 Guns from positions in E.3. B and E.3.D. to fire on Cross Roads in E.4.B.

After initial barrage guns as in (a) come under orders of O.C. 7th.Lan Fus. Guns as in (b) under orders of O.C.8th.Lan Fus for use during the advance and for consolidation.

8. (a). 5 Brigades of Field Artillery together with 42nd Division M.T.M. Batteries will support the attack of the Brigade.
(b). The barrage will fall at ZERO plus 80 on the initial line E.16.A.0.7. - E.9.D.7.7. - E.4.A.4.5. - W.27.D.65.45.
(c). The creeping barrage will advance at the uniform rate of 100 yds in 6 minutes, on the flanks, but will be slower in the centre, to the protective line of the BLUE objective.
(d). Smoke shell will be fired to indicate the arrival of the barrage on the BLUE protective Line. Smoke shells will also be fired to screen the troops on the BLUE Line after daylight until the N.Z.Division has passed through.
(e). At 0825 a barrage will be put down ~~300~~ 200 yds East of BLUE LINE. At 0840 this barrage will lift and the 2nd N.Z. Inf Bde will pass through the 125th.Inf Bde and continue the advance.

9. Direction during the advance will be kept by the following means:-

(a). Compass bearing. All officers will have Compass Bearings of their objective.
(b). Thermite will be fired along both Division boundaries, 500 yds in front of the advancing infantry. A thermite beacon will also be fired by 1 gun on E.4.B.3.6., to give general direction of Inter Bn boundary. This beacon will be fired on a point 500 yds further East, when Infantry get within 500 yds of E 4.B.3.6.
It will be necessary to pay the greatest attention to direction owing to the fact that the barrage is falling in Echelon to the line of advance.

10. Handshakes with flanking Divisions will be as follows :-

SOUTHERN DIVISION.

(a). E.10.C.4.0.
(b). E.10.Central.
(c). Road junction E.10.B.9.7.
(d). E.5.C.6.6.

NORTHERN DIVISION.

(a). Corner of Wood. W.27.D.3.5.
(b). Road W.27.D.9.8.
(c). Railway W.28.A.4.6.
(d). Junction of Road and Railway W.28.B.2.8.

11. Signal arrangements will be issued separately.

12. Contact Aeroplane will call for flares at 0700 hours.

13. A Brigade representative will visit units of Bde Group to synchronise WATCHES BEFORE 2200 HOURS TO NIGHT

14. Brigade H.Qrs. will remain at COPSE E.19.A.3.3.

15. ACKNOWLEDGE.

P.B.B. Nichols.
Captain,
Brigade Major,
125th. Inf Bde.

Issued at 1840. thro' Signals.

Copies to:-

1.	5th. Lan Fus.	10.	127th. Inf Bde.
2.	7th. Lan Fus.	* 11.	76th. Inf Bde.
3.	8th. Lan Fus.	* 12.	15th. Inf Bde.
4.	125th. T.M. Battery.	* 13.	2nd N.Z. Inf Bde.
5.	'C' Coy., 42nd M.G. Bn.	14.	42nd Division.
6.	'D' Coy, 42nd M.G. Bn.	15.	Staff Captain.
7.	O.C. Group R.F.A.	16.	Bde Signal Officer.
8.	C.R.E., 2nd Division.	17.	War Diary.
9.	126th. Inf Bde.	18.	War Diary.
		19.	F I L E.

* Trace attached.

TIME TABLE FOR 125TH. INFANTRY BRIGADE ORDER NO. 122.

ZERO HOUR for all Armies is 0200.

ZERO plus 80. .... Initial barrage falls.
(0320).

ZERO plus 86.... 3 Coys 8th. Lan Fus on Left and 2 Coys 7th. Lan Fus on right with special parties for ringed points leave assembly positions.
(0326)

ZERO plus 104... Left of 8th. Lan Fus arrives on Left of Black Dotted line. Party for Wood and Cross Roads at W.27.d.9.0. remains and mops up.
(0344).

ZERO plus 122. Left of 7th. Lan Fus arrives at Cross Roads in E.4.b.1.4. Special party for Cross Roads remains and mops up.
(0402).

ZERO plus 140... Right of 7th. Lan Fus arrives at RED Dotted Line. Party for E.10.central remains and mops up.
(0420)

ZERO plus 152... Left of 8th. Lan Fus arrives on Left of the BLUE Line. Special party mops up on Left.
(0432).

ZERO plus 182... Right of 7th. Lan Fus arrives at Cross Roads in E.10.b.8.7.
(0502).

ZERO plus 218... Right of 7th. Lan Fus arrives on BLUE Line.
(0538).

ZERO plus 146... Final Barrage becomes protective in Centre.
(0426).

ZERO plus 152... Final Barrage becomes protective on Left.
(0432).

ZERO plus 218... Final Barrage becomes protective on Right.
(0538).

ZERO plus 240... Protective barrage dies away. Posts thrown forward, which will be withdrawn at 0800.
(0600).

ZERO plus 400... New Zealanders pass through.
(0840).

(11)

SECRET.

125TH.INFANTRY BRIGADE ORDER NO. 124.

Copy No. 13

Ref Sheet 57B. 1/40,000.

23rd Oct:1918.

1. The 125th.Inf Bde Group will move from VIESLY to BEAUVOIS tomorrow 24th inst.

2. Personnel will move by cross country tracks, transport by FRAYELLE-BETHENCOURT Road.

3. Starting point :- Cross Roads D.28.C.2.8.

4. Units will pass starting point at following times :-

Bde H.Qrs.and 125th.L.T.M.B........	1030.
5th.Lan Fus........................	1100.
7th.Lan Fus........................	1130.
8th.Lan Fus........................	1200.
'C' Coy.,42nd M.G.Bn...............	1230.

5. Completion of moves to be reported to Brigade H.Qrs.

6. Brigade H.Qrs. will close at VIESLY at 1000 and reopen at BEAUVOIS on arrival.

7. Units of 125th.Inf Bde Group to ACKNOWLEDGE.

P.B.B. Nichols
Captain,
Brigade Major,
125th.Inf Bde.

Issued thro' Signals at 1600.

Copies to :-

1. 5th.Lan Fus.
2. 7th.Lan Fus.
3. 8th.Lan Fus.
4. 125th.T.M.Battery.
5. 'C' Coy,42nd.M.G.Bn.
6. No.2 Coy,42nd Div Train.
7. 126th.Inf Bde.
8. 127th.Inf Bde.
9. A.P.M.,42nd Division.
10. 42nd Division. (for information)
11. Staff Captain.
12. Bde Signal Officer.
13. War Diary.
14. War Diary.
15. F I L E.

lwb

SECRET.
****

AMENDMENT NO.1. TO
125th. INFANTRY BRIGADE ORDER NO.124
****

Copy No......14

23rd Oct:1918.

PARAS. 1 and 6.

For BEAUVOIS.

Read. FONTAINE.

P.B.B. Nich...
Captain,
Brigade Major,
125th.Inf Bde.

Copy to to all recipients of
125th.Inf Bde.Order No.124.

S E C R E T.
****

5th.Lan Fus.
7th.Lan Fus.
8th.Lan Fus.
125th.T.M.B.
'C'Coy,42nd.M.G.Bn.
'D'Coy,42nd.M.G.Bn.
2nd N.Z.Bde.
42nd Division.

C.15.

Herewith Instructions No.1. "Signal Arrangements" to accompany 125th.Inf Bde.Order No.122.

Captain,
Brigade Major
125th.Inf Bde.

22/10/18.
A.L.

INSTRUCTIONS NO 1.

SIGNALLING ARRANGEMENTS
****

1. A Brigade report centre will be established at MAROU E.9.c.95.90. in Cellar at present occupied by 'B' Company 1/7th.Lan Fus.

2. A relay post will also be established in the SUNKEN ROAD at E.14.a.3.4. near present 7th.Lan Fus Headquarters.

3. Communication will be established between the report centre and Brigade Headquarters by wire.

4. Between the report centre and the relay post communication will be by runner, power buzzer and amplifier and by rocket.

5. Between relay post and Brigade Headquarters by runner, power buzzer and amplifier and messenger dogs.

6. When the Battalion Headquarters move forward they will immediately inform Brigade report centre, who will run a line to their new position.

7. The Brigade report centre will open at 2200 hours on 22nd inst, and will be marked by a Blue and White Flag.

8. The 7th.Lan Fus are establishing a report centre at the commencement of operations along with the Brigade report centre, this will advance when the situation permits; this is advancing to the Cross Roads in E.4.b.

The 8th.Lan Fus are establishing a report centre at the Cross Roads in E.3.b.

****

17

CONFIDENTIAL

9/R 22

125 Inf Bde HQ

WAR DIARY

NOVEMBER 1918

VOL 52

Instructions regarding War Diaries and Intelligence Summaries are contained in F. S. Regs., Part II, and the Staff Manual respectively. Title pages will be prepared in manuscript.

WAR DIARY
or
~~INTELLIGENCE SUMMARY.~~
(Erase heading not required.)

Army Form C. 2118.

125 Inf. Bde HQ. Nov. 1918.

PAGE 1. Vol. 52.

Place	Date	Hour	Summary of Events and Information	Remarks and references to Appendices
Map 57B I 15 d 26.	1 & 2.		Div in reserve. Recreation & training. Bde in billets in FONTAINE.	
	3.	1000	On receipt of orders from Div. Bde O.O. No 125 issued, ordering move of Bde to SOLESMES on Nov 4 in conjunction with advance by N.Z. DIV.	1.
SOLESMES.	4	1630.	Bde moved to SOLESMES. HQ. opened at 1630.	
— " —	4.	2345	On receipt of operation orders from Div. Bde OO No 126 issued, ordering move of Bde group to BEAUDIGNIES area.	2.
51A R32 BEAUDIGNIES.	5		Bde. moved to BEAUDIGNIES. HQ opened at 1300. Div relieved N.Z. Div in line	
		2315	Bde in Reserve. Orders received for Bde to move to HERPIGNIES. Bde OO. No 127 issued. Heavy rain all day.	3
51 — " — HERPIGNIES.	6.	1230	Bde moved to HERPIGNIES. HQ opened at 1230 Heavy rain all day. Bde in reserve	
		1630.	Wire from Div. placing Bde in support & warning it to be at 1 hours notice. Batts notified	
		1900	Div. order No 88 received, conforming change from reserve to support, ready to reinforce either flank. Batts. informed. Necessary reconnaissances made.	
		2120.	Orders received from Div that Bde should be ready to move forward at 0600 hours on 7th Batts informed.	
	7	1106	Orders received from Div. for Bde to move to billets in OBIES & be prepared to take over line on night 8/9th. BM 78 issued.	4
		1215	Wire from Div cancelling move to OBIES, & substituting HARGNIES & VIEUX MESNIL. Bde was diverted en route.	
		1630.	HARGNIES & VIEUX MESNIL reported being shelled & unsuitable for billets. GOC spoke to GSO.1 & orders were received for Bde group to billets in PETIT BAYAY & LA HAUTE RUE. Bde group again diverted en route. C. Coy MG Bn was not met & therefore did not know of this diversion.	
O 34 a 97		1700.	Bde HQ established at O 34 a 97.	

Instructions regarding War Diaries and Intelligence Summaries are contained in F. S. Regs., Part II, and the Staff Manual respectively. Title pages will be prepared in manuscript.

WAR DIARY
or
~~INTELLIGENCE SUMMARY.~~
(Erase heading not required.)

Army Form C. 2118.

125 Inf Bde HQ. NOVEMBER. 1918

PAGE 2. VOL 52.

Place	Date	Hour	Summary of Events and Information	Remarks and references to Appendices
51/40000 034a97	7	2220	Div. Order No 89 received. Bde ordered to advance through 126 Bde early on 8th, with final objective high ground E of AVESNES – MAUBERGE road. This to be consolidated in depth.	
		2300	Order received for 126 Bde to deal with HAUTMONT, when high ground in P35 & P29 has been taken.	
		2300.	Bde Group less C Coy MG Bn in billets	
		2300.	Conference of C.O's at Bde HQ. Summoned. GOC's of 125 & 126 Bde decided on plan of operation. C Coy MG still being unlocated, another Coy was placed at disposal of Bde by 126 Bde.	
	8.	0200.	Conference of C.O's Plan of operations given them.	
		0400.	Bde O.O. No 129 issued, with orders for the operations.	5
		0750.	Owing to accident with pontoons, RE unable to get bridge at P32d established in time. Batts therefore diverted en route & ordered to cross by bridges at PONT SUR SAMBRE.	
		0830.	BDE HQ established at HOISIES FARM.	
		11.45.	Situation left batt. practically through BOIS DU QUESNOY. Slight MG fire from NE. No report from right batt. HAUTMONT probably evacuated by enemy.	
		1242.	All 3 batt. HQ moving to P33 Central.	
		1335.	Message received 1247 from ~~right~~ left batt, stating capture of 1st objective	
		1355	Message received 1314 from right batt, stating capture of 1st objective: casualties nil, & patrols pushing on.	
BOUSSIERES P31d88		1430	BDE HQ established at BOUSSIERES	
		1530	Left Batt report patrols held up by MG fire in P29 b&d. Fire coming from X roads P30b. Attempt being made to outflank this.	
			Arrangements made for bombardment of final objective from 2200 – 2300. This was cancelled at 2130.	
		1700.	Situation right batt. patrols have reached P36 Central & P35 b59 at latter point MG opposition from NE. Support Coy on 1st obj. in touch with left batt. Left Batt on line approx P.30 Central to road P30a66, held	

Instructions regarding War Diaries and Intelligence Summaries are contained in F. S. Regs., Part II, and the Staff Manual respectively. Title pages will be prepared in manuscript.

WAR DIARY
or
~~INTELLIGENCE SUMMARY.~~
(Erase heading not required.)

125 Inf Bde HQ

PAGE 3 . VOL 52

Army Form C. 2118.

Nov. 1918.

Place	Date	Hour	Summary of Events and Information	Remarks and references to Appendices
Ref. 51. 1/40000 BOUSSIERES P31d88.	8.		up by Strong point at X Road P30b. Enemy seen moving on high ground in Q31 Central. as arty. was moving up, no guns were available.	
		1740	right Coy right batt held up by MG fire from FME DE FORÊT. attempts being made to surround it.	
		2030.	approx outpost line of right batt. P30b70 - P36a79 - P36d98.	
		2150.	FERME DE FORÊT & FORT HAUTMONT in our hands. patrols pushing on to final objective.	
		2235	3rd Hussars warned to be ready to go forward to keep touch with enemy at 0630 9th, in the event of the final objective being captured before that hour & contact lost.	
	9	0515	Right batt. line FORT HAUTMONT along road to Q26a22, then S down AVESNES Rd to Div. Boundary. In touch on left. Patrols pushing E of final objective	
		0600	Left Batt. line P30a05 - P30b83. Patrols have been in P30 Centr. MG fire on X roads P30b.	
		0600	Right batt. report no touch with enemy on final objective. Patrols pushing out E. It is believed enemy have withdrawn	
		0630	Final obj. gained on whole front at 0440. Defensive flank formed on N boundary. No touch on right. patrols pushing forward	
		0645.	3rd Hussars ordered to go through & gain touch with enemy.	
		0745	Patrols have reached LOUVROIL.	
		0825.	1 OFF 20 OR. captured by left Batt.	
		1245	Cavalry patrols report R19a 25 clear of enemy	
		1300	~~Report timed 1130 states cavalry have gained touch with enemy in R27C~~	
		1315	Left Batt patrols have reached FERRIERE LA GRANDE & TRIEUX, where 3 trains of ammunition were captured	
		1400	Bde O.O. No 130 issued, ordering 7LF to take over Bde front, to be held as outpost line.	6
		1830	message timed 1700 from cavalry patrols report R19 20 14c & C 26 25 31 & Q30 free of enemy	
		2325	Bde ordered to take over Corps front on 10th.	
HAUTMONT P29C88	10	0400	Cavalry have established post at R22d, & are pushing forward. No touch with enemy.	7
		1000	Bde HQ established at HAUTMONT.	
		1200.	Bde OO No 131 issued. ordering 7th LF to take over whole Corps front.	
		1120.	Cavalry patrols have reached high ground W of COUSOIRE. Slight enemy opposition & shelling of COLLERET.	

(A9475) Wt W2358/P360 600,000 12/17 D. D. & L. Sch. 52a. Forms/C2118/15

Instructions regarding War Diaries and Intelligence Summaries are contained in F. S. Regs., Part II. and the Staff Manual respectively. Title pages will be prepared in manuscript.

WAR DIARY
or
~~INTELLIGENCE SUMMARY.~~
(Erase heading not required.)

Army Form C. 2118.

125 Inf. Bde HQ. Nov 1918.
PAGE 4. Vol 52

Place	Date	Hour	Summary of Events and Information	Remarks and references to Appendices
HAUTMONT 1/40000 of 51. & 52.	10.	1400.	Report timed 1135 recd from Cavalry states BARELLE - AIBES RD clear. Enemy still holding LES HAIES DE COUSOLRES & BOIS DE FORET.	–
		1400 - 1545	3rd Hussars transferred to VI Corps. 1 Coy Cyclist allotted to Bde. Orders issued to Cyclist Coy, to hold outpost line.	
	11.	0700.	Message received ordering cessation of hostilities at 1100	
		1245	BDE O.O. 132 issued, ordering Cyclists to take over from 7th LF.	8.
51. P23c70.	12.	1000	Bde HQ. moved to another part of HAUTMONT.	
	13.		Rest & recreation, memorial service held for those who had died in HAUTMONT.	
	14/18.		Training & recreation.	
	19.		Brig. Gen. H FARGUS. CMG DSO took over command of Div, in absence on leave of D.C. LT. Col. J. McLEOD in command of 125 Bde.	
	20/25		Training & recreation.	
	26.		Bde route march	
	27/29		Training & recreation.	
	30.		Bde route march. Bde ration strength 110 OFF. 1711 O.R.	

James S. Macleod Lt. Col
Cmdg. 125 Inf Bde.
3/12/18.

(A9475) Wt W2358/P360 600,000 12/17 D. D. & L. Sch. 52a. Forms/C2118/13

(1)

SECRET.

125TH.INFANTRY BRIGADE ORDER NO.125.

COPY NO.....

Ref Sheets 37.S., 51.A. and 51.

Nov:3rd 1918.

1. The advance will be resumed by the Fourth, Third and First Armies on the 4th November. French Armies are also co-operating.

2.(a). The attack on the IV Corps front is being carried out by the 37th Division on the Right and the N.Z.Division on the left. Boundaries and objectives are shown on the attached tracing. (To Bns and M.G.COY only).

(b). As soon as the RED LINE has been made good, the advance is being vigorously pressed to line of the ST REMY - CHAUSSEE - PONT-SUR-SAMBRE - BAVAI ROAD.

3. Seven Brigades R.F.A. are supporting the Left Division; 4 Brigades Heavy Artillery are supporting the attack on IV Corps Front.

4. The 5th and 42nd Divisions are to be prepared to pass through the 37th and N.Z.Divisions respectively and to continue the advance.

5. The strictest measures will be taken to maintain secrecy.

6. Four O.R's per Platoon will carry hatchets and bill hooks for cutting gaps in hedges.

7(a) The 125th.Inf Brigade Group will move to SOLESMES on Nov: 4th.

(b). STARTING POINT - Main Road I.10.B.6.5.

(c). Units pass starting point at following times :-

125th.Inf Bde.H.Qrs..............1245.
5th.Lan Fus......................1300.
7th.Lan Fus......................1317.
8th.Lan Fus......................1334.
125th.L.T.M.B....................1400.
'C' Coy.,42nd.M.G.Bn.............1405.

(d). ROUTE.- BETHENCOURT - VIESLY - BELLE VUE.

(e). First Line Transport and baggage wagons accompany their respective units.

8. Brigade H.Qrs. will close at FONTAINE-au-PIRE at 1200 hours on Nov 4th and reopen at SOLESMES on arrival.

9. ZERO Hour will be 0530 on Nov 4th.

10. ACKNOWLEDGE.

T.B.B. Nichols
Captain,
Brigade Major,
125th.Inf Bde.

Issued at thro' Signals at 1600.

Copies to :-

1. 5th.Lan Fus.
2. 7th.Lan Fus.
3. 8th.Lan Fus.
4. 125th.L.T.M.B.
5. 'C' Coy,42nd M.G.Bn.
6. 126th.Inf Brigade.
7. No.2 Coy,42nd Div Train.
8. 127th.Inf Bde.
9. A.P.M.42nd Division.
10. 42nd Division (for information).
11. Staff Captain.
12. Bde Signal Officer.
13. Bde Transport Officer.
14. War Diary.
15. War Diary.
16. FILE.

(2)

SECRET. 100

125TH. INFANTRY BRIGADE ORDER NO. 126.

Copy No....17

Ref Sheets 51.A.S.E.)
57.B.N.E.) 1/20.000.

4/11/18.

1. The 125th. Inf Bde Group will move tomorrow 5th inst to BEAUDIGNIES or, if BEAUDIGNIES is occupied by 127th Inf Bde Group, to the VERTIGNEUL - PONT-a-PIERRES Area.

2. STARTING POINT - Road junction E.2.C.5.3.

3. Units pass starting point at following times :-

5th. Lan Fus.............0800 .hours.
7th. Lan Fus.............0817 .hours.
8th. Lan Fus.............0834 .hours.
125th. Inf Bde. H. Qrs...0900 .hours.
125th. L.T.M.B...........0905 .hours.
'C' Coy, 42nd M.G. Bn...0910 .hours.
1/2nd. (E.L.) Fd. Amb...0920 .hours.

4. ROUTE.- Cross Roads E.4.B. - VERTIGNEUL - thence Infantry will use track W.23.B.9.1. to W.18.B.4.2.; transport will move via Cross Roads W.23.D.9.9. thence by W.17.C.1.2.

5. Transport will accompany units.

6. If Bde Group does not more further than VERTIGNEUL - PONT-a-PIERRES Area, distribution of units will be as follows :-

5th. Lan Fus.) at PONT-a-PIERRES.
7th. Lan Fus.)
Remainder including Bde. H. Qrs. at : VERTIGNEUL.

7. Bde H. Qrs. will close at SOLESMES at 0800 hours; new location will be notified later.

8. ACKNOELEDGE. (Units of Bde Group only).

P.B.B. Nichols.
Captain,
Brigade Major,
125th. Inf Bde.

Issued thro' Signals at 2345 hrs

Copies to :-

P.T.O.

- 2 -

1. 5th.Lan Fus.
2. 7th.Lan Fus.
3. 8th.Lan Fus.
4. 125th.L.T.M.B.
5. No.2 Coy, 42nd Div Train.
6. 'C' Coy, 42nd M.G.Bn.
7. 1/2nd.(E.L.)Fd.Amb.
8. 126th.Inf Bde.
9. 127th.Inf Bde.
10. A.P.M., 42nd Division.
11. 42nd Division (for information).
12. N.Z.Division. (for information).
13. Staff Captain.
14. Bde Signal Officer.
15. Bde T.O.
16. War Diary.
17. War Diary.
18. F I L E.

War Diary.
"A" Form
MESSAGES AND SIGNALS.

Army Form C. 2121
(in pads of 100).
No. of Message..................

Prefix............Code............m.
Office of Origin and Service Instructions.
Special D.R.
Ref sheets.
51.A.S.E. & 51.S.W. 1/20,000.

Words | Charge.
Sent
At..........
To..........
By..........

This message is on a/c of:
SECRET. Service.
****
(Signature of "Franking Officer.")

Recd. at..........m.
Date..........
From..........
By..........

TO MOLA DURI VAVU
MOWE PIRI WULI.
MOHU ZUVU

Sender's Number.	Day of Month.	In reply to Number.	AAA
* B.M.65.	5.		

JUNE Order No.127. AAA Bde Group moves to HERBIGNIES tomorrow 6th inst AAA Starting Point Cross Roads R.33.A.65.30. AAA Units pass S.P. at following times AAA MOLA 0800 MOWE 0817 MOHU 0834 JUNE H.Qrs. 0900 DURI 0905 PIRI 0910 AAA ROUTE - Road skirting N. of LE QUESNOY to R.34.C.4.9. - M.19.D.2.5. - Cross Roads M.15.C.0.4. - VILLEREAU AAA Transport accompanies units AAA Bde H.Qrs. close BEAUDIGNIES 0800 hrs reopen HERBIGNIES on arrival AAA Units of Bde Group to ACKNOWLEDGE AAA Addsd MOLA MOWE MOHU DURI PIRI ZUVU reptd VAVU WULI.

From J U N E.
Place
Time 1115. 2315

The above may be forwarded as now corrected.
Censor.

(Z) Captain.
Signature of Addressor or person authorised to telegraph in his name.

* This line should be erased if not required.

(18965.) Wt. W12952/M1294. 187,500 Pads. 1/17 McC. & Co., Ltd. (E. 818.)

Army Form C. 2121
(in pads of 100).

"A" Form
MESSAGES AND SIGNALS.

No. of Message..................

Prefix.............Code......... ......m. | Words | Charge.

Office of Origin and Service Instructions.

Special D.R.

SECRET & URGENT.
Ref sheet 51.[illegible] 1/40,000.

Sent
At..................m.
To....................
By....................

This message is on a/c of:
..........................*Service.*
(Signature of "Franking Officer.")

Recd. at..........m.
Date................
From................
By..................

TO
MOLA DURI WUJE
MOWE FIRI VAVU
MOHU VUDE Bde T.O.

Sender's Number.	Day of Month.	In reply to Number.	AAA
* B.M.78.	7.		

JUNE order No.128.AAA Bde Group will move to OBIES today AAA Starting point MAISON ROUGE N.31.A.3.8. AAA Units pass S.P. at following hours AAA JUNE H.Qrs. 1200 MOLA 1205 MOWE 1220 MOHU 1225 DURI 1300 FIRI 1305 AAA Route Later AAA Transport accompanies units AAA Billetting representatives meet Staff Captain at church OBIES at 1200 AAA Bde H.Qrs. close HARMIGNIES 1130 reopen OBIES on arrival. AAA Bde is to be prepared to take over line tomorrow night AAA Bde Units to ACKNOWLEDGE AAA Added 3 Bns DURI FIRI Bde.T.O. reptd VAVU WUJE VUDE.

From J U N E.
Place
Time

The above may be forwarded as now corrected. (Z)
Censor.

Captain.

Signature of Addressor or person authorised to telegraph in his name.

* This line should be erased if not required.

(18965.) Wt. W12952/M1294. 187,500 Pads. 1/17 McC. & Co., Ltd. **(E. 818.)**

"A" Form

MESSAGES AND SIGNALS.

Army Form C. 2121 (In pads of 100)

No. of Message............

Prefix............ Code..............m. Words. Charge.

Office of Origin and Service Instructions

Special D.R.

SECRET & URGENT.

Ref sheet 41. 1/40.000.

Sent At..............m. To................ By................

This message is on a/c of: .... Service.

(5)

(Signature of "Franking Officer.")

Recd. at...........m. Date.............. From.............. By..............

TO 5th.L.F. 125th.L.T.M.B. 42nd Div

7th.L.F. 'C' Coy,42nd 126th.Inf Bde.

8th.L.F. M.G.Bn. 95th.Inf Bde.

187th.Inf Bde.

427 Fd Coy R.E.

C Squad 3 Hussrs

A Coy 1/2 L.F.

Group R.A.

Sender's Number. Day of Month. In reply to Number.

* B.M.84. 8.

JUNE Order No.129. AAA

1. The 125th.Inf Bde will pass through the 126th.Inf Bde today and continue the advance.

2. The advance will be made in two bounds. First bound High Ground in P.35. and P.29. Final objective Hi h Ground East of AVESNE – MAUBEUGE Road between Divl Boundaries.

3.(a). 125th.Inf Bde will advanc in Battle patrol formation with 5th.L.F. on right 7th.L.F. on left and 8th.L.F. in support..

(b). Forward inter Bn boundary will be the WARGNORIES stream thence road from S.E. Corner of BOIS D'-QUESNOY through P.30.B.4.4. to Q.26.A.3.3. all inclusive to Right Bn.

(c). The 8th.L.F. will follow forward Bns at 500 yds distance and as soon as the advance from first bound has taken place will ~~assemble~~ encircle HAUTMONT from the East covering all exits with their fire, and induce the garrison to surrender by all possible means.

From

Place

Time

The above may be forwarded as now corrected.

(Z)

Censor.

Signature of Addressor or person authorised to telegraph in his name.

* This line should be erased if not required.

(4615) Wt. W3253/P511 1,113,336 Shts. 2/18 C. & Co. (2634)

"A" Form

MESSAGES AND SIGNALS.

Army Form C. 2121
(In pads of 100)

No. of Message..............

Prefix............ Code............m	Words. Charge.	This message is on a/c of:	Recd. at............m.
Office of Origin and Service Instructions	Sent	.... Service.	Date..............
	At..................m.		From ....
	To....................		
	By....................	(Signature of "Franking Officer.")	By ....

TO

– 2 –

Sender's Number.	Day of Month.	In reply to Number.	AAA
*			

B.M.84 8.

4. Assembly will be as follows :-
5th.L.F. F.51.a. 7th.L.F. F.51.A. 8th.L.F. F.58.B. and will be complete by following y time :- 5th.L.F. [illegible] hrs 7th.L.F. [illegible] hrs 8th.L.F. [illegible] hrs.

5. One, probably two, pontoon bridges are being put across the SAMBRE in F.58.D. tonight and early tomorrow morning.
These bridges will be used by the Bde.

6. 5th.L.F. will move off from assembly positions as soon as the bridges are completed, 7th.L.F. and 8th.L.F. will follow.

7. There will be no artillery barrage, but a liaison officer R.A. will go forward with 2 forward Bns, who will make their H.Qrs. together in BOUSSIERES for first bound.

8. 1 section of M.G's. will accompany each Bn and will report to Bns before they leave present positions.

9. 1 Trench Mortar with 32 rounds will be accompany each Bn.

10. The 126th.Inf Bde are advancing their line this morning through the BOIS D' HAUTMONT with a view to encircling HAUTMONT from the WEST.

From

Place

Time

The above may be forwarded as now corrected. (Z)

Censor. Signature of Addressor or person authorised to telegraph in his name.

* This line should be erased if not required.

(4715) Wt. W3253/P511 1,113,336 Shts. 2/18 C. & Co. (E634)

"A" Form

MESSAGES AND SIGNALS.

Army Form C. 2121
(In pads of 100)

No. of Message..............

Prefix.............. Code..............m. Office of Origin and Service Instructions	Words. Charge. Sent At..............m. To.............. By..............	This message is on a/c of: .... Service. .... (Signature of "Franking Officer.")	Recd. at..........m. Date.............. From.............. By..............

TO - 3 -

Sender's Number.	Day of Month.	In reply to Number.	AAA
* B.M.84.	8.		

11. An Advd Bde Report Centre is being established in BOUSSIERES in P.32.A. Exact location later but house will be marked with flags.
12. Bde Battle H.Qrs. will open at HOISING FARM C.22.A. at 0830 hours.
13. ACKNOWLEDGE. (Units of Bde group only).

From

Place JUNE.

Time 0400.

The above may be forwarded as now corrected. (Z)

Captain.

Censor. Signature of Addressor or person authorised to telegraph in his name.

Bde Major.

* This line should be erased if not required.

(4715) Wt. W3253/P511 1,113,336 Shts 2/18 C. & Co. (2634)

Army Form C. 2121
(In pads of 100.)

MESSAGES AND SIGNALS.

No. of Message...........

Prefix..............Code..............m. | Words | Charge.

Office of Origin and Service Instructions

PRIORITY.

Sent

At ....m.

To ....

By ....

This message is on a/c of :

(6)

.......................Service.

(Signature of "Franking Officer")

Recd. at......m.

Date..............

From ....

By...............

TO { MOLA FIRI 187th.Inf Bde.
MOWE GIHU 13th.Inf Bde.
MOHU VAVU Grou R.F.A.
DURI WULI 3rd Hussars.

Sender's Number.	Day of Month.	In reply to Number.	AAA
B.M.128.	9.		

JUNE ORDER No.130. AAA on receipt of this order MOWE will take over the whole front of the Bde making arrangements direct with MOLA AAA Line will be held as outpost position with outpost line along high ground about 1000 yds E. of AVESNES - MAUBEUGE Rd and picquet line immediately E. of this road AAA On relief MOLA will withdraw to billets in HAUTMONT AAA MOHU will also billet in HAUTMONT AAA FIRI and GIHU will carry out relief and guns will then be disposed in accordance with verbal arrangement made this morning AAA MOWE will maintain touch with Bdes on flanks AAA Completion of reliefs and moves and location of Bn. H.Qrs. will be reported to this office AAA Bde H.Qrs. will move to P.29.C.8.6. tomorrow at a time to be notified later AAA Bde units to ACKNOWLEDGE AAA Added 3 Bns DURI FIRI GIHU repeated VAVU WULI 187 and 13th.Inf Bdes, Group R.F.A. 3rd Hussars.

From

Place J U N E.

Time

The above may be forwarded as now corrected. (Z)

.... Captain.

Censor. Signature of Addressor or person authorised to telegraph in his name

* This line should be erased if not required.

Order No. 1625 Wt. W3253/ P 511 27/2 H. & K.. Ltd. (E. 2634).

"A" Form

Army Form C. 2121
(In pads of 100.)

MESSAGES AND SIGNALS.

No. of Message............

Prefix..............Code..............m. Office of Origin and Service Instructions	Words	Charge.	This message is on a/c of:	Recd. at......m.
(7)	Sent At ....m. To .... By		......W-D......Service. (Signature of "Franking Officer")	Date.............. From .... By................

TO 5th.L.F. A Coy.42nd.M.G.C. 127.I.B. 3rd.
7th.L.F. C Coy.42nd M.G.C. 127.I.B. Hussars.
8th.L.F. 427th.Fd.Coy.R.E. 126.I.B. C Sqdn
125th.L.T.M.B. 13.I.B. [illegible] R.F.A. 3rd Hussars

Sender's Number.	Day of Month.	In reply to Number.	AAA
B.M.140.	10. VAVU		

125th.Inf Bde.Order No.131.AAA 125th.Inf Bde will take over front held by 5th Division today and will then hold Corps Front AAA 7th.L.F. will take over front at present held by 13th Inf Bde by 1430 hrs AAA Dispositions as follows AAA 1 Coy as outpost Coy with forward outposts in squares W.9. W.3. and W.33 guarding Road approaches and with support posts on AVESNES - MAUBERGE Rd AAA 1 Coy as inlying picquet at 1hrs notice billetted in FONTAINE AAA Outpost Coy H.Qrs. in LE FAYE W.1.B. where officer i/c 2 forward sections of 119 and 120th Bdes R.F.A. should report AAA 'A' Coy42nd M.G.C. will move from present positions and arrange to cover front taken over with 3 sections in line and 1 section in reserve AAA Positions to be chosen primarily with regard to comfort of men AAA 7th.L.F. and A Coy 42nd M.G.C. will report to this office when they are in new positions and will forward disposition maps by 1600 hrs AAA 7th.L.F. and A Coy.42nd M.G.C. to ACKNOWLEDGE.

From
Place 125th.Inf Bde.
Time 12 Noon.

The above may be forwarded as now corrected. (Z)

Censor.

[signature] Captain,
Bde Major,
125th.Inf Bde.

Signature of Addressor or person authorised to telegraph in his name

* This line should be erased if not required.

Order No. 1625 Wt. W3253/ P 511 27/2 H. & K.. Ltd. (E. 2634).

(8)

S E C R E T.
****

125TH. INFANTRY BRIGADE ORDER NO.132.
****

Copy No. 17

Ref Sheet 51.1/40.000.

11/11/18.

1. The IV Corps Cyclist Bn will take over the examining posts on the Corps Front at present manned by the 7th.Lan Fus today.

2. On relief the 7th.Lan Fus will withdraw into billets in HAUTMONT.

3. The posts will be taken over as they now stand by the IV Corps Cyclist Bn, who will, by means of these posts, ensure that no civilians move about the area without the necessary passes. All suspicious persons will be detained.

4. The 7th.Lan Fus will detail 1 Coy daily as inlying picquet, to be at 1 hours notice.

5. 'A' and 'C' Coys, 42nd M.G.Bn will today withdraw the sections at present covering the Corps Front into billets in HAUTMONT.

6. Completion of relief and moves to be reported to this office.

7. 7th.Lan Fus, 4th Corps Cyclist Bn, 'A' and 'C' Coys, 42nd M.G.Bn. to ACKNOWLEDGE.

P.B.B. Nichols.
Captain,
Brigade Major,
125th.Inf Bde.

Issued at 1245 thro' Signals.
Copies to :-

1. 5th.Lan Fus.
2. 7th.Lan Fus.
3. 8th.Lan Fus.
4. 125th.L.T.M.B.
5. 'A' Coy.42nd.M.G.Bn.
6. 'C' Coy,42nd.M.G.Bn.
7. IV Corps Cyclist Bn.
8. Group R.F.A.
9. 52nd.Inf Bde.
10. 187th.Inf Bde.
11. 126th.Inf Bde.
12. 127th.Inf Bde
13. 42nd.M.G.Bn.
14. 42nd Division.
15. Staff Captain.
16. Bde Signal Officer.
17. War Diary.
18. War Diary.
19. F I L E.

42nd (EAST LANCASHIRE) DIVISION.

SUMMARY OF OPERATIONS.

5th to 11th November, 1918.

On 3rd November the Division was concentrated in BEAUVOIS. On the eve of the operations of 4th November it commenced its forward move and passed through the N.Z. Division in the Eastern part of the FORET DE MORMAL on the night 5th/6th November. It was then disposed with 126th Inf. Brigade in front (Map 'A'), 127th Inf. Brigade in Support in HERBIGNIES and 125th Inf. Brigade in Reserve in BEAUDIGNIES.

The long approach marches on the night 3rd/4th, the days 4th and 5th and the night 5th/6th were carried out under very trying and exhausting conditions. Rain fell continuously. The roads and tracks were deep in mud, crowded with troops and transport, and broken by numerous mine craters which caused tedious waits and detours and necessitated the man-handling of M.Gs, L.Gs and L.T.Ms, ammunition and supplies for the last stages. The nights 3rd/4th, 4th/5th were spent in crowded billets, which allowed but little rest to the troops.

The work of relieving the troops of N.Z. Division in the FORET DE MORMAL was peculiarly difficult owing to the extreme darkness, the uncertainty of the location of the troops to be relieved, and the state of the Forest roads and tracks.

The Right Division of the VI Corps on our Left was echeloned some 3,000 yards to the rear. To cover the flank thus exposed a second M.G. Coy. was allotted to 126th Inf. Brigade.

At 0630 hours on November 6th, four hours after completion of relief, 126th Inf. Brigade resumed the advance with 5th Bn. E. Lancs. on the Right, and 8th Bn. Manchester Regt. on the Left.

On the Right the troops succeeded in reaching their objective. In the centre and the Left intense M.G. fire was met with from the direction of HOISIES FARM, HARGNIES and COUTANT. The Left Bn. suffered particularly from fire from its Left flank which was entirely exposed. In attempting to make progress in face of this heavy fire, considerable casualties were suffered and troops were eventually held up on the line shown (Map 'A'.). They remained on this line in the open for the remainder of the day and the following night. M.G. and artillery fire was very severe making all movement E. of and in the Eastern portions of the forest very difficult. Communications in these circumstances were much impeded, and despite the greatest efforts artillery support was reduced to an almost negligible quantity.

During the day the 127th Inf. Brigade moved to billets in LE CARNOY. This Brigade had been on the line of march in heavy rain all day and 125th Inf. Brigade in HERBIGNIES were accordingly made support Brigade.

On the evening of the 6th orders were received that the advance was being continued the following day by divisions on the Right and Left, but that the Division would not attempt to push forward until the Right Division of the VI Corps on our Left had made progress. At 08.45 hours on the 7th, this Division having come up into line, 126th Inf. Brigade again advanced and occupied HARGNIES, VIEUX MESNIL and the high ground E. of the latter village. At first little opposition was encountered. Later, VIEUX MESNIL was heavily shelled and the Left flank, which was again exposed, suffered from M.G. fire.

On the evening of the 7th, 126th Inf. Brigade were given a further objective, the high ground immediately E. of the River SAMBRE, and 125th Inf. Brigade, which had meantime moved to LA HAUT RUE, and PETIT BAVAY, were ordered to pass through them on the morning of the 8th and advance to the final objective E. of AVESNES - MAUBEUGE Road.

Before daybreak on the 8th, 126th Inf. Brigade had seized BOIS D'HAUTMONT and sent patrols into the Western part of HAUTMONT itself surprising a small enemy rearguard and killing two. All the bridges over the SAMBRE were found to have been destroyed but the leading Company immediately improvised a crossing and engaged the enemy rearguards which were holding out with M.Gs in the town and field artillery near FORT D'HAUTMONT.

Meantime, 125th Inf. Brigade crossed the River SAMBRE near PONT SUR SAMBRE at about 0800 hours. Shortly afterwards a footbridge was thrown over the River at BOUSSIERES. Enemy shell fire was extremely heavy - his batteries occupying forward positions and remaining in action until our infantry were close upon them.

Progress was made until enemy rearguard, holding strong positions about FME DE FORET, FORT D'HAUTMONT and the cross roads in P.30.b. and well supported by Field Artillery, were encountered during the afternoon. Immediately dusk fell fighting patrols worked forward and succeeded in ejecting the enemy from all these positions, and the Right battalion passed on and occupied its final objective with a defensive flank thrown back to FORT D'HAUTMONT. At the same time the 1/10th Manchesters, 126th Inf. Brigade, who were still engaging the enemy at the cemetery E. of HAUTMONT were relieved by troops of the 8th Lancashire Fusiliers. The Division was now disposed with 125th Inf. Brigade in the line, 126th Inf. Brigade in HAUTMONT and 127th Inf. Brigade in HARGNIES and VIEUX MESNIL.

By 04.40 hours on the 9th the final objective was occupied on the whole front. The Right Division of the VI Corps on our Left was still echeloned to the rear and patrols from the Left Battalion, 125th Inf. Brigade, reconnoitring to their flank found LOUVROIL evacuated. During the morning cavalry patrols passed through the leading infantry to gain touch with the enemy, eventually reaching their first objective, the River THURE, by early the following day.

No further infantry advance being intended that day, the 3rd Hussars and IV Corps Cyclists were sent forward and gained touch with the enemy on the line of the River THURE, and the outpost line of the Divisional front was taken over by one battalion and the remaining troops withdrawn into billets.

Orders were received during the morning for the Division to take over the infantry outpost line on the whole Corps front. This was carried out during the day, one battalion 125th Inf. Brigade covering the front with two outpost companies and two companies in support.

At 11.00 hours on the 11th the armistice came into force and operations ceased. The "standfast" and "cease fire" being sounded by massed bugles throughout the Divisional area.

Thus the Division, which after 3 continuous months in the trenches at HEBUTERNE, commenced the advance on the 21st August finished up still in touch with the enemy at 11.00 hours on 11/11/18.

CASUALTIES.

	Officers.	Other Ranks.
Killed.	4.	66.
Wounded & Missing.	12.	248.
TOTALS.	16.	314.

CAPTURES.

Prisoners,	1 Officer.	29 Other Ranks.
Field Guns.	3.	
Machine Guns.	84.	
Trench Mortars.	12.	
Motor Lorries.	2.	

35 Trucks of Ammunition (various sizes).

and other various booty.

A. Solly-Flood

Major General,
Commanding 42nd Division.

16/11/18.

17

VOL: 53.

CONFIDENTIAL

VR 23

WAR DIARY.

DECEMBER 1918.

125 INFY. BDE. H. Qrs.

Instructions regarding War Diaries and Intelligence Summaries are contained in F. S. Regs., Part II. and the Staff Manual respectively. Title pages will be prepared in manuscript.

WAR DIARY
or
~~INTELLIGENCE~~ ~~SUMMARY.~~ VOL 53

(Erase heading not required.)

December 1918

125 Inf. Bde H.Q.

Army Form C. 2118.

Place	Date	Hour	Summary of Events and Information	Remarks and references to Appendices
Ref 51. 1/40000	1	1100	H.M. The King passed along MAUBERGE – AVESNES RD. Brigade lined E. Side of road. Brig Gen H. Fargus CMG DSO. was presented to the King.	
HAUTMONT P 23 C 70.	2/8		Training in morning; recreation in afternoon.	
	3.		Brig Gen H. Fargus CMG DSO. proceeded on leave to U.K. Lt Col J. McLeod assumed command of Bde.	
	3/8		Training in morning. recreation in afternoon.	
	9.		Warning order for move of Div to CHARLEROI area received.	
	10.		Bde O.O. No 135 issued, ordering move to CHARLEROI.	1.
	11/13.		Training & recreation.	
MAUBERGE	14.		Brigade Group moved to MAUBERGE by march route.	
ESTINNE AU MONT	15.		Brigade Group moved to ESTINNE AU MONT by march route.	
ANDERLUES	16.		Brigade Group moved to ANDERLUES by march route.	
— " —	17.		Rest.	
CHARLEROI.	18.		Brigade Group moved to CHARLEROI by march route. All battalions in the barracks (infantry)	
	19		Brig. Gen. FARGUS CMG DSO. returned from leave.	
	20/24.		Battalions engaged on improving accomodation in barracks. Two Coys of 7 LF move to cavalry barracks	
	25/26		Holiday.	
	27/28		Training education in morning. Recreation in afternoon.	

(A9175) Wt W2353/P360 600,000 12/17 D. D. & L. Sch 52a. Forms/C2118/15

Instructions regarding War Diaries and Intelligence Summaries are contained in F. S. Regs., Part II, and the Staff Manual respectively. Title pages will be prepared in manuscript.

Army Form C. 2118.

(2)

WAR DIARY
~~or~~
~~INTELLIGENCE SUMMARY.~~

(*Erase heading not required.*)

Place	Date	Hour	Summary of Events and Information	Remarks and references to Appendices
CHARLEROI	29.		Church parade.	
	30/31.		Training & education in morning. Recreation in afternoon	

P.B.B. Nicholls Capt.
for Brig. Genl. Comd.
125th Inf Bde.

(A9175) Wt W2358/P360 600,000 12/17 D. D. & L. Sch 52a. Forms/C2118/15

(1)

S E C R E T.

COPY NO. 18

125th. INFANTRY BRIGADE ORDER NO. 135.

Reference Sheets 12 & 8 1/100,000. 10th. December, 1918.

1. (a). The 125th. Infantry Brigade Group will march to CHARLEROI, commencing December 14th., in accordance with the attached March Table.

2. The following units will march with the Brigade:-

427th. Field Coy., R.E. less 1 Section.
1 Section 1/3rd. E.L. Fd. Ambulance.
No. 2. Coy., Divisional Train.

3. Detailed orders in connection with move are given in Appendix 'A'.

Administrative Orders will be issued separately.

4. Completion of moves will be notified to Brigade Headquarters.

5. A C K N O W L E D G E. (Units of Bde. Group only).

T.B.B. Nichols.
Captain,
Bde. Major,
125th. Bde.

Issued at 1900 thro' Signals.

Copy No.			
1. 5th. L.F.		11. A.P.M., 42 Div.	
2. 7th. L.F.		12. 42nd. Division.	
3. 8th. L.F.		13. "	
4. 125th. T.M.B.		14. Staff Capt.	
5. No. 2. Coy., Div. Train.		15. Bde Signal Offr.	
6. 427th. Fd. Coy. R.E.		16. Bde. T.O.	
7. 1/3rd. E.L. Fd. Amb.		17. W.D.	
8. 126th. Inf. Bde.		18. W.D.	
9. 127th. Inf. Bde.		19. File.	
10. C.R.A., 42 Div.			

APPENDIX TO 125th INFANTRY BRIGADE ORDER NO.135.

1. The comfort of the troops will be the first consideration during the march.

2. S.A.A. to be carried on the man during the march will be reduced to 60 rounds.

3. DRESS.

(a). Full Marching Order. Caps will be worn, and steel helmets carried against the back of the pack by means of the supporting straps. Mess Tins will be carried below the pack. Box Respirators will be carried on top of the pack, Waterproof sheets showing below the flap of the pack. Jerkins and greatcoats in pack.

(b). Transport Drivers will wear Jerkins, and haversacks on back in place of packs. Greatcoats strapped in front on saddle.

4. MARCH DISCIPLINE. The provision of 4th Army No.G.S.128 will be strictly adhered to, special attention being paid to the following points:-

(1). During halts, chargers and pack animals must be well on the right hand side of the road, with their heads facing in towards the road.

(2). Rear Parties of 6 Other Ranks under an N.C.O. will march immediately in rear of the transport of each unit; this party will be responsible for clearing the road of any broken vehicles etc., and generally ensuring that the road is not blocked for units in rear.

(3). Men left behind in billets, or for any purpose, will be properly marched under an officer or N.C.O.

(4). When marching at ease, the rifle will be slung on either shoulder.

(5). In order to give space on the road, bands will march in sections of threes and not in sections of fours.

(6). DISTANCES. Will be as laid down in above mentioned Letter, with the following additions:-

Between unit and its Transport 50 yards.
Between Sections of Transport 50 yards.

5. After 1700 hours daily, by which time the march will have been completed, all roads will be kept clear for the advance of the Supply Column.

6. First Line Transport will accompany units on the march; baggage wagons of the Train will march with 1st Line Transport.

7. A.A. Lewis Guns of Battalions will not be carried on the march but will be left at Div. Depot under orders to be issued by Staff Captain.

(P.T.O).

8.(a). As soon as possible after arrival in a billeting area, all units of the Bde. Group will send 2 orderlies, who know their own Headquarters, to Brigade Headquarters; one orderly will then return to his unit, the other remaining at Brigade Headquarters.

In addition Bde. Signal Officer will detail 1 Cyclist Orderly to accompany each Battalion daily on the march; this orderly will return to Brigade Headquarters as soon as he knows the new location of the H.Q. of the Battalion to which he is attached.

(b). All sentries, Traffic Control Posts, and Police, will be instructed as to the position of, and routes to, all H.Q. in the vicinity.

9. A Bde. Report Centre will be established in each Billeting Area to which units can send all reports, until such time as the position of Brigade Headquarters is notified to all concerned, when reports will be sent to Brigade Headquarters.

Positions of Bde. Report Centre will be as follows;-

December 14th. Road junction at N. of MAUBERGE.

" 15th. ESTINNE-AU-MONT Church.

" 16th. ANDERLUES Church.

10. All references in orders, and reports will be to the 1/100,000 Map.

11. A watch will be circulated to all units each evening, while on the march, with correct time.

MARCH TABLE TO ACCOMPANY 125th.BDE ORDER NO.135.

1. The Bde.Group will march in the same order each day, and with the same intervals of time in passing the Starting Point, as follows:-

125th.Inf.Bde.H.Q.	Z.	8th.L.F.	Z.plus 18 mins.
125th.L.T.M.B.	Z. plus 1 mins.	427th.Fd.Coy.	Z.plus 26 mins.
		1 Sec.1/3 E.L.F.A.	Z. plus 31 mins.
5th.L.F.	Z. plus 2 mins.	No.2.Coy.Div.Train.	Z.plus 33.
7th.L.F.	Z. plus 10 mins.		

2. In each case Z Hour is the hour of passing the Starting Point as given in Table below:-

Serial No.	Date.	Starting Point.	Hour of passing S.P.	From.	To.	Route.	Remarks.
1.	14th.Dec.	Road Junction ½ mile South of first O in LOUVROIL.	1200.	HAUTMONT.	MAUBERGE FAUBG de MONS.	LOUVRIL.	No unit to move N. of HAUTMONT BRIDGE-FORT HAUTMONT ROAD before 1115.
2.	15th.Dec.	Road Junction ¼ mile East of last S. in LES PASSES LA BANLIEUE.	1030.	MAUBERGE FAUBG de MONS.	ESTINNE AU MONT. ESTINNE AU VAL.	VILLERS SIRE NICOLE-Pte 10, ½ mile S.of GIVRY Village.	
3.	16th.Dec.	Cross Roads 1 mile N.of A in ESTINNE AU MONT.	0915.	ESTINNE AU MONT. ESTINNE AU VAL	ANDERLUES.	BINCHE	
4.	17th.Dec.	-	-	-	-	-	Halt for the day.
5.	18th.Dec.	X Rds., ¼ Mile N.E. of T in ANDERLUES STA.	0915.	ANDERLUES	CHARLEROI	Main MONS-CHARLEROI Rd.	

S.E.C.R.E.T.

NO. 2.
AMENDMENT TO 125th.INF.BRIGADE ORDER NO.135.

13/10/18.

MARCH TABLE.

Serial No.2., Col.4. In order to clear the area for a Division following, hour of passing Starting Point will be advanced by 30 minutes viz:-

For 1000

Read 0930.

P.B.B. Nichols.
Capt.,
Bde.Major,
125th.Inf.Bde.

Copies to all Recipients of 125th.Inf.Bde.Order No.135.

S E C R E T.

ADDENDUM AND AMENDMENT NO.1 TO 125TH. INFANTRY BRIGADE ORDER NO.135.

11th. Dec. 1918.

1. APPENDIX 'A'.

Para. 3. Sub-Para. 'A'. Delete last sentence. Substitute. "Greatcoats in pack, Jerkins will not be carried.

Add Sub-Para. (c). " Bands and transport drivers will carry steel helmet slung from left shoulder strap. Mounted officers will carry steel helmet attached to saddle."

2. MARCH TABLE.

Serial No. 2. Col. 4.

For. 1030
Read 1000.

3. A C K N O W L E D G E. (Units of Bde. Group only).

F.B.B. Nichols.
Captain,
Bde. Major,
125th. Bde.

DISTRIBUTION:- Copies to all recipients of 125th. Bde. Order No. 135.

Vol 54
9

Confidential

VR 24

War Diary
for
January 1919.

125 Inf Bde H. Qrs.

Instructions regarding War Diaries and Intelligence Summaries are contained in F. S. Regs., Part II. and the Staff Manual respectively. Title pages will be prepared in manuscript.

WAR DIARY
or
~~INTELLIGENCE~~ SUMMARY.
(Erase heading not required.)

VOL: 54.

Army Form C. 2118.

JANUARY 1919.

Place	Date	Hour	Summary of Events and Information	Remarks and references to Appendices
RUE de MONTIGNY				
CHARLEROI	Jan: 1st		It was decided at a Divn Conference to do Military Training 3 mornings a week and	
			Educational Training 3 mornings a week.	
		0930-1230	Military Training.	
	Jan 2nd	0930-1230	Educational Training -	
	Jan 3rd	Morning	Bde Route March, South of CHARLEROI; distance 8 or 9 miles -	
	Jan 4th	0930-1230	Educational Training. Strength of Bde as follows:- (Numbers actually with units) -	
			5th L.7. 26 and 518; 7th L.7. 25 and 488; 8th L.7 27 and 519; TMB 3 and 41 - Total 81 + 1586	
	Jan 5th		Church Parade.	
	Jan 6th	0930-1230	Military Training - Demobilization of Pivotals, Demobilizers + Guarantee letter men proceeding -	
	Jan 7th	0930-1230	Educational Training. Divl Commander visited Bde Educational Classes -	
	Jan 8th	0930-1230	Military Training. Final of Divn Platoon Soccer Competition - 5th L.7. were Runners Up -	
	Jan 9th	0930-1230	Educational Training. Lecture by Lt Col NAPIER on the "CAUCASUS" -	
	Jan 10th	0930-1230	Military Training - Release of Groups 1, 2, 10, 22, 30, 33 + 35 authorised + commenced -	
	Jan 11th	0930-1230	Educational Training. Strength of Bde (Numbers actually with units) as follows:-	
			5th L.7. 26 + 524; 7th L.7. 28 and 473; 8th L.7. 26 and 509; TMB 2 + 36; Total 82 + 1542	
	Jan 12th		Church Parade -	

(A9175) Wt W2358/P360 600,000 12/17 D. D. & L. Sch 52a. Forms/C2118/15

Instructions regarding War Diaries and Intelligence Summaries are contained in F. S. Regs., Part II, and the Staff Manual respectively. Title pages will be prepared in manuscript.

WAR DIARY
or
INTELLIGENCE SUMMARY.
(*Erase heading not required.*)

Army Form C. 2118.

Place	Date	Hour	Summary of Events and Information	Remarks and references to Appendices
RUE de MONTIGNY CHARLEROI	Jan 13th		Military Training.	
	Jan 14th		Educational Training. Daily allotment for Demobilization made to Bde from Div: 16.	
	Jan 15th		Bde Route March cancelled owing to rain. Daily allotment 16. Revision of whole of releasable categories by G.R.O. 6051.	
	Jan 16th		Educational Training. 12 noon, Lecture on 'Naval Raid at Zeebrugge'. Daily allotment 16.	
	Jan 17th		Military Training. 12 noon, Lecture on 'South Africa'. Daily allotment 16.	
	Jan 18th		Educational Training. Medal Presentation to Bde by Div Commander. 12 noon, Lecture on 'Demobilization + Reconstruction' by Lt Col APLIN DSO. Daily allotment 16. Strength of Bde (Numbers actually with units) as follows: 5th Y. 24 + 504; 7th Y. 24 + 455; 8th Y. 19 + 515; TMB 2 + 36; Total 69 + 1510	
	Jan 19th		Church Parade. Daily allotment 30.	
	Jan 20th		Military Training. Inspection of 5th Y., including Barrack Rooms + Institutes by B.G.C. 12 noon, Lecture by Lt. Comm^d. EVERARD RN. on "Navy's Work". Daily allotment 30.	
	Jan 21st		Educational Training. Corps Commander gave a lecture on the Battle of Waterloo, at Waterloo. Daily allotment 30.	
	Jan 22nd		Military Training. Inspection of 7th Y., including Barrack Rooms + Institutes by B.G.C. Daily allotment 30.	

Instructions regarding War Diaries and Intelligence Summaries are contained in F. S. Regs., Part II, and the Staff Manual respectively. Title pages will be prepared in manuscript.

WAR DIARY
or
INTELLIGENCE SUMMARY.
(Erase heading not required.)

Army Form C. 2118.

Place	Date	Hour	Summary of Events and Information	Remarks and references to Appendices
ROUX les MONTIGNY CHARLEROI	Jan. 23rd		Educational Training – No demobilization Train –	
	24th		Military Training – Inspection of 8th L.F. including Barrack Rooms + ~~Institutes~~ by B.G.C. – No demobilization Train – 250 men of Bde went on Training guards at MONTIGNIES.	
	Jan 25th		Educational Training – Group 1 (Agriculture) takes place of Coalminers in Priority Groups –	
		12 noon	Lecture by Capt. GUEST "Rhodes in South Africa" – Daily allotment 40 –	
	Jan 26th		Church Parade – Daily allotment 40. Snow fall all day – Strength of Bde (numbers actually with units on 24th inst, excluding guards (250 men) at MONTIGNIES) as follows:– 5th L.F. 18 + 327; 7th L.F. 20 + 314; 8th L.F. 16 + 378; TMB 3 + 28; Total 57 + 1047 –	
	Jan 27th		Military Training – Still snowing – Daily allotment 40 –	
	Jan 28th		Educational Training. Daily allotment 40 –	
	Jan 29th		Bde Route March cancelled owing to lack of numbers, due to demobilization and large numbers of duties + guards to be found – Ann. Novices Boxing Competition.	
	Jan 30th		Educational Training. Hard frost – No demobilization Train – Final Ann. Novices Boxing –	
	Jan 31st		Military Training – No demobilization Train – Strength of Bde (numbers actually with units, excluding guard (250) at MONTIGNIES) as follows:– 5th L.F. 18 + 292; 7th L.F. 19 + 336; 8th L.F. 18 + 394; TMB 2 + 21. Total 57 + 1043 – Guard of 250 men returned from MONTIGNIES –	

P.B.B. Nichols Capt.
Bde Major
for Brig. Genl. Comd. 125 Inf Bde.

(A9475) Wt W2358/P360 600,000 12/17 D. D. & L. Sch 52a. Forms/C2118/15

Instructions regarding War Diaries and Intelligence Summaries are contained in F. S. Regs., Part II. and the Staff Manual respectively. Title pages will be prepared in manuscript.

WAR DIARY

~~or~~

~~INTELLIGENCE SUMMARY.~~

(*Erase heading not required.*)

Army Form C. 2118.

Place	Date	Hour	Summary of Events and Information	Remarks and references to Appendices
			125 LIGHT TRENCH MORTAR BATTERY.	
			From 1st January 1919	
			to 31st January 1919.	
			VOLUME No. 24.	
			Confidential	

D. D. & L., London, E.C.
(A8001) Wt. W1771/M2031 750,000 5/17 Sch. 52 Forms/C2118/14

Instructions regarding War Diaries and Intelligence Summaries are contained in F. S. Regs., Part II. and the Staff Manual respectively. Title pages will be prepared in manuscript.

WAR DIARY

~~or~~

~~INTELLIGENCE SUMMARY.~~

(Erase heading not required.)

Army Form C. 2118.

Place	Date	Hour	Summary of Events and Information	Remarks and references to Appendices
	1/1/19 – 31/1/19		Battery stationed at CHARLEROI. (H.Q.rs at 50 RUE DE L'ATHENEE)	

[illegible] Lt.
12 S[illegible]

D. D. & L., London, E.C.
(A8001) Wt. W1771/M2031 750,000 5/17 Sch. 52 Forms/C2118/14

14

VOL: 55.

CONFIDENTIAL.

WR 25

125 Inf Bde H Qrs

War Diary

for

February 1919.

Instructions regarding War Diaries and Intelligence Summaries are contained in F. S. Regs., Part II. and the Staff Manual respectively. Title pages will be prepared in manuscript.

WAR DIARY
or
INTELLIGENCE SUMMARY.
(Erase heading not required.)

Army Form C. 2118.

VOL: 55

FEBRUARY 1919.

Place	Date	Hour	Summary of Events and Information	Remarks and references to Appendices
RUE DE MONTIGNY CHARLEROI	Feb 1st		In accordance with instructions from Divn, 7th L.T moved from Barracks CHARLEROI to MONCEAU (3 to 4 kilometres outside the town of CHARLEROI), in order to take over the Corps Concentration Camp. Relief to be complete by Feb 8th.	
		12 noon	Lecture on "Drawing to Scale + Sketching".	MMcN.
			Daily allotment to Bde for Demobilization purposes: 76	
	Feb 2nd		Church Parades. Daily allotment 75.	MMcN
	Feb 3rd		Very little military or Educational Training is now possible owing to rapid demobilization + large numbers of duties + guards to be found.	
		1400	B.G.C. attended a Divn Conference, at which the questions of the formation of Cadres for Bns + disposal of Surplus Stores were discussed, + verbal orders issued. Daily allotment 67	MMcN
	Feb 4th	12 noon	Lecture by Revd E.D. MARTIN on "The League of Nations". Daily allotment nil.	MMcN
	Feb 5th	12 noon	Lecture by Revd STUDDART KENNEDY on "Lies + Lies". Daily allotment nil. Orders received for dispatch of Regular Officers who wish to serve with their units overseas.	MMcN.
	Feb 6th		Heavy snowfall in the night. Daily allotment 52. Preliminary verbal warning order received from Divn re dispatch of Personnel to Army of Occupation.	MMcN
	Feb 7th		Orders issued for Disbandment (due to low numbers caused by Demobilization) of	

(A9175) Wt W2358/P360 600,000 12/17 D. D. & L. Sch 52a. Forms/C2118/15

Army Form C. 2118.

Instructions regarding War Diaries and Intelligence Summaries are contained in F. S. Regs., Part II. and the Staff Manual respectively. Title pages will be prepared in manuscript.

WAR DIARY
or
INTELLIGENCE SUMMARY.
(Erase heading not required.)

Place	Date	Hour	Summary of Events and Information	Remarks and references to Appendices
RUE de MONTIGNY CHARLEROI	Feb 7th		125 L.T.M.B. Orders also received for dispatch in a few days time of draft of 20 officers + 400 ORs to 15th + 16th Bns Lancashire Fusiliers. Daily allotment = 52.	MWN
	Feb 8th		Severe frost. Orders issued for move of 5th L.F. from Barracks, CHARLEROI to MARCHIENNE-AU-PONT, where they will be closed up with the 7th L.F., + help to find personnel to run the IV Corps Concentration Camp. Daily allotment = 26.	MWN.
	Feb 9th		Church Parade. Actual Number with Units on noon 8th Feb as follows: 5th L.F. 16 + 293; 7th L.F. 18 + 292; 8th L.F. 15 + 323; TMB 2 + 17; Total 51 + 925	MWN.
	Feb 10th		5th L.F. moved to MARCHIENNE-AU-PONT less draft for 15th + 16th L.F.s, which remained in CHARLEROI. Daily allotment nil.	MWN.
	Feb 11th		Staff of IV Corps Concentration Camp taken over by men of 5th + 7th L.F.s. Orders received that draft for 15th + 16th L.F. will not proceed until further orders. Daily allotment nil.	MWN
	Feb 12th		Daily allotment 22. The 8th L.F., the only Bn now left in CHARLEROI, is almost entirely taken up in finding guards, duties etc.	MWN.
	Feb 13th		Daily allotment 19.	MWN
	Feb 14th		8th L.F. moved from Infantry to Cavalry Barracks, CHARLEROI, in order	

Army Form C. 2118.

Instructions regarding War Diaries and Intelligence Summaries are contained in F. S. Regs., Part II. and the Staff Manual respectively. Title pages will be prepared in manuscript.

WAR DIARY
or
INTELLIGENCE SUMMARY.
(Erase heading not required.)

Place	Date	Hour	Summary of Events and Information	Remarks and references to Appendices
RUE de MONTIGNY.				
CHARLEROI	Feb 14th		to clear former for use as Corps Demobilization Store. Daily allotment 19.	MMN.
	Feb 15th		Daily allotment – Strength actually with Bns as follows:–	
			5th L.F. 15 + 220; 7th L.F. 17 + 229; 8th L.F. 15 + 275; Total 47 + 724.	
			The 125 L.T.M.B. was reduced to Cadre 'A' strength viz:– 1 OR – remainder	
			rejoining their Bns.	MMN
	Feb 16th		Church Parade. Daily allotment 22. Frost has ceased & weather is now mild.	MMN
	Feb 17th		Remainder of 5th L.F. moved to MARCHIENNE-AU-PONT. 10 Prisoners of War	
			arrived for work on Bde Transport. CAPT B. SHELMERDINE M.C., 7th L.F.,	
			appointed Staff Capt vice CAPT J. MARSHALL, demobilized, assumed duties.	
			Lt-Col G.S. BREWN DSO, comm'd 7th L.F., took over temporary command of IX Corps Concentration Camp.	
			Daily allotment nil.	MMN
	Feb 18th		Demobilization of horses of Bde begun by sending of 8 'Y' horses to Base.	
			Daily allotment nil.	MMN.
	Feb 19th		Orders received to hold draft for 16th L.F. ready to move at short notice.	
			Daily allotment 22.	MMN
	Feb 20th		Daily allotment 19.	MMN.

(A9175) Wt W2358/P360 600,000 12/17 D. D. & L. Sch 52a. Forms/C2118/15

Army Form C. 2118.

WAR DIARY
or
INTELLIGENCE SUMMARY.
(Erase heading not required.)

Instructions regarding War Diaries and Intelligence Summaries are contained in F. S. Regs., Part II. and the Staff Manual respectively. Title pages will be prepared in manuscript.

Place	Date	Hour	Summary of Events and Information	Remarks and references to Appendices
RUE de MONTIGNY CHARLEROI	Feb. 21st		4 'Y' horses sent to Base - Daily allotment 16 - Orders received to send away all remaining releasable men for demobilization tomorrow - Nos actually with units as follows:- 5th L.F. 18 and 181; 7th L.F. 17 + 219; 8th L.F. 14 + 244; Total 49 & 644 -	MWN.
	Feb 22nd		All releasable men proceeded to Corps Concentration Camp for Demobilization; nos so proceeding from Bde are 115 -	MWN.
	Feb 23rd		An additional 40 releasable men left for Demobilization, who did not proceed yesterday -	MWN
	Feb 24th		Orders received to provide 50 volunteers or releasable men for duty at Corps Concentration Camp, to replace any cadre men or men detailed for drafts, who are to be withdrawn -	MWN.
	Feb 25th		Orders received for cadres of Bns, less 7th L.F., to be prepared to concentrate in CHARLEROI, ready to entrain, at short notice. Probable date given for entrainment - middle of March - 49 'Z' animals of the Bde were sold locally -	MWN
	Feb 26th		Orders received and issued to Bns for the parking of all transport vehicles surplus to present requirements on the ground in front of the Infantry Barracks, CHARLEROI, commencing tomorrow -	MWN

(A9475) Wt W2358/P360 600,000 12/17 D. D. & L. Sch 52a. Forms/C2118/15

Instructions regarding War Diaries and Intelligence Summaries are contained in F. S. Regs., Part II, and the Staff Manual respectively. Title pages will be prepared in manuscript.

WAR DIARY
or
INTELLIGENCE SUMMARY.
(Erase heading not required.)

Army Form C. 2118.

Place	Date	Hour	Summary of Events and Information	Remarks and references to Appendices
RUE de MONTIGNY CHARLEROI	Feb 27th		Mobilization stores being stored in rooms in Infantry Barracks. Each Bn has a separate room.	[illegible]
	Feb 28th		Nos actually with Units as follows: 5th R.F. 14 + 184; 7th R.F. 16 + 222; 8th R.F. 14 + 201; Total 44 + 607. Compared with last weeks total, the large no of men demobilized this week has been balanced in some degree by return of detached men to their Bns.	[illegible]

T.B.B. Nichols Capt.
Bde Major
for Brig. Genl. Comm. 125 Inf Bde.

(A9175) Wt W2358/P360 600,000 12/17 D. D. & L. Sch 52a. Forms/C2118/15

Vol 56

Confidential Vol 26

125 Inf Bde H.Qrs

War Diary

for

March 1919

Instructions regarding War Diaries and Intelligence Summaries are contained in F. S. Regs., Part II. and the Staff Manual respectively. Title pages will be prepared in manuscript.

WAR DIARY
or
INTELLIGENCE SUMMARY.
(Erase heading not required.)

Army Form C. 2118.

VOL: 56.

MARCH 1919.

Place	Date	Hour	Summary of Events and Information	Remarks and references to Appendices
RUE de MONTIGNY				
CHARLEROI	March 1st		Bde still waiting to send drafts to Army of Occupation; when this has been done + about 50 more men demobilized, the Bde will be down to Cadre strength.	
			Brig. Genl. H. FARGUS CMG. DSO has been appointed to take charge of Cadres of Divn.	[illegible]
	March 2nd		Owing to prevalence of Influenza, Church Parades were held in the open.	[illegible]
	March 3rd		45 more P.O.W. arrived for use by the Bde.	[illegible]
	March 4th		27 'Z' horses + mules of Bde sold in CHARLEROI.	[illegible]
	March 5th		Nothing of interest.	[illegible]
	March 6th		All remaining releasable men in Bde were again sent off for Demobilization viz 95 all ranks.	[illegible]
	March 7th		21 'Z' animals of Bde sold in CHARLEROI.	[illegible]
	March 8th		All 'X' horses paraded and 5 chosen to accompany 210th + 211th Bdes RFA to Army of Occupation. Nos actually with units as follows: 5th Z.7 12 + 178; 7th Z.7 17 + 192; 8th Z.7 12 + 176; Total 41 + 546.	[illegible]
	March 9th		Church Parade	[illegible]
	March 10th		Inspection of 'X' mules for 210 + 211 Bdes RFA.	
	March 11th		Capt P. BB. NICHOLS MC Brigade Major proceeded to UK for demobilization.	[illegible]

(A9475) Wt W2358/P360 600,000 12/17 D. D. & L. Sch. 52a. Forms/C2118/15

Army Form C. 2118.

WAR DIARY
or
INTELLIGENCE SUMMARY.
(Erase heading not required.)

Instructions regarding War Diaries and Intelligence Summaries are contained in F. S. Regs., Part II. and the Staff Manual respectively. Title pages will be prepared in manuscript.

Place	Date	Hour	Summary of Events and Information	Remarks and references to Appendices
Rue de Montigny CHARLEROI	March 12th		4 officers (3 from 8LF 1 from 7LF) volunteers for army of occupation posted to 15th & 16th LF with orders to proceed to new units forthwith	[initials]
"	March 13th		Orders received to transfer 'X' animals already chosen to 210 & 211 Bdes RFA proceeding on March 15th	[initials]
"	March 14th		Orders received that HQ 42 Division will cease to exist at midnight 15/16th March ~~[illegible]~~ Brig: General H FARGUS CMG DSO to take over command of the division less RA & Eng. from that time.	[initials]
"	March 15th		Transfer of 'X' animals to 210 & 211 Bdes RFA cancelled	[initials]
"	March 16th		Lt Col J Macleod 1/8 Lan Fus takes over command of Brigade cadres	[initials]
"	March 17th		4 officers 1/5 Lan Fus volunteers for army of occupation posted to 15th LF. with orders to proceed to new unit forthwith.	[initials]
	March 18th		Orders received to clear cavalry barracks of British troops. 8 LF to move to Jesuit college & move to be completed by 20th.	
	March 19th		All remaining releasable & available men sent to concentration camp for demobilization. Total 2 officers 14 OR.	[initials]
	March 20th		1 'Y' SS horse despatched to base. 26 'X' animals transferred to 42 Bn M.G.C.	[initials]

(A9175) Wt W2358/P360 600,000 12/17 D. D. & L. Sch 53a. Forms/C2118/15

Instructions regarding War Diaries and Intelligence Summaries are contained in F. S. Regs., Part II. and the Staff Manual respectively. Title pages will be prepared in manuscript.

WAR DIARY
or
INTELLIGENCE SUMMARY.
(Erase heading not required.)

Army Form C. 2118.

Place	Date	Hour	Summary of Events and Information	Remarks and references to Appendices
Rue de Montigny Charleroi	March 21st		Preliminary orders for entrainment of cadres received. Route to be Antwerp & Cumminghame.	
"	March 22nd		All demobilization & leave stopped owing to threatened strikes in England.	
"	March 23rd		20 'X' animals entrained for the base leaving only 2 mules per battalion & 5 riders in the brigade	
"	March 24th		Leave & demobilization normal traffic resumed.	
	March 25th		Orders for movement of cadres received 4/5 LF on 5th train under orders of 126 Bde.	
	March 26th		8 LF to replace 1/7 NF (P) on 2nd train under 127 Bde. Entrainment commences 28th (one train per day)	
	March 27th		2 officers & 14 OR. sent to concentration camp for demobilization.	
	March 28th		5 riders Class 'X' transferred to R.G.A.	
	March 29th		8 L F cadre (strength 6 officers 49 OR) together with L.T.M. Battery (strength 1 OR) entrain for Antwerp. All officers (1) over 35 years of age (2) joined the army in 1914 & 1915. who have not volunteered for army of occupation to proceed to concentration camp for demobilization	
	March 30th		5 officers to concentration camp for demobilization	
	March 31st		Orders received that draft for 15th & 16th Lan Fus will proceed as soon as train can be arranged	

[illegible signature]
Capt.
for Lt Colonel
Comdg 125 Inf Bde (Cadres)

(A9175) Wt W2358/P360 600,000 12/17 D. D. & L. Sch 52a. Forms/C2118/15

Instructions regarding War Diaries and Intelligence Summaries are contained in F. S. Regs., Part II, and the Staff Manual respectively. Title pages will be prepared in manuscript.

24

WAR DIARY
or
INTELLIGENCE SUMMARY.
(Erase heading not required.)

HQ 125 Infy Bde

Army Form C. 2118.

42

VOL: 57.

APRIL. 1919.

27

Place	Date	Hour	Summary of Events and Information	Remarks and references to Appendices
Rue de Montigny CHARLEROI				
"	April 1st		Orders received to despatch draft of retainable men to 15th & 16th LF on 2nd.	
"	April 2nd		6 officers 289 OR from Brigade entrain 0900 Charleroi SUD for 15th & 16th LF. 11 officers and 138 OR also transferred to same battalions but owing to employment unable to proceed	
			5 LF cadre entrained for Antwerp.	
"	April 3rd		Ration Strength of remainder of Brigade 13 officers 119 OR	
"	April 4th		no change	
"	April 5th		Two riders class 'X' retained for use at Bde returned to the ? battalion who are moving to the Rhine on 7th. 6 'X' mules now only animals left.	
"	April 6th		Received orders that remainder of Bde cadres will probably entrain for Antwerp on 12th inst	
	April 7th		no change	
	April 8th		8 other ranks despatched on posting to 15 & 16 LF.	
	April 9th		2 mules 'X' class taken over from DW Signal Coy	
	April 10th		Orders received for Bde HQ & 7 LF cadres to entrain 12th for Antwerp	
	April 11th		Brig: General FARGUS CMG DSO entrains with 42 DW cadre for Antwerp all mules Z class — 8 — handed over to 123 Bde RFA.	

(Signed) [illegible]
Capt.
Staff Capt
for Lt Col Comdg 125 Bde (Cadre)

(B9175) Wt W2338/P360 600,000 12/17 D. D. & L. Sch 52a. Forms/C2118/15

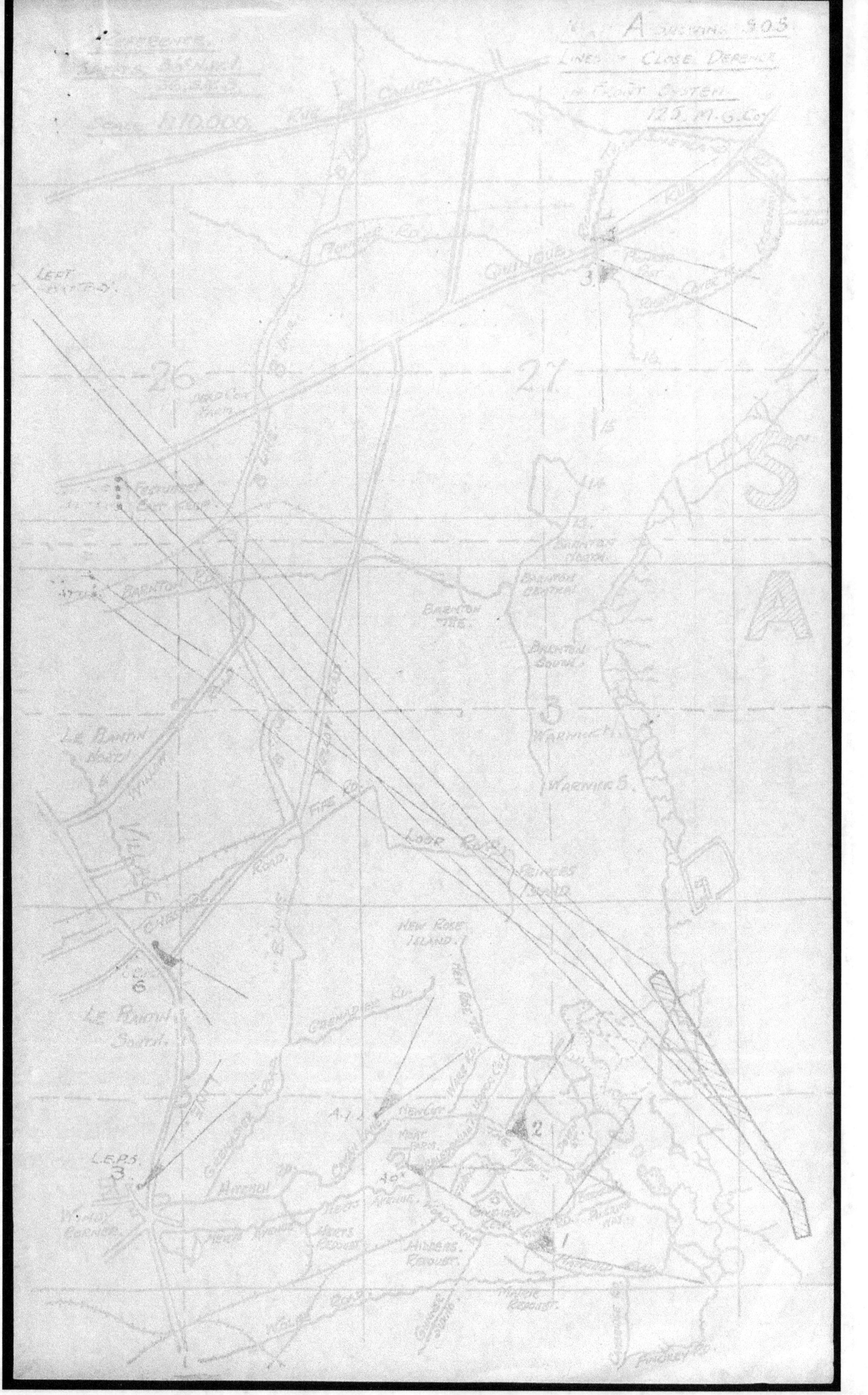

A Section S.O.S.
Lines of Close Defence
in Front System
125 M.G. Coy

Scale 1/10,000

26
27
Left
Quinque Rue
Barnton Rd.
Barnton Tee
Barnton South
Warwick
Warwick S.
Le Plantin North
Le Plantin South
Fire Rd.
Loop Rd.
Princes Island
New Rose Island
Grenadier Rd.
A.1.
New Cut
L.E.P.S.
3.
Windy Corner
Herts Avenue
Herts Redoubt
Finchley Rd.
1
2
3
6

MAP "B" SHOWING S.O.S.
LINES OF 125 T.M.B.
SOS.
REFERENCE.
SHEETS 36 N.W.1.
SCALE:- 1:10.000
RUE DE CAILLOUX
ARES THAT CAN BE REACHED
AMM. DUMP.
SHETLAND
No 8.
No 7.
QUINQUE
OFFENSIVE.
26
27
AMM. DUMP.
BARNTON NORTH.
BARNTON CENTRAL.
BARNTON TEE
No 5
WARWICK
LOOP ROAD
PRINCES ISLAND.
NEW ROSE ISLAND.
LE PLANTIN NORTH
LE PLANTIN SOUTH
WILLOW ROAD
FIFE ROAD
CHESHIRE ROAD
HATFIELD ROAD
No 1
MAPLE REDOUBT
HILDERS REDOUBT

www.ingramcontent.com/pod-product-compliance
Lightning Source LLC
Chambersburg PA
CBHW081426300426
44108CB00016BA/2313
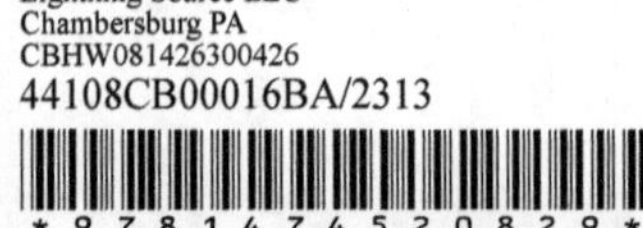
* 9 7 8 1 4 7 4 5 2 0 8 2 9 *